"IT MAY BE THE MOST IMPORT̶ KIND BY AN AMERICAN SINCE ̶̶̶̶ ̶̶̶̶ ̶̶̶̶.

—*Chicago Tribune*

THE CLOSING OF THE AMERICAN MIND

Allan Bloom

"Commands one's attention and concentrates one's mind more effectively than any other book I can think of in the past five years."

—Christopher Lehmann-Haupt, *The New York Times*

"A penetrating look at the state of modern American society . . . filled to overflowing with trenchant insights into American life. . . . Required reading for every thoughtful citizen concerned with the decline of American society. . . . It will challenge you to think."

—*The New American*

"Essential reading for anyone concerned with the state of liberal education in this society."

—*The New York Times Book Review*

"Important and controversial . . . could—and should—serve as a major resource in the effort to rethink the very nature and purpose of American higher education."

—*San Francisco Chronicle Book Review*

"Every chapter, if not every page, offers something delightful, something puzzling, something outrageous."

—*St. Louis Post-Dispatch*

"Elegant, passionate, wide-ranging. . . . His prose is rhapsodic, compelling, personal and reassuring. He writes from a deep love of history and intellectual tradition."

—*Los Angeles Times Book Review*

"Graceful and grave . . . a serious-minded, sinewy and wise work."

—*Virginia Pilot & The Ledger-Star*

"Has the density of fiction, the sting of satire, the lucidity of philosophy . . . all the compact fluidity and dazzle of Emerson's essays."

—*The Christian Science Monitor Book Review*

How Higher Education Has Failed Democracy and Impoverished the Souls of Today's Students

THE
CLOSING
OF THE
AMERICAN
MIND

◆

Allan Bloom

Foreword by Saul Bellow

Afterword by Andrew Ferguson

SIMON & SCHUSTER PAPERBACKS

New York   London   Toronto   Sydney   New Delhi

To My Students

Simon & Schuster Paperbacks
A Division of Simon & Schuster, Inc.
1230 Avenue of the Americas
New York, NY 10020

This Simon & Schuster trade paperback edition April 2012

SIMON & SCHUSTER PAPERBACKS and colophon are registered trademarks
of Simon & Schuster, Inc.

For information about special discounts for bulk purchases, please contact
Simon & Schuster Special Sales at 1-866-506-1949
or business@simonandschuster.com.

Designed by Eve Kirch

20 19 18 17 16

The Library of Congress had cataloged the hardcover edition as follows:

Bloom, Allan David, date.
     The closing of the American mind.
     Includes index.
         1. United States—Intellectual life—20th century.
2. Education, Higher—United States—Philosophy.
I. Title
LA227.3.B584   1987
378'.012'0973dc20   86-24768

ISBN 978-0-671-47990-9
ISBN 978-1-4516-8320-2 (pbk)
ISBN 978-1-4391-2626-4 (ebook)

Contents

PART THREE. THE UNIVERSITY

Foreword

Professor Bloom has his own way of doing things. Writing about the higher education in America, he does not observe the forms, manners and ceremonies of what is called (usually by itself) the community of scholars. Yet his credentials are irreproachable. He is the author of an excellent book on Shakespeare's politics, and has translated Plato's *Republic* and Rousseau's *Emile*. It will be difficult for nettled colleagues to wave him away, and many will want to do just that, for he is shrewd and mettlesome, as well as learned, and a great observer of what Mencken would call, when he was being mean, "the higher learning."

But Professor Bloom is neither a debunker nor a satirist, and his conception of seriousness carries him far beyond the positions of academia. He is not addressing himself primarily to the professors. They are welcome to listen—and they will listen because they come under heavy fire—but he places himself in a larger community, invoking Socrates, Plato, Machiavelli, Rousseau and Kant more often than he does our contemporaries: "The real community of man, in the midst of all the self-contradictory simulacra of community, is the community of those who seek the truth, of the potential knowers . . . of all men to the extent they desire to know. But in fact, this includes only a few, the true friends, as Plato was to Aristotle at the very moment they were disagreeing about the nature of the good. . . . They were absolutely one soul as they looked at the problem. This, according to Plato, is the only real friendship, the only real common good. It is here that the contact people so desperately

11

seek is to be found. . . . This is the meaning of the riddle of the improbable philosopher-kings. They have a true community that is exemplary for all the other communities."

A style of this sort will seem to modern readers marred by classical stiffness—"Truth," "Knowers," "the Good," "Man"—but we can by no means deny that behind our objection to such language is a guilty consciousness of the flimsiness, and not infrequently the trashiness, of our modern talk about "values."

The sentences above are taken from the conclusion of Bloom's book. Parting from his readers, he is at his most earnest. He writes in a different vein when he is discussing the power of professional economists, the separation of modern science from the "natural philosophy" that preceded it, the phenomenon called "cultural relativism," or the real, the bottom-line, significance of an M.B.A. degree. He often flashes out provocatively and wickedly. Speaking of the place of the humanities in the universities, he calls them a "submerged old Atlantis," to which we turn again to try to "find ourselves now that everybody else has given up." "The humanities are like the great old Paris Flea Market where, amidst masses of junk, people with a good eye found cast away treasures. . . ." Or else, "They are like a refugee camp where all the geniuses driven out of their jobs and countries by unfriendly regimes are idling. . . . The other two divisions of the university have no use for the past . . ." When he is not busy with the nature of the Good, he can hit, with the best (or should I say the worst) of them, very hard. As a scholar he intends to enlighten us, and as a writer he has learned from Aristophanes and other models that enlightenment should also be enjoyable. To me, this is not the book of a professor, but that of a thinker who is willing to take the risks more frequently taken by writers. It is risky in a book of ideas to speak in one's own voice, but it reminds us that the sources of the truest truths are inevitably profoundly personal. Bloom tells us: "Throughout this book I have referred to Plato's *Republic*, which is for me *the* book on education, because it really explains to me what I experience as a man and a teacher." Academics, even those describing themselves as existentialists, very seldom offer themselves publicly and frankly as individuals, as persons. So Professor Bloom is a front-line fighter in the mental wars of our times, and as such, singularly congenial to me. (If he can be personal, I see no reason why I should remain the anonymous commentator.)

In his concluding pages, Bloom tells of a student who, after a reading of the *Symposium,* said that it was hard today to imagine the magic Athenian atmosphere, "in which friendly men, educated, lively, on a footing of equality, civilized but natural, came together and told wonderful stories about the meaning of their longing. But [adds Bloom] such experiences are always accessible. Actually, this playful discussion took place in the midst of a terrible war that Athens was destined to lose, and Aristophanes and Socrates at least could foresee that this meant the decline of Greek civilization. But they were not given to culture despair, and in these terrible political circumstances, their abandon to the joy of nature proved the viability of what is best in man, independent of accidents, of circumstance. We feel ourselves too dependent on history and culture. . . . What is essential about . . . any of the Platonic dialogues is reproducible in almost all times and places. . . . This thinking might be what it is all for. That's where we are beginning to fail. But it is right under our noses, improbable but always present."

I take this statement very seriously and am greatly moved by it, seeing in it the seed from which my life grew. For as a Midwesterner, the son of immigrant parents, I recognized at an early age that I was called upon to decide for myself to what extent my Jewish origins, my surroundings (the accidental circumstances of Chicago), my schooling, were to be allowed to determine the course of my life. I did not intend to be wholly dependent on history and culture. Full dependency must mean that I was done for. The commonest teaching of the civilized world in our time can be stated simply: "Tell me where you come from and I will tell you what you are." There was not a chance in the world that Chicago, with the agreement of my eagerly Americanizing extended family, would make me in its image. Before I was capable of thinking clearly, my resistance to its material weight took the form of obstinacy. I couldn't say why I would not allow myself to become the product of an *environment.* But gainfulness, utility, prudence, business, had no hold on me. My mother wanted me to be a fiddler or, failing that, a rabbi. I had my choice between playing dinner music at the Palmer House or presiding over a synagogue. In traditional orthodox families small boys were taught to translate *Genesis* and *Exodus,* so I might easily have gone on to the rabbinate if the great world, the world of the streets, had not been so seductive. Besides, a life of pious observance was not for me. Anyway, I had begun at an early age to read widely, and I was quickly carried away from the ancient religion. Reluctantly, my father allowed me at seventeen to enter the university, where I was an enthusiastic (wildly excited) but erratic and contrary student. If I signed up for Economics 201, I was sure to spend all my time reading Ibsen and Shaw. Registering for a poetry course, I was soon bored by meters and stanzas, and shifted my attention to Kropotkin's *Memoirs of a Revolutionist* and Lenin's *What Is to Be Done?* My tastes and habits were those of a writer. I preferred to read poetry on my own without the benefit of lectures on the caesura. To rest my book-strained eyes I played pool and Ping-Pong at the men's club.

I was soon aware that in the view of advanced European thinkers, the cultural expectations of a young man from Chicago, that center of brutal materialism, were bound to be disappointed. Put together the slaughterhouses, the steel mills, the freight yards, the primitive bungalows of the industrial villages that comprised the city, the gloom of the financial district, the ballparks and prizefights, the machine politicians, the prohibition gang wars, and you had a solid cover of "Social-Darwinist" darkness, impenetrable by the rays of culture. Hopeless, in the judgment of highly refined Englishmen, Frenchmen, Germans and Italians, the spokesmen for art in its most advanced modern forms. For some of these foreign observers, America had many advantages over Europe, it was more productive, more energetic, more free, largely immune from pathogenic politics and ruinous wars, but as far as art was concerned it would be better, as Wyndham Lewis put it, to have been born an Eskimo than a Minnesota Presbyterian who wanted to be a painter. Civilized Europeans, often exceptionally free from the class prejudices of their own countries, were able conveniently to lodge their not fully mastered biases in the free-for-all U.S.A. What no one was able to foresee was that all civilized countries were destined to descend to a common cosmopolitanism and that the lamentable weakening of the older branches of civilization would open fresh opportunities and free us from our dependency on history and culture—a concealed benefit of decline. There would be barbarous manifestations certainly, but there would be also the possibility of new kinds of independence.

In this regard I find myself, as Americans have taken to saying, between a rock and a hard place. European observers sometimes classify me as a hybrid curiosity, neither fully American nor satisfactorily European, stuffed with references to the philosophers, the historians, and poets I had consumed higgledy-piggledy, in my Midwestern lair. I am of course, an autodidact, as modern writers always are. That spirited newcomer, the nineteenth-century novelist, guessed, ventured, conjectured daringly. Independent intelligence made its synthesis. Balzac declared, "The world belongs to me because I *understand* it." Professor Bloom's book makes me fear that the book of the world, so richly studied by autodidacts, is being closed by the "learned" who are raising walls of opinions to shut the world out.

From a different standpoint, American readers sometimes object to a kind of foreignness in my books. I mention Old World writers, I have highbrow airs, and appear to put on the dog. I readily concede that here and there I am probably hard to read, and I am likely to become harder as the illiteracy of the public increases. It is never an easy task to take the mental measure of your readers. There are things that people *should* know if they are to read books at all, and out of respect for them, or to save appearances, one is apt to assume more familiarity on their part with the history of the twentieth century than is objectively justified. Besides, a certain psychic unity is always taken for granted by writers. "Others are in essence like me and I am basically like them, give or take a few minor differences." A piece of writing is an offering. You bring it to the altar and hope it will be accepted. You pray at least that rejection will not throw you into a rage and turn you into a Cain. Perhaps naively, you produce your favorite treasures and pile them in an indiscriminate heap. Those who do not recognize their value now may do so later. And you do not always feel that you are writing for any of your contemporaries. It may well be that your true readers are not here as yet and that your books will cause them to materialize.

There are times when I enjoy making fun of the educated American. *Herzog,* for instance, was meant to be a comic novel: a Ph.D. from a good American university falls apart when his wife leaves him for another man. He is taken by an epistolary fit and writes grieving, biting, ironic and rambunctious letters not only to his friends and acquaintances, but also to the great men, the giants of thought, who formed his mind. What is he to do in this moment of crisis, pull Aristotle or Spinoza from the shelf and storm through the pages looking for consolation and advice? The stricken man, as he tries to put himself together again, interpret his experience, make sense of life, becomes clearly aware of the preposterousness of such an effort. "What this country needs," he writes at last, surrendering to the absurdity of his state, "is a good five-cent synthesis." Here he echoes Mr. Marshall, Woodrow Wilson's Vice President, who had said at about the time of the Great War, "What this country needs is a good five-cent cigar." Certain readers of Herzog complained the book was difficult. Much as they might have sympathized with the unhappy and comical history professor, they were occasionally put off by his long and erudite letters. Some felt that they were being asked to sit for a difficult exam in a survey course in intellectual history and thought it mean of me to mingle sympathy and wit with obscurity and pedantry.

But I was making fun of pedantry!

The reply: "If that was your purpose, you didn't altogether succeed. Some of your readers thought you were setting up a challenge, something resembling an obstacle course, or an egghead crossword puzzle for members of MENSA." A few may have been flattered, while others resented being tested. People reserve their best thinking for their professional specialties and, next in line, for serious matters confronting the alert citizen—economics, politics, the disposal of nuclear waste, etc. The day's work done, they want to be entertained. They can't see why their entertainment should not simply be entertaining, and in some ways I agree, for I myself, in reading Montaigne as I sometimes do, am tempted to skip his long citations from the classics, which put my high school Latin under some strain, and it is not amusing to send oneself back to high school.

To finish with Herzog, I meant the novel to show how little strength "higher education" had to offer a troubled man. In the end he is aware that he has had no education in the conduct of life (at the university who was there to teach him how to deal with his erotic needs, with women, with family matters?) and he returns, in the language of games, to square one—or as I put it to myself while writing the book, to some primal point of balance. Herzog's confusion is barbarous. Well, what else can it be? But there is one point at which, assisted by his comic sense, he is able to hold fast. In the greatest confusion there is still an open channel to the soul. It may be difficult to find because by midlife it is overgrown, and some of the wildest thickets that surround it grow out of what we describe as our education. But the channel is always there, and it is our business to keep it open, to have access to the deepest part of ourselves—to that part of us which is conscious of a higher consciousness, by means of which we make final judgments and put everything together. The independence of this consciousness, which has the strength to be immune to the noise of history and the distractions of our immediate surroundings, is what the life struggle is all about. The soul has to find and hold its ground against hostile forces, sometimes embodied in ideas which frequently deny its very existence, and which indeed often seem to be trying to annul it altogether.

Romantic poets and other edifying theorists of the nineteenth century had it wrong—poets and novelists will never be the legislators and teachers of mankind. That poets—artists—should give new eyes to human beings, inducing them to view the world differently, converting them from fixed modes of experience, is ambition enough, if one must offer a purposive account of the artist's project. What makes that project singularly difficult is the disheartening expansion of trained ignorance and bad thought. For to put the matter at its baldest, we live in a thought-world, and the thinking has gone very bad indeed. Therefore the artist, whether or not he views himself as an intellectual, is involved in thought-struggles. Thinking alone will never cure what ails him, and any artist should be grateful for a naive grace which puts him beyond the need to reason elaborately. For me, the university has been the place of divestiture where I am able to find help in the laborious task of discarding bad thought. It was at the university that I began to work through the modern ideologies, Capitalist as well as Marxist, and the psychologies, the social and historical theories, as well as the philosophies (logical positivism, naturalism, existentialism, etc.). Shedding superfluities so that my mental body could recover its ability to breathe, and protecting the root-simplicit-ies of being, I have never viewed the university as a sanctuary or shelter from "the outer world." Life in a strictly academic village, in isolation from a great turbulent city, would have been a torment to me. So I have never been, as a "radical" Central European novelist recently called me, a "campus writer." Rather, I have trained myself to pick up the endless variations on radical and right-wing themes so that I have become able (not an enviable skill) to detect the untreated sewage odors of a century of revolutionary rhetoric or, from another direction, to identify in Gore Vidal's recent outburst of "original" geopolitics nothing other than the Hearst Sunday Supplement theme of the "Yellow Peril," the odor of which is no more pleasant now than it was in the thirties. There is nothing at all new in the fiery posturing of these agitational and "activist" writers. If they were able to come up with something of their own, the universities would not hold their monopoly on the intellectual life.

The heart of Professor Bloom's argument is that the university, in a society ruled by public opinion, was to have been an island of intellectual freedom where all views were investigated without restriction. Liberal democracy in its generosity made this possible, but by consenting to play an active or "positive," a participatory role in society, the university has become inundated and saturated with the backflow of society's "problems." Preoccupied with questions of Health, Sex, Race, War, academics make their reputations and their fortunes and the university has become society's conceptual warehouse of often harmful influences. Any proposed reforms of liberal education which might bring the university into conflict with the whole of the U.S.A. are unthinkable. Increasingly, the people "inside" are identical in their appetites and motives with the people "outside" the university. This is what I take Bloom to be saying, and if he were making a polemical statement merely it would be easy enough to set aside. What makes it formidably serious is the accurate historical background accompanying the argument. He explains with an admirable command of political theory how all this came to be, how modern democracy originated, what Machiavelli, Hobbes, Locke, Rousseau and the other philosophers of enlightenment intended, and how their intentions succeeded or failed.

The heat of the dispute between Left and Right has grown so fierce in the last decade that the habits of civilized discourse have suffered a scorching. Antagonists seem no longer to listen to one another. It would be a pity if intelligent adversaries were not to read Professor Bloom's book with disinterested attention. It makes an important statement and deserves careful study. What it provides, whether or not one agrees with its conclusions, is an indispensable guide for discussion, not a mere skimming of the tradition, but a completely articulated, historically accurate summary, a trustworthy resumé of the development of the higher mental life in the democratic U.S.A.

SAUL BELLOW

Preface

This essay—a meditation on the state of our souls, particularly those of the young, and their education—is written from the perspective of a teacher. Such a perspective, although it has grave limitations and is accompanied by dangerous temptations, is a privileged one. The teacher, particularly the teacher dedicated to liberal education, must constantly try to look toward the goal of human completeness and back at the natures of his students here and now, ever seeking to understand the former and to assess the capacities of the latter to approach it. Attention to the young, knowing what their hungers are and what they can digest, is the essence of the craft. One must spy out and elicit those hungers. For there is no real education that does not respond to felt need; anything else acquired is trifling display. What each generation is can be best discovered in its relation to the permanent concerns of mankind. This in turn can best be discovered in each generation's tastes, amusements, and especially angers (this is above all true in an age that prides itself on calm self-awareness). Particularly revealing are the various impostors whose business it is to appeal to the young. These culture peddlers have the strongest of motives for finding out the appetites of the young—so they are useful guides into the labyrinths of the spirit of the times.

The teacher's standpoint is not arbitrary. It is neither simply dependent on what students think they want or happen to be in this place or time, nor is it imposed on him by the demands of a particular society or the vagaries of the market. Although much effort has been expended in trying to prove that the teacher is always the agent of such forces, in fact he is, willy-nilly, guided by the awareness, or the divination, that there is a human nature, and that assisting its fulfillment is his task. He does not come to this by way of abstractions or complicated reasoning. He sees it in the eyes of his students. Those students are only potential, but potential points beyond itself; and this is the source of the hope, almost always disappointed but ever renascent, that man is not just a creature of accident, chained to and formed by the particular cave in which he is born. Midwifery—i.e., the delivery of real babies of which not the midwife but nature is the cause—describes teaching more adequately than does the word socialization. The birth of a robust child, independent of the midwife, is the teacher's true joy, a pleasure far more effective in motivating him than any disinterested moral duty would be, his primary experience of a contemplation more satisfying than any action. No real teacher can doubt that his task is to assist his pupil to fulfill human nature against all the deforming forces of convention and prejudice. The vision of what that nature is may be clouded, the teacher may be more or less limited, but his activity is solicited by something beyond him that at the same time provides him with a standard for judging his students' capacity and achievement. Moreover there is no real teacher who in practice does not believe in the existence of the soul, or in a magic that acts on it through speech. The soul, so the teacher must think, may at the outset of education require extrinsic rewards and punishments to motivate its activity; but in the end that activity is its own reward and is self-sufficient.

These are the reasons that help to explain the perversity of an adult who prefers the company of youths to that of grownups. He prefers the promising "might be" to the defective "is." Such an adult is subject to many temptations—particularly vanity and the desire to propagandize rather than teach—and the very activity brings with it the danger of preferring teaching to knowing, of adapting oneself to what the students can or want to learn, of knowing oneself only by one's students.

Thus, teaching can be a threat to philosophy because philosophizing is a solitary quest, and he who pursues it must never look to an audience. But it is too much to ask that teachers be philosophers, and a bit of attachment to one's audience is almost inevitable. And if it is well resisted, the very vice can turn into something of a virtue and encourage philosophizing. Fascination with one's students leads to an awareness of the various kinds of soul and their various capacities for truth and error as well as learning. Such experience is a condition of investigating *the* question, "What is man?," in relation to his highest aspirations as opposed to his low and common needs.

A liberal education means precisely helping students to pose this question to themselves, to become aware that the answer is neither obvious nor simply unavailable, and that there is no serious life in which this question is not a continuous concern. Despite all the efforts to pervert it (a few of which will be discussed in this book), the question that every young person asks, "Who am I?," the powerful urge to follow the Delphic command, "Know thyself," which is born in each of us, means in the first place "What is man?" And in our chronic lack of certainty, this comes down to knowing the alternative answers and thinking about them. Liberal education provides access to these alternatives, many of which go against the grain of our nature or our times. The liberally educated person is one who is able to resist the easy and preferred answers, not because he is obstinate but because he knows others worthy of consideration. Although it is foolish to believe that book learning is anything like the whole of education, it is always necessary, particularly in ages when there is a poverty of living examples of the possible high human types. And book learning is most of what a teacher can give—properly administered in an atmosphere in which its relation to life is plausible. Life will happen to his students. The most he can hope is that what he might give will inform life. Most students will be content with what our present considers relevant; others will have a spirit of enthusiasm that subsides as family and ambition provide them with other objects of interest; a small number will spend their lives in an effort to be autonomous. It is for these last, especially, that liberal education exists. They become the models for the use of the noblest human faculties and hence are benefactors to all of us, more for what they are than for what they do. Without their presence (and, one should add, without their being respectable), no society—no matter how rich or comfortable, no matter how technically adept or full of tender sentiments—can be called civilized.

From the teacher's standpoint, thus understood, I have for more than thirty years, with the most intense interest, watched and listened to students. What they bring to their higher education, in passions, curiosities, longings, and especially previous experience, has changed; and therewith the task of educating them has changed. In this book I am attempting to make a contribution to understanding this generation. I am not moralizing; I no more want to be Jeremiah than Pollyanna. More than anything else, this book is to be taken as a report from the front. The reader can judge for himself the gravity of our situation. Every age has its problems, and I do not claim that things were wonderful in the past. I am describing our present situation and do not intend any comparison with the past to be used as grounds for congratulating or blaming ourselves but only for the sake of clarifying what counts for us and what is special in our situation.

A word about my "sample" in this study. It consists of thousands of students of comparatively high intelligence, materially and spiritually free to do pretty much what they want with the few years of college they are privileged to have—in short, the kind of young persons who populate the twenty or thirty best universities. There are other kinds of students whom circumstances of one sort or another prevent from having the freedom required to pursue a liberal education. They have their own needs and may very well have very different characters from those I describe here. My sample, whatever its limits, has the advantage of concentrating on those who are most likely to take advantage of a liberal education and to have the greatest moral and intellectual effect on the nation. It is sometimes said that these advantaged youths have less need of our attention and resources, that they already have enough. But they, above all, most need education, inasmuch as the greatest talents are most difficult to perfect, and the more complex the nature the more susceptible it is to perversion.

There is no need to prove the importance of education; but it should be remarked that for modern nations, which have founded themselves on reason in its various uses more than did any nations in the past, a crisis in the university, the home of reason, is perhaps the profoundest crisis they face.

This book has concentrated my mind on the experiences of a lifetime of teaching. Because my career has been an unusually happy one, gratitude is the leading sentiment evoked in reviewing it. My acknowledgments, therefore, reflect contributions to that total experience rather than to this particular book. So above all, I must thank all the students to whom I have had the privilege of teaching classic texts for more than thirty years, especially those I came to know well and from whom I learned so much about the questions discussed here.

Among them are those old students, now very independent thinkers and friends, who have told me of their experiences and observations and helped me interpret mine: Christopher J. Bruell, Hillel G. Fradkin, James H. Nichols, Jr., Clifford Orwin, Thomas L. Pangle, Abram N. Shulsky, Nathan and Susan Tarcov. David S. Bolotin, in particular, responded to my thesis and in turn persuaded me of its seriousness. All of them contributed to and tempered my enthusiasms, each in his own special way. Michael Z. Wu has assisted me enormously with his sharp insight and criticism.

Among my colleagues with whom I share conversation and students, I want to make mention of Saul Bellow and Werner J. Dannhauser. The former, with his special generosity, entered into my thoughts and encouraged me in paths I had never before taken; the latter, my intellectual companion throughout my adult life, undertook as usual to read my manuscript and gave me the benefit of his penetration and honesty.

In the preparation of the manuscript, Judy Chernick, Terese Denov, and Erica Aronson worked as loyal friends with total reliability, making the most boring phases in the production of a book seem exciting. I have been particularly happy in my editors, Robert Asahina, of Simon and Schuster, and Bernard de Fallois, of Editions Julliard, who pushed me to write the book and then spent more time working on it than I could have imagined. The Earhart Foundation and the John M. Olin Foundation have supported me as teacher and scholar for a long time, and I am very grateful to their officers.

Finally, I want to express my admiration for Allan P. Sindler, who has been for me the model of the selfless university man. His lifelong behavior proves that the enterprise is still possible and worthwhile.

I must say, and not only *pro forma,* that my mention of these persons in no way implies that they endorse my views.

ALLAN BLOOM

Chicago, May 1986

Introduction:
Our Virtue

There is one thing a professor can be absolutely certain of: almost every student entering the university believes, or says he believes, that truth is relative. If this belief is put to the test, one can count on the students' reaction: they will be uncomprehending. That anyone should regard the proposition as not self-evident astonishes them, as though he were calling into question $2 + 2 = 4$. These are things you don't think about. The students' backgrounds are as various as America can provide. Some are religious, some atheists; some are to the Left, some to the Right; some intend to be scientists, some humanists or professionals or businessmen; some are poor, some rich. They are unified only in their relativism and in their allegiance to equality. And the two are related in a moral intention. The relativity of truth is not a theoretical insight but a moral postulate, the condition of a free society, or so they see it. They have all been equipped with this framework early on, and it is the modern replacement for the inalienable natural rights that used to be the traditional American grounds for a free society. That it is a moral issue for students is revealed by the character of their response when challenged—a combination of disbelief and indignation: "Are you an absolutist?," the only alternative they know, uttered in the same tone as "Are you a monarchist?" or "Do you really believe in witches?" This latter leads into the indignation, for someone who believes in witches might well be a witch-hunter or a Salem judge. The danger they have been taught to fear from absolutism is not error but intolerance. Relativism is necessary to openness; and this is the virtue, the only virtue, which all primary education for more than fifty years has dedicated itself to inculcating. Openness— and the relativism that makes it the only plausible stance in the face of various claims to truth and various ways of life and kinds of human beings —is the great insight of our times. The true believer is the real danger. The study of history and of culture teaches that all the world was mad in the past; men always thought they were right, and that led to wars, persecutions, slavery, xenophobia, racism, and chauvinism. The point is not to correct the mistakes and really be right; rather it is not to think you are right at all.

The students, of course, cannot defend their opinion. It is something with which they have been indoctrinated. The best they can do is point out all the opinions and cultures there are and have been. What right, they ask, do I or anyone else have to say one is better than the others? If I pose the routine questions designed to confute them and make them think, such as, "If you had been a British administrator in India, would you have let the natives under your governance burn the widow at the funeral of a man who had died?," they either remain silent or reply that the British should never have been there in the first place. It is not that they know very much about other nations, or about their own. The purpose of their education is not to make them scholars but to provide them with a moral virtue—openness.

Every educational system has a moral goal that it tries to attain and that informs its curriculum. It wants to produce a certain kind of human being. This intention is more or less explicit, more or less a result of reflection; but even the neutral subjects, like reading and writing and arithmetic, take their place in a vision of the educated person. In some nations the goal was the pious person, in others the warlike, in others the industrious. Always important is the political regime, which needs citizens who are in accord with its fundamental principle. Aristocracies want gentlemen, oligarchies men who respect and pursue money, and democ- racies lovers of equality. Democratic education, whether it admits it or not, wants and needs to produce men and women who have the tastes, knowledge, and character supportive of a democratic regime. Over the history of our republic, there have obviously been changes of opinion as to what kind of man is best for our regime. We began with the model of the rational and industrious man, who was honest, respected the laws, and was dedicated to the family (his own family—what has in its decay been dubbed the nuclear family). Above all he was to know the rights doctrine; the Constitution, which embodied it; and American history, which presented and celebrated the founding of a nation "conceived in liberty and dedicated to the proposition that all men are created equal." A powerful attachment to the letter and the spirit of the Declaration of Independence gently conveyed, appealing to each man's reason, was the goal of the education of democratic man. This called for something very different from the kinds of attachment required for traditional communities where myth and passion as well as severe discipline, authority, and the extended family produced an instinctive, unqualified, even fanatic patriotism, unlike the reflected, rational, calm, even self-interested loyalty—not so much to the country but to the form of government and its rational principles—required in the United States. This was an entirely new experiment in politics, and with it came a new education. This education has evolved in the last half-century from the education of democratic man to the education of the democratic personality.

The palpable difference between these two can easily be found in the changed understanding of what it means to be an American. The old view was that, by recognizing and accepting man's natural rights, men found a fundamental basis of unity and sameness. Class, race, religion, national origin or culture all disappear or become dim when bathed in the light of natural rights, which give men common interests and make them truly brothers. The immigrant had to put behind him the claims of the Old World in favor of a new and easily acquired education. This did not necessarily mean abandoning old daily habits or religions, but it did mean subordinating them to new principles. There was a tendency, if not a necessity, to homogenize nature itself.

The recent education of openness has rejected all that. It pays no attention to natural rights or the historical origins of our regime, which are now thought to have been essentially flawed and regressive. It is progressive and forward-looking. It does not demand fundamental agreement or the abandonment of old or new beliefs in favor of the natural ones. It is open to all kinds of men, all kinds of life-styles, all ideologies. There is no enemy other than the man who is not open to everything. But when there are no shared goals or vision of the public good, is the social contract any longer possible?

From the earliest beginnings of liberal thought there was a tendency in the direction of indiscriminate freedom. Hobbes and Locke, and the American Founders following them, intended to palliate extreme beliefs, particularly religious beliefs, which lead to civil strife. The members of sects had to obey the laws and be loyal to the Constitution; if they did so, others had to leave them alone, however distasteful their beliefs might be. In order to make this arrangement work, there was a conscious, if covert, effort to weaken religious beliefs, partly by assigning—as a result of a great epistemological effort—religion to the realm of opinion as opposed to knowledge. But the right to freedom of religion belonged to the realm of knowledge. Such rights are not matters of opinion. No weakness of conviction was desired here. All to the contrary, the sphere of rights was to be the arena of moral passion in a democracy.

It was possible to expand the space exempt from legitimate social and political regulation only by contracting the claims to moral and political knowledge. The insatiable appetite for freedom to live as one pleases thrives on this aspect of modern democratic thought. In the end it begins to appear that full freedom can be attained only when there is no such knowledge at all. The effective way to defang the oppressors is to persuade them they are ignorant of the good. The inflamed sensitivity induced by radicalized democratic theory finally experiences any limit as arbitrary and tyrannical. There are no absolutes; freedom is absolute. Of course the result is that, on the one hand, the argument justifying freedom disappears and, on the other, all beliefs begin to have the attenuated character that was initially supposed to be limited to religious belief.

The gradual movement away from rights to openness was apparent, for example, when Oliver Wendell Holmes renounced seeking for a principle to determine which speech or conduct is not tolerable in a democratic society and invoked instead an imprecise and practically meaningless standard—clear and present danger—which to all intents and purposes makes the preservation of public order the only common good. Behind his opinion there was an optimistic view about progress, one in which the complete decay of democratic principle and a collapse into barbarism are impossible and in which the truth unaided always triumphs in the marketplace of ideas. This optimism had not been shared by the Founders, who insisted that the principles of democratic government must be returned to and consulted even though the consequences might be harsh for certain points of view, some merely tolerated and not respected, others forbidden outright. To their way of thinking there should be no tolerance for the intolerant. The notion that there should be no limitation on free expression unless it can be shown to be a clear and present danger would have made it impossible for Lincoln to insist that there could be no compromise with the *principle* of equality, that it did not depend on the people's choice or election but is the condition of their having elections in the first place, that popular sovereignty on the question of black slavery was impermissible even if it would enable us to avoid the clear and present danger of a bloody civil war.

But openness, nevertheless, eventually won out over natural rights, partly through a theoretical critique, partly because of a political rebellion against nature's last constraints. Civic education turned away from concentrating on the Founding to concentrating on openness based on history and social science. There was even a general tendency to debunk the Founding, to prove the beginnings were flawed in order to license a greater openness to the new. What began in Charles Beard's Marxism and Carl Becker's historicism became routine. We are used to hearing the Founders charged with being racists, murderers of Indians, representatives of class interests. I asked my first history professor in the university, a very famous scholar, whether the picture he gave us of George Washington did not have the effect of making us despise our regime. "Not at all," he said, "it doesn't depend on individuals but on our having good democratic values." To which I rejoined, "But you just showed us that Washington was only using those values to further the class interests of the Virginia squirearchy." He got angry, and that was the end of it. He was comforted by a gentle assurance that the values of democracy are part of the movement of history and did not require his elucidation or defense. He could carry on his historical studies with the moral certitude that they would lead to greater openness and hence more democracy. The lessons of fascism and the vulnerability of democracy, which we had all just experienced, had no effect on him.

Liberalism without natural rights, the kind that we knew from John Stuart Mill and John Dewey, taught us that the only danger confronting us is being closed to the emergent, the new, the manifestations of progress. No attention had to be paid to the fundamental principles or the moral virtues that inclined men to live according to them. To use language now popular, civic culture was neglected. And this turn in liberalism is what prepared us for cultural relativism and the fact-value distinction, which seemed to carry that viewpoint further and give it greater intellectual weight.

History and social science are used in a variety of ways to overcome prejudice. We should not be ethnocentric, a term drawn from anthropology, which tells us more about the meaning of openness. We should not think our way is better than others. The intention is not so much to teach the students about other times and places as to make them aware of the fact that their preferences are only that—accidents of their time and place. Their beliefs do not entitle them as individuals, or collectively as a nation, to think they are superior to anyone else. John Rawls is almost a parody of this tendency, writing hundreds of pages to persuade men, and proposing a scheme of government that would force them, not to despise anyone. In *A Theory of Justice,* he writes that the physicist or the poet should not look down on the man who spends his life counting blades of grass or performing any other frivolous or corrupt activity. Indeed, he should be esteemed, since esteem from others, as opposed to self-esteem, is a basic need of all men. So indiscriminateness is a moral imperative because its opposite is discrimination. This folly means that men are not permitted to seek for the natural human good and admire it when found, for such discovery is coeval with the discovery of the bad and contempt for it. Instinct and intellect must be suppressed by education. The natural soul is to be replaced with an artificial one.

At the root of this change in morals was the presence in the United States of men and women of a great variety of nations, religions, and races, and the fact that many were badly treated because they belonged to these groups. Franklin Roosevelt declared that we want "a society which leaves no one out." Although the natural rights inherent in our regime are perfectly adequate to the solution of this problem, provided these outsiders adhere to them (i.e., they become insiders by adhering to them), this did not satisfy the thinkers who influenced our educators, for the right to vote and the other political rights did not automatically produce social acceptance. The equal protection of the laws did not protect a man from contempt and hatred as a Jew, an Italian, or a Black.

The reaction to this problem was, in the first place, resistance to the notion that outsiders had to give up their "cultural" individuality and make themselves into that universal, abstract being who participates in natural rights or else be doomed to an existence on the fringe; in the second place, anger at the majority who imposed a "cultural" life on the nation to which the Constitution is indifferent. Openness was designed to provide a respectable place for these "groups" or "minorities"—to wrest respect from those who were not disposed to give it— and to weaken the sense of superiority of the dominant majority (more recently dubbed WASPs, a name the success of which shows something of the success of sociology in reinterpreting the national consciousness). That dominant majority gave the country a dominant culture with its traditions, its literature, its tastes, its special claim to know and supervise the language, and its Protestant religions. Much of the intellectual machinery of twentieth-century American political thought and social science was constructed for the purposes of making an assault on that majority. It treated the founding principles as impediments and tried to overcome the other strand of our political heritage, majoritarianism, in favor of a nation of minorities and groups each following its own beliefs and inclinations. In particular, the intellectual minority expected to enhance its status, presenting itself as the defender and spokesman of all the others.

This reversal of the founding intention with respect to minorities is most striking. For the Founders, minorities are in general bad things, mostly identical to factions, selfish groups who have no concern as such for the common good. Unlike older political thinkers, they entertained no hopes of suppressing factions and educating a united or homogeneous citizenry. Instead they constructed an elaborate machinery to contain factions in such a way that they would cancel one another and allow for the pursuit of the common good. The good is still the guiding consideration in their thought, although it is arrived at, less directly than in classical political thought, by tolerating faction. The Founders wished to achieve a national majority concerning the fundamental rights and then prevent that majority from using its power to overturn those fundamental rights. In twentieth-century social science, however, the common good disappears and along with it the negative view of minorities. The very idea of majority—now understood to be selfish interest—is done away with in order to protect the minorities. This breaks the delicate balance between majority and minority in Constitutional thought. In such a perspective, where there is no common good, minorities are no longer problematic, and the protection of them emerges as the central function of government. Where this leads is apparent in, for example, Robert Dahl's *A Preface to Democratic Theory*. Groups or individuals who really care, as opposed to those who have lukewarm feelings, deserve special attention or special rights for their "intensity" or "commitment," the new political validation, which replaces reason. The Founding Fathers wished to reduce and defang fanaticism, whereas Dahl encourages it.

The appeal of the minority formula was enormous for all kinds of people, reactionary and progressive, all those who in the twenties and thirties still did not accept the political solution imposed by the Constitution. The reactionaries did not like the suppression of class privilege and religious establishment. For a variety of reasons they simply did not accept equality. Southerners knew full well that the Constitution's heart was a moral commitment to equality and hence condemned segregation of blacks. The Constitution was not just a set of rules of government but implied a moral order that was to be enforced throughout the entire Union. Yet the influence, which has not been sufficiently noted, of Southern writers and historians on the American view of their history has been powerful. They were remarkably successful in characterizing their "peculiar institution" as part of a charming diversity and individuality of culture to which the Constitution was worse than indifferent. The ideal of openness, lack of ethnocentricity, is just what they needed for a modern defense of their way of life against all the intrusions of outsiders who claimed equal rights with the folks back home. The Southerners' romantic characterization of the alleged failings of the Constitution, and their hostility to "mass society" with its technology, its money-grubbing way of life, egoistic individuals and concomitant destruction of community, organic and rooted, appealed to malcontents of all political colorations. The New Left in the sixties expressed exactly the same ideology that had been developed to protect the South from the threat to its practices posed by the Constitutional rights and the Federal Government's power to enforce them. It is the old alliance of Right and Left against liberal democracy, parodied as "bourgeois society."

The progressives of the twenties and thirties did not like the Constitutional protection of private property or the restraints on majority will and on living as one pleased. For them, equality had not gone far enough. Stalinists also found the definition of democracy as openness useful. The Constitution clashed too violently with the theory and practice of the

Soviet Union. But if democracy means open-endedness, and respect for other cultures prevents doctrinaire, natural-rights-based condemnation of the Soviet reality, then someday their ways may become ours. I remember my grade-school history textbook, newly printed on fine glossy paper, showing intriguing pictures of collective farms where farmers worked and lived together without the profit motive. (Children cannot understand the issues, but they are easy to propagandize.) This was very different from our way of life, but we were not to be closed to it, to react to it merely on the basis of our cultural prejudices.

Sexual adventurers like Margaret Mead and others who found America too narrow told us that not only must we know other cultures and learn to respect them, but we could also profit from them. We could follow their lead and loosen up, liberating ourselves from the opinion that our taboos are anything other than social constraints. We could go to the bazaar of cultures and find reinforcement for inclinations that are repressed by puritanical guilt feelings. All such teachers of openness had either no interest in or were actively hostile to the Declaration of Independence and the Constitution.

The civil rights movement provides a good example of this change in thought. In its early days almost all the significant leaders, in spite of tactical and temperamental differences, relied on the Declaration of Independence and the Constitution. They could charge whites not only with the most monstrous injustices but also with contradicting their own most sacred principles. The blacks were the true Americans in demanding the equality that belongs to them as human beings by natural and political right. This stance implied a firm conviction of the truth of the principles of natural right and of their fundamental efficacy within the Constitutional tradition, which, although tarnished, tends in the long run toward fulfilling those principles. They therefore worked through Congress, the Presidency, and, above all, the Judiciary. By contrast, the Black Power movement that supplanted the older civil rights movement—leaving aside both its excesses and its very understandable emphasis on self-respect and refusal to beg for acceptance—had at its core the view that the Constitutional tradition was always corrupt and was constructed as a defense of slavery. Its demand was for black identity, not universal rights. Not rights but power counted. It insisted on respect for blacks as blacks, not as human beings simply.

Yet the Constitution does not promise respect for blacks, whites, yellows, Catholics, Protestants, or Jews. It guarantees the protection of the rights of individual human beings. This has not proved to be enough, however, to what is perhaps by now a majority of Americans.

The upshot of all this for the education of young Americans is that they know much less about American history and those who were held to be its heroes. This was one of the few things that they used to come to college with that had something to do with their lives. Nothing has taken its place except a smattering of facts learned about other nations or cultures and a few social science formulas. None of this means much, partly because little attention has been paid to what is required in order truly to convey the spirit of other places and other times to young people, or for that matter to anyone, partly because the students see no relevance in any of it to the lives they are going to lead or to their prevailing passions. It is the rarest of occurrences to find a youngster who has been infused by this education with a longing to know all about China or the Romans or the Jews.

All to the contrary. There is an indifference to such things, for relativism has extinguished the real motive of education, the search for a good life. Young Americans have less and less knowledge of and interest in foreign places. In the past there were many students who actually knew something about and loved England, France, Germany, or Italy, for they dreamed of living there or thought their lives would be made more interesting by assimilating their languages and literatures. Such students have almost disappeared, replaced at most by students who are interested in the political problems of Third World countries and in helping them to modernize, with due respect to their old cultures, of course. This is not learning from others but condescension and a disguised form of a new imperialism. It is the Peace Corps mentality, which is not a spur to learning but to a secularized version of doing good works.

Actually openness results in American conformism—out there in the rest of the world is a drab diversity that teaches only that values are relative, whereas here we can create all the life-styles we want. Our openness means we do not need others. Thus what is advertised as a great opening is a great closing. No longer is there a hope that there are great wise men in other places and times who can reveal the truth about life —except for the few remaining young people who look for a quick fix from a guru. Gone is the real historical sense of a Machiavelli who wrested a few hours from each busy day in which "to don regal and courtly garments, enter the courts of the ancients and speak with them."

None of this concerns those who promote the new curriculum. The point is to propagandize acceptance of different ways, and indifference to their real content is as good a means as any. It was not necessarily the best of times in America when Catholics and Protestants were suspicious of and hated one another; but at least they were taking their beliefs seriously, and the more or less satisfactory accommodations they worked out were not simply the result of apathy about the state of their souls. Practically all that young Americans have today is an insubstantial awareness that there are many cultures, accompanied by a saccharine moral drawn from that awareness: We should all get along. Why fight? In 1980, during the crisis with Iran, the mother of one of the hostages expressed our current educational principles very well. She went to Iran to beg for her son's release, against the express wishes of the government of her country, the very week a rescue of the hostages was attempted. She justified her conduct by explaining that a mother has a right to try to save her son and also to learn a new culture. These are two basic rights, and her trip enabled her to kill two birds with one stone.

Actually the problem of cultural difference could have been faced more easily here in America forty years ago. When I was in college, a young Mississippian was lodged in my dormitory room for a few days during a visit of the University of Virginia debating team, of which he was a member. It was my first meeting with an intelligent, educated Southerner. He explained the inferiority of blacks to me, the reasons for Jim Crow, and how all that was a part of a unique way of life. He was an attractive, lively, amiable, healthy youngster. I, however, was horrified by him because I was still ethnocentric. I took my Northern beliefs to be universal. The "different strokes for different folks" philosophy had not yet taken full hold. Fortunately the homogenization of American culture that has occurred since that enables us to avoid such nasty confrontations. Only obviously pathological lower-class types now hold the racist views of my young visitor. Southerners helped to fashion our theoretical view of culture, but the Southern culture they intended to defend disappeared.

One of the techniques of opening young people up is to require a college course in a non-Western culture. Although many of the persons teaching such courses are real scholars and lovers of the areas they study, in every case I have seen this requirement—when there are so many other things that can and should be learned but are not required, when philosophy and religion are no longer required—has a demagogic intention. The point is to force students to recognize that there are other ways of thinking and that Western ways are not better. It is again not the content that counts but the lesson to be drawn. Such requirements are part of the effort to establish a world community and train its member—the person devoid of prejudice. But if the students were really to learn something of the minds of any of these non-Western cultures—which they do not—they would find that each and every one of these cultures is ethnocentric. All of them think their way is the best way, and all others are inferior. Herodotus tells us that the Persians thought that they were the best, that those nations bordering on them were next best, that those nations bordering on the nations bordering on them were third best, and so on, their worth declining as the concentric circles were farther from the Persian center. This is the very definition of ethnocentrism. Something like this is as ubiquitous as the prohibition against incest between mother and son.

Only in the Western nations, i.e., those influenced by Greek philosophy, is there some willingness to doubt the identification of the good with one's own way. One should conclude from the study of non-Western cultures that not only to prefer one's own way but to believe it best, superior to all others, is primary and even natural—exactly the opposite of what is intended by requiring students to study these cultures. What we are really doing is applying a Western prejudice—which we covertly take to indicate the superiority of our culture—and deforming the evidence of those other cultures to attest to its validity. The scientific study of other cultures is almost exclusively a Western phenomenon, and in its origin was obviously connected with the search for new and better ways, or at least for validation of the hope that our own culture really is the better way, a validation for which there is no felt need in other cultures. If we are to learn from those cultures, we must wonder whether such scientific study is a good idea. Consistency would seem to require professors of openness to respect the ethnocentrism or closedness they find everywhere else. However, in attacking ethnocentrism, what they actually do is to assert unawares the superiority of their scientific understanding and the inferiority of the other cultures which do not recognize it at the same time that they reject all such claims to superiority. They both affirm and deny the goodness of their science. They face a problem akin to that faced by Pascal in the conflict between reason and revelation, without the intellectual intransigence that forced him to abandon science in favor of faith.

The reason for the non-Western closedness, or ethnocentrism, is clear. Men must love and be loyal to their families and their peoples in order to preserve them. Only if they think their own things are good can they rest content with them. A father must prefer his child to other children, a citizen his country to others. That is why there are myths— to justify these attachments. And a man needs a place and opinions by which to orient himself. This is strongly asserted by those who talk about the importance of roots. The problem of getting along with outsiders is secondary to, and sometimes in conflict with, having an inside, a people, a culture, a way of life. A very great narrowness is not incompatible with the health of an individual or a people, whereas with great openness it is hard to avoid decomposition. The firm binding of the good with one's own, the refusal to see a distinction between the two, a vision of the cosmos that has a special place for one's people, seem to be conditions of culture. This is what really follows from the study of non-Western cultures proposed for undergraduates. It points them back to passionate attachment to their own and away from the science which liberates them from it. Science now appears as a threat to culture and a dangerous uprooting charm. In short, they are lost in a no-man's-land between the goodness of knowing and the goodness of culture, where they have been placed by their teachers who no longer have the resources to guide them. Help must be sought elsewhere.

Greek philosophers were the first men we know to address the problem of ethnocentrism. Distinctions between the good and one's own, between nature and convention, between the just and the legal are the signs of this movement of thought. They related the good to the fulfillment of the whole natural human potential and were aware that few, if any, of the nations of men had ways that allowed such fulfillment. They were open to the good. They had to use the good, which was not their own, to judge their own. This was a dangerous business because it tended to weaken wholehearted attachment to their own, hence to weaken their peoples as well as to expose themselves to the anger of family, friends, and countrymen. Loyalty versus quest for the good introduced an unresolvable tension into life. But the awareness of the good as such and the desire to possess it are priceless humanizing acquisitions.

This is the sound motive contained, along with many other less sound ones, in openness as we understand it. Men cannot remain content with what is given them by their culture if they are to be fully human. This is what Plato meant to show by the image of the cave in the *Republic* and by representing us as prisoners in it. A culture is a cave. He did not suggest going around to other cultures as a solution to the limitations of the cave. Nature should be the standard by which we judge our own lives and the lives of peoples. That is why philosophy, not history or anthropology, is the most important human science. Only dogmatic assurance that thought is culture-bound, that there is no nature, is what makes our educators so certain that the only way to escape the limitations of our time and place is to study other cultures. History and anthropology were understood by the Greeks to be useful only in discovering what the past and other peoples had to contribute to the discovery of nature. Historians and anthropologists were to put peoples and their conventions to the test, as Socrates did individuals, and go beyond them. These scientists were superior to their subjects because they saw a problem where others refused to see one, and they were engaged in the quest to solve it. They wanted to be able to evaluate themselves and others.

This point of view, particularly the need to know nature in order to have a standard, is uncomfortably buried beneath our human sciences, whether they like it or not, and accounts for the ambiguities and contradictions I have been pointing out. They want to make us culture-beings with the instruments that were invented to liberate us from culture. Openness used to be the virtue that permitted us to seek the good by using reason. It now means accepting everything and denying reason's power. The unrestrained and thoughtless pursuit of openness, without recognizing the inherent political, social, or cultural problem of openness as the goal of nature, has rendered openness meaningless. Cultural relativism destroys both one's own and the good. What is most characteristic of the West is science, particularly understood as the quest to know nature and the consequent denigration of convention—i.e., culture or the West understood as a culture—in favor of what is accessible to all men as men through their common and distinctive faculty, reason. Science's latest attempts to grasp the human situation—cultural relativism, historicism, the fact-value distinction—are the suicide of science. Culture, hence closedness, reigns supreme. Openness to closedness is what we teach.

Cultural relativism succeeds in destroying the West's universal or intellectually imperialistic claims, leaving it to be just another culture. So there is equality in the republic of cultures. Unfortunately the West is defined by its need for justification of its ways or values, by its need for discovery of nature, by its need for philosophy and science. This is its cultural imperative. Deprived of that, it will collapse. The United States is one of the highest and most extreme achievements of the rational quest for the good life according to nature. What makes its political structure possible is the use of the rational principles of natural right to found a people, thus uniting the good with one's own. Or, to put it otherwise, the regime established here promised untrammeled freedom to reason—not to everything indiscriminately, but to reason, the essential freedom that justifies the other freedoms, and on the basis of which, and for the sake of which, much deviance is also tolerated. An openness that denies the special claim of reason bursts the mainspring keeping the mechanism of this regime in motion. And this regime, contrary to all claims to the contrary, was founded to overcome ethnocentrism, which is in no sense a discovery of social science.

It is important to emphasize that the lesson the students are drawing from their studies is simply untrue. History and the study of cultures do not teach or prove that values or cultures are relative. All to the contrary, that is a philosophical premise that we now bring to our study of them. This premise is unproven and dogmatically asserted for what are largely political reasons. History and culture are interpreted in the light of it, and then are said to prove the premise. Yet the fact that there have been different opinions about good and bad in different times and places in no way proves that none is true or superior to others. To say that it does so prove is as absurd as to say that the diversity of points of view expressed in a college bull session proves there is no truth. On the face of it, the difference of opinion would seem to raise the question as to which is true or right rather than to banish it. The natural reaction is to try to resolve the difference, to examine the claims and reasons for each opinion.

Only the unhistorical and inhuman belief that opinions are held for no reason would prevent the undertaking of such an exciting activity. Men and nations always think they have reasons, and it could be understood to be historians' and social scientists' most important responsibility to make explicit and test those reasons. It was always known that there were many and conflicting opinions about the good, and nations embodying each of them. Herodotus was at least as aware as we are of the rich diversity of cultures. But he took that observation to be an invitation to investigate all of them to see what was good and bad about each and find out what he could learn about good and bad from them. Modern relativists take that same observation as proof that such investigation is impossible and that we must be respectful of them all. Thus students, and the rest of us, are deprived of the primary excitement derived from the discovery of diversity, the impulse of Odysseus, who, according to Dante, traveled the world to see the virtues and vices of men. History and anthropology cannot provide the answers, but they can provide the material on which judgment can work.

I know that men are likely to bring what are only their prejudices to the judgment of alien peoples. Avoiding that is one of the main purposes of education. But trying to prevent it by removing the authority of men's reason is to render ineffective the instrument that can correct their prejudices. True openness is the accompaniment of the desire to know, hence of the awareness of ignorance. To deny the possibility of knowing good and bad is to suppress true openness. A proper historical attitude would lead one to doubt the truth of historicism (the view that all thought is essentially related to and cannot transcend its own time) and treat it as a peculiarity of contemporary history. Historicism and cultural relativism actually are a means to avoid testing our own prejudices and asking, for example, whether men are really equal or whether that opinion is merely a democratic prejudice.

One might well wonder whether our historical and anthropological wisdom is not just a disguised and rather muddled version of the Romantic dilemma that seemed so compelling and tragic at the beginning of the nineteenth century and produced a longing for the distant past or exotic new lands and an art to satisfy that longing. As the heirs of science, so the argument goes, we know more than did the peoples of other times and places with their unscientific prejudices and illusions, but they were, or are, happier. This dilemma is expressed in the distinction between naive and sentimental art. Lévi-Strauss is an unwilling witness to my hypothesis. With a half-digested Rousseauism, he thinks the best culture is to be found at that moment when men have left the state of nature and live together in simple communities, without real private property or the explosion of *amour-propre*. Such a view requires science, which in turn requires developed and corrupted society, in order to emerge. Science is itself one of the modifications of *amour-propre*, the love of inequality. So this view simultaneously produces melancholy about science. But the dilemma seems so compelling only if we are certain that we know so much, which depends on science. Abandon that certainty, and we might be willing to test the beliefs of those happier peoples in order to see if they know something we do not know. Maybe Homer's genius was not so naive as Schiller thought it was. If we abandon this pride in our knowledge, which presents itself as humility, the discussion takes on a new dimension. Then we could go in one of two directions: abandonment of science, or the reestablishment of the theoretical life as both possible and itself productive of self-sufficient happiness. The Romantic posture is a way of not facing these extremes that masquerades as heroic endurance. Our shuttling back and forth between science and culture is a trivialized spin-off from that posture.

Thus there are two kinds of openness, the openness of indifference —promoted with the twin purposes of humbling our intellectual pride and letting us be whatever we want to be, just as long as we don't want to be knowers—and the openness that invites us to the quest for knowledge and certitude, for which history and the various cultures provide a brilliant array of examples for examination. This second kind of openness encourages the desire that animates and makes interesting every serious student—"I want to know what is good for me, what will make me happy" —while the former stunts that desire.

Openness, as currently conceived, is a way of making surrender to whatever is most powerful, or worship of vulgar success, look principled. It is historicism's ruse to remove all resistance to history, which in our day means public opinion, a day when public opinion already rules. How often I have heard the abandonment of requirements to learn languages or philosophy or science lauded as a progress of openness. Here is where the two kinds of openness clash. To be open to knowing, there are certain kinds of things one must know which most people don't want to bother to learn and which appear boring and irrelevant. Even the life of reason is often unappealing; and useless knowledge, i.e., knowledge that is not obviously useful for a career, has no place in the student's vision of the curriculum. So the university that stands intransigently for humane learning must necessarily look closed and rigid. If openness means to "go with the flow," it is necessarily an accommodation to the present. That present is so closed to doubt about so many things impeding the progress of its principles that unqualified openness to it would mean forgetting the despised alternatives to it, knowledge of which makes us aware of what is doubtful in it. True openness means closedness to all the charms that make us comfortable with the present.

When I was a young teacher at Cornell, I once had a debate about education with a professor of psychology. He said that it was his function to get rid of prejudices in his students. He knocked them down like tenpins. I began to wonder what he replaced those prejudices with. He did not seem to have much of an idea of what the opposite of a prejudice might be. He reminded me of the little boy who gravely informed me when I was four that there is no Santa Claus, who wanted me to bathe in the brilliant light of truth. Did this professor know what those prejudices meant for the students and what effect being deprived of them would have? Did he believe that there are truths that could guide their lives as did their prejudices? Had he considered how to give students the love of the truth necessary to seek unprejudiced beliefs, or would he render them passive, disconsolate, indifferent, and subject to authorities like himself, or the best of contemporary thought? My informant about Santa Claus was just showing off, proving his superiority to me. He had not created the Santa Claus that had to be there in order to be refuted. Think of all we learn about the world from men's belief in Santa Clauses, and all that we learn about the soul from those who believe in them. By contrast, merely methodological excision from the soul of the imagination that projects Gods and heroes onto the wall of the cave does not promote knowledge of the soul; it only lobotomizes it, cripples its powers.

I found myself responding to the professor of psychology that I personally tried to teach my students prejudices, since nowadays—with the general success of his method—they had learned to doubt beliefs even before they believed in anything. Without people like me, he would be out of business. Descartes had a whole wonderful world of old beliefs, of prescientific experience and articulations of the order of things, beliefs firmly and even fanatically held, before he even began his systematic and radical doubt. One has to have the experience of really believing before one can have the thrill of liberation. So I proposed a division of labor in which I would help to grow the flowers in the field and he could mow them down.

Prejudices, strong prejudices, are visions about the way things are. They are divinations of the order of the whole of things, and hence the road to a knowledge of that whole is by way of erroneous opinions about it. Error is indeed our enemy, but it alone points to the truth and therefore deserves our respectful treatment. The mind that has no prejudices at the outset is empty. It can only have been constituted by a method that is unaware of how difficult it is to recognize that a prejudice is a prejudice. Only Socrates knew, after a lifetime of unceasing labor, that he was ignorant. Now every high-school student knows that. How did it become so easy? What accounts for our amazing progress? Could it be that our experience has been so impoverished by our various methods, of which openness is only the latest, that there is nothing substantial enough left there to resist criticism, and we therefore have no world left of which to be really ignorant? Have we so simplified the soul that it is no longer difficult to explain? To an eye of dogmatic skepticism, nature herself, in all her lush profusion of expressions, might appear to be a prejudice. In her place we put a gray network of critical concepts, which were invented to interpret nature's phenomena but which strangled them and therewith destroyed their own *raison d'être*. Perhaps it is our first task to resuscitate those phenomena so that we may again have a world to which we can put our questions and be able to philosophize. This seems to me to be our educational challenge.

PART ONE

◆

STUDENTS

THE CLEAN SLATE

I used to think that young Americans began whatever education they were to get at the age of eighteen, that their early lives were spiritually empty and that they arrived at the university clean slates unaware of their deeper selves and the world beyond their superficial experience. The contrast between them and their European counterparts was set in high relief in the European novels and movies into which we were initiated at the university. The Europeans got most of the culture they were going to get from their homes and their public schools, lyceés, or gymnasiums, where their souls were incorporated into their specific literary traditions, which in turn expressed, and even founded, their traditions as peoples. It was not simply or primarily that these European schoolchildren had a vastly more sophisticated knowledge of the human heart than we were accustomed to in the young or, for that matter, the old. It was that their self-knowledge was mediated by their book learning and that their ambitions were formed as much by models first experienced in books as in everyday life. Their books had a substantial existence in everyday life and constituted much of what their society as a whole looked up to. It was commonplace for children of what they called good families to fill their imaginations with hopes of serious literary or philosophic careers, as do ours with hopes of careers in entertainment or business. All this was given to them early on, and by the time they were in their late teens it was part of the equipment of their souls, a lens through which they saw everything and which would affect all their later learning and experience. They went to the university to specialize.

Young Americans seemed, in comparison, to be natural savages when they came to the university. They had hardly heard the names of the writers who were the daily fare of their counterparts across the Atlantic, let alone took it into their heads that they could have a relationship to them. "What's Hecuba to him or he to Hecuba?" They belonged to the whole world, using their reason to see the things all men have in common, to solve the problems of survival, all the time innocently and unaware trampling on the altars sacred to the diverse peoples and nations of the earth who believe themselves constituted by their particular gods and heroes rather than by the common currency of the body. This American intellectual obtuseness could seem horrifying and barbarous, a stunting of full humanity, an incapacity to experience the beautiful, an utter lack of engagement in the civilization's ongoing discourse.

But for me, and for many better observers, this constituted a large part of the charm of American students. Very often natural curiosity and love of knowing appeared to come into their own in the first flush of maturity. Without traditional constraints or encouragements, without society's rewards and punishments, without snobbism or exclusivity, some Americans discovered that they had a boundless thirst for significant awareness, that their souls had spaces of which they were unaware and which cried out for furnishing. European students whom I taught always knew all about Rousseau and Kant, but such writers had been drummed into them from childhood and, in the new world after the war, they had become routine, as much a part of childhood's limitations as short pants, no longer a source of inspiration. So these students became suckers for the new, the experimental. But for Americans the works of the great writers could be the bright sunlit uplands where they could find the outside, the authentic liberation for which this essay is a plea. The old was new for these American students, and in that they were right, for every important old insight is perennially fresh. It is possible that Americans would always lack the immediate, rooted link to the philosophic and artistic achievements that appear to be part of the growth of particular cultures. But their approach to these works bespoke a free choice and the potential for man as man, regardless of time, place, station or wealth, to participate in what is highest. It would be a sad commentary on the human condition if the brotherhood of man is founded on what is lowest in him, while the higher cultivation required unbridgeably separate "cultures." The American disposition gave witness to an optimistic belief that the two universalities, of the body and of the soul, are possible, that access to the best is not dependent on chance. Young Americans, that is, some young Americans, gave promise of a continuing vitality for the tradition because they did not take it to be tradition.

The enchanting prospect provided by the American student was particularly powerful when I first started teaching good undergraduates in this country in the years just after Sputnik. In 1965 I wrote:

> The current generation of students is unique and very different in outlook from its teachers. I am referring to the good students in the better colleges and universities, those to whom a liberal education is primarily directed and who are the objects of a training which presupposes the best possible material. These young people have never experienced the anxieties about simple physical well-being that their parents experienced during the depression. They have been raised in comfort and with the expectation of ever increasing comfort. Hence they are largely indifferent to it; they are not proud of having acquired it and have not occupied themselves with the petty and sometimes deforming concerns necessary to its acquisition. And, because they do not particularly care about it, they are more willing to give it up in the name of grand ideals; as a matter of fact, they are eager to do so in the hope of proving that they are not attached to it and are open to higher callings. In short, these students are a kind of democratic version of an aristocracy. The unbroken prosperity of the last twenty years gives them the confidence that they can always make a living. So they are ready to undertake any career or adventure if it can be made to appear serious. The ties of tradition, family, and financial responsibility are weak. And, along with all this, goes an open, generous character. They tend to be excellent students and extremely grateful for anything they learn. A look at this special group tends to favor a hopeful prognosis for the country's moral and intellectual health.

There was, at that moment, a spiritual yearning, a powerful tension of the soul which made the university atmosphere electric. The Soviets' beating us into space shocked the nation and, for a moment, leveling education was set back on its heels. There seemed to be no time for that nonsense. Survival itself depended on better education for the best people. External necessity injected into the easygoing educational world the urgency that should always be there. Money and standards emerged in the twinkling of an eye. The goal was to produce scientific technicians who would save us from being at the mercy of tyrants. The high schools concentrated on math and physics, and there was honor and the promise of great futures for those who excelled in them. The Scholastic Aptitude Test became authoritative. Intellectual effort became a national pastime. The mere exercise of unused and flabby muscles is salutary, and the national effort both trained and inspired the mind. The students were better, more highly motivated.

Then I began to notice strange things. For example, for the first time, American students were really learning languages. And there were the signs of an incipient longing for something else. Science had been oversold. The true scientific vocation is very rare, and in the high schools it was presented in technical and uninspired fashion. The students apparently learned what they were asked to learn, but boredom was not wholly compensated for by great expectations. The new mental activity and desire for achievement had not quite found their objects. I observed that many of the best students' dedication to science was very thin. The great theoretical difficulty of modern natural science—that it cannot explain why it is good—was having its practical effect. The *why* question was coming close to the surface. As a result, although the sole interest of the public officials was in natural science, social science and the humanities also began to profit (inasmuch as the universities could not avoid saying they counted too). A little liberal learning easily attracted many of the most gifted away from natural science. They felt the alternatives had been hidden from them. And, once in the university, they could, this being a free country, change their minds about their interests when they discovered that there is something in addition to science. It was a tense moment, full of cravings that lacked clearly perceived goals.

I was convinced in the early sixties that what was wanted was a liberal education to give such students the wherewithal to examine their lives and survey their potential. This was the one thing the universities were unequipped and unwilling to offer them. The students' wandering and wayward energies finally found a political outlet. By the mid-sixties universities were offering them every concession other than education, but appeasement failed and soon the whole experiment in excellence was washed away, leaving not a trace. The various liberations wasted that marvelous energy and tension, leaving the students' souls exhausted and flaccid, capable of calculating, but not of passionate insight.

It may very well be that I was wrong, that what was building up in the early sixties was only a final assault on the last remaining inhibitions, that the appearance of intellectual longing was really only a version of the most powerful of modern longings—for the overcoming of necessity, tension, and conflict, a resting of the soul from its eternal travail. I still think, however, that there was much of true intellectual longing, and it only ended in relaxation as a result of our wasted opportunities.

But the students who have succeeded that generation of the late fifties and early sixties, when the culture leeches, professional and amateur, began their great spiritual bleeding, have induced me to wonder whether my conviction—the old Great Books conviction—was correct. That conviction was that nature is the only thing that counts in education, that the human desire to know is permanent, that all it really needs is the proper nourishment, and that education is merely putting the feast on the table. At the very best, it is clear to me now that nature needs the cooperation of convention, just as man's art is needed to found the political order that is the condition of his natural completeness. At worst, I fear that spiritual entropy or an evaporation of the soul's boiling blood is taking place, a fear that Nietzsche thought justified and made the center of all his thought. He argued that the spirit's bow was being unbent and risked being permanently unstrung. Its activity, he believed, comes from culture, and the decay of culture meant not only the decay of man in this culture but the decay of man simply. This is the crisis he tried to face resolutely: the very existence of man as man, as a noble being, depended on him and on men like him—so he thought. He may not have been right, but his case looks stronger all the time. At all events, the impression of natural savagery that Americans used to make was deceptive. It was only relative to the impression made by the Europeans. Today's select students know so much less, are so much more cut off from the tradition, are so much slacker intellectually, that they make their predecessors look like prodigies of culture. The soil is ever thinner, and I doubt whether it can now sustain the taller growths.

Consider by contrast the education that still persists, in very attenuated form, in France. To overstate only a bit, there are two writers who between them shape and set the limits to the minds of educated French-

men. Every Frenchman is born, or at least early on becomes, Cartesian
or Pascalian. (Something similar could be said about Shakespeare as educator of the English, Goethe of the Germans, and Dante and Machiavelli
of the Italians.) Descartes and Pascal are national authors, and they tell
the French people what their alternatives are, and afford a peculiar and
powerful perspective on life's perennial problems. They weave the fabric
of souls. On my last trip to France I heard a waiter call one of his fellow
waiters "a Cartesian." It was not pretentiousness; he was just referring to
what was for him a type. It is not so much that the French get principles
from these sources; rather they produce a cast of mind. Descartes and
Pascal represent a choice between reason and revelation, science and
piety, the choice from which everything else follows. One or the other of
these total visions almost always presents itself to the minds of Frenchmen
when they think about themselves and their problems. These great opponents whom no synthesis can unite—the opposition between *bon sens*
and faith against all odds—set in motion a dualism that we recognize
when we speak both of French clarity and of French passion. No country
has had such a persistent and irreconcilable quarrel between the secular
and the religious as France, where the two parties find no common
ground, where the aspirations of citizens who share the same country have
such different senses about the meaning of life. Shakespeare provided a
mediation of these two poles for the English, but no one succeeded in
doing it for the French, although Rousseau, a Swiss, made a noble attempt. Both Enlightenment and Catholic thought have found their special home in France for more than three centuries. Descartes and Pascal
gave accounts for the French of the West's common faith, Christianity,
and at the same time situated them with respect to that other, more
distant, source of inspiration, Greece. The succeeding generations of
writers who began from the Descartes-Pascal tension developed and varied their themes, and the essential spiritual experiences are repeated in
Voltaire, Montesquieu, Constant, Balzac and Zola, on the one hand, and
Malebranche, Chateaubriand, De Maistre, Baudelaire, Proust and Céline,
on the other, each aware of the others and carrying on a dialogue with
or confronting his opposite number.

    It was, therefore, very French of Tocqueville to say that the Ameri-
cans' method of thought was Cartesian without their ever having read
Descartes, and to wonder whether they could understand a Pascal or

produce one. America was not for him a people with a book. A Frenchman was a creature of sentiments informed by a literary tradition, while an American was a man of rational principles. These principles were first elaborated, of course, by writers but were such, as Kant said about his own moral philosophy, as to express what every well-brought-up child knows. Reciprocal recognition of rights needs little training, no philosophy, and abstracts from all differences of national character. Americans were, in effect, told that they could be whatever they wanted to be or happened to be as long as they recognized that the same applied to all other men and they were willing to support and defend the government that guaranteed that dispensation. It is possible to become an American in a day. And this is not to make light of what it means to be an American. The cooperation of natural passion and natural reason defies the ancient maxims that insisted that a city be like an organic unity, generated by the motherland, with a citizen's relation to it like a leaf's to a tree. It is, however, impossible, or it was until only yesterday, to become a Frenchman, for a Frenchman is a complex harmony, or dissonance, of historic echoes, from birth on. The French language, which the French used to learn very well, did not exist for the sake of conveying information, for communicating men's common needs; it was indistinguishable from a historical consciousness. Frenchness is defined by participation in this language, its literature and the entire range of effects it produces. Somehow the legalistic arguments about rights do not touch the privilege conveyed by participation in it. In America there are in principle no real outsiders, while in France persons who, although citizens, are marginal to this tradition, for example, Jews, have always had to think hard about what it is they belong to. In France, the Jew's relation to what is constitutively French is a great and complex literary theme. The response to the issue is not universal and causes the development of an interesting spectrum of human types. A Jew in America, by contrast, is as American as anyone; and if he is singled out or treated differently, unconditional outrage is the appropriate response.

The lack of American equivalents to Descartes, Rascal, or, for that matter, Montaigne, Rabelais, Racine, Montesquieu and Rousseau is not a question of quality, but of whether there are any writers who are necessary to building our spiritual edifice, whom one must have read, or rather lived with, to be called educated, and who are the interpreters and even makers of our national life. One can think of American writers and writings that should be read and frequently are read; but, to the extent that Americans are readers, the whole world is their bookshelf; there has not been the deep necessity to absorb their own country's writings that citizens of other nations experience. A phenomenon like Wagner's *Gesamtkunstwerk*, a high work of art which is intended to be wholly German, of Germans, for Germans and by Germans, and is an expression of collective consciousness, is inconceivable to Americans. And it is astonishing how little a Frenchman knows, or has a feeling for, things that are not French. But to Americans, Homer, Virgil, Dante, Shakespeare, Goethe belong to everyone or to "civilization." And perhaps they do, in the long run. But this was not the view of Greeks, Romans, Italians, Englishmen and Germans, or of the Jews with their book that belonged to *them*, that told *their* story, and embodied, so to speak, their instinct. Americans believe in equal access. Mortimer Adler's business genius recognized this and made a roaring commercial success out of the Great Books. He was not even concerned about the translations he used, let alone about learning languages. Most writers in older lands despaired of being understood by those who had not *lived* their language. Heidegger, who desperately tried to maintain and revitalize this view, thought that "Language is the house of Being," that it is the height of superficiality to suppose that translation is even possible.

Yet my early experience of American simplicity had persuaded me that we were right, that we could begin with nothing, that uncultivated nature sufficed. I had not, however, paid sufficient attention to what students actually used to bring with them, the education that was once in the air that helped launch them. Most students could be counted on to know the Bible, that ubiquitous source of the older traditions. In America it was not filtered through great national interpreters, but approached directly in the manner of early Protestantism, every man his own interpreter. The Bible was thus a mirror of that indifference to national cultures inherent in the American method. Most students also participated in a remarkably unified and explicit political tradition that possesses one writing known to everyone and probably believed by most, the Declaration of Independence.

Contrary to much contemporary wisdom, the United States has one of the longest uninterrupted political traditions of any nation in the world.

What is more, that tradition is unambiguous; its meaning is articulated in simple, rational speech that is immediately comprehensible and powerfully persuasive to all normal human beings. America tells one story: the unbroken, ineluctable progress of freedom and equality. From its first settlers and its political foundings on, there has been no dispute that freedom and equality are the essence of justice for us. No one serious or notable has stood outside this consensus. You had to be a crank or a buffoon (e.g., Henry Adams or H. L. Mencken, respectively) to get attention as a nonbeliever in the democracy. All significant political disputes have been about the meaning of freedom and equality, not about their rightness. Nowhere else is there a tradition or a culture whose message is so distinct and unequivocal—certainly not in France, Italy, Germany, or even England. There the greatest events and the greatest men speak for monarchy and aristocracy as well as for democracy, for established religion as well as for tolerance, for patriotism that takes primacy over liberty, for privilege that takes primacy over equality of right. Belonging to one of these peoples may be explained as a sentiment, an attachment to one's own, akin to the attachment to father and mother, but Frenchness, Englishness, Germanness remain, nonetheless, ineffable. Everybody can, however, articulate what Americanness is. And that Americanness generated a race of heroes—Franklin, Washington, Hamilton, Jefferson, Lincoln and so on—all of whom contributed to equality. Our imagination is not turned toward a Joan of Arc, a Louis XIV or a Napoleon who counterbalance our equivalent of 1789. Our heroes and the language of the Declaration contribute to a national reverence for our Constitution, also a unique phenomenon. All this is material for self-consciousness and provides a superior moral significance to humdrum lives as well as something to study.

But the unity, grandeur and attendant folklore of the founding heritage was attacked from so many directions in the last half-century that it gradually disappeared from daily life and from textbooks. It all began to seem like Washington and the cherry tree—not the sort of thing to teach children seriously. What is influential in the higher intellectual circles always ends up in the schools. The leading ideas of the Declaration began to be understood as eighteenth-century myths or ideologies. Historicism, in Carl Becker's version (*The Declaration of Independence: A Study in the History of Political Ideas*, 1922), both cast doubt on the truth of the natural rights teaching and optimistically promised that it would provide a substitute. Similarly Dewey's pragmatism—the method of science as the method of democracy, individual growth without limits, especially natural limits—saw the past as radically imperfect and regarded our history as irrelevant or as a hindrance to rational analysis of our present. Then there was Marxist debunking of the Charles Beard variety, trying to demonstrate that there was no public spirit, only private concern for property, in the Founding Fathers, thus weakening our convictions of the truth or superiority of American principles and our heroes (*An Economic Interpretation of the Constitution*, 1913). Then the Southern historians and writers avenged the victory of the antislavery Union by providing low motives for the North (incorporating European critiques of commerce and technology) and idealizing the South's way of life. Finally, in curious harmony with the Southerners, the radicals in the civil rights movement succeeded in promoting a popular conviction that the Founding was, and the American principles are, racist. The bad conscience they promoted killed off the one continuing bit of popular culture that celebrated the national story—the Western.

Thus, openness has driven out the local deities, leaving only the speechless, meaningless country. There is no immediate, sensual experience of the nation's meaning or its project, which would provide the basis for adult reflection on regimes and statesmanship. Students now arrive at the university ignorant and cynical about our political heritage, lacking the wherewithal to be either inspired by it or seriously critical of it.

The other element of fundamental primary learning that has disappeared is religion. As the respect for the Sacred—the latest fad—has soared, real religion and knowledge of the Bible have diminished to the vanishing point. The gods never walked very tall in our political life or in our schools. The Lord's Prayer we mumbled in grade school when I was a child affected us less than the Pledge of Allegiance we also recited. It was the home—and the houses of worship related to it—where religion lived. The holy days and the common language and set of references that permeated most households constituted a large part of the family bond and gave it a substantial content. Moses and the Tables of the Law, Jesus and his preaching of brotherly love, had an imaginative existence. Passages from the Psalms and the Gospels echoed in children's heads. Attending church or synagogue, praying at the table, were a way of life, inseparable from the moral education that was supposed to be the family's special responsibility in this democracy. Actually, the moral teaching was the religious teaching. There was no abstract doctrine. The things one was supposed to do, the sense that the world supported them and punished disobedience, were all incarnated in the Biblical stories. The loss of the gripping inner life vouchsafed those who were nurtured by the Bible must be primarily attributed not to our schools or political life, but to the family, which, with all its rights to privacy, has proved unable to maintain any content of its own. The dreariness of the family's spiritual landscape passes belief. It is as monochrome and unrelated to those who pass through it as are the barren steppes frequented by nomads who take their mere subsistence and move on. The delicate fabric of the civilization into which the successive generations are woven has unraveled, and children are raised, not educated.

I am speaking here not of the unhappy, broken homes that are such a prominent part of American life, but the relatively happy ones, where husband and wife like each other and care about their children, very often unselfishly devoting the best parts of their lives to them. But they have nothing to give their children in the way of a vision of the world, of high models of action or profound sense of connection with others. The family requires the most delicate mixture of nature and convention, of human and divine, to subsist and perform its function. Its base is merely bodily reproduction, but its purpose is the formation of civilized human beings. In teaching a language and providing names for all things, it transmits an interpretation of the order of the whole of things. It feeds on books, in which the little polity—the family—believes, which tell about right and wrong, good and bad and explain why they are so. The family requires a certain authority and wisdom about the ways of the heavens and of men. The parents must have knowledge of what has happened in the past, and prescriptions for what ought to be, in order to resist the philistinism or the wickedness of the present. Ritual and ceremony are now often said to be necessary for the family, and they are now lacking. The family, however, has to be a sacred unity believing in the permanence of what it teaches, if its ritual and ceremony are to express and transmit the wonder of the moral law, which it alone is capable of transmitting and which makes it special in a world devoted to the humanly, all too humanly, useful. When that belief disappears, as it has, the family has, at best, a transitory togetherness. People sup together, play together, travel together, but they do not think together. Hardly any homes have any intellectual life whatsoever, let alone one that informs the vital interests of life. Educational TV marks the high tide for family intellectual life.

The cause of this decay of the family's traditional role as the transmitter of tradition is the same as that of the decay of the humanities: nobody believes that the old books do, or even could, contain the truth. So books have become, at best, "culture," i.e., boring. As Tocqueville put it, in a democracy tradition is nothing more than information. With the "information explosion," tradition has become superfluous. As soon as tradition has come to be recognized as tradition, it is dead, something to which lip service is paid in the vain hope of edifying the kids. In the United States, practically speaking, the Bible was the only common culture, one that united simple and sophisticated, rich and poor, young and old, and—as the very model for a vision of the order of the whole of things, as well as the key to the rest of Western art, the greatest works of which were in one way or another responsive to the Bible—provided access to the seriousness of books. With its gradual and inevitable disappearance, the very idea of such a total book and the possibility and necessity of world-explanation is disappearing. And fathers and mothers have lost the idea that the highest aspiration they might have for their children is for them to be wise—as priests, prophets or philosophers are wise. Specialized competence and success are all that they can imagine. Contrary to what is commonly thought, without the book even the idea of the order of the whole is lost.

Parents do not have the legal or moral authority they had in the Old World. They lack self-confidence as educators of their children, generously believing that they will be better than their parents, not only in well-being, but in moral, bodily and intellectual virtue. There is always a more or less open belief in progress, which means the past appears poor and contemptible. The future, which is open-ended, cannot be prescribed to by parents, and it eclipses the past which they know to be inferior.

Along with the constant newness of everything and the ceaseless moving from place to place, first radio, then television, have assaulted and overturned the privacy of the home, the real American privacy, which permitted the development of a higher and more independent life within democratic society. Parents can no longer control the atmosphere of the home and have even lost the will to do so. With great subtlety and energy, television enters not only the room, but also the tastes of old and young alike, appealing to the immediately pleasant and subverting whatever does not conform to it. Nietzsche said the newspaper had replaced the prayer in the life of the modern bourgeois, meaning that the busy, the cheap, the ephemeral, had usurped all that remained of the eternal in his daily life. Now television has replaced the newspaper. It is not so much the low quality of the fare provided that is troubling. It is much more the difficulty of imagining any order of taste, any way of life with pleasures and learning that naturally fit the lives of the family's members, keeping itself distinct from the popular culture and resisting the visions of what is admirable and interesting with which they are bombarded from within the household itself.

The improved education of the vastly expanded middle class in the last half-century has also weakened the family's authority. Almost every-one in the middle class has a college degree, and most have an advanced degree of some kind. Those of us who can look back to the humble stations of our parents or grandparents, who never saw the inside of an institution of higher learning, can have cause for self-congratulation. But—inevitably but—the impression that our general populace is better educated depends on an ambiguity in the meaning of the word education, or a fudging of the distinction between liberal and technical education. A highly trained computer specialist need not have had any more learning about morals, politics or religion than the most ignorant of persons. All to the contrary, his narrow education, with the prejudices and the pride accompanying it, and its literature which comes to be and passes away in a day and uncriti-cally accepts the premises of current wisdom, can cut him off from the liberal learning that simpler folk used to absorb from a variety of tradi-tional sources. It is not evident to me that someone whose regular reading consists of *Time, Playboy* and *Scientific American* has any profounder wisdom about the world than the rural schoolboy of yore with his McGuffey's reader. When a youngster like Lincoln sought to educate himself, the immediately available obvious things for him to learn were the Bible, Shakespeare and Euclid. Was he really worse off than those who try to find their way through the technical smorgasbord of the current school system, with its utter inability to distinguish between important and unimportant in any way other than by the demands of the market?

My grandparents were ignorant people by our standards, and my grandfather held only lowly jobs. But their home was spiritually rich because all the things done in it, not only what was specifically ritual, found their origin in the Bible's commandments, and their explanation in the Bible's stories and the commentaries on them, and had their imaginative counterparts in the deeds of the myriad of exemplary heroes. My grandparents found reasons for the existence of their family and the fulfillment of their duties in serious writings, and they interpreted their special sufferings with respect to a great and ennobling past. Their simple faith and practices linked them to great scholars and thinkers who dealt with the same material, not from outside or from an alien perspective, but believing as they did, while simply going deeper and providing guidance. There was a respect for real learning, because it had a felt connection with their lives. This is what a community and a history mean, a common experience inviting high and low into a single body of belief.

I do not believe that my generation, my cousins who have been educated in the American way, all of whom are M.D.s or Ph.D.s, have any comparable learning. When they talk about heaven and earth, the relations between men and women, parents and children, the human condition, I hear nothing but cliches, superficialities, the material of satire. I am not saying anything so trite as that life is fuller when people have myths to live by. I mean rather that a life based on the Book is closer to the truth, that it provides the material for deeper research in and access to the real nature of things. Without the great revelations, epics and philosophies as part of our natural vision, there is nothing to see out there, and eventually little left inside. The Bible is not the only means to furnish a mind, but without a book of similar gravity, read with the gravity of the potential believer, it will remain unfurnished.

The moral education that is today supposed to be the great responsibility of the family cannot exist if it cannot present to the imagination of the young a vision of a moral cosmos and of the rewards and punishments for good and evil, sublime speeches that accompany and interpret deeds, protagonists and antagonists in the drama of moral choice, a sense of the stakes involved in such choice, and the despair that results when the world is "disenchanted." Otherwise, education becomes the vain attempt to give children "values." Beyond the fact that parents do not know what they believe, and surely do not have the self-confidence to tell their children much more than that they want them to be happy and fulfill whatever potential they may have, values are such pallid things. What are they and how are they communicated? The courses in "value-clarification" springing up in schools are supposed to provide models for parents and get children to talk about abortion, sexism or the arms race, issues the significance of which they cannot possibly understand. Such education is little more than propaganda, and propaganda that does not work, because the opinions or values arrived at are will-o'-the-wisps, insubstantial, without ground in experience or passion, which are the bases of moral reasoning. Such "values" will inevitably change as public opinion changes. The new moral education has none of the genius that engenders moral instinct or second nature, the prerequisite not only of character but also of thought. Actually, the family's moral training now comes down to inculcating the bare minima of social behavior, not lying or stealing, and produces university students who can say nothing more about the ground of their moral action than "If I did that to him, he could do it to me" —an explanation which does not even satisfy those who utter it.

This gradual stilling of the old political and religious echoes in the souls of the young accounts for the difference between the students I knew at the beginning of my teaching career and those I face now. The loss of the books has made them narrower and flatter. Narrower because they lack what is most necessary, a real basis for discontent with the present and awareness that there are alternatives to it. They are both more contented with what is and despairing of ever escaping from it. The longing for the beyond has been attenuated. The very models of admiration and contempt have vanished. Flatter, because without interpretations of things, without the poetry or the imagination's activity, their souls are like mirrors, not of nature, but of what is around. The refinement of the mind's eye that permits it to see the delicate distinctions among men, among their deeds and their motives, and constitutes real taste, is impossible without the assistance of literature in the grand style.

So there is less soil in which university teaching can take root, less of the enthusiasm and curiosity of young Glaucon in Plato's *Republic*, whose *eros* makes him imagine that there are splendid satisfactions in store for him about which he does not wish to be fooled and for knowledge of which he seeks a teacher. It is much more difficult today to attach the classic books to any experience or felt need the students have.

BOOKS

I have begun to wonder whether the experience of the greatest texts from early childhood is not a prerequisite for a concern throughout life for them and for lesser but important literature. The soul's longing, its intolerable irritation under the constraints of the conditional and limited, may very well require encouragement at the outset. At all events, whatever the cause, our students have lost the practice of and the taste for reading. They have not learned how to read, nor do they have the expectation of delight or improvement from reading. They are "authentic," as against the immediately preceding university generations, in having few cultural pretensions and in refusing hypocritical ritual bows to high culture.

When I first noticed the decline in reading during the late sixties, I began asking my large introductory classes, and any other group of younger students to which I spoke, what books really count for them. Most are silent, puzzled by the question. The notion of books as companions is foreign to them. Justice Black with his tattered copy of the Constitution in his pocket at all times is not an example that would mean much to them. There is no printed word to which they look for counsel, inspiration or joy. Sometimes one student will say "the Bible." (He learned it at home, and his Biblical studies are not usually continued at the university.) There is always a girl who mentions Ayn Rand's *The Fountainhead*, a book, although hardly literature, which, with its sub-Nietzschean assertiveness, excites somewhat eccentric youngsters to a new way of life. A few students mention recent books that struck them and supported their own self-interpretation, like *The Catcher in the Rye*. (Theirs is usually the most genuine response and also shows a felt need for help in self-interpretation. But it is an uneducated response. Teachers should take advantage of the need expressed in it to show such students that better writers can help them more.) After such sessions I am pursued by a student or two who wants to make it clear that he or she is really influenced by books, not just by one or two but by many. Then he recites a list of classics he may have grazed in high school.

Imagine such a young person walking through the Louvre or the Uffizi, and you can immediately grasp the condition of his soul. In his innocence of the stories of Biblical and Greek or Roman antiquity, Raphael, Leonardo, Michelangelo, Rembrandt and all the others can say nothing to him. All he sees are colors and forms—modern art. In short, like almost everything else in his spiritual life, the paintings and statues are abstract. No matter what much of modern wisdom asserts, these artists counted on immediate recognition of their subjects and, what is more, on their having a powerful meaning for their viewers. The works were the fulfillment of those meanings, giving them a sensuous reality and hence completing them. Without those meanings, and without their being something essential to the viewer as a moral, political and religious being, the works lose their essence. It is not merely the tradition that is lost when the voice of civilization elaborated over millennia has been stilled in this way. It is being itself that vanishes beyond the dissolving horizon. One of the most flattering things that ever happened to me as a teacher occurred when I received a postcard from a very good student on his first visit to Italy, who wrote, "You are not a professor of political philosophy but a travel agent." Nothing could have better expressed my intention as an educator. He thought I had prepared him to see. Then he could begin thinking for himself with something to think about. The real sensation of the Florence in which Machiavelli is believable is worth all the formulas of metaphysics ten times over. Education in our times must try to find whatever there is in students that might yearn for completion, and to reconstruct the learning that would enable them autonomously to seek that completion.

In a less grandiose vein, students today have nothing like the Dickens who gave so many of us the unforgettable Pecksniffs, Micawbers, Pips, with which we sharpened our vision, allowing us some subtlety in our distinction of human types. It is a complex set of experiences that enables one to say so simply, "He is a Scrooge." Without literature, no such observations are possible and the fine art of comparison is lost. The psychological obtuseness of our students is appalling, because they have only pop psychology to tell them what people are like, and the range of their motives. As the awareness that we owed almost exclusively to literary genius falters, people become more alike, for want of knowing they can be otherwise. What poor substitutes for real diversity are the wild rainbows of dyed hair and other external differences that tell the observer nothing about what is inside.

Lack of education simply results in students' seeking for enlightenment wherever it is readily available, without being able to distinguish between the sublime and trash, insight and propaganda. For the most part students turn to the movies, ready prey to interested moralisms such as the depictions of Gandhi or Thomas More—largely designed to further passing political movements and to appeal to simplistic needs for greatness —or to insinuating flattery of their secret aspirations and vices, giving them a sense of significance. *Kramer vs. Kramer* may be up-to-date about divorces and sex roles, but anyone who does not have *Anna Karenina* or *The Red and the Black* as part of his viewing equipment cannot sense what might be lacking, or the difference between an honest presentation and an exercise in consciousness-raising, trashy sentimentality and elevated sentiment. As films have emancipated themselves from the literary tyranny under which they suffered and which gave them a bad conscience, the ones with serious pretensions have become intolerably ignorant and manipulative. The distance from the contemporary and its high seriousness that students most need in order not to indulge their petty desires and to discover what is most serious about themselves cannot be found in the cinema, which now only knows the present. Thus, the failure to read good books both enfeebles the vision and strengthens our most fatal tendency—the belief that the here and now is all there is.

The only way to counteract this tendency is to intervene most vigorously in the education of those few who come to the university with a strong urge for *un je ne sais quoi,* who fear that they may fail to discover it, and that the cultivation of their minds is required for the success of their quest. We are long past the age when a whole tradition could be stored up in all students, to be fruitfully used later by some. Only those who are willing to take risks and are ready to believe the implausible are now fit for a bookish adventure. The desire must come from within. People do what they want, and now the most needful things appear so implausible to them that it is hopeless to attempt universal reform. Teachers of writing in state universities, among the noblest and most despised laborers in the academy, have told me that they cannot teach writing to students who do not read, and that it is practically impossible to get them to read, let alone like it. This is where high schools have failed most, filled with teachers who are products of the sixties and reflecting the pallor of university-level humanities. The old teachers who loved Shakespeare or Austen or Donne, and whose only reward for teaching was the perpetuation of their taste, have all but disappeared.

The latest enemy of the vitality of classic texts is feminism. The struggles against elitism and racism in the sixties and seventies had little direct effect on students' relations to books. The democratization of the university helped dismantle its structure and caused it to lose its focus. But the activists had no special quarrel with the classic texts, and they were even a bit infected by their Frankfurt School masters' habit of parading their intimacy with high culture. Radicals had at an earlier stage of egalitarianism already dealt with the monarchic, aristocratic and antidemocratic character of most literary classics by no longer paying attention to their manifest political content. Literary criticism concentrated on the private, the intimate, the feelings, thoughts and relations of individuals, while reducing to the status of a literary convention of the past the fact that the heroes of many classic works were soldiers and statesmen engaged in ruling and faced with political problems. Shakespeare, as he has been read for most of this century, does not constitute a threat to egalitarian right thinking. And as for racism, it just did not play a role in the classic literature, at least in the forms in which we are concerned about it today, and no great work of literature is ordinarily considered racist.

But *all* literature up to today is sexist. The Muses never sang to the poets about liberated women. It's the same old *chanson* from the Bible and Homer through Joyce and Proust. And this is particularly grave for literature, since the love interest was most of what remained in the classics after politics was purged in the academy, and was also what drew students to reading them. These books appealed to eros while educating it. So activism has been directed against the content of books. The latest translation of Biblical text—sponsored by the National Council of the Churches of Christ—suppresses gender references to God, so that future generations will not have to grapple with the fact that God was once a sexist. But this technique has only limited applicability. Another tactic is to expunge the most offensive authors—for example, Rousseau—from the education of the young or to include feminist responses in college courses, pointing out the distorting prejudices, and using the books only as evidence of the misunderstanding of woman's nature and the history of injustice to it. Moreover, the great female characters can be used as examples of the various ways women have coped with their enslavement to the sexual role. But never, never, must a student be attracted to those old ways and take them as models for him or herself. However, all this effort is wasted. Students cannot imagine that the old literature could teach them anything about the relations they want to have or will be permitted to have. So they are indifferent.

Having heard over a period of years the same kinds of responses to my question about favorite books, I began to ask students who their heroes are. Again, there is usually silence, and most frequently nothing follows. Why should anyone have heroes? One should be oneself and not form oneself in an alien mold. Here positive ideology supports them: their lack of hero-worship is a sign of maturity. They posit their own values. They have turned into a channel first established in the *Republic* by Socrates, who liberated himself from Achilles, and picked up in earnest by Rousseau in *Emile.* Following on Rousseau, Tolstoy depicts Prince Andrei in *War and Peace,* who was educated in Plutarch and is alienated from himself by his admiration for Napoleon. But we tend to forget that Andrei is a very noble man indeed and that his heroic longings give him a splendor of soul that dwarfs the petty, vain, self-regarding concerns of the bourgeoisie that surrounds him. Only a combination of natural sentiment and unity with the spirit of Russia and its history can, for Tolstoy, produce human beings superior to Andrei, and even they are only ambiguously superior. But in America we have only the bourgeoisie, and the love of the heroic is one of the few counterpoises available to us. In us the contempt for the heroic is only an extension of the perversion of the democratic principle that denies greatness and wants everyone to feel comfortable in his skin without having to suffer unpleasant comparisons. Students have not the slightest notion of what an achievement it is to free oneself from public guidance and find resources for guidance within oneself. From what source within themselves would they draw the goals they think they set for themselves? Liberation from the heroic only means that they have no resource whatsoever against conformity to the current "role models." They are constantly thinking of themselves in terms of fixed standards that they did not make. Instead of being overwhelmed by Cyrus, Theseus, Moses or Romulus, they unconsciously act out the roles of the doctors, lawyers, businessmen or TV personalities around them. One can only pity young people without admirations they can respect or avow, who are artificially restrained from the enthusiasm for great virtue.

In encouraging this deformity, democratic relativism joins a branch of conservatism that is impressed by the dangerous political consequences of idealism. These conservatives want young people to know that this tawdry old world cannot respond to their demands for perfection. In the choice between the somewhat arbitrarily distinguished realism and idealism, a sensible person would want to be both, or neither. But, momentarily accepting a distinction I reject, idealism as it is commonly conceived should have primacy in an education, for man is a being who must take his orientation by his possible perfection. To attempt to suppress this most natural of all inclinations because of possible abuses is, almost literally, to throw out the baby with the bath. Utopianism is, as Plato taught us at the outset, the fire with which we must play because it is the only way we can find out what we are. We need to criticize false understandings of Utopia, but the easy way out provided by realism is deadly. As it now stands, students have powerful images of what a perfect body is and pursue it incessantly. But deprived of literary guidance, they no longer have any image of a perfect soul, and hence do not long to have one. They do not even imagine that there is such a thing.

Following on what I learned from this second question, I began asking a third: Who do you think is evil? To this one there is an immediate response: Hitler. (Stalin is hardly mentioned.) After him, who else? Up until a couple of years ago, a few students said Nixon, but he has been forgotten and at the same time is being rehabilitated. And there it stops. They have no idea of evil; they doubt its existence. Hitler is just another abstraction, an item to fill up an empty category. Although they live in a world in which the most terrible deeds are being performed and they see brutal crime in the streets, they turn aside. Perhaps they believe that evil deeds are performed by persons who, if they got the proper therapy, would not do them again—that there are evil deeds, not evil people. There is no *Inferno* in this comedy. Thus, the most common student view lacks an awareness of the depths as well as the heights, and hence lacks gravity.

MUSIC

Though students do not have books, they most emphatically do have
music. Nothing is more singular about this generation than its addiction
to music. This is the age of music and the states of soul that accompany
it. To find a rival to this enthusiasm, one would have to go back at least
a century to Germany and the passion for Wagner's operas. They had the
religious sense that Wagner was creating the meaning of life and that they
were not merely listening to his works but experiencing that meaning.
Today, a very large proportion of young people between the ages of ten
and twenty live for music. It is their passion; nothing else excites them
as it does; they cannot take seriously anything alien to music. When they
are in school and with their families, they are longing to plug themselves
back into their music. Nothing surrounding them—school, family, church
—has anything to do with their musical world. At best that ordinary life
is neutral, but mostly it is an impediment, drained of vital content, even
a thing to be rebelled against. Of course, the enthusiasm for Wagner was
limited to a small class, could be indulged only rarely and only in a few
places, and had to wait on the composer's slow output. The music of the
new votaries, on the other hand, knows neither class nor nation. It is
available twenty-four hours a day, everywhere. There is the stereo in the
home, in the car; there are concerts; there are music videos, with special
channels exclusively devoted to them, on the air nonstop; there are the
Walkmans so that no place—not public transportation, not the library—
prevents students from communing with the Muse, even while studying.
And, above all, the musical soil has become tropically rich. No need to

wait for one unpredictable genius. Now there are many geniuses, producing all the time, two new ones rising to take the place of every fallen hero. There is no dearth of the new and the startling.

The power of music in the soul—described to Jessica marvelously by Lorenzo in the *Merchant of Venice*—has been recovered after a long period of desuetude. And it is rock music alone that has effected this restoration. Classical music is dead among the young. This assertion will, I know, be hotly disputed by many who, unwilling to admit tidal changes, can point to the proliferation on campuses of classes in classical music appreciation and practice, as well as performance groups of all kinds. Their presence is undeniable, but they involve not more than 5 to 10 percent of the students. Classical music is now a special taste, like Greek language or pre-Columbian archeology, not a common culture of reciprocal communication and psychological shorthand. Thirty years ago, most middle-class families made some of the old European music a part of the home, partly because they liked it, partly because they thought it was good for the kids. University students usually had some early emotive association with Beethoven, Chopin and Brahms, which was a permanent part of their makeup and to which they were likely to respond throughout their lives. This was probably the only regularly recognizable class distinction between educated and uneducated in America. Many, or even most, of the young people of that generation also swung with Benny Goodman, but with an element of self-consciousness—to be hip, to prove they weren't snobs, to show solidarity with the democratic ideal of a pop culture out of which would grow a new high culture. So there remained a class distinction between high and low, although private taste was beginning to create doubts about whether one really liked the high very much. But all that has changed. Rock music is as unquestioned and unproblematic as the air the students breathe, and very few have any acquaintance at all with classical music. This is a constant surprise to me. And one of the strange aspects of my relations with good students I come to know well is that I frequently introduce them to Mozart. This is a pleasure for me, inasmuch as it is always pleasant to give people gifts that please them. It is interesting to see whether and in what ways their studies are complemented by such music. But this is something utterly new to me as a teacher; formerly my students usually knew much more classical music than I did.

Music was not all that important for the generation of students preceding the current one. The romanticism that had dominated serious music since Beethoven appealed to refinements—perhaps overrefinements—of sentiments that are hardly to be found in the contemporary world. The lives people lead or wish to lead and their prevailing passions are of a different sort than those of the highly educated German and French bourgeoisie, who were avidly reading Rousseau and Baudelaire, Goethe and Heine, for their spiritual satisfaction. The music that had been designed to produce, as well as to please, such exquisite sensibilities had a very tenuous relation to American lives of any kind. So romantic musical culture in America had had for a long time the character of a veneer, as easily susceptible to ridicule as were Margaret Dumont's displays of coquettish chasteness, so aptly exploited by Groucho Marx in *A Night At The Opera*. I noticed this when I first started teaching and lived in a house for gifted students. The "good" ones studied their physics and then listened to classical music. The students who did not fit so easily into the groove, some of them just vulgar and restive under the cultural tyranny, but some of them also serious, were looking for things that really responded to their needs. Almost always they responded to the beat of the newly emerging rock music. They were a bit ashamed of their taste, for it was not respectable. But I instinctively sided with this second group, with real, if coarse, feelings as opposed to artificial and dead ones. Then their musical sans-culotteism won the revolution and reigns unabashed today. No classical music has been produced that can speak to this generation.

Symptomatic of this change is how seriously students now take the famous passages on musical education in Plato's *Republic*. In the past, students, good liberals that they always are, were indignant at the censorship of poetry, as a threat to free inquiry. But they were really thinking of science and politics. They hardly paid attention to the discussion of music itself and, to the extent that they even thought about it, were really puzzled by Plato's devoting time to rhythm and melody in a serious treatise on political philosophy. Their experience of music was as an entertainment, a matter of indifference to political and moral life. Students today, on the contrary, know exactly why Plato takes music so seriously. They know it affects life very profoundly and are indignant because Plato seems to want to rob them of their most intimate pleasure. They are drawn into argument with Plato about the experience of music, and the dispute centers on how to evaluate it and deal with it. This encounter not only helps to illuminate the phenomenon of contemporary music, but also provides a model of how contemporary students can profitably engage with a classic text. The very fact of their fury shows how much Plato threatens what is dear and intimate to them. They are little able to defend their experience, which had seemed unquestionable until questioned, and it is most resistant to cool analysis. Yet if a student can —and this is most difficult and unusual—draw back, get a critical distance on what he clings to, come to doubt the ultimate value of what he loves, he has taken the first and most difficult step toward the philosophic conversion. Indignation is the soul's defense against the wound of doubt about its own; it reorders the cosmos to support the justice of its cause. It justifies putting Socrates to death. Recognizing indignation for what it is constitutes knowledge of the soul, and is thus an experience more philosophic than the study of mathematics. It is Plato's teaching that music, by its nature, encompasses all that is today most resistant to philosophy. So it may well be that through the thicket of our greatest corruption runs the path to awareness of the oldest truths.

Plato's teaching about music is, put simply, that rhythm and melody, accompanied by dance, are the barbarous expression of the soul. Barbarous, not animal. Music is the medium of the *human* soul in its most ecstatic condition of wonder and terror. Nietzsche, who in large measure agrees with Plato's analysis, says in *The Birth of Tragedy* (not to be forgotten is the rest of the title, *Out of the Spirit of Music*) that a mixture of cruelty and coarse sensuality characterized this state, which of course was religious, in the service of gods. Music is the soul's primitive and primary speech and it is *alogon*, without articulate speech or reason. It is not only not reasonable, it is hostile to reason. Even when articulate speech is added, it is utterly subordinate to and determined by the music and the passions it expresses.

Civilization or, to say the same thing, education is the taming or domestication of the soul's raw passions—not suppressing or excising them, which would deprive the soul of its energy—but forming and informing them as art. The goal of harmonizing the enthusiastic part of the soul with what develops later, the rational part, is perhaps impossible to attain. But without it, man can never be whole. Music, or poetry, which is what music becomes as reason emerges, always involves a delicate balance between passion and reason, and, even in its highest and most developed forms—religious, warlike and erotic—that balance is always tipped, if ever so slightly, toward the passionate. Music, as everyone experiences, provides an unquestionable justification and a fulfilling pleasure for the activities it accompanies: the soldier who hears the marching band is enthralled and reassured; the religious man is exalted in his prayer by the sound of the organ in the church; and the lover is carried away and his conscience stilled by the romantic guitar. Armed with music, man can damn rational doubt. Out of the music emerge the gods that suit it, and they educate men by their example and their commandments.

Plato's Socrates disciplines the ecstasies and thereby provides little consolation or hope to men. According to the Socratic formula, the lyrics —speech and, hence, reason—must determine the music—harmony and rhythm. Pure music can never endure this constraint. Students are not in a position to know the pleasures of reason; they can only see it as a disciplinary and repressive parent. But they do see, in the case of Plato, that that parent has figured out what they are up to. Plato teaches that, in order to take the spiritual temperature of an individual or a society, one must "mark the music." To Plato and Nietzsche, the history of music is a series of attempts to give form and beauty to the dark, chaotic, premonitory forces in the soul—to make them serve a higher purpose, an ideal, to give man's duties a fullness. Bach's religious intentions and Beethoven's revolutionary and humane ones are clear enough examples. Such cultivation of the soul uses the passions and satisfies them while sublimating them and giving them an artistic unity. A man whose noblest activities are accompanied by a music that expresses them while providing a pleasure extending from the lowest bodily to the highest spiritual, is whole, and there is no tension in him between the pleasant and the good. By contrast a man whose business life is prosaic and unmusical and whose leisure is made up of coarse, intense entertainments, is divided, and each side of his existence is undermined by the other.

Hence, for those who are interested in psychological health, music is at the center of education, both for giving the passions their due and for preparing the soul for the unhampered use of reason. The centrality of such education was recognized by all the ancient educators. It is hardly noticed today that in Aristotle's *Politics* the most important passages about the best regime concern musical education, or that the *Poetics* is an appendix to the *Politics.* Classical philosophy did not censor the singers. It persuaded them. And it gave them a goal, one that was understood by them, until only yesterday. But those who do not notice the role of music in Aristotle and despise it in Plato went to school with Hobbes, Locke and Smith, where such considerations have become unnecessary. The triumphant Enlightenment rationalism thought that it had discovered other ways to deal with the irrational part of the soul, and that reason needed less support from it. Only in those great critics of Enlightenment and rationalism, Rousseau and Nietzsche, does music return, and they were the most musical of philosophers. Both thought that the passions—and along with them their ministerial arts—had become thin under the rule of reason and that, therefore, man himself and what he sees in the world have become correspondingly thin. They wanted to cultivate the enthusiastic states of the soul and to re-experience the Corybantic possession deemed a pathology by Plato. Nietzsche, particularly, sought to tap again the irrational sources of vitality, to replenish our dried-up stream from barbaric sources, and thus encouraged the Dionysian and the music derivative from it.

This is the significance of rock music. I do not suggest that it has any high intellectual sources. But it has risen to its current heights in the education of the young on the ashes of classical music, and in an atmosphere in which there is no intellectual resistance to attempts to tap the rawest passions. Modern-day rationalists, such as economists, are indifferent to it and what it represents. The irrationalists are all for it. There is no need to fear that "the blond beasts" are going to come forth from the bland souls of our adolescents. But rock music has one appeal only, a barbaric appeal, to sexual desire—not love, not *eros,* but sexual desire undeveloped and untutored. It acknowledges the first emanations of children's emerging sensuality and addresses them seriously, eliciting them and legitimating them, not as little sprouts that must be carefully tended in order to grow into gorgeous flowers, but as the real thing. Rock gives children, on a silver platter, with all the public authority of the entertainment industry, everything their parents always used to tell them they had to wait for until they grew up and would understand later.

Young people know that rock has the beat of sexual intercourse. That is why Ravel's *Bolero* is the one piece of classical music that is commonly known and liked by them. In alliance with some real art and a lot of pseudo-art, an enormous industry cultivates the taste for the orgiastic state of feeling connected with sex, providing a constant flood of fresh material for voracious appetites. Never was there an art form directed so exclusively to children.

Ministering to and according with the arousing and cathartic music, the lyrics celebrate puppy love as well as polymorphous attractions, and fortify them against traditional ridicule and shame. The words implicitly and explicitly describe bodily acts that satisfy sexual desire and treat them as its only natural and routine culmination for children who do not yet have the slightest imagination of love, marriage or family. This has a much more powerful effect than does pornography on youngsters, who have no need to watch others do grossly what they can so easily do themselves. Voyeurism is for old perverts; active sexual relations are for the young. All they need is encouragement.

The inevitable corollary of such sexual interest is rebellion against the parental authority that represses it. Selfishness thus becomes indignation and then transforms itself into morality. The sexual revolution must overthrow all the forces of domination, the enemies of nature and happiness. From love comes hate, masquerading as social reform. A worldview is balanced on the sexual fulcrum. What were once unconscious or half-conscious childish resentments become the new Scripture. And then comes the longing for the classless, prejudice-free, conflictless, universal society that necessarily results from liberated consciousness—"We Are the World," a pubescent version of *Alle Menschen werden Brüder,* the fulfillment of which has been inhibited by the political equivalents of Mom and Dad. These are the three great lyrical themes: sex, hate and a smarmy, hypocritical version of brotherly love. Such polluted sources issue in a muddy stream where only monsters can swim. A glance at the videos that project images on the wall of Plato's cave since MTV took it over suffices to prove this. Hitler's image recurs frequently enough in exciting contexts to give one pause. Nothing noble, sublime, profound, delicate, tasteful or even decent can find a place in such tableaux. There is room only for the intense, changing, crude and immediate, which Tocqueville warned us would be the character of democratic art, combined with a pervasiveness, importance and content beyond Tocqueville's wildest imagination.

Picture a thirteen-year-old boy sitting in the living room of his family home doing his math assignment while wearing his Walkman headphones or watching MTV. He enjoys the liberties hard won over centuries by the alliance of philosophic genius and political heroism, consecrated by the blood of martyrs; he is provided with comfort and leisure by the most productive economy ever known to mankind; science has penetrated the secrets of nature in order to provide him with the marvelous, lifelike electronic sound and image reproduction he is enjoying. And in what does progress culminate? A pubescent child whose body throbs with orgasmic rhythms; whose feelings are made articulate in hymns to the joys of onanism or the killing of parents; whose ambition is to win fame and wealth in imitating the drag-queen who makes the music. In short, life is made into a nonstop, commercially prepackaged masturbational fantasy.

This description may seem exaggerated, but only because some would prefer to regard it as such. The continuing exposure to rock music is a reality, not one confined to a particular class or type of child. One need only ask first-year university students what music they listen to, how much of it and what it means to them, in order to discover that the phenomenon is universal in America, that it begins in adolescence or a bit before and continues through the college years. It is *the* youth culture and, as I have so often insisted, there is now no other countervailing nourishment for the spirit. Some of this culture's power comes from the fact that it is so loud. It makes conversation impossible, so that much of friendship must be without the shared speech that Aristotle asserts is the essence of friendship and the only true common ground. With rock, illusions of shared feelings, bodily contact and grunted formulas, which are supposed to contain so much meaning beyond speech, are the basis of association. None of this contradicts going about the business of life, attending classes and doing the assignments for them. But the meaningful inner life is with the music.

This phenomenon is both astounding and indigestible, and is hardly noticed, routine and habitual. But it is of historic proportions that a society's best young and their best energies should be so occupied. People of future civilizations will wonder at this and find it as incomprehensible as we do the caste system, witch-burning, harems, cannibalism and gladiatorial combats. It may well be that a society's greatest madness seems normal to itself. The child I described has parents who have sacrificed to provide him with a good life and who have a great stake in his future happiness. They cannot believe that the musical vocation will contribute very much to that happiness. But there is nothing they can do about it. The family spiritual void has left the field open to rock music, and they cannot possibly forbid their children to listen to it. It is everywhere; all children listen to it; forbidding it would simply cause them to lose their children's affection and obedience. When they turn on the television, they will see President Reagan warmly grasping the daintily proffered gloved hand of Michael Jackson and praising him enthusiastically. Better to set the faculty of denial in motion—avoid noticing what the words say, assume the kid will get over it. If he has early sex, that won't get in the way of his having stable relationships later. His drug use will certainly stop at pot. School is providing real values. And popular historicism provides the final salvation: there are new life-styles for new situations, and the older generation is there not to impose its values but to help the younger one to find its own. TV, which compared to music plays a comparatively small role in the formation of young people's character and taste, is a consensus monster—the Right monitors its content for sex, the Left for violence, and many other interested sects for many other things. But the music has hardly been touched, and what efforts have been made are both ineffectual and misguided about the nature and extent of the problem.

The result is nothing less than parents' loss of control over their children's moral education at a time when no one else is seriously concerned with it. This has been achieved by an alliance between the strange young males who have the gift of divining the mob's emergent wishes—our versions of Thrasymachus, Socrates' rhetorical adversary—and the record-company executives, the new robber barons, who mine gold out of rock. They discovered a few years back that children are one of the few groups in the country with considerable disposable income, in the form of allowances. Their parents spend all they have providing for the kids. Appealing to them over their parents' heads, creating a world of delight for them, constitutes one of the richest markets in the postwar world. The rock business is perfect capitalism, supplying to demand and helping to create it. It has all the moral dignity of drug trafficking, but it was so totally new and unexpected that nobody thought to control it, and now it is too late. Progress may be made against cigarette smoking because our absence of standards or our relativism does not extend to matters of bodily health. In all other things the market determines the value. (Yoko Ono is among America's small group of billionaires, along with oil and computer magnates, her late husband having produced and sold a commodity of worth comparable to theirs.) Rock is very big business, bigger than the movies, bigger than professional sports, bigger than television, and this accounts for much of the respectability of the music business. It is difficult to adjust our vision to the changes in the economy and to see what is really important. McDonald's now has more employees than U.S. Steel, and likewise the purveyors of junk food for the soul have supplanted what still seem to be more basic callings.

This change has been happening for some time. In the late fifties, De Gaulle gave Brigitte Bardot one of France's highest honors. I could not understand this, but it turned out that she, along with Peugeot, was France's biggest export item. As Western nations became more prosperous, leisure, which had been put off for several centuries in favor of the pursuit of property, the means to leisure, finally began to be of primary concern. But, in the meantime, any notion of the serious life of leisure, as well as men's taste and capacity to live it, had disappeared. Leisure became entertainment. The end for which they had labored for so long has turned out to be amusement, a justified conclusion if the means justify the ends. The music business is peculiar only in that it caters almost exclusively to children, treating legally and naturally imperfect human beings as though they were ready to enjoy the final or complete satisfaction. It perhaps thus reveals the nature of all our entertainment and our loss of a clear view of what adulthood or maturity is, and our incapacity to conceive ends. The emptiness of *values* results in the acceptance of the natural *facts* as the ends. In this case infantile sexuality is the end, and I suspect that, in the absence of other ends, many adults have come to agree that it is.

It is interesting to note that the Left, which prides itself on its critical approach to "late capitalism" and is unrelenting and unsparing in its analysis of our other cultural phenomena, has in general given rock music a free ride. Abstracting from the capitalist element in which it flourishes, they regard it as a people's art, coming from beneath the bourgeoisie's layers of cultural repression. Its antinomianism and its longing for a world without constraint might seem to be the clarion of the proletarian revolution, and Marxists certainly do see that rock music dissolves the beliefs and morals necessary for liberal society and would approve of it for that alone. But the harmony between the young intellectual Left and rock is probably profounder than that. Herbert Marcuse appealed to university students in the sixties with a combination of Marx and Freud. In *Eros and Civilization* and *One Dimensional Man* he promised that the overcoming of capitalism and its false consciousness will result in a society where the greatest satisfactions are sexual, of a sort that the bourgeois moralist Freud called polymorphous and infantile. Rock music touches the same chord in the young. Free sexual expression, anarchism, mining of the irrational unconscious and giving it free rein are what they have in common. The high intellectual life I shall describe in Part Two and the low rock world are partners in the same entertainment enterprise. They must both be interpreted as parts of the cultural fabric of late capitalism. Their success comes from the bourgeois' need to feel that he is not bourgeois, to have undangerous experiments with the unlimited. He is willing to pay dearly for them. The Left is better interpreted by Nietzsche than by Marx. The critical theory of late capitalism is at once late capitalism's subtlest and crudest expression. Anti-bourgeois ire is the opiate of the Last Man.

This strong stimulant, which Nietzsche called Nihiline, was for a very long time, almost fifteen years, epitomized in a single figure, Mick Jagger. A shrewd, middle-class boy, he played the possessed lower-class demon and teen-aged satyr up until he was forty, with one eye on the mobs of children of both sexes whom he stimulated to a sensual frenzy and the other eye winking at the unerotic, commercially motivated adults who handled the money. In his act he was male and female, heterosexual and homosexual; unencumbered by modesty, he could enter everyone's dreams, promising to do everything with everyone; and, above all, he legitimated drugs, which were the real thrill that parents and policemen conspired to deny his youthful audience. He was beyond the law, moral and political, and thumbed his nose at it. Along with all this, there were nasty little appeals to the suppressed inclinations toward sexism, racism and violence, indulgence in which is not now publicly respectable. Nevertheless, he managed not to appear to contradict the rock ideal of a universal classless society founded on love, with the distinction between brotherly and bodily blurred. He was the hero and the model for countless young persons in universities, as well as elsewhere. I discovered that students who boasted of having no heroes secretly had a passion to be like Mick Jagger, to live his life, have his fame. They were ashamed to admit this in a university, although I am not certain that the reason has anything to do with a higher standard of taste. It is probably that they are not supposed to have heroes. Rock music itself and talking about it with infinite seriousness are perfectly respectable. It has proved to be the ultimate leveler of intellectual snobbism. But it is not respectable to think of it as providing weak and ordinary persons with a fashionable behavior, the imitation of which will make others esteem them and boost their own self-esteem. Unaware and unwillingly, however, Mick Jagger played the role in their lives that Napoleon played in the lives of ordinary young Frenchmen throughout the nineteenth century. Everyone else was so boring and unable to charm youthful passions. Jagger caught on.

In the last couple of years, Jagger has begun to fade. Whether Michael Jackson, Prince or Boy George can take his place is uncertain. They are even weirder than he is, and one wonders what new strata of taste they have discovered. Although each differs from the others, the essential character of musical entertainment is not changing. There is only a constant search for variations on the theme. And this gutter phenomenon is apparently the fulfillment of the promise made by so much psychology and literature that our weak and exhausted Western civilization would find refreshment in the true source, the unconscious, which appeared to the late romantic imagination to be identical to Africa, the dark and unexplored continent. Now all has been explored; light has been cast everywhere; the unconscious has been made conscious, the repressed expressed. And what have we found? Not creative devils, but show business glitz. Mick Jagger tarting it up on the stage is all that we brought back from the voyage to the underworld.

My concern here is not with the moral effects of this music— whether it leads to sex, violence or drugs. The issue here is its effect on education, and I believe it ruins the imagination of young people and makes it very difficult for them to have a passionate relationship to the art and thought that are the substance of liberal education. The first sensuous experiences are decisive in determining the taste for the whole of life, and they are the link between the animal and spiritual in us. The period of nascent sensuality has always been used for sublimation, in the sense of making sublime, for attaching youthful inclinations and longings to music, pictures and stories that provide the transition to the fulfillment of the human duties and the enjoyment of the human pleasures. Lessing, speaking of Greek sculpture, said "beautiful men made beautiful statues, and the city had beautiful statues in part to thank for beautiful citizens." This formula encapsulates the fundamental principle of the esthetic education of man. Young men and women were attracted by the beauty of heroes whose very bodies expressed their nobility. The deeper understanding of the meaning of nobility comes later, but is prepared for by the sensuous experience and is actually contained in it. What the senses long for as well as what reason later sees as good are thereby not at tension with one another. Education is not sermonizing to children against their instincts and pleasures, but providing a natural continuity between what they feel and what they can and should be. But this is a lost art. Now we have come to exactly the opposite point. Rock music encourages passions and provides models that have no relation to any life the young people who go to universities can possibly lead, or to the kinds of admiration encouraged by liberal studies. Without the cooperation of the sentiments, anything other than technical education is a dead letter.

Rock music provides premature ecstasy and, in this respect, is like the drugs with which it is allied. It artificially induces the exaltation naturally attached to the completion of the greatest endeavors—victory in a just war, consummated love, artistic creation, religious devotion and discovery of the truth. Without effort, without talent, without virtue, without exercise of the faculties, anyone and everyone is accorded the equal right to the enjoyment of their fruits. In my experience, students who have had a serious fling with drugs—and gotten over it—find it difficult to have enthusiasms or great expectations. It is as though the color has been drained out of their lives and they see everything in black and white. The pleasure they experienced in the beginning was so intense that they no longer look for it at the end, or as the end. They may function perfectly well, but dryly, routinely. Their energy has been sapped, and they do not expect their life's activity to produce anything but a living, whereas liberal education is supposed to encourage the belief that the good life is the pleasant life and that the best life is the most pleasant life. I suspect that the rock addiction, particularly in the absence of strong counterattractions, has an effect similar to that of drugs. The students will get over this music, or at least the exclusive passion for it. But they will do so in the same way Freud says that men accept the reality principle —as something harsh, grim and essentially unattractive, a mere necessity. These students will assiduously study economics or the professions and the Michael Jackson costume will slip off to reveal a Brooks Brothers suit beneath. They will want to get ahead and live comfortably. But this life is as empty and false as the one they left behind. The choice is not between quick fixes and dull calculation. This is what liberal education is meant to show them. But as long as they have the Walkman on, they cannot hear what the great tradition has to say. And, after its prolonged use, when they take it off, they find they are deaf.

RELATIONSHIPS

Self-Centeredness

Students these days are, in general, nice. I choose the word carefully. They are not particularly moral or noble. Such niceness is a facet of democratic character when times are good. Neither war nor tyranny nor want has hardened them or made demands on them. The wounds and rivalries caused by class distinction have disappeared along with any strong sense of class (as it once existed in universities in America and as it still does, poisonously, in England). Students are free of most constraints, and their families make sacrifices for them without asking for much in the way of obedience or respect. Religion and national origin have almost no noticeable effect on their social life or their career prospects. Although few really believe in "the system," they do not have any burning sentiment that injustice is being done to them. The drugs and the sex once thought to be forbidden are available in the quantities required for sensible use. A few radical feminists still feel the old-time religion, but most of the women are comfortably assured that not much stands in the way of their careers. There is an atmosphere of easy familiarity with their elders, and even of the kind of respect of free young people for them that Tocqueville asserted equality encourages. Above all, there are none of the longings, romantic or otherwise, that used to make bourgeois society, or society in general, repugnant to the young. The impossible dreams of the sixties proved to be quite possible within the loosened fabric of American life.

Students these days are pleasant, friendly and, if not great-souled, at least not particularly mean-spirited. Their primary preoccupation is themselves, understood in the narrowest sense.

I had a revelatory experience when I chatted quite frankly one evening with a group of bright students at an Ivy League college where I was a visiting professor for a short time. I had succeeded in establishing a certain common ground with them in class, for serious reading of Plato frequently has the effect of making students speak, at least for the moment, outside of their conventions. We had a farewell picnic and the atmosphere was easy and conducive to candor. Somewhat disingenuously I introduced some themes into the conversation about which I was eager to know the current state of opinion. I had been primed for this encounter by a conversation I had had the previous evening at a dinner with members of the faculty and the administration. The wife of one of the high officials told me of her son's activities. He had a law degree, but, she said, he and his friends had little ambition and had moved from one thing to another. She did not seem to be very distressed by his behavior—perhaps even a bit proud of it—a modern parent willing to believe in the superiority of the younger generation to her own, especially when the former is most disrespectful of the latter's standards. So I asked her why she thought they behaved this way. She responded firmly, quietly and without hesitation, "Fear of nuclear war."

This prompted me to ask my group of students whether they were frightened of nuclear war. The response was a universal, somewhat embarrassed giggle. They knew what their daily thoughts were about, and those thoughts had hardly anything to do with public questions. And they also knew that there are a great many right-thinking adults who expect them to use the nuclear threat as an excuse for demanding a transformation of the world political order and who also want to produce their maimed souls in evidence against our politicians' mad pursuit of the "arms race." Students today—and I have now asked the question over and over again—are morally unpretentious, and they look at themselves with irony when it comes to the big moral questions. Some look back with nostalgia at students of the sixties as persons who believed in something. The prospect of being drafted to fight in Vietnam was really frightening. But youngsters today are, with few exceptions, no more taken in by the psychological quacks who explain their apathy with respect to nuclear war as "denial," who enlist science in the service of proving that there are causes without effects, than was the American public by a President who tried to persuade it that he sat around discussing nuclear war with his little daughter. Their concerns lie elsewhere. There is, indeed, a certain listlessness about them, an absence of a broad view of the future, but it is as plausible to attribute that to the lack of a frontier to conquer in the American West, or the death of God, as to fear of nuclear war.

It is difficult to say just why this generation tends to be so honest in comparison with the preceding one. And, of course, there are plenty of public posturers among them, as is evident from the vote of the student body at Brown (an institution that was at the forefront of dismantling liberal education in the sixties), which demanded that cyanide be made available by the university in case of nuclear attack. This was a "statement" telling us all about the torment to which we subject young people. But the great majority of students, although they as much as anyone want to think well of themselves, are aware that they are busy with their own careers and their relationships. There is a certain rhetoric of self-fulfillment that gives a patina of glamor to this life, but they can see that there is nothing particularly noble about it. Survivalism has taken the place of heroism as the admired quality. This turning in on themselves is not, as some would have it, a return to normalcy after the hectic fever of the sixties, nor is it preternatural selfishness. It is a new degree of isolation that leaves young people with no alternative to looking inward. The things that almost naturally elicit attention to broader concerns are simply not present. Starvation in Ethiopia, mass murder in Cambodia, as well as nuclear war, are all real calamities worthy of attention. But they are not immediate, not organically connected to students' lives. The affairs of daily life rarely involve concern for a larger community in such a way as to make the public and private merge in one's thought. It is not merely that one is free to participate or not to participate, that there is no need to do so, but that everything militates against one's doing so. Tocqueville describes the tip of the iceberg of advanced egalitarianism when he discusses the difficulty that a man without family lands, or a family tradition for whose continuation he is responsible, will have in avoiding individualism and seeing himself as an integral part of a past and a future, rather than as an anonymous atom in a merely changing continuum. The modern economic principle that private vice makes public virtue has penetrated all aspects of daily life in such a way that there seems to be no reason to be a conscious part of civic existence. As Saul Bellow has put it, public virtue is a kind of ghost town into which anyone can move and declare himself sheriff.

Country, religion, family, ideas of civilization, all the sentimental and historical forces that stood between cosmic infinity and the individual, providing some notion of a place within the whole, have been rationalized and have lost their compelling force. America is experienced not as a common project but as a framework within which people are only individuals, where they are left alone. To the extent that there is a project, it is to put those who are said to be disadvantaged in a position to live as they please too. The advanced Left talks about self-fulfillment; the Right, in its most popular form, is Libertarian, i.e., the right-wing form of the Left, in favor of everybody's living as he pleases. The only forms of intrusion on the private-life characteristic of liberal democracies—taxes and military service—are not now present in student life. If there is an inherent political impulse in man, it is certainly being frustrated. But this impulse has already been so attenuated by modernity that it is hardly experienced.

Students may indeed feel a sense of impotence, a sense that they have little or no influence over the collective life, but essentially they live comfortably within the administrative state that has replaced politics. Nuclear war is indeed a frightening prospect, but only when it appears imminent does it cross their minds. Even such a powerful, concerted effort as the nuclear-freeze commotion, with its attendant entertainments like *The Day After,* has nothing to do with the lives students lead and is little more than a distraction. Very few of them are destined for a political life; and if they do actually enter politics, it is by accident, and does not follow from their early training or expectations. In the universities about which I am speaking, there are almost no students born of families that have inherited the privilege and responsibility of public service, for almost no such families remain. Neither duty nor pleasure involves students with the political, and our lives exhibit in the extreme what Burke and Tocqueville said about the disappearance of citizens and statesmen. The petty personal interests of youth—"making it," finding a place for oneself—persevere throughout life. The honesty of this generation of students causes them to laugh when asked to act as though they were powerful agents in world history. They know the truth of Tocqueville's dictum that "in democratic societies, each citizen is habitually busy with the contemplation of a very petty object, which is himself," a contemplation now intensified by a greater indifference to the past and the loss of a national view of the future. The only common project engaging the youthful imagination is the exploration of space, which everyone knows to be empty.

The resulting inevitable individualism, endemic to our regime, has been reinforced by another unintended and unexpected development, the decline of the family, which was the intermediary between individual and society, providing quasi-natural attachments beyond the individual, that gave men and women unqualified concern for at least some others and created an entirely different relation to society from that which the isolated individual has. Parents, husbands, wives and children are hostages to the community. They palliate indifference to it and provide a material stake in its future. This is not quite instinctive love of country, but it is love of country for love of one's own. It is the gentle form of patriotism, one that flows most easily out of self-interest, without the demand for much self-denial. The decay of the family means that community would require extreme self-abnegation in an era when there is no good reason for anything but self-indulgence.

Apart from the fact that many students have experienced the divorce of their parents and are informed by statistics that there is a strong possibility of divorce in their futures, they hardly have an expectation that they will have to care for their parents or any other blood relatives, or that they will even see much of them as they grow older. Social security, retirement funds and health insurance for old people free their children from even having to give them financial support, let alone taking them into their own homes to live. When a child goes away to college, it is really the beginning of the end of his vital connection with his family, though he scarcely realizes it at the time. Parents have little authority over their children when they leave home, and the children are forced to look outward and forward. They are not coldhearted; the substance of their interests merely lies elsewhere. Spiritually, the family was pretty empty, anyway, and new objects fill their field of vision as the old ones fade. American geography plays a role in this separation. This is a large country, and people are very mobile, particularly since World War II and the

expansion of air travel. Practically no student knows where he is going to
live when he has completed his education. Very likely it will be far away
from his parents and his birthplace. In Canada or France, by contrast,
even if the same fundamental cultural winds are blowing, people have
almost no place to go. For an English-speaking Canadian born in Toronto
there is, practically speaking, only Vancouver as an attractive alternative,
and for a Parisian there is no alternative whatsoever. The unlimited, or
dissolving, horizon, which is the hallmark of our age, is in these places
somewhat less visible. People are not really more rooted in them, but they
are stuck. Hence they continue to see their relatives and all the people
they grew up with. Their landscape is unchanging. But a young American
really begins all over again, and everything is open. He can live in the
North, South, East or West, in the city, the suburbs, or the country—
who knows which? There are arguments for each, and he is absolutely
unconstrained in his choice. The accidents of where he finds a job and
of variable inclination are likely to take him far away from all he has been
connected with, and he is psychically prepared for this. His investments
in his past and those who peopled it are necessarily limited.

This indeterminate or open-ended future and the lack of a binding
past mean that the souls of young people are in a condition like that of
the first men in the state of nature—spiritually unclad, unconnected,
isolated, with no inherited or unconditional connection with anything or
anyone. They can be anything they want to be, but they have no particular
reason to want to be anything in particular. Not only are they free to
decide their place, but they are also free to decide whether they will
believe in God or be atheists, or leave their options open by being agnos-
tic; whether they will be straight or gay, or, again, keep their options open;
whether they will marry and whether they will stay married; whether they
will have children—and so on endlessly. There is no necessity, no morality, no social pressure, no sacrifice to be made that militates going in or
turning away from any of these directions, and there are desires pointing
toward each, with mutually contradictory arguments to buttress them.
The young are exaggerated versions of Plato's description of the young in
democracies:

> [The democratic youth] lives along day by day, gratifying the desire that
> occurs to him, at one time drinking and listening to the flute, at another

downing water and reducing, now practicing gymnastic, and again idling and neglecting everything; and sometimes spending his time as though he were occupied with philosophy. Often he engages in politics and, jumping up, says and does whatever chances to come to him; and if he admires any soldiers, he turns in that direction; and if it's moneymakers, in that one, and there is neither order nor necessity in his life, but calling it sweet, free and blessed, he follows it throughout. (*Republic*, 561c-d)

Why are we surprised that such unfurnished persons should be preoccupied principally with themselves and with finding means to avoid permanent free fall? No wonder that the one novel that remains continuously popular with students is Camus's *The Stranger*.

Equality

In addition to their self-ironical niceness, the other striking quality of these students is their egalitarianism. Whatever their politics, they believe that all men—and women—are created equal and have equal rights. It is more than a belief, it is an instinct, felt in their bones. Whenever they meet anyone, considerations of sex, color, religion, family, money, nationality, play no role in their reactions. The very understanding that such considerations once really counted for something has departed; it belongs to mythology. This may seem surprising inasmuch as there is such interest in roots, ethnicity and the sacred—the things that once separated men. But it is precisely because they are no longer real that they fascinate. A real Italian immigrant in 1920 did not worry about ethnicity. He had it, and although he was an American, his life was by necessity and choice Italian, and he lived with Italians. His grandson at Harvard today might wish to recover Italianness—the social disadvantages of which his father struggled to shake off—but his friends will be the individuals he likes, willy-nilly, not because of his Italian origin but as a result of the common features of American life. His sexual attractions, and hence his marriage, will not be influenced by his national origin or even by his traditional Catholicism. And this will not be because he is attracted by opposites or is trying to join the establishment. It is simply because such things do not really count now, even if there is a conscious effort to make them count. There is no society out there that will banish him for marrying out of order, or even parents who will object very strenuously. He is not in any important way looked on as an Italian by his peers. Even if students have gone to parochial schools, where they were religiously and in effect ethnically segregated, the general culture usually prevails, and when they enter the university they almost immediately find themselves associating primarily with those who were formerly outsiders to them. They simply drop their cultural baggage. There is none of the solemnity of the interfaith or interethnic get-togethers I knew as a child, where people who felt themselves to be very different and who were quite often both prejudiced and victims of prejudice, pointed piously to the brotherhood of man. These kids just do not have prejudices against anyone. Whether this is because man has been reduced to a naked animal without any of the trappings of civilization that differentiate him, or because we have recognized our essential humankindness, is a matter of interpretation. But the fact is that everyone is an individual—if not very individual —in our major universities. They are all just *persons.* Being human is enough for what is important. It does not occur to students to think that any of the things that classically divided people, even in egalitarian America, should keep them away from anyone else.

Thus Harvard, Yale and Princeton are not what they used to be— the last resorts of aristocratic sentiment within the democracy. The differentiations based on old family or old wealth have vanished. The old wounds that used to be inflicted by the clubbable on the unclubbable, in our muted version of the English class system, have healed because the clubs are not anything to be cared about seriously. All this began after World War II, with the GI Bill. College was for everyone. And the top universities gradually abandoned preference for the children of their alumni and the exclusion of outsiders, especially Jews. Academic records and tests became the criterion for selection. New kinds of preference— particularly for blacks—replaced the old ones, which were class preserving, whereas these are class destroying. Now the student bodies of all the major universities are pretty much alike, drawn from the best applicants, with "good" meaning good at the academic disciplines. There is hardly a Harvard man or a Yale man any more. No longer do any universities have the vocation of producing gentlemen as well as scholars. Snobbism of the old sort is dead. Of course students are, no matter what they say, proud to be at one of these select universities. They are distinguished by it. But they believe, and they are probably right, that they are there not because of anything other than natural talent and hard work at their earlier studies. To the extent that their parents' wealth may have contributed to their excelling in high school whereas poorer children were disadvantaged, they believe this to be a social injustice. But they are not very much bothered, at least not so far as whites are concerned, for the country is largely middle class now, and scholarship aid is easily available for those unable to pay. They see around them students who come from all kinds of families. Very few feel themselves culturally deprived, outsiders looking resentfully in at the privileged whose society is closed to them. Nor are there social climbers, for there is no vision of a high society into which to climb. Similarly, there are no longer schools of thought, as there always used to be, that despise democracy and equality. Again, World War II finished all that. *All* the students are egalitarian meritocrats, who believe each individual should be allowed to develop his special—and unequal—talents without reference to race, sex, religion, family, wealth or national origin. This is the only form of justice they know, and they cannot even imagine that there could be any substantial argument in favor of aristocracy or monarchy. These were inexplicable follies of the past.

Again, although the difference between girls and boys still has a living meaning—unlike the difference between Jew and Catholic, German and Irish, old family and new family, which are mere memories of their parents' day and do not constitute differences in present way of life —students take women's equality in education, their legitimate pursuit of exactly the same careers as men and their equal and often superior performance in them, completely in stride. There are no jokes, no self-consciousness, in short, no awareness that this state of affairs is any less normal in human history than is breathing. None of their beliefs result from principle, a project, an effort. They are pure feeling, a way of life, the actualization of the democratic dream of each man taken as man, the essential, abstracted from everything else. Except no abstraction is taking place. Contrary to fashionable opinion, universities are melting pots, no matter what may be true of the rest of society. Ethnicity is no more important a fact than tall or short, black-haired or blond. What these young people have in common infinitely outweighs what separates them. The quest for traditions and rituals both proves my point and may teach something about the price paid for this homogenization. The lack of prejudice is a result of students' failing to see differences and of the gradual eradication of differences. When students talk about one another, one almost never hears them saying things that divide others into groups or kinds. They always speak about the individual. The sensitivity to national character, sometimes known as stereotyping, has disappeared.

Race

The one eccentric element in this portrait, the one failure—a particularly grave one inasmuch as it was the part most fraught with hope—is the relation between blacks and whites. White and black students do not in general become real friends with one another. Here the gulf of difference has proved unbridgeable. The forgetting of race in the university, which was predicted and confidently expected when the barriers were let down, has not occurred. There is now a large black presence in major universities, frequently equivalent to their proportion in the general population. But they have, by and large, proved indigestible. Most keep to themselves. White students act as though their relations with black students were just as immediate and unself-conscious as with others (including Orientals). But although the words are right, the music is off-key. Here there is an atmosphere of right-thinking, principle and project—of effort rather than instinct. The automatic character of current student camaraderie is absent; and the really intimate attachment that knows no barriers stops here. The programmatic brotherhood of the sixties did not culminate in integration but veered off toward black separation. White students feel uncomfortable about this and do not like to talk about it. This is not the way things are supposed to be. It does not fit their prevailing view that human beings are all pretty much alike, and that friendship is another aspect of equal opportunity. They pretend not to notice the segregated tables in dining halls where no white student would comfortably sit down. This is only one of the more visible aspects of a prevailing segregation in the real life of universities—which includes separation in housing and in areas of study, particularly noticeable in the paucity of blacks in theoretical sciences and humanities. The universities are formally integrated, and blacks and whites are used to seeing each other. But the substantial human contact, indifferent to race, soul to soul, that prevails in all other aspects of student life simply does not usually exist between the two races. There are exceptions, perfectly integrated black students, but they are rare and in a difficult position.

I do not believe this somber situation is the fault of the white students, who are rather straightforward in such matters and frequently embarrassingly eager to prove their liberal credentials in the one area where Americans are especially sensitive to a history of past injustice. These students have made the adjustment, without missing a beat, to a variety of religions and nationalities, the integration of Orientals and the change in women's aspirations and roles. It would require a great deal of proof to persuade me that they remain subtly racist. Although preferential treatment of blacks goes against a deep-seated conviction that equal rights belong to individuals and are color-blind, white students have been willing by and large to talk themselves into accepting affirmative action as a temporary measure on the way to equality. Still this makes them uncomfortable because, although they are very used to propaganda and to the imposition of new moralities on them, in daily life they like to act as they think and feel. And they do not think that black is beautiful any more than they think white is beautiful, and they do not think that a student who is not qualified is qualified. So the tendency among white students is to suppress the whole question, act as though it were not there, and associate with the minority of blacks who want to be associated with and forget the rest. They cannot befriend blacks as blacks, and the heady days of a common purpose are gone. The discriminatory laws are ancient history, and there are large numbers of blacks in the universities. There is nothing more that white students can do to make great changes in their relations to black students.

Thus, just at the moment when everyone else has become a "person," blacks have become blacks. I am not speaking about doctrine, although there was much doctrine at the beginning, but about feeling. "They stick together" was a phrase often used in the past by the prejudiced about this or that distinctive group, but it has become true, by and large, of the black students. In general, the expectation of anything other than routine contact in classes or at campus jobs—usually quite polite—has vanished. This is peculiar inasmuch as race is less spiritually substantial than religion, and also inasmuch as integration was both the goal and the practice of blacks in universities prior to the late sixties, when numbers were smaller and human difficulties greater. Further, it is peculiar in that blacks seem to be the only group that has picked up "ethnicity"—the discovery or the creation of the sixties—in an instinctive way. At the same time, there has been a progressive abandonment on their part of belief or interest in a distinctive black "culture." Blacks are not sharing a special positive intellectual or moral experience; they partake fully in the common culture, with the same goals and tastes as everyone else, but they are doing it by themselves. They continue to have the inward sentiments of separateness caused by exclusion when it no longer effectively exists. The heat is under the pot, but they do not melt as have *all* other groups.

There are obviously some good reasons for this, and it is the right of any part of the large community in a pluralistic society to separate itself. But the movement of the blacks goes counter not only to that of the rest of society, and tends to put them at odds with it, but also to their own noblest claims and traditions in this country. And it is connected with a dangerous severing of the races in the intellectual world, where there can be no justification for separatism and where the ideal of common humanity must prevail. The confrontations and indignations of the political realm have become firmly fixed in the university. For this the university's loss of conviction in its universalizing mission must bear a part of the blame. Since the end of World War II there was in most major universities an effort—ever increasing in intensity—to educate more blacks, in the sincere American belief that education is good and the inclusion of blacks at the highest levels of intellectual achievement would be decisive in the resolving the American dilemma. Practically nobody hesitated, and there were private discussions about whether, at least in the beginning, standards should not be informally lowered for talented but deprived blacks in order to help them catch up. Decent men took different sides on this question, some believing that blacks, for the sake of the example they were to set and for their own self-respect, should be held to the highest standards of achievement, others believing that gains would be incremental over generations. No person of goodwill doubted that one way or another it would work out, that what had happened with respect to religion and nationality would also happen with race. At the peak of the civil rights movement there was a sense of urgency about enrolling greater numbers of blacks in order to prove the absence of discrimination. A sign of the times was the reappearance of pictures on applications so that blacks could be identified, whereas pictures had been banished a decade previously so that blacks could not be identified. High school records and standardized tests began to be criticized as insufficient guides to real talent. But the goal was unchanged—to educate black students as any student is educated and to evaluate them according to the same standards. Everyone was still integrationist. The belief was that insufficient energy had been devoted to the recruitment of talented black students. Cornell, where I taught for several years, was one of many institutions that announced great increases in goals for enrollment of blacks. The president, adding a characteristic twist, also announced that not only would it seek blacks, but that it would find them not among privileged blacks but in the inner cities. At the beginning of the 1967 academic year there were many more blacks on campus and, of course, in order to get so many, particularly poor blacks, standards of admission had silently and drastically been altered. Nothing had been done to prepare these students for the great intellectual and social challenges awaiting them in the university. Cornell now had a large number of students who were manifestly unqualified and unprepared, and therefore it faced an inevitable choice: fail most of them or pass them without their having learned. Moralism and press relations made the former intolerable; the latter was only partially possible (it required consenting faculty and employers after college who expected and would accept incompetence) and was unbearably shameful to black students and university alike. It really meant that blacks would be recognizably second-class citizens.

Black power, which hit the universities like a tidal wave at just that moment, provided a third way. Integrationism was just an ideology for whites and Uncle Toms. Who says that what universities teach is the truth rather than just the myths necessary to support the system of domination? Black students are second-class not because they are academically poor but because they are being forced to imitate white culture. Relativism and Marxism made some of this claim believable. And the discomfort of the times made it more so. Blacks were to be proud, and from them the university could learn its failings. Such a perspective was decidedly attractive to the kids who were the victims of the university's manipulations. Courses in black studies and black English, and many other such concessions, became the way out. It was hopefully assumed that these would not fundamentally transform the university or the educational goals of black students. They were merely supposed to be an enrichment. But this was really a cop-out, and the license for a new segregationism that would allow the white impresarios to escape from the corner they had painted themselves into. The way was opened for black students to live and study the black experience, to be comfortable, rather than be constrained by the learning accessible to man as man.

When the black students at Cornell became aware that they could intimidate the university and that they were not just students but negotiating partners in the process of determining what an education is, they demanded the dismissal of the tough-minded, old-style integrationist black woman who was assistant dean of students. In short order the administration complied with this demand. From that moment on, the various conciliatory arrangements with which we are now so familiar came into being.

The black studies programs largely failed because what was serious in them did not interest the students, and the rest was unprofitable hokum. So the university curriculum returned to a debilitated normalcy. But a kind of black domain, not quite institutional, but accepted, a shadow of the university life, was created: permanent quotas in admission, preference in financial assistance, racially motivated hiring of faculty, difficulty in giving blacks failing marks, and an organized system of grievance and feeling aggrieved. And everywhere hypocrisy, contempt-producing lies about what is going on and how the whole scheme is working. This little black empire has gained its legitimacy from the alleged racism surrounding it and from which it defends its subjects. Its visible manifestations are to be found in those separate tables in the dining halls, which reproduce the separate facilities of the Jim Crow South. At Cornell and elsewhere, the black militants had to threaten—and to do—bodily harm to black students with independent inclinations in order to found this system. Now the system is routine. For the majority of black students, going to the university is therefore a different experience from that of the other students, and the product of the education is also different. The black student who wishes to be just a student and to avoid allegiance to the black group has to pay a terrific price, because he is judged negatively by his black peers and because his behavior is atypical in the eyes of whites. White students have silently and unconsciously adjusted to a group presence of blacks, and they must readjust for a black who does not define himself by the group. He is painfully conscious that many whites, well-meaning ones, judge him by special standards. All this is daunting. The university's acquiescence in the interference with its primary responsibility of providing educational opportunity to those capable of education should be a heavy burden on its collective conscience.

Affirmative action now institutionalizes the worst aspects of separatism. The fact is that the average black student's achievements do not equal those of the average white student in the good universities, and everybody knows it. It is also a fact that the university degree of a black student is also tainted, and employers look on it with suspicion, or become guilty accomplices in the toleration of incompetence. The worst part of all this is that the black students, most of whom avidly support this system, hate its consequences. A disposition composed of equal parts of shame and resentment has settled on many black students who are beneficiaries of preferential treatment. They do not like the notion that whites are in the position to do them favors. They believe that everyone doubts their merit, their capacity for equal achievement. Their successes become questionable in their own eyes. Those who are good students fear that they are equated with those who are not, that their hard-won credentials are not credible. They are the victims of a stereotype, but one that has been chosen by black leadership. Those who are not good students, but have the same advantages as those who are, want to protect their position but are haunted by the sense of not deserving it. This gives them a powerful incentive to avoid close associations with whites, who might be better qualified than they are and who might be looking down on them. Better to stick together, so these subtle but painful difficulties will not arise. It is no surprise that extremist black politics now gets a kind of support among middle and upper-class blacks unheard of in the past. The common source that united the races at the peaks in the past has been polluted. Reason cannot accommodate the claims of any kind of power whatever, and democratic society cannot accept any principle of achievement other than merit. White students, as I have said, do not really believe in the justice of affirmative action, do not wish to deal with the facts, and turn without mentioning it to their all-white—or, rather, because there are now so many Orientals, non-black—society. Affirmative action (quotas), at least in universities, is the source of what I fear is a long-term deterioration of the relations between the races in America.

Sex

Contrary to the popular prejudice that America is the nation of unintellectual and anti-intellectual people, where ideas are at best means to ends, America is actually nothing but a great stage on which theories have been played as tragedy and comedy. This is a regime founded by philosophers and their students. All the recalcitrant matter of the historical *is* gave way here before the practical and philosophical *ought to be*, as the raw natural givens of this wild continent meekly submitted to the yoke of theoretical science. Other peoples were autochthonous, deriving guidance from the gods of their various places. When they too decided to follow the principles we pioneered, they hobbled along awkwardly, unable to extricate themselves gracefully from their pasts. Our story is the majestic and triumphant march of the principles of freedom and equality, giving meaning to all that we have done or are doing. There are almost no accidents; everything that happens among us is a consequence of one or both of our principles—a triumph over some opposition to them, a discovery of a fresh meaning in them, a dispute about which of the two has primacy, etc.

Now we have arrived at one of the ultimate acts in our drama, the informing and reforming of our most intimate private lives by our principles. Sex and its consequences—love, marriage and family—have finally become the theme of the national project, and here the problem of nature, always present but always repressed in the reconstruction of man demanded by freedom and equality, becomes insistent. In order to intuit the meaning of equality, we have no need for the wild imaginative genius of Aristophanes, who in *The Assembly of Women* contrives the old hags entitled by law to sexual satisfaction from handsome young males, or of Plato, who in the *Republic* prescribed naked exercises for men and women together. We only have to look around us, if we have eyes to see.

The change in sexual relations, which now provide an unending challenge to human ingenuity, came over us in two successive waves in the last two decades. The first was the sexual revolution; the second, feminism. The sexual revolution marched under the banner of freedom; feminism under that of equality. Although they went arm in arm for a while, their differences eventually put them at odds with each other, as Tocqueville said freedom and equality would always be. This is manifest in the squabble over pornography, which pits liberated sexual desire against feminist resentment about stereotyping. We are presented with the amusing spectacle of pornography clad in armor borrowed from the heroic struggles for freedom of speech, and using Miltonic rhetoric, doing battle with feminism, newly draped in the robes of community morality, using arguments associated with conservatives who defend traditional sex roles, and also defying an authoritative tradition in which it was taboo to suggest any relation between what a person reads and sees and his sexual practices. In the background stand the liberals, wringing their hands in confusion because they wish to favor both sides and cannot.

Sexual liberation presented itself as a bold affirmation of the senses and of undeniable natural impulse against our puritanical heritage, society's conventions and repressions, bolstered by Biblical myths about original sin. From the early sixties on there was a gradual testing of the limits on sexual expression, and they melted away or had already disappeared without anybody's having noticed it. The disapproval of parents and teachers of youngsters' sleeping or living together was easily overcome. The moral inhibitions, the fear of disease, the risk of pregnancy, the family and social consequences of premarital intercourse and the difficulty of finding places in which to have it—everything that stood in its way suddenly was no longer there. Students, particularly the girls, were no longer ashamed to give public evidence of sexual attraction or of its fulfillment. The kind of cohabitations that were dangerous in the twenties, and risqué or bohemian in the thirties and forties, became as normal as membership in the Girl Scouts. I say "particularly" girls because young men were always supposed to be eager for immediate gratification, whereas young women, inspired by modesty, were supposed to resist it. It was a modification or phasing out of female modesty that made the new arrangements possible. Since, however, modesty was supposed to be mere convention or habit, no effort was required to overcome it. This emancipation had in its intention and its effect the accentuation of the difference between the sexes. Making love was to be the primary activity, so men and women were to be more emphatically male and female. Of course, homosexuals were also liberated, but for the great mass of people, being free and natural meant achieving heterosexual satisfactions, opposite sexes made for each other.

The immediate promise of sexual liberation was, simply, happiness understood as the release of energies that had been stored up over millennia during the dark night of repression, in a great continuous Bacchanalia. However, the lion roaring behind the door of the closet turned out, when that door was opened, to be a little, domesticated cat. In fact, seen from a long historical perspective, sexual liberation might be interpreted as the recognition that sexual passion is no longer dangerous in us, and that it is safer to give it free course than to risk rebellion by restraining it. I once asked a class how it could be that not too long ago parents would have said, "Never darken our door again," to wayward daughters, whereas now they rarely protest when boyfriends sleep over in their homes. A very nice, very normal, young woman responded, "Because it's no big deal." That says it all. This passionlessness is the most striking effect, or revelation, of the sexual revolution, and it makes the younger generation more or less incomprehensible to older folks.

In all this, the sexual revolution was precisely what it said it was—a liberation. But some of the harshness of nature asserted itself beneath the shattered conventions: the young were more apt to profit from the revolution than the old, the beautiful more than the ugly. The old veil of discretion had had the effect of making these raw and ill-distributed natural advantages less important in life and marriage. But now there was little attempt to apply egalitarian justice in these matters, as did Aristophanes' older Athenian women who, because of their very repulsiveness, had a right to enjoy handsome young men before beautiful young women did. The undemocratic aspects of free sex were compensated for in our harmless and mildly ridiculous way: "Beauty is in the eye of the beholder" was preached more vigorously than formerly; the cosmetics industry had a big boom; and education and therapy in the style of Masters and Johnson, promising great orgasms to every subscriber, became common. My favorite was a course in sex for the elderly given at a local YMCA and advertised over the radio with the slogan "Use It or Lose It." These were the days when pornography slipped its leash.

Feminism, on the other hand, was, to the extent it presented itself as liberation, much more a liberation from nature than from convention or society. Therefore it was grimmer, unerotic, more of an abstract project, and required not so much the abolition of law but the institution of law and political activism. Instinct did not suffice. The negative sentiment of imprisonment was there, but what was wanted, as Freud suggested, was unclear. The programmatic language shifted from "living naturally" (with reference to very definite bodily functions) to vaguer terms such as "self-definition," "self-fulfillment," "establishing priorities," "fashioning a life-style," etc. The women's movement is not founded on nature. Although feminism sees the position of women as a result of nurture and not nature, its crucial contention is that biology should not be destiny, and biology is surely natural. It is not self-evident, although it may be true, that women's roles were always determined by human relations of domination, like those underlying slavery. This thesis requires interpretation and argument, and is not affirmed by the bodily desires of all concerned, as was the sexual revolution. Moreover, it is very often asserted that science's *conquest* of nature—in the form of the pill and labor-saving devices—has made woman's emancipation from the home possible. It is certain that feminism has brought with it an unrelenting process of consciousness-raising and -changing that begins in what is probably a permanent human inclination and is surely a modern one—the longing for the unlimited, the unconstrained. It ends, as do many modern movements that seek abstract justice, in forgetting nature and using force to refashion human beings to secure that justice.

Feminism is in accord with and encourages many elements of the sexual revolution, but uses them to different ends. Libertinism allows for what even Rousseau called the greatest pleasure. But in making sex easy, it can trivialize, de-eroticize and demystify sexual relations. A woman who can easily satisfy her desires and does not invest her emotions in exclusive relationships is liberated from the psychological tyranny of men, to do more important things. Feminism acted as a depressant on the Bacchanalian mood of the sexual revolution, as nakedness in Plato's *Republic* led not to great indulgences but to an unromantic regulation and manipulation of sexual desire for public purposes. Just as smoking and drinking overcame puritanical condemnation only to find themselves, after a brief moment of freedom, under equally moralistic attacks in the name not of God but of the more respectable and powerful names of health and safety, so sex had a short day in the sun before it had to be reined in to accommodate the feminist sensibility. As a people, we are good not at gratifying ourselves but at delaying gratification for the sake of projects which promise future good. In this case the project is overcoming what is variously called male dominance, machismo, phallocracy, patriarchy, etc., to which men and their female collaborators seem very attached, inasmuch as so many machines of war must be mounted against them.

Male sexual passion has become sinful again because it culminates in sexism. Women are made into objects, they are raped by their husbands as well as by strangers, they are sexually harassed by professors and employers at school and at work, and their children, whom they leave in day-care centers in order to pursue their careers, are sexually abused by teachers. All these crimes must be legislated against and punished. What sensitive male can avoid realizing how dangerous his sexual passion is? Is there perhaps really original sin? Men had failed to read the fine print in the Emancipation Proclamation. The new interference with sexual desire is more comprehensive, more intense, more difficult to escape than the older conventions, the grip of which was so recently relaxed. The July 14 of the sexual revolution was really only a day between the overthrow of the Ancien Régime and the onset of the Terror. The new reign of virtue, accompanied by relentless propaganda on radio and television and in the press, has its own catechism, inducing an examination of the conscience and the inmost sentiments for traces of possessiveness, jealousy, protectiveness—all those things men used to feel for women. There are, of course, a multitude of properly indignant censors equipped with loudspeakers and inquisitional tribunals.

Central to the feminist project is the suppression of modesty, in which the sexual revolution played a critical preparatory role, just as capitalism, in the Marxist scheme, prepared the way for socialism by tearing the sacred veils from the charade of feudal chivalry. The sexual revolution, however, wanted men and women to get together bodily, while feminism wanted them to be able easily to get along separately. Modesty in the old dispensation was *the* female virtue, because it governed the powerful desire that related men to women, providing a gratification in harmony with the procreation and rearing of children, the risk and responsibility of which fell naturally—that is, biologically—on women. Although modesty impeded sexual intercourse, its result was to make such gratification central to a serious life and to enhance the delicate interplay between the sexes, which makes acquiescence of the will as important as possession of the body. Diminution or suppression of modesty certainly makes attaining the end of desire easier—which was the intention of the sexual revolution—but it also dismantles the structure of involvement and attachment, reducing sex to the thing-in-itself. This is where feminism enters.

Female modesty extends sexual differentiation from the sexual act to the whole of life. It makes men and women always men and women. The consciousness of directedness toward one another, and its attractions and inhibitions, inform every common deed. As long as modesty operates, men and women together are never just lawyers or pilots together. They have something else, always potentially very important, in common— ultimate ends, or as they say, "life goals." Is winning this case or landing this plane what is most important, or is it love and family? As lawyers or pilots, men and women are the same, subservient to the one goal. As lovers or parents they are very different, but inwardly related by sharing the naturally given end of continuing the species. Yet their working together immediately poses the questions of "roles" and, hence, "priorities," in a way that men working together or women working together does not. Modesty is a constant reminder of their peculiar relatedness and its outer forms and inner sentiments, which impede the self's free creation or capitalism's technical division of labor. It is a voice constantly repeating that a man and a woman have a work to do together that is far different from that found in the marketplace, and of a far greater importance.

This is why modesty is the first sacrifice demanded by Socrates in Plato's *Republic* for the establishment of a city where women have the same education, live the same lives and do the same jobs as men. If the difference between men and women is not to determine their ends, if it is not to be more significant than the difference between bald men and men with hair, then they must strip and exercise naked together just as Greek men did. With some qualifications, feminists praise this passage in Plato and look upon it as prescient, for it culminates in an absolute liberation of women from the subjection of marriage and childbearing and -rearing, which become no more important than any other necessary and momentary biological event. Socrates provides birth control, abortion and day-care centers, as well as marriages that last a day or a night and have as their only end the production of sound new citizens to replenish the city's stock, cared for by the city. He even adds infanticide to the list of conveniences available. A woman will probably have to spend no more time and effort on children's business than a man would in curing a case of the measles. Only then can women be thought to be naturally fit to do the same things as men. Socrates' radicalism extends to the relation of parent and child. The citizens are not to know their own children, for, if they were to love them above others, then the means that brought them into being, the intercourse of this man and this woman, would be judged to be of special significance. Then we would be back to the private family and the kinds of relatedness peculiar to it.

Socrates' proposal especially refers to one of the most problematic cases for those who seek equal treatment for women—the military. These citizens are warriors, and he argues that just as women can be liberated from subjection to men and take their places alongside them, men must be liberated from their special concern for women. A man must have no more compunction about killing the advancing female enemy than the male, and he must be no more protective of the heroine fighting on his right side than of the hero on his left. Equal opportunity and equal risk. The only concern is the common good, and the only relationship is to the community, bypassing the intermediate relationships that tend to take on a life of their own and were formerly thought to have natural roots in sexual attraction and love of one's own children. Socrates consciously rips asunder the delicate web of relations among human beings woven out of their sexual nature. Without it, the isolation of individuals is inevitable. He makes explicit how equal treatment of women necessitates the removal of meaning from the old kind of sexual relations—whether they were founded on nature or convention—and a consequent loss of the human connections that resulted from them which he replaces with the common good of the city.

In this light we can discern the outlines of what has been going on recently among us. Conservatives who have been heartened by the latest developments within the women's movement are mistaken if they think that they and the movement are on common ground. Certainly both sides are against pornography. But the feminists are against it because it is a reminiscence of the old love relationship, which involved differentiated sexual roles—roles now interpreted as bondage and domination. Pornography demystifies that relationship, leaving the merely sexual component of male-female relationships without their erotic, romantic, moral and ideal accompaniments. It caters to and encourages the longing men have for women and its unrestrained if impoverished satisfaction. This is what feminist anti-pornographers are against—not the debasement of sentiment or the threat to the family. That is why they exempt homosexual pornography from censorship. It is by definition not an accomplice to the domination of females by males and even helps to undermine it. Actually, feminists favor the demystifying role of pornography. It unmasks the true nature of the old relationships. Their purpose is not to remystify the worn-out systems but to push on toward the realm of freedom. They are not for a return to the old romances, *Brief Encounter,* for example, which gave charm to love in the old way. They know that is dead, and they are now wiping up the last desperate, untutored, semicriminal traces of a kind of desire that no longer has a place in the world.

It is one thing, however, to want to prevent women from being ravished and brutalized because modesty and purity should be respected and their weakness protected by responsible males, and quite another to protect them from male desire altogether so that they can live as they please. Feminism makes use of conservative moralism to further its own ends. This is akin to, and actually part of, the fatal old alliance between traditional conservatives and radicals, which has had such far-reaching effects for more than a century. They had nothing in common but their hatred of capitalism, the conservatives looking back to the revival of throne and altar in the various European nations, and to piety, the radicals looking forward to the universal, homogeneous society and to freedom—reactionaries and progressives united against the present. They feed off the inner contradictions of the bourgeoisie. Of course fundamentalists and feminists can collaborate to pass local ordinances banning smut, but the feminists do so to demonstrate their political clout in furthering their campaign against "bourgeois rights," which are, sad to say, enjoyed by people who want to see dirty movies or buy equipment to act out comically distorted fantasies. It is doubtful whether the fundamentalists gain much from this deal, because it guarantees the victory of a surging moral force that is "antifamily and antilife." See how they do together on the abortion issue! People who watch pornography, on the other hand, are always at least a little ashamed and unwilling to defend it as such. At best, they sound a weak and uncertain trumpet for the sanctity of the Constitution and the First Amendment, of which they hope to be perceived as defenders. They pose no threat in principle to anything.

Similarly, some conservatives are heartened by recent feminist discussion about the differences between men and women and about the special fulfillment of "parenting," forbidden subjects at earlier stages of the movement, when equal rights was the primary theme. However, this discussion has really only been made possible by the success of those earlier stages. There may indeed be a feminine nature or self, but it has been definitively shaken loose from its teleological moorings. The feminine nature is not in any reciprocal relation to the male nature, and they do not define one another. The male and female sexual organs themselves now have no more evident purposiveness than do white and black skin, are no more naturally pointed toward one another than white master and black slave, or so the legend goes. Women do have different physical structures, but they can make of them what they will—without paying a price. The feminine nature is a mystery to be worked out on its own, which can now be done because the male claim to it has been overcome. The fact that there is today a more affirmative disposition toward childbearing does not imply that there is any natural impulse or compulsion to establish anything like a traditional fatherhood to complement motherhood. The children are to be had on the female's terms, with or without fathers, who are not to get in the way of the mother's free development. Children have always been, and still are, more the mother's anyway. Ninety per cent or more of children of divorced parents stay with their mothers, whose preeminent stake in children has been enhanced by feminist demands and by a consequent easy rationalization of male irresponsibility. So we have reproduction without family—if family includes the presence of a male who has any kind of a definite function. The return to motherhood as a feminist ideal is only possible because feminism has triumphed over the family as it was once known, and women's freedom will not be limited by it. None of this means returning to family values or even bodes particularly well for the family as an institution, although it does mean that women have become freer to come to terms with the complexity of their situation.

The uneasy bedfellowship of the sexual revolution and feminism produced an odd tension in which all the moral restraints governing nature disappeared, but so did nature. The exhilaration of liberation has evaporated, however, for it is unclear what exactly was liberated or whether new and more onerous responsibilities have not been placed on us. And this is where we return to the students, for whom everything is new. They are not sure what they feel for one another and are without guidance about what to do with whatever they may feel.

The students of whom I am speaking are aware of all the sexual alternatives, and have been from very early on in their lives, and they feel that all sexual acts which do not involve real harm to others are licit. They do not think they should feel guilt or shame about sex. They have had sex education in school, of "the biological facts, let them decide the values for themselves" variety, if not "the options and orientations" variety. They have lived in a world where the most explicit discussions and depictions of sex are all around them. They have had little fear of venereal disease.[1] Birth-control devices and ready abortion have been available to them since puberty. For the great majority, sexual intercourse was a normal part of their lives prior to college, and there was no fear of social stigma or even much parental opposition. Girls have had less supervision in their relations with boys than at any time in history. They are not precisely pagan, but there is an easy familiarity with others' bodies and less inhibition about using their own for a broad range of erotic purposes. There is no special value placed on virginity in oneself or in one's partners. It is expected that there were others before and, incredibly to older folks, this does not seem to bother them, even though it provides a ground for predictions about the future. They are not promiscuous or given to orgies or casual sex, as it used to be understood. In general, they have one connection at a time, but most have had several serially. They are used to coed dormitories. Many live together, almost always without expectation of marriage. It is just a convenient arrangement. They are not couples in the sense of having simulacra of marriage or a way of life different from that of other students not presently so attached. They are roommates, which is what they call themselves, with sex and utilities included in the rent. Every single obstacle to sexual relationships between young unmarried persons has disappeared, and these relationships are routine. To strangers from another planet, what would be the most striking thing is that sexual passion no longer includes the illusion of eternity.

---

[1] It remains to be seen what effect AIDS will have. The wave of publicity about herpes a couple of years ago had almost no discernible psychological fallout.

Men and women are now used to living in exactly the same way and studying exactly the same things and having exactly the same career expectations. No man would think of ridiculing a female premed or prelaw student, or believe that these are fields not proper for women, or assert that a woman should put family before career. The law schools and medical schools are full of women, and their numbers are beginning to approach their proportion in the general population. There is very little ideology or militant feminism in most of the women, because they do not need it. The strident voices are present, and they get attention in the university newspapers and in student governments. But, again, the battle here has been won. Women students do not generally feel discriminated against or despised for their professional aspirations. The economy will absorb them, and they have rising expectations. They do not need the protection of NOW any more than do women in general, who see they are doing at least as well with Reagan as they did with Carter. Academically, students are comfortably unisexual; they revert to dual sexuality only for the sex act. Sex no longer has any political agenda in universities except among homosexuals, who are not yet quite satisfied with their situation. But the fact that there is an open homosexual presence, with rights at least formally recognized by university authorities and almost all students, tells us much about current university life.

Students today understandably believe that they are the beneficiaries of progress. They have a certain benign contempt for their parents, particularly for their poor mothers, who were sexually inexperienced and had no profession to be taken as seriously as their fathers'. Superior sexual experience was always one of the palpable advantages that parents and teachers had over youngsters who were eager to penetrate the mysteries of life. But this is no longer the case, nor do students believe it to be so. They quietly smile at professors who try to shock them or talk explicitly about the facts of life in the way once so effective in enticing more innocent generations of students to pay attention to the words of their elders. Freud and D. H. Lawrence are very old hat. Better not to try.

Even less do students expect to learn anything about their situation from old literature, which from the Garden of Eden on made coupling a very dark and complicated business. On reflection, today's students wonder what all the fuss was about. Many think their older brothers and sisters discovered sex, as we now know it to be, in the sixties. I was impressed by students who, in a course on Rousseau's *Confessions*, were astounded to learn that he had lived with a woman out of wedlock in the eighteenth century. Where could he have gotten the idea?

There is, of course, literature that affects a generation profoundly but has no interest at all for the next generation because its central theme proved ephemeral, whereas the greatest literature addresses the permanent problems of man. Ibsen's *Ghosts*, for example, lost all its force for young people when syphilis ceased to be a threat. Aristotle teaches that pity for the plight of others requires that the same thing could happen to us. Now, however, the same things that used to happen to people, at least in the relations between the sexes, do not happen to students anymore. And one must begin to wonder whether there is any permanent literature for them, because there do not seem to them to be permanent problems for them. As I have suggested earlier, this is the first fully historical or historicized generation, not only in theory but also in practice, and the result is not the cultivation of the vastest sympathies for long ago and far away, but rather an exclusive interest in themselves. Anna Karenina and Madame Bovary are adulteresses, but the cosmos no longer rebels at their deed. Anna's son today would probably have been awarded to her in the amicable divorce arrangements of the Karenins. All the romantic novels with their depictions of highly differentiated men and women, their steamy, sublimated sensuality and their insistence on the sacredness of the marriage bond just do not speak to any reality that concerns today's young people. Neither do Romeo and Juliet, who must struggle against parental opposition, Othello and his jealousy, or Miranda's carefully guarded innocence. Saint Augustine, as a seminarian told me, had sexual hang-ups. And let us not speak of the Bible, every *no* in which is now a *yes*. With the possible exception of Oedipus, they are all gone, and they departed in the company of modesty.

When young people today have crushing problems in what used to be called sexual relationships, they cannot trace them back to any moral ambiguity in man's sexual nature. That was, of course, what was erroneously done in the past.

Separateness

Civilization has seemingly led us around full circle, back to the state of nature taught to us by the founding fathers of modern thought. But now it is present not in rhetoric but in reality. Those who first taught the state of nature proposed it as a hypothesis. Liberated from all the conventional attachments to religion, country and family that men actually did have, how would they live and how would they freely reconstruct those attachments? It was an experiment designed to make people recognize what they really care about and engage their loyalties on the basis of this caring. But a young person today, to exaggerate only a little, actually begins *de novo*, without the givens or imperatives that he would have had only yesterday. His country demands little of him and provides well for him, his religion is a matter of absolutely free choice and—this is what is really fresh—so are his sexual involvements. He can now choose, but he finds he no longer has a sufficient motive for choice that is more than whim, that is binding. Reconstruction is proving impossible.

The state of nature should culminate in a contract, which constitutes a society out of individuals. A contract requires not only a common interest between the contracting parties but also an authority to enforce its fulfillment by them. In the absence of the former, there is no relationship; in the absence of the latter, there can be no trust, only diffidence. In the state of nature concerning friendships and love today, there is doubt about both, and the result is a longing for the vanished common ground, called roots, without the means to recover it, and timidity and self-protectiveness in associations guaranteed by neither nature nor convention. The pervasive feeling that love and friendship are groundless, perhaps the most notable aspect of the current feeling of groundlessness, has caused them to give way to the much vaguer and more personal idea of commitment, that choice in the void whose cause resides only in the will or the self. The young want to make commitments, which constitute the meaning of life, because love and nature do not suffice. This is what they talk about, but they are haunted by the awareness that the talk does not mean very much and that commitments are lighter than air.

At the origins of modern natural rights teachings, freedom and equality were political principles intended to bring both justice and effectiveness to the relationships of ruling and being ruled, which in the conventional order were constituted by pretended rights of strength, wealth, tradition, age and birth. The relations of king and subject, master and slave, lord and vassal, patrician and pleb, rich and poor, were revealed to be purely manmade and hence not morally binding, apart from the consent of the parties to them, which became the only source of political legitimacy. Civil society was to be reconstructed on the natural ground of man's common humanity. Then it would appear that all relationships or relatedness within civil society would also depend on the free consent of individuals. Yet the relationships between man and woman, parent and child, are less doubtfully natural and less arguably conventional than the relations between rulers and ruled, especially as they are understood by modern natural rights teachings. They cannot be understood simply as contractual relationships, as resulting from acts of human freedom, since they would thereby lose their character and dissolve. Instead they seem to constrain that freedom, to argue against the free arrangements of consent dominant in the political order. But it is difficult to argue that nature both does and does not prescribe certain relations in civil society. The radical transformation of the relations between men and women and parents and children was the inevitable consequence of the success of the new politics of consent.

It might be said, with some exaggeration, that the first state-of-nature teachers paid little attention to the natural teleology of sex because they were primarily concerned with analyzing away the false appearances of teleology in the existing political arrangements. (I mean by teleology nothing but the evident, everyday observation and sense of purposiveness, which may be only illusory, but which ordinarily guides human life, the kind everyone sees in the reproductive process.) Hobbes and Locke marshaled their great talents to explode myths of rulership that protected corrupt and selfish regimes, such as Menenius' tale:

> There was a time when all the body's members
> Rebelled against the belly; thus accused it:
> That only like a gulf it did remain
> I' the midst o' the body, idle and unactive,
> Still cupboarding the viand, never bearing

Like labor with the rest; where the other instruments
Did see and hear, devise, instruct, walk, feel,
And, mutually participate, did minister
Unto the appetite and affection common
Of the whole body. The belly answered . . .
To the discontented members, the mutinous parts
That envied his receipt; even so most fitly
As you malign our senators for that
They are not such as you . . .
'True is it, my incorporate friends,' quoth he,
'That I receive the general food at first
Which you do live upon; and fit it is,
Because I am the storehouse and the shop
Of the whole body. But, if you do remember,
I send it through the rivers of your blood,
Even to the court, the heart, to the seat o' the brain;
And, through the cranks and offices of man,
The strongest nerves and small inferior veins
From me receive that natural competency
Whereby they live. And . . .
. . . though all at once cannot
See what I do deliver out to each,
Yet I can make my audit up, that all
From me do back receive the flour of all,
And leave me but the bran. . . .
The senators of Rome are this good belly,
And you the mutinous members; for, examine
Their counsels and their cares, digest things rightly
Touching the weal o' the common, you shall find
No public benefit which you receive
But it proceeds or comes from them to you,
And no way from yourselves.
                    (Shakespeare, *Coriolanus*, 1. 95–156)

In the place of such an "organic" tale they provided a rational account
of legitimacy that made each individual the judge of his own best interests
and gave him the right to choose rulers who were bound to protect him,
abstracting from the habits of thought and feeling that permitted patri-
cians under the colors of the common good to make use of plebs for their

own greedy purposes. Hobbes and Locke gave the plebs equal rights to selfishness. The ruled are not directed by nature to the rulers any more than the rulers naturally care only for the good of the ruled. Rulers and ruled can consciously craft a compact by which the separate interests of each are protected. But they are never one, sharing the same highest end, like the organs in Menenius' body. There is no body politic, only individuals who have come together voluntarily and can separate voluntarily without maiming themselves.

Hobbes and Locke supposed that, although the political order would be constituted out of individuals, the subpolitical units would remain largely unaffected. Indeed, they counted on the family, as an intermediate between individual and the state, partially to replace what was being lost in passionate attachment to the polity. The immediate and reliable love of one's own property, wife and children can more effectively counterpoise purely individual selfishness than does the distant and abstract love of country. Moreover, concern for the safety of one's family is a powerful reason for loyalty to the state, which protects them. The nation as a community of families is a formula that until recently worked very well in the United States. However, it is very questionable whether this solution is viable over the very long run, because there are two contrary views of nature present here. And, as the political philosophers have always taught, the one that is authoritative in the political regime will ultimately inform its parts. In the social contract view, nature has nothing to say about relationships and rank order; in the older view, which is part and parcel of ancient political philosophy, nature is prescriptive. Are the relations between men and women and parents and children determined by natural impulse or are they the product of choice and consent? In Aristotle's *Politics,* the subpolitical or prepolitical family relations point to the necessity of political rule and are perfected by it, whereas in the state-of-nature teachings, political rule is derived entirely from the need for protection of individuals, bypassing their social relations completely. Are we dealing with political actors or with men and women? In the former case, persons are free to construct whatever relations they please with one another; in the latter, prior to any choice, a preexisting frame largely determines the relations of men and women.

There are three classic images of the polity that clarify this issue. The first is the ship of state, which is one thing if it is to be forever at sea, and quite another if it is to reach port and the passengers go their separate ways. They think about one another and their relationships on the ship very differently in the two cases. The former case is the ancient city; the latter, the modern state. The other two images are the herd and the hive, which oppose each other. The herd may need a shepherd, but each of the animals is grazing for itself and can easily be separated from the herd. In the hive, by contrast, there are workers, drones and a queen; there is a division of labor and a product toward which they all work in common; separation from the hive is extinction. The herd is modern, the hive ancient. Of course, neither image is an accurate description of human society. Men are neither atoms nor parts of a body. But this is why there have to be such images, since for the brutes these things are not a matter for discussion or deliberation. Man is ambiguous. In the tightest communities, at least since the days of Odysseus, there is something in man that wants out and senses that his development is stunted by being just a part of a whole, rather than a whole itself. And in the freest and most independent situations men long for unconditional attachments. The tension between freedom and attachment, and attempts to achieve the impossible union of the two, are the permanent condition of man. But in modern political regimes, where rights precede duties, freedom definitely has primacy over community, family and even nature.

The spirit of this choice must inevitably penetrate into all the details of life. The ambiguity of man is well illustrated in the sexual passion and the sentiments that accompany it. Sex may be treated as a pleasure out of which men and women may make what they will, its promptings followed or rejected, its forms matters of taste, its importance or unimportance in life decided freely by individuals. As such, at least according to thinkers like Hobbes and Locke, it would have to give precedence to objective natural necessity, to the imperatives of self-love or self-preservation. Or sex can be immediately constitutive of a whole law of life, to which self-preservation is subordinated and in which love, marriage and the rearing of infants is the most important business. It cannot be both. The direction in which we have been going is obvious.

Now, it is not entirely correct to say that mankind at large is able to treat sex as a matter of free choice, one which initially does not obligate us to others. In a world where the natural basis of sexual differentiation has crumbled, this choice is readily available to men, but less so to women. Man in the state of nature, either in the first one or the one we have now, can walk away from a sexual encounter and never give it another thought. But a woman may have a child, and in fact, as becomes ever clearer, may want to have a child. Sex can be an indifferent thing for men, but it really cannot quite be so for women. This is what might be called the female drama. Modernity promised that all human beings would be treated equally. Women took that promise seriously and rebelled against the old order. But as they have succeeded, men have also been liberated from their old constraints. And women, now liberated and with equal careers, nevertheless find they still desire to have children, but have no basis for claiming that men should share their desire for children or assume a responsibility for them. So nature weighs more heavily on women. In the old order they were subordinated and dependent on men; in the new order they are isolated, needing men, but not able to count on them, and hampered in the free development of their individuality. The promise of modernity is not really fulfilled for women.

The decay of the natural ground for the family relationships was largely unanticipated and unprepared for in the early modern thinkers. But they did suggest a certain reform of the family, reflecting the movement away from the constraints of duty, toward reliance on those elements of the family that could be understood to flow out of free expressions of personal sentiment. In Locke, paternal authority is turned into parental authority, a rejection of a father's divine or natural right to rule and to rule permanently, in favor of a father's and a mother's right to care for their children as long as they need care, for the sake of the children's freedom—which the child will immediately recognize, when he reaches majority, to have been for his own benefit. There is nothing left of the reverence toward the father as the symbol of the divine on earth, the unquestioned bearer of authority. Rather, sons and daughters will calculate that they have benefited from their parents' care, which prepared them for the freedom they enjoy, and they will be grateful, although they have no reciprocal duty, except insofar as they wish to leave behind a plausible model for the conduct of their own children toward them. They may, if they please, obey their father in order to inherit his estate, if he has one, which he can dispose of as he pleases. From the point of view of the children, the family retains its validity on the basis of modern principles, and Locke prepares the way for the democratic family, so movingly described by Tocqueville in *Democracy in America.*

So far, so good. The children are reconciled to the family. But the problem, it seems to me, is in the motive of the parents to care for their children. The children can say to their parents: "You are strong, and we are weak. Use your strength to help us. You are rich, and we are poor. Spend your money on us. You are wise, and we are ignorant. Teach us." But why should mother and father want to do so much, involving so much sacrifice without any reward? Perhaps parental care is a duty, or family life has great joys. But neither of these is a conclusive reason when rights and individual autonomy hold sway. The children have unconditional need for and receive unquestionable benefits from the parents; the same cannot be asserted about parents.

Locke believed, and the events of our time seem to confirm his belief, that women have an instinctive attachment to children that cannot be explained as self-interest or calculation. The attachment of mother and child is perhaps the only undeniable natural social bond. It is not always effective, and it can, with effort, be suppressed, but it is always a force. And this is what we see today. But what about the father? Maybe he loves imagining his own eternity through the generations stemming from him. But this is only an act of imagination, one that can be attenuated by other concerns and calculations, as well as by his losing faith in the continuation of his name for very long in the shifting conditions of democracy. Of necessity, therefore, it was understood to be the woman's job to get and hold the man by her charms and wiles because, by nature, nothing else would induce him to give up his freedom in favor of the heavy duties of family. But women no longer wish to do this, and they, with justice, consider it unfair according to the principles governing us. So the cement that bound the family together crumbled. It is not the children who break away; it is the parents who abandon them. Women are no longer willing to make unconditional and perpetual commitments on unequal terms, and, no matter what they hope, nothing can effectively make most men share equally the responsibilities of childbearing and child-rearing. The divorce rate is only the most striking symptom of this breakdown.

None of this results from the sixties, or from the appeal to masculine vanity begun by advertisers in the fifties, or from any other superficial, pop-culture events. More than two hundred years ago Rousseau saw with alarm the seeds of the breakdown of the family in liberal society, and he dedicated much of his genius to trying to correct it. He found that the critical connection between man and woman was being broken by individualism, and focused his efforts, theoretical and practical, on encouraging passionate romantic love in them. He wanted to rebuild and reinforce that connection, previously encumbered by now discredited religious and civil regulation, on modern grounds of desire and consent. He retraced the picture of nature that had become a palimpsest under the abrasion of modern criticism, and he enticed men and women into admiring its teleological ordering, specifically the complementarity between the two sexes, which mesh and set the machine of life in motion, each differing from and needing the other, from the depths of the body to the heights of the soul. He set utter abandon to the sentiments and imaginations of idealized love against calculation of individual interest. Rousseau inspired a whole genre of novelistic and poetic literature that lived feverishly for over a century, coexisting with the writings of the Benthams and the Mills who were earnestly at work homogenizing the sexes. His undertaking had the heaviest significance because human community was at risk. In essence he was persuading women freely to be different from men and to take on the burden of entering a positive contract with the family, as opposed to a negative, individual, self-protective contract with the state. Tocqueville picked up this theme, described the absolute differentiation of husband's and wife's functions and ways of life in the American family, and attributed the success of American democracy to its women, who freely choose their lot. This he contrasted to the disorder, nay, chaos, of Europe, which he attributed to a misunderstanding or misapplication of the principle of equality—only an abstraction when not informed by nature's imperatives.

This whole effort failed and now arouses either women's anger, as an attempt to take from them rights guaranteed to all human beings, or their indifference, as irrelevant in a time when women do exactly the same things as men and face the same difficulties in ensuring their independence. Rousseau, Tocqueville and all the others now have only historical significance and at most provide us with a serious alternative perspective for analyzing our situation. Romantic love is now as alien to us as knight-errantry, and young men are no more likely to court a woman than to wear a suit of armor, not only because it is not fitting, but because it would be offensive to women. As a student exclaimed to me, with approval of his fellows, "What do you expect me to do? Play a guitar under some girl's window?" Such a thing seemed as absurd to him as swallowing goldfish.

But the parents of this same young man, it turned out, were divorced. He strongly, if incoherently, expressed his distress and performed the now ritualistic incantation for roots. Here Rousseau is most helpful, for he honestly exposed the nerve of that incantation, whereas the discussion of roots is an evasion. There is a passage in *Emile*, his educational novel, which keeps coming back to me as I look at my students. It occurs in the context of the teacher's arrangements with the parents of the pupil whose total education he is undertaking, and in the absence of any organic relation between husbands and wives and parents and children after having passed through the solvent of modern theory and practice:

> I would even want the pupil and the governor to regard themselves as so inseparable that the lot of each in life is always a common object for them. As soon as they envisage from afar their separation, as soon as they foresee the moment which is going to make them strangers to one another, they are already strangers. Each sets up his own little separate system; and both engrossed by the time they will no longer be together, stay only reluctantly. (*Emile*, p. 53, ed. Bloom, Basic Books, 1979)

That is it. Everyone has "his own little separate system." The aptest description I can find for the state of students' souls is the psychology of separateness.

The possibility of separation is already the fact of separation, inasmuch as people today must plan to be whole and self-sufficient, and cannot risk interdependence. Imagination compels everyone to look forward to the day of separation in order to see how he will do. The energies people should use in the common enterprise are exhausted in preparation for independence. What would, in the case of union, be a building stone becomes a stumbling block on the path to secession. The goals of those who are together naturally and necessarily must become a common good; what one must live with can be accepted. But there is no common good for those who are to separate. The presence of choice already changes the character of relatedness. And the more separation there is, the more there will be. Death of a parent, child, husband, wife or friend is always a possibility and sometimes a fact, but separation is something very different because it is an intentional rebuff to the demand for reciprocity of attachment which is the heart of these relations. People can continue to live while related to the dead beloved; they cannot continue to be related to a living beloved who no longer loves or wishes to be loved. This continual shifting of the sands in our desert—separation from places, persons, beliefs—produces the psychic state of nature where reserve and timidity are the prevailing dispositions. We are social solitaries.

Divorce

The most visible sign of our increasing separateness and, in its turn, the cause of ever greater separateness is divorce. It has a deep influence on our universities because more and more of the students are products of it, and they not only have problems themselves but also affect other students and the general atmosphere. Divorce in America is the most palpable indication that people are not made to live together, and that, although they want and need to create a general will out of the particular wills, those particular wills constantly reassert themselves. There is a quest, but ever more hopeless, for arrangements and ways of putting the broken pieces back together. The task is equivalent to squaring the circle, because everyone loves himself most but wants others to love him more than they love themselves. Such is particularly the demand of children, against which parents are now rebelling. In the absence of a common good or common object, as Rousseau puts it, the disintegration of society into particular wills is inevitable. Selfishness in this case is not a moral vice or a sin but a natural necessity. The "Me generation" and "narcissism" are merely descriptions, not causes. The solitary savage in the state of nature cannot be blamed for thinking primarily of himself, nor can a person who lives in a world where the primacy of self-concern is only too evident in the most fundamental institutions, where the original selfishness of the state of nature remains, where concern for the common good is hypocritical, and where morality seems to be squarely on the side of selfishness. Or, to put it otherwise, the concern with self-development, self-expression, or growth, which flourished as a result of the optimistic faith in a pre-established harmony between such a concern and society or community, has gradually revealed itself to be inimical to community. A young person's qualified or conditional attachment to divorced parents merely reciprocates what he necessarily sees as their conditional attachment to him, and is entirely different from the classic problem of loyalty to families, or other institutions, which were clearly dedicated to their members. In the past, such breaking away was sometimes necessary but always morally problematic. Today it is normal, and this is another reason why the classic literature is alien to so many of our young, for it is largely concerned with liberation from real claims—like family, faith, or country—whereas now the movement is in the opposite direction, a search for claims on oneself that have some validity. Children who have gone to the school of conditional relationships should be expected to view the world in the light of what they learned there.

Children may be told over and over again that their parents have a right to their own lives, that they will enjoy quality time instead of quantity time, that they are really loved by their parents even after divorce, but children do not believe any of this. They think they have a right to total attention and believe their parents must live for them. There is no explaining otherwise to them, and anything less inevitably produces indignation and an inextirpable sense of injustice. To children, the voluntary separation of parents seems worse than their death precisely because it is voluntary. The capriciousness of wills, their lack of directedness to the common good, the fact that they could be otherwise but are not— these are the real source of the war of all against all. Children learn a fear of enslavement to the wills of others, along with a need to dominate those wills, in the context of the family, the one place where they are supposed to learn the opposite. Of course, many families are unhappy. But that is irrelevant. The important lesson that the family taught was the existence of the only unbreakable bond, for better or for worse, between human beings.

The decomposition of this bond is surely America's most urgent social problem. But nobody even tries to do anything about it. The tide seems to be irresistible. Among the many items on the agenda of those promoting America's moral regeneration, I never find marriage and divorce. The last time anyone in public office took a crack at anything like this issue was when Jimmy Carter urged Federal civil servants living together out of wedlock to get married. Meanwhile, the first conservative

President elected in a half-century is a divorced man, and his Secretary of Health and Human Services, the public officer most closely connected with family matters, said she took heart from his example during her own well-publicized divorce.

A university teacher of liberal arts cannot help confronting special handicaps, a slight deformity of the spirit, in the students, ever more numerous, whose parents are divorced. I do not have the slightest doubt that they do as well as others in all kinds of specialized subjects, but I find they are not as open to the serious study of philosophy and literature as some other students are. I would guess this is because they are less eager to look into the meaning of their lives, or to risk shaking their received opinions. In order to live with the chaos of their experience, they tend to have rigid frameworks about what is right and wrong and how they ought to live. They are full of desperate platitudes about self-determination, respect for other people's rights and decisions, the need to work out one's individual values and commitments, etc. All this is a thin veneer over boundless seas of rage, doubt and fear.

Young people habitually are able to jettison their habits of belief for an exciting idea. They have little to lose. Although this is not really philosophy, because they are not aware of how high the stakes are, in this period of their lives they can experiment with the unconventional and acquire deeper habits of belief and some learning to go along with them. But children of divorced parents often lack this intellectual daring because they lack the natural youthful confidence in the future. Fear of both isolation and attachment clouds their prospects. A large measure of their enthusiasm has been extinguished and replaced by self-protectiveness. Similarly, their open confidence in friendship as part of the newly discovered search for the good is somewhat stunted. The Glauconian *eros* for the discovery of nature has suffered more damage in them than in most. Such students can make their disarray in the cosmos the theme of their reflection and study. But it is a grim and dangerous business, and more than any students I have known, they evoke pity. They are indeed victims.

An additional factor in the state of these students' souls is the fact that they have undergone therapy. They have been told how to feel and what to think about themselves by psychologists who are paid by their parents to make everything work out as painlessly as possible for the parents, as part of no-fault divorce. If ever there was a conflict of interest, this is it. There are big bucks for therapists in divorce, since the divorcés are eager to get back to persecuting the wretches who smoke or to ending the arms race or to saving "civilization as we know it." Meanwhile, psychologists provide much of the ideology justifying divorce—e.g., that it is worse for kids to stay in stressful homes (thus motivating the potential escapees—that is, the parents—to make it as unpleasant as possible there). Psychologists are the sworn enemies of guilt. And they have an artificial language for the artificial feelings with which they equip children. But it unfortunately does not permit such children to get a firm grip on anything. Of course, not every psychologist who deals with these matters simply plays the tune called by those who pay the piper, but the givens of the market and the capacity for self-deception, called creativity, surely influence such therapy. After all, parents can shop around for a psychologist just as some Catholics used to shop for a confessor. When these students arrive at the university, they are not only reeling from the destructive effects of the overturning of faith and the ambiguity of loyalty that result from divorce, but deafened by self-serving lies and hypocrisies expressed in a pseudoscientific jargon. Modern psychology at its best has a questionable understanding of the soul. It has no place for the natural superiority of the philosophic life, and no understanding of education. So children who are impregnated with that psychology live in a sub-basement and have a long climb just to get back up to the cave, or the world of common sense, which is the proper beginning for their ascent toward wisdom. They do not have confidence in what they feel or what they see, and they have an ideology that provides not a reason but a rationalization for their timidity.

These students are the symbols of the intellectual-political problems of our time. They represent in extreme form the spiritual vortex set in motion by loss of contact with other human beings and with the natural order. But all students are affected, in the most practical everyday way, unaware that their situation is peculiar, because their education does not give them perspective on it.

Love

The best point of entry into the very special world inhabited by today's students is the astonishing fact that they usually do not, in what were once called love affairs, say, "I love you," and never, "I'll always love you." One student told me that, of course, he says "I love you," to girlfriends, "when we are breaking up." It is the clean and easy break—no damage, no fault—at which they are adept. This is understood to be morality, respect for other persons' freedom.

Perhaps young people do not say "I love you" because they are honest. They do not experience love—too familiar with sex to confuse it with love, too preoccupied with their own fates to be victimized by love's mad self-forgetting, the last of the genuine fanaticisms. Then there is distaste for love's fatal historical baggage—sex roles, making women into possessions and objects without respect for their self-determination. Young people today are afraid of making commitments, and the point is that love *is* commitment, and much more. Commitment is a word invented in our abstract modernity to signify the absence of any real motives in the soul for moral dedication. Commitment is gratuitous, motiveless, because the real passions are all low and selfish. One may be sexually attracted, but that does not, so people think, provide any sufficient motive for real and lasting concern for another. Young people, and not only young people, have studied and practiced a crippled *eros* that can no longer take wing, and does not contain within it the longing for eternity and the divination of one's relatedness to being. They are practical Kantians: whatever is tainted with lust or pleasure cannot be moral. However, they have not discovered the pure morality. It remains an empty category used to discredit all substantial inclinations that were once moralizing. Too much emphasis on authenticity has made it impossible to trust one's instincts, and too much seriousness about sex has made it impossible to take sex seriously. Young men and women distrust eroticism too much to think it a sufficient pointer toward a way of life. The burdens implied in and blessed by eros are only burdens without it. It is not cowardice to avoid taking on responsibilities that have no charm even in anticipation.

When marriage occurs it does not usually seem to result from a decision and a conscious will to take on its responsibilities. The couple have lived together for a long time, and by an almost imperceptible process, they find themselves married, as much out of convenience as passion, as much negatively as positively (not really expecting to do much better, since they have looked around and seen how imperfect all fits seem to be). Among the educated, marriage these days seems to be best acquired, as Macaulay said about the British Empire, in a fit of absence of mind.

Part of the inability to make sexual commitments results from an ideology of the feelings. Young people are always telling me such reasonable things about jealousy and possessiveness and even their dreams about the future. But as to dreams about the future with a partner, they have none. That would be to impose a rigid, authoritarian pattern on the future, which should emerge spontaneously. This means they can foresee no future, or that the one they would naturally foresee is forbidden them by current piety, as sexist. Similarly, why should a man or a woman be jealous if his or her partner has sexual relations with someone else? A serious person today does not want to force the feelings of others. The same goes for possessiveness. When I hear such things, all so sensible and in harmony with a liberal society, I feel that I am in the presence of robots. This ideology only works for people who have had no experience of the feelings, have never loved, have abstracted from the texture of life. These prodigies of reason need never fear Othello's fate. Kill for love! What can that mean? It may very well be that their *apatheia* is a suppression of feeling, anxiety about getting hurt. But it might also be the real thing. People may, having digested the incompatibility of ends, have developed a new kind of soul. None of the sexual possibilities students have actualized was unknown to me. But their lack of passion, of hope, of despair, of a sense of the twinship of love and death, is incomprehensible to me. When I see a young couple who have lived together throughout their college years leave each other with a handshake and move out into life, I am struck dumb.

Students do not date anymore. Dating was the petrified skeleton of courtship. They live in herds or packs with no more sexual differentiation than any herds have when not in heat. Human beings can, of course, engage in sexual intercourse at any time. But today there are none of the conventions invented by civilization to take the place of heat, to guide mating, and perhaps to channel it. Nobody is sure who is to make the advances, whether there are to be a pursuer and a pursued, what the event is to mean. They have to improvise, for roles are banned, and a man pays a high price for misjudging his partner's attitude. The act takes place but it does not separate the couple from the flock, to which they immediately return as they were before, undifferentiated.

It is easier for men to get gratification than it used to be, and many men have the advantage of being pursued. Certainly they do not have to make all kinds of efforts and pay all kinds of attention, as men once did. There is an easy familiarity. But at least some of these advantages for men are offset by nervousness about their sexual performance. In the past a man could think he was doing a wonderful thing for a woman, and expect to be admired for what he brought. But that was before he could be pretty sure that he was being compared and judged, which is daunting. And certain aspects of the undeniably male biology sometimes make it difficult for him to perform and cause him to prefer being the one to express the desire.

Women are still pleased by their freedom and their capacity to chart an independent course for themselves. But they frequently suspect that they are being used, that in the long run they may need men more than men need them, and that they cannot expect much from the feckless contemporary male. They despise what men used to think women had to offer (that is partly why it is now offered so freely), but they are dogged by doubt whether men are very impressed by what they are now offering instead. Distrust suffuses the apparently easy commerce between the sexes. There is an awful lot of breaking up, surely disagreeable, though nothing earthshaking. Exam time is a great moment for students to separate. They are under too much stress and too busy to put up with much trouble from a relationship.

"Relationships," not love affairs, are what they have. Love suggests something wonderful, exciting, positive and firmly seated in the passions. A relationship is gray, amorphous, suggestive of a project, without a given content, and tentative. You work at a relationship, whereas love takes care of itself. In a relationship the difficulties come first, and there is a search for common grounds. Love presents illusions of perfection to the imagination and is forgetful of all the natural fissures in human connection. About relationships there is ceaseless anxious talk, the kind one cannot help overhearing in student hangouts or restaurants frequented by men and women who are "involved" with one another, the kind of obsessive prattle so marvelously captured in old Nichols and May routines or Woody Allen films. In one Nichols and May bit, a couple who have just slept together for the first time, assert with all the emptiness of doubt, "We are going to have a *relationship*." This insight was typical of the University of Chicago in the fifties, of *The Lonely Crowd*. The only mistake was to encourage the belief that by becoming more "inner-directed," going farther down the path of the isolated self, people will be less lonely. The problem, however, is not that people are not authentic enough, but that they have no common object, no common good, no natural complementarity. Selves, of course, have no relation to anything but themselves, and this is why "communication" is their problem. Gregariousness, like that of the animals in the herd, is admitted by all. Grazing together side by side and rubbing against one another are the given, but there is a desire and a necessity to have something more, to make the transition from the herd to the hive, where there is real interconnection. Hence, the hive—community, roots, extended family—is much praised, but no one is willing to transform his indeterminate self into an all too determinate worker, drone or queen, to submit to the rank-ordering and division of labor necessary to any whole that is more than just a heap of discrete parts. Selves want to be wholes, but have lately also taken to longing to be parts. This is the reason why conversation about relationships remains so vacuous, abstract and unprogrammatic, with its whole content stored in a bottle labeled "commitment." It is also why there is so much talk about phenomena like "bonding." In the absence of any connectedness in their souls, human beings seek reassurance in fruitless analogy to mechanisms found in brutes. But this will not work because human attachment always has an element of deliberate choice, denied by such analogy. One need only compare the countless novels and movies about male bonding with Aristotle's discussion of friendship in the *Ethics*. Friendship, like its related phenomenon, love, is no longer within our ken because both require notions of soul and nature that, for a mixture of theoretical and political reasons, we cannot even consider.

The reliance on relationships is a self-delusion because it is founded on an inner contradiction. Relations between the sexes have always been difficult, and that is why so much of our literature is about men and women quarreling. There is certainly legitimate ground to doubt their suitability for each other given the spectrum—from the harem to Plato's *Republic*—of imaginable and actually existing relations between them, whether nature acted the stepmother or God botched the creation by an afterthought, as some Romantics believed. That man is not made to be alone is all very well, but who is made to live with him? This is why men and women hesitated before marriage, and courtship was thought necessary to find out whether the couple was compatible, and perhaps to give them basic training in compatibility. No one wanted to be stuck forever with an impossible partner. But, for all that, they knew pretty much what they wanted from one another. The question was whether they could get it (whereas our question today is much more what is wanted). A man was to make a living and protect his wife and children, and a woman was to provide for the domestic economy, particularly in caring for husband and children. Frequently this did not work out very well for one or both of the partners, because they either were not good at their functions or were not eager to perform them. In order to assure the proper ordering of things, the transvestite women in Shakespeare, like Portia and Rosalind, are forced to masquerade as men because the real men are inadequate and need to be corrected. This happens only in comedies; when there are no such intrepid women, the situation turns into tragedy. But the assumption of male garb observes the proprieties or conventions. Men should be doing what the impersonating women are doing; and when the women have set things right, they become women again and submit to the men, albeit with a tactful, ironical consciousness that they are at least partially playacting in order to preserve a viable order. The arrangement implicit in marriage, even if it is only conventional, tells those who enter into it what to expect and what the satisfactions are supposed to be. Very simply, the family is a sort of miniature body politic in which the husband's will is the will of the whole. The woman can influence her husband's will, and it is supposed to be informed by love of wife and children.

Now all of this has simply disintegrated. It does not exist, nor is it considered good that it should. But nothing certain has taken its place. Neither men nor women have any idea what they are getting into anymore, or, rather, they have reason to fear the worst. There are two equal wills, and no mediating principle to link them and no tribunal of last resort. What is more, neither of the wills is certain of itself. This is where the "ordering of priorities" comes in, particularly with women, who have not yet decided which comes first, career or children. People are no longer raised to think they ought to regard marriage as the primary goal and responsibility, and their uncertainty is mightily reinforced by the divorce statistics, which imply that putting all of one's psychological eggs in the marriage basket is a poor risk. The goals and wills of men and women have become like parallel lines, and it requires a Lobachevskyan imagination to hope they may meet.

The inharmoniousness of final ends finds its most concrete expression in the female career, which is now precisely the same as the male career. There are two equal careers in almost every household composed of educated persons under thirty-five. And those careers are not mere means to family ends. They are personal fulfillments. In this nomadic country it is more than likely that one of the partners will be forced, or have the opportunity, to take a job in a city other than the one where his or her spouse works. What to do? They can stay together with one partner sacrificing his career to the other, they can commute, or they can separate. None of these solutions is satisfactory. More important, what is going to happen is unpredictable. Is it the marriage or the career that will count most? Women's careers today are qualitatively different from what they were up to twenty years ago, and such conflict is now inevitable. The result is that both marriage and career are devalued.

For a long time middle-class women, with the encouragement of their husbands, had been pursuing careers. It was thought they had a right to cultivate their higher talents instead of being household drudges. Implicit in this was, of course, the view that the bourgeois professions indeed offered an opportunity to fulfill the human potential, while family and particularly the woman's work involved in it were merely in the realm of necessity, limited and limiting. Serious men of good conscience believed that they must allow their wives to develop themselves. But, with rare exceptions, both parties still took it for granted that the family was the woman's responsibility and that, in the case of potential conflict, she would subordinate or give up her career. It was not quite serious, and she usually knew it. This arrangement was ultimately untenable, and it was clear in which way the balance would tip. Couples agreed that the household was not spiritually fulfilling for women and that women have equal rights. The notion of a domestic life appropriate to women had become incredible. Why should not women take their careers as seriously as men take theirs, and have them be taken as seriously by men? Terrific resentment at the injustice done to women under the prevailing understanding of justice found its expression in demands seen as perfectly legitimate by both men and women, that men weaken the attachment to their careers, that they share equally in the household and the care of the children. Women's abandonment of the female persona was reinforced by the persona's abandoning them. Economic changes made it desirable and necessary that women work; lowering of infant mortality rates meant that women had to have fewer pregnancies; greater longevity and better health meant that women devoted a much smaller portion of their lives to having and rearing children; and the altered relationships within the family meant that they were less likely to find continuing occupation with their children and their children's children. At forty-five they were finding themselves with nothing to do, and forty more years to do it in. Their formative career years had been lost, and they were, hence, unable to compete with men. A woman who now wanted to be a woman in the old sense would find it very difficult to do so, even if she were to brave the hostile public opinion. In all of these ways the feminist case is very strong indeed. But, though the terms of marriage had been radically altered, no new ones were defined.

The feminist response that justice requires equal sharing of all domestic responsibility by men and women is not a solution, but only a compromise, an attenuation of men's dedication to their careers and of women's to family, with arguably an enrichment in diversity of both parties but just as arguably a fragmentation of their lives. The question of who goes with whom in the case of jobs in different cities is unresolved and is, whatever may be said about it, a festering sore, a source of suspicion and resentment, and the potential for war. Moreover, this compromise does not decide anything about the care of the children. Are both parents going to care more about their careers than about the children? Previously children at least had the unqualified dedication of one person, the woman, for whom their care was the most important thing in life. Is half the attention of two the same as the whole attention of one? Is this not a formula for neglecting children? Under such arrangements the family is not a unity, and marriage is an unattractive struggle that is easy to get out of, especially for men.

And here is where the whole business turns nasty. The souls of men —their ambitious, warlike, protective, possessive character—must be dismantled in order to liberate women from their domination. Machismo— the polemical description of maleness or spiritedness, which was the central *natural* passion in men's souls in the psychology of the ancients, the passion of attachment and loyalty—was the villain, the source of the difference between the sexes. The feminists were only completing a job begun by Hobbes in his project of taming the harsh elements in the soul. With machismo discredited, the positive task is to make men caring, sensitive, even nurturing, to fit the restructured family. Thus once again men must be re-educated according to an abstract project. They must accept the "feminine elements" in their nature. A host of Dustin Hoffman and Meryl Streep types invade the schools, popular psychology, TV and the movies, making the project respectable. Men tend to undergo this re-education somewhat sullenly but studiously, in order to avoid the opprobrium of the sexist label and to keep peace with their wives and girlfriends. And it is indeed possible to soften men. But to make them "care" is another thing, and the project must inevitably fail.

It must fail because in an age of individualism, persons of either sex cannot be forced to be public-spirited, particularly by those who are becoming less so. Further, caring is either a passion or a virtue, not a description like "sensitive." A virtue governs a passion, as moderation governs lust, or courage governs fear. But what passion does caring govern? One might say possessiveness, but possessiveness is not to be governed these days—it is to be rooted out. What is wanted is an antidote to natural selfishness, but wishes do not give birth to horses, however much abstract moralism may demand them. The old moral order, however imperfect it may have been, at least moved toward the virtues by way of the passions. If men were self-concerned, that order tried to expand the scope of self-concern to include others, rather than commanding men to cease being concerned with themselves. To attempt the latter is both tyrannical and ineffective. A true political or social order requires the soul to be like a Gothic cathedral, with selfish stresses and strains helping to hold it up. Abstract moralism condemns certain keystones, removes them, and then blames both the nature of the stones and the structure when it collapses. The failure of agriculture in socialist collective farming is the best political example of this. An imaginary motive takes the place of a real one, and when the imaginary motive fails to produce the real effect, those who have not been motivated by it are blamed and persecuted. In family questions, inasmuch as men were understood to be so strongly motivated by property, an older wisdom tried to attach concern for the family to that motive: the man was allowed and encouraged to regard his family as his property, so he would care for the former as he would instinctively care for the latter. This was effective, although it obviously had disadvantages from the point of view of justice. When wives and children come to the husband and father and say, "We are not your property; we are ends in ourselves and demand to be treated as such," the anonymous observer cannot help being impressed. But the difficulty comes when wives and children further demand that the man continue to care for them as before, just when they are giving an example of caring for themselves. They object to the father's flawed motive and ask that it be miraculously replaced by a pure one, of which they wish to make use for their own ends. The father will almost inevitably constrict his quest for property, cease being a father and become a mere man again, rather than turning into a providential God, as others ask him to be. What is so intolerable about the *Republic*, as Plato shows, is the demand that men give up their land, their money, their wives, their children, for the sake of the public good, their concern for which had previously been buttressed by these lower attachments. The hope is to have a happy city made up entirely of unhappy men. Similar demands are made today in an age of slack morality and self-indulgence. Plato taught that, however laudable justice may be, one cannot expect prodigies of virtue from ordinary people. Better a real city tainted by selfish motives than one that cannot exist, except in speech, and that promotes real tyranny.

I am not arguing here that the old family arrangements were good or that we should or could go back to them. I am only insisting that we not cloud our vision to such an extent that we believe that there are viable substitutes for them just because we want or need them. The peculiar attachment of mothers for their children existed, and in some degree still exists, whether it was the product of nature or nurture. That fathers should have exactly the same kind of attachment is much less evident. We can insist on it, but if nature does not cooperate, all our efforts will have been in vain. Biology forces women to take maternity leaves. Law can enjoin men to take paternity leaves, but it cannot make them have the desired sentiments. Only the rankest ideologue could fail to see the difference between the two kinds of leave, and the contrived and somewhat ridiculous character of the latter. Law may prescribe that the male nipples be made equal to the female ones, but they still will not give milk. Female attachment to children is to be at least partly replaced with promissory notes on male attachment. Will they be redeemed? Or won't everyone set up his own little separate psychological banking system?

Similarly, women, due to the unreliability of men, have had to provide the means for their own independence. This has simply given men the excuse for being even less concerned with women's well-being. A dependent, weak woman is indeed vulnerable and puts herself at men's mercy. But that appeal did influence a lot of men a lot of the time. The cure now prescribed for male irresponsibility is to make them more irresponsible. And a woman who can be independent of men has much less motive to entice a man into taking care of her and her children. In the same vein, I heard a female lieutenant-colonel on the radio explaining that the only thing standing in the way of woman's full equality in the military is male protectiveness. So, do away with it! Yet male protectiveness, based on masculine pride, and desire to gain the glory for defending a blushing woman's honor and life, was a form of relatedness, as well as a way of sublimating selfishness. These days, why should a man risk his life protecting a karate champion who knows just what part of the male anatomy to go after in defending herself? What substitute is there for the forms of relatedness that are dismantled in the name of the new justice?

All our reforms have helped strip the teeth of our gears, which can therefore no longer mesh. They spin idly, side by side, unable to set the social machine in motion. It is at this exercise in futility that young people must look when thinking about their future. Women are pleased by their successes, their new opportunities, their agenda, their moral superiority. But underneath everything lies the more or less conscious awareness that they are still dual beings by nature, capable of doing most things men do and also wanting to have children. They may hope otherwise, but they fully expect to pursue careers, to have to pursue careers, while caring for children alone. And what they expect and plan for is likely to happen. The men have none of the current ideological advantages of the women, but they can opt out without too much cost. In their relations with women they have little to say; convinced of the injustice of the old order, for which they were responsible, and practically incapable of changing the direction of the juggernaut, they wait to hear what is wanted, try to adjust but are ready to take off in an instant. They want relationships, but the situation is so unclear. They anticipate a huge investment of emotional energy that is just as likely as not to end in bankruptcy, to a sacrifice of their career goals without any clarity about what reward they will reap, other than a vague togetherness. Meanwhile, one of the strongest, oldest motives for marriage is no longer operative. Men can now easily enjoy the sex that previously could only be had in marriage. It is strange that the tiredest and stupidest bromide mothers and fathers preached to their daughters—"He won't respect you or marry you if you give him what he wants too easily"—turns out to be the truest and most probing analysis of the current situation. Women can say they do not care, that they want men to have the right motives or none at all, but everyone, and they best of all, knows that they are being, at most, only half truthful with themselves.

Eros

This is the campus sexual scene. Relativism in theory and lack of relatedness in practice make students unable to think about or look into their futures, and they shrivel up within the confines of the present and material *I*. They are willing to mutter the prescribed catechism, the substitute for thought, which promises them salvation, but there is little faith. As a very intelligent student said to me, "We are all obsessively going to the well, but we always come up dry." The rhetoric of the campus gays only confirms this. After all the demands and the complaints against the existing order—"Don't discriminate against us; don't legislate morality; don't put a policeman in every bedroom; respect our orientation"—they fall back into the empty talk about finding life-styles. There is not, and cannot be, anything more specific. All relationships have been homogenized in their indeterminacy.

The eroticism of our students is lame. It is not the divine madness Socrates praised; or the enticing awareness of incompleteness and the quest to overcome it; or nature's grace, which permits a partial being to recover his wholeness in the embrace of another, or a temporal being to long for eternity in the perpetuity of his seed; or the hope that all men will remember his deeds; or his contemplation of perfection. Eroticism is a discomfort, but one that in itself promises relief and affirms the goodness of things. It is the proof, subjective but incontrovertible, of man's relatedness, imperfect though it may be, to others and to the whole of nature. Wonder, the source of both poetry and philosophy, is its characteristic expression. Eros demands daring from its votaries and provides a good reason for it. This longing for completeness is the longing for education, and the study of it is education. Socrates' knowledge of ignorance is identical with his perfect knowledge of erotics. The longing for his conversations with which he infected his companions, and which was intensified after his death and has endured throughout the centuries, proved him to have been both the neediest and most grasping of lovers, and the richest and most giving of beloveds. The sex lives of our students and their reflection on them disarm such longing and make it incomprehensible to them. Reduction has robbed eros of its divinatory powers. Because they do not trust it, students have no reverence for themselves. There is almost no remaining link visible to them between what they learn in sex education and Plato's *Symposium.*

Yet only from such dangerous heights can our situation be seen in proper perspective. The fact that this perspective is no longer credible is the measure of our crisis. When we recognize the *Phaedrus* and the *Symposium* as interpreting our experiences, we can be sure that we are having those experiences in their fullness, and that we have the minimum of education. Rousseau, the founder of the most potent of reductionist teachings about eros, said that the *Symposium* is always the book of lovers. Are we lovers anymore? This is my way of putting the educational question of our times.

In all species other than man, when an animal reaches puberty, it is all that it will ever be. This stage is the clear end toward which all of its growth and learning is directed. The animal's activity is reproduction. It lives on this plateau until it starts downhill. Only in man is puberty just the beginning. The greater and more interesting part of his learning, moral and intellectual, comes afterward, and in civilized man is incorporated into his erotic desire. His taste and hence his choices are determined during this "sentimental education." It is as though his learning were for the sake of his sexuality. Reciprocally, much of the energy for that learning obviously comes from his sexuality. Nobody takes human children who have reached puberty to be adults. We properly sense that there is a long road to adulthood, the condition in which they are able to govern themselves and be true mothers and fathers. This road is the serious part of education, where animal sexuality becomes human sexuality, where instinct gives way in man to choice with regard to the true, the good and the beautiful. Puberty does not provide man, as it does other animals, with all that he needs to leave behind others of his kind. This means that the animal part of his sexuality is intertwined in the most complex way with the higher reaches of his soul, which must inform the desires with its insight, and that the most delicate part of education is to keep the two in harmony.

I cannot pretend that I understand very much of this mystery, but knowing that I do not know keeps me attentive to, and far from the current simplifications of, the phenomena of this aspect of our nature that links the highest and the lowest in us. I believe that the most interesting students are those who have not settled the sexual problem, who are still young, even look young for their age, who think there is much to look forward to and much they must yet grow up to, fresh and naive, excited by the mysteries to which they have not yet been fully initiated. There are some who are men and women at the age of sixteen, who have nothing more to learn about the erotic. They are adult in the sense that they will no longer change very much. They may become competent specialists, but they are flat-souled. The world is for them what it presents itself to the senses to be; it is unadorned by imagination and devoid of ideals. This flat soul is what the sexual wisdom of our time conspires to make universal.

The easy sex of teen-agers snips the golden thread linking eros to education. And popularized Freud finishes it for good by putting the seal of science on an unerotic understanding of sex. A youngster whose sexual longings consciously or unconsciously inform his studies has a very different set of experiences from one in whom such motives are not active. A trip to Florence or to Athens is one thing for a young man who hopes to meet his Beatrice on the Ponte Santa Trinità or his Socrates in the Agora, and quite another for one who goes without such aching need. The latter is only a tourist, the former is looking for completion. Flaubert, a great expert on the fate of longing in the modern world, sends his awestruck Emma Bovary to a ball at the estate of decadent aristocrats where she sees:

... at the head of the table, alone among all of these men and women, bent over, his full plate with his napkin knotted around his neck like a child, an old man ate, letting drops of gravy trickle from his mouth. He had bloodshot eyes and wore a little pigtail fastened with a black ribbon. It was the Marquis' father-in-law, the old Duc de Laverdière, the former favorite of the Comte d'Artois at the time of the hunts at the Vaudreuil home of the Marquis de Conflans, and who had been, it was said, the lover of Queen Marie-Antoinette between M. de Coigny and M. de Lauzun. He had led a wild life of debauch, full of duels, wagers, abducted women, had devoured his fortune and terrified his whole family. A domestic, behind his chair, speaking loudly into his ear, named the dishes for him to which he pointed while stuttering. And constantly Emma's eyes, of their own accord, returned to this old man with drooping lips as to something extraordinary and august. He had lived at court and slept in the bed of queens.

Others see only a repulsive old man, but Emma sees the *ancien régime.* Her vision is truer, for there once really was an *ancien régime,* and in it there were great lovers. The constricted present cannot teach it to us without the longing that makes us dissatisfied with the present. Such longing is what students most need, because the great remains of the tradition have grown senile in our care. Imagination is required to restore their youth, beauty and vitality, and then experience their inspiration.

The student who made fun of playing the guitar under a girl's window will never read or write poetry under her influence. His defective eros cannot provide his soul with images of the beautiful, and it will remain coarse and slack. It is not that he will fail to adorn or idealize the world; it is that he will not see what is there.

A significant number of students used to arrive at the university physically and spiritually virginal, expecting to lose their innocence there. Their lust was mixed into everything they thought and did. They were painfully aware that they wanted something but were not quite sure exactly what it was, what form it would take and what it all meant. The range of satisfactions intimated by their desire moved from prostitutes to Plato, and back, from the criminal to the sublime. Above all they looked for instruction. Practically everything they read in the humanities and social sciences might be a source of learning about their pain, and a path to its healing. This powerful tension, this literal lust for knowledge, was what a teacher could see in the eyes of those who flattered him by giving such evidence of their need for him. His own satisfaction was promised by having something with which to feed their hunger, an overflow to bestow on their emptiness. His joy was in hearing the ecstatic "Oh, yes!" as he dished up Shakespeare and Hegel to minister to their need. Pimp and midwife really described him well. The itch for what appeared to be only sexual intercourse was the material manifestation of the Delphic oracle's command, which is but a reminder of the most fundamental human desire, to "know thyself."

Sated with easy, clinical and sterile satisfactions of body and soul, the students arriving at the university today hardly walk on the enchanted ground they once did. They pass by the ruins without imagining what was once there. Spiritually detumescent, they do not seek wholeness in the university. These most productive years of learning, the time when Alcibiades was growing his first beard, are wasted because of artificial precociousness and a sophistic wisdom acquired in high school. The real moment for sexual education goes by, and hardly anybody has an idea of what it would be.

Reciprocally, the university does not see itself as ministering to such needs and does not believe the mummies on display in its museum can speak to the visitors or, horrors, go home to live with them. The humanists are old maid librarians. As I reflect on it, the last fertile moment when student and university made a match was the fling with Freud during the forties and fifties. He advertised a real psychology, a version of the age-old investigation of the soul's phenomena adjusted to the palate of modern man. Today one can hardly imagine the excitement. What a thrill it was when my first college girlfriend told me that the university's bell tower was a phallic symbol. This was a real mix of my secret obsessions and the high seriousness I expected to get from the university. High school was never like this. It was hard to tell whether the meaning of it all was that I was about to lose my virginity or to penetrate the mysteries of being. An admirable confusion. At last everything was out on the table. The dirty things had disappeared from the philosophy of the *mind,* and Freud promised to restore the *soul* and take seriously what happened in it. He fancied himself a new and truer Plato and allowed us to praise Plato again as Freud's precursor.

But it turned out to be psychology without the *psyche,* i.e., without the soul. Freud just did not give a satisfying account of all the things we experience. Everything higher had to be a repression of something lower, and a symbol of something else rather than itself. The best a Freudian vision could do for man's real intellectual longings was *Death in Venice*, clearly not a very rich row to hoe for the finer spirits. Aristotle said that man has two peaks, each accompanied by intense pleasure: sexual intercourse and thinking. The human soul is a kind of ellipse or hyperbola, and its phenomena are spread between its two foci, displaying their tropical variety and ambiguity. Freud saw only one focus in the soul, the same one as the brutes have, and had to explain all psychology's higher phenomena by society's repression or other such versions of the Indian rope trick. He really did not believe in the soul, but in the body, along with its passive instrument of consciousness, the mind. This blunted his vision of the higher phenomena, as is apparent from his crude observations about art and philosophy. It was not merely sexual satisfaction students were seeking, whether they were aware of it or not, but knowledge of themselves, and Freud did not provide it. People found that Freud's "know thyself" led them to the couch, where they emptied their tank of the compressed fuel, which was intended to power them on their flight from opinion to knowledge. "Know thyself" did not mean to Freud knowing man's place within the order of the whole of things. It is long since that academic psychology has had any appeal for students who have a philosophic urge. Freudian psychology has become a big business and entered into the mainstream of public life with a status equal to that of engineering and banking. But it has no more intellectual appeal than do they. We must look elsewhere for ourselves.

PART TWO

NIHILISM, AMERICAN STYLE

THE GERMAN CONNECTION

When President Ronald Reagan called the Soviet Union "the evil empire," right-thinking persons joined in an angry chorus of protest against such provocative rhetoric. At other times Mr. Reagan has said that the United States and the Soviet Union "have different *values*" (italics added), an assertion that those same persons greet at worst with silence and frequently with approval. I believe he thought he was saying the same thing in both instances, and the different reaction to his different words introduces us to *the* most important and most astonishing phenomenon of our time, all the more astonishing in being almost unnoticed: there is now an entirely new language of good and evil, originating in an attempt to get "beyond good and evil" and preventing us from talking with any conviction about good and evil anymore. Even those who deplore our current moral condition do so in the very language that exemplifies that condition.

The new language is that of *value* relativism, and it constitutes a change in our view of things moral and political as great as the one that took place when Christianity replaced Greek and Roman paganism. A new language always reflects a new point of view, and the gradual, unconscious popularization of new words, or of old words used in new ways, is a sure sign of a profound change in people's articulation of the world. When bishops, a generation after Hobbes's death, almost naturally spoke the language of the state of nature, contract and rights, it was clear that he had defeated the ecclesiastical authorities, who were no longer able to understand themselves as they once had. It was henceforward inevitable that the modern archbishops of Canterbury would have no more in common with the ancient ones than does the second Elizabeth with the first.

What was offensive to contemporary ears in President Reagan's use of the word "evil" was its cultural arrogance, the presumption that he, and America, know what is good; its closedness to the dignity of other ways of life; its implicit contempt for those who do not share our ways. The political corollary is that he is not open to negotiation. The opposition between good and evil is not negotiable and is a cause of war. Those who are interested in "conflict resolution" find it much easier to reduce the tension between values than the tension between good and evil. Values are insubstantial stuff, existing primarily in the imagination, while death is real. The term "value," meaning the radical subjectivity of all belief about good and evil, serves the easygoing quest for comfortable self-preservation.

Value relativism can be taken to be a great release from the perpetual tyranny of good and evil, with their cargo of shame and guilt, and the endless efforts that the pursuit of the one and the avoidance of the other enjoin. Intractable good and evil cause infinite distress—like war and sexual repression—which is almost instantly relieved when more flexible values are introduced. One need not feel bad about or uncomfortable with oneself when just a little value adjustment is necessary. And this longing to shuck off constraints and have one peaceful, happy world is the first of the affinities between our real American world and that of German philosophy in its most advanced form, given expression by the critics of the President's speech.

But there is a second side to the coin. Persons deeply committed to values are admired. Their intense belief, their caring or concern, their believing in something, is the proof of autonomy, freedom and creativity. Such persons are the contrary of easygoing, and they have standards, all the more worthy because they are not received from tradition, and are not based on a reality all can see, or derived from thin rationalizing confined to calculation about material interests. The heroic and artistic types dedicate themselves to ideals of their own making. They are the antibourgeois. Value here serves those who are looking for fresh inspiration, for new beliefs about good and evil at least as powerful as the old ones that have been disenchanted, demystified, demythologized by scientific reason. This interpretation seems to say that dying for values is the noblest of acts and that the old realism or objectivism led to weak attachments to one's goals. Nature is indifferent to good and evil; man's interpretations prescribe a law of life to nature.

Thus our use of the value language leads us in two opposite directions —to follow the line of least resistance, and to adopt strong poses and fanatic resolutions. But these are merely different deductions from a common premise. Values are not discovered by reason, and it is fruitless to seek them, to find the truth or the good life. The quest begun by Odysseus and continued over three millennia has come to an end with the observation that there is nothing to seek. This alleged fact was announced by Nietzsche just over a century ago when he said, "God is dead." Good and evil now for the first time appeared as values, of which there have been a thousand and one, none rationally or objectively preferable to any other. The salutary illusion about the existence of good and evil has been definitively dispelled. For Nietzsche this was an unparalleled catastrophe; it meant the decomposition of culture and the loss of human aspiration. The Socratic "examined" life was no longer possible or desirable. It was itself unexamined, and if there was any possibility of a human life in the future it must begin from the naive capacity to live an unexamined life. The philosophic way of life had become simply poisonous. In short, Nietzsche with the utmost gravity told modern man that he was free-falling in the abyss of nihilism. Perhaps after having lived through this terrible experience, drunk it to the dregs, people might hope for a fresh era of value creation, the emergence of new gods.

Modern democracy was, of course, the target of Nietzsche's criticism. Its rationalism and its egalitarianism are the contrary of creativity. Its daily life is for him the civilized reanimalization of man. Nobody really believes in anything anymore, and everyone spends his life in frenzied work and frenzied play so as not to face the fact, not to look into the abyss. Nietzsche's call to revolt against liberal democracy is more powerful and more radical than is Marx's. And Nietzsche adds that the Left, socialism, is not the opposite of the special kind of Right that is capitalism, but is its fulfillment. The Left means equality, the Right inequality. Nietzsche's call is from the Right, but a new Right transcending capitalism and socialism, which are the powers moving in the world.

But in spite of this, or perhaps because of it, the latest models of modern democratic or egalitarian man find much that is attractive in Nietzsche's understanding of things. It is the sign of the strength of equality, and of the failure of Nietzsche's war against it, that he is now far better known and really influential on the Left than on the Right.

This may at first appear surprising, inasmuch as Nietzsche looks toward the extraordinary, not the ordinary, the unequal, not the equal. But the democratic man requires flattery, like any ruler, and the earliest versions of democratic theory did not provide it. They justified democracy as the regime in which very ordinary people were protected in their attempt to achieve very ordinary and common goals. It was also the regime dominated by public opinion, where the common denominator set the rule for everyone. Democracy presented itself as decent mediocrity as over against the splendid corruption of older regimes. But it is quite another thing to have a regime in which all the citizens can be thought to be at least potentially autonomous, creating values for themselves. A value-creating man is a plausible substitute for a good man, and some such substitute becomes practically inevitable in pop relativism, since very few persons can think of themselves as just nothing. The respectable and accessible nobility of man is to be found not in the quest for or discovery of the good life, but in creating one's own "life-style," of which there is not just one but many possible, none comparable to another. He who has a "life-style" is in competition with, and hence inferior to, no one, and because he has one he can command his own esteem and that of others.

All this has become everyday fare in the United States, and the most popular schools of psychology and their therapies take value positing as the standard of healthy personality. Woody Allen's comedy is nothing but a set of variations on the theme of the man who does not have a real "self" or "identity," and feels superior to the inauthentically self-satisfied people because he is conscious of his situation and at the same time inferior to them because they are "adjusted." This borrowed psychology turns into a textbook in *Zelig*, which is the story of an "other-directed" man, as opposed to an "inner-directed" man, terms popularized in the 1950s by David Riesman's *The Lonely Crowd*, borrowed by him from his analyst, Erich Fromm, who himself absorbed them (e.g., *innige Mensch*) from a really serious thinker, Nietzsche's heir, Martin Heidegger. I was astounded to see how doctrinaire Woody Allen is, and how normal his way of looking at things—which has immediate roots in the most profound German philosophy—has become in the American entertainment market. One of the links between Germany and the United States, the psychologist Bruno Bettelheim, actually plays a cameo role in *Zelig*.

Zelig is a man who literally becomes whoever or whatever is expected of him—a Republican when with the rich; a gangster when with Mafiosi; black, Chinese or female, when with blacks, Chinese or females. He is nothing in himself, just a collection of roles prescribed by others. He inevitably enters into psychiatric treatment, where we learn that he was once "tradition-directed," i.e., from a family of silly, dancing rabbinic Jews. "Tradition-directed" means to be guided by old values, received from old beliefs, usually religious, which give a man a role that he takes to be more than a role and a place in the world. It goes without saying that a return to that old mode of adjustment and apparent health is neither possible nor desirable. One is supposed to laugh at the dancing Jew, although it is not clear whether from the point of view of alienation or health. It is sure that the Jew is a pariah, Max Weber's category given special notoriety by Hannah Arendt, here meaning interesting only as an outsider who has a special insight into the insider, but whose Jewishness has no merit in itself. His value is defined by the world currently of interest to him. His health is restored when he becomes "inner-directed," when he follows his real instincts and sets his own values. When Zelig hears people say that it is a nice day, when it manifestly is, he responds that it is not a nice day. So he is immediately clapped back into a mental institution by those whom he previously tried to imitate and with whose opinions he is now at war. This is the way society imposes its values on the creator. At the end he gets around, on his own, to reading *Moby Dick*, which he had previously discussed without having read, in order to impress people. His health is a mixture of petulance and facile, self-conscious smugness.

Woody Allen's haunted comedy diagnoses our ills as stemming from value relativism, for which the cure is value positing. And his great strength is in depicting the self-conscious role-player, never quite at home in his role, interesting because he is trying so hard to be like the others, who are ridiculous because they are unaware of their emptiness. But Allen is tasteless and superficial in playing with his Jewishness, which apparently has no inner dignity for him. And where he fails completely is in his presentation of the healthy inner-directed man, who is neither funny nor interesting. This is the figure against which the others are understood and judged, as misers are ridiculous only compared to the man who knows the real value of money. But Allen's inner-directed man is simply empty or nonexistent, forcing one to wonder how profound his creator's understanding can be. Here is where we confront the nothing, but it is not clear that Allen knows it. Inner-directedness is an egalitarian promise that enables us easily to despise and ridicule "the bourgeois" we actually see around us. This is all terribly lightweight and disappointing, for it really tries to assure us that the agonies of the nihilism we are living are just neuroses that can be cured by a little therapy and by a little stiffening of our backs. Erich Fromm's *Escape from Freedom* is just Dale Carnegie with a bit of middle-European cultural whipped cream on top. Get rid of capitalist alienation and Puritan repression, and all will be well as each man chooses for himself. But Woody Allen really has nothing to tell us about inner-directedness. Nor does Riesman nor, going further back, does Fromm. One has to get to Heidegger to learn something of all the grim facts of what inner-directedness might really mean. Allen is never nearly as funny as was Kafka, who really took the problem seriously, without the propagandistic reassurance that Left progressivism would solve it. Zelig has a flirtation with Hitler—whose appeal, it almost goes without saying, is to "other-directed persons," or to use an equivalent expression popularized by another German psychosociologist, Theodore Adorno, to "authoritarian personalities"[2]—but is rescued by his *psychiatricus ex machina.* (Flirtation with Stalin never needs explanation in this intellectual universe.) Woody Allen helps to make us feel comfortable with nihilism, to Americanize it. *I*'m O.K., *thou* art O.K. too, if *we* agree to be a bit haunted together.

In politics, in entertainment, in religion, everywhere, we find the language connected with Nietzsche's value revolution, a language necessitated by a new perspective on the things of most concern to us. Words such as "charisma," "life-style," "commitment," "identity" and many others, all of which can easily be traced to Nietzsche, are now practically American slang, although they, and the things to which they refer, would

[2]Exactly the same point, but without Allen's saving wit, is stressed by Bertolucci in *The Conformist.*

have been incomprehensible to our fathers, not to speak of our Founding Fathers. A few years ago I chatted with a taxi driver in Atlanta who told me he had just gotten out of prison, where he served time for peddling dope. Happily he had undergone "therapy." I asked him what kind. He responded, "All kinds—depth-psychology, transactional analysis, but what I liked best was *Gestalt.*" Some of the German ideas did not even require English words to become the language of the people. What an extraordinary thing it is that high-class talk from what was the peak of Western intellectual life, in Germany, has become as natural as chewing gum on American streets. It indeed had its effect on this taxi driver. He said that he had found his identity and learned to like himself. A generation earlier he would have found God and learned to despise himself as a sinner. The problem lay with his sense of *self,* not with any original sin or devils in him. We have here the peculiarly American way of digesting Continental despair. It is nihilism with a happy ending.

This popularization of German philosophy in the United States is of peculiar interest to me because I have watched it occur during my own intellectual lifetime, and I feel a little like someone who knew Napoleon when he was six. I have seen value relativism and its concomitants grow greater in the land than anyone imagined. Who in 1920 would have believed that Max Weber's technical sociological terminology would someday be the everyday language of the United States, the land of the Philistines, itself in the meantime become the most powerful nation in the world? The self-understanding of hippies, yippies, yuppies, panthers, prelates and presidents has unconsciously been formed by German thought of a half-century earlier; Herbert Marcuse's accent has been turned into a Middle Western twang; the *echt Deutsch* label has been replaced by a *Made in America* label; and the new American life-style has become a Disneyland version of the Weimar Republic for the whole family. So my studies have led me ineluctably back to the half-hidden and thrilling origins of all this, providing me a standpoint from which I look in both directions, forward to our evolving American life and backward to the profound philosophical reflection that broke with and then buried the philosophic tradition, with the most ambiguous intellectual, moral and political consequences. Knowledge of this fascinating intellectual history is required in order to understand ourselves and provide ourselves with real alternatives—if only intellectual historians could be persuaded that the intellect has an effect on history, that, as Nietzsche said, "the greatest deeds are thoughts," that "the world revolves around the inventors of new values, revolves silently." Nietzsche was such an inventor, and we are still revolving around him, although rather squeakily. This is our scene, and the spectacle consists in how his views have been trivialized by democratic man desirous of tricking himself out in borrowed finery, in how democracy has been corrupted by alien views and alien tastes.

I got my first look at this scene at the midpoint of its development, when American university life was being revolutionized by German thought, which was still the preserve of earnest intellectuals. When I came to the University of Chicago in the mid-forties, just after the war, terms like "value judgment" were fresh, confined to an elite and promising special insight. There were great expectations in the social sciences that a new era was beginning in which man and society would be understood better than they had ever been understood before. The academic character of the philosophy departments, with their tired and tiresome methodology and positivism, had caused people interested in the perennial and live questions about man to migrate to the social sciences. There were two writers who dominated and generated real enthusiasm—Freud and Weber. Marx was revered but, as had been true for a long time, was little read and did not provide inspiration for dealing with the problems really facing us. Although it is even now still insufficiently appreciated, Freud and Weber were both thinkers who were profoundly influenced by Nietzsche, as is obvious to anyone who knows Nietzsche and knows what was going on in the German-speaking world in the late nineteenth century. In a strange way they divided up Nietzsche's psychological and social concerns between them. Freud concentrated on the id, or unconscious, the sexual as the motor of the most interesting spiritual phenomena, and the related ideas of sublimation and neurosis. Weber was most concerned with the problem of values, the role of religion in their formation, and community. Together Freud and Weber are the immediate source of most of the language with which we are so familiar.

Everyone knew that they were German thinkers, and that the professors teaching them were a mix of German refugees from Hitler and of Americans who had either studied in Germany prior to Hitler or who had learned from these emigrés. It was not problematic to any of them that these ideas were German. Freud and Weber were part of that great pre-Hitlerian German classical tradition, which everyone respected. Nietzsche himself was not at that time very respectable because his thought seemed to have some discomfiting relation to fascism, and many of those who had favored Nietzsche in the Anglo-Saxon world (where he had had his greatest direct influence on artists, most notably, of course, Ezra Pound) had not been sufficiently alert to the dangers of fascism and anti-Semitism (although Nietzsche himself was the very opposite of an anti-Semite). The fact that German thought had taken an antirational and antiliberal turn with Nietzsche, and even more so with Heidegger, was evident. But this was simply repressed, and a blind eye was turned to their influence on their contemporaries. There were some superficial attempts to blame Hegel, Fichte and Nietzsche for what happened in Germany, but the German classical tradition in general, as well as German historicism, remained in favor, and the special stars in our firmament were either treated as spinoffs from them or as having been generated spontaneously. The trouble with Weimar was simply that the bad guys won.

My professors, many of whom were to become very famous, did not tend to be philosophic and did not dig back into the sources of the new language and categories they were using. They thought that these were scientific discoveries like any others, which were to be used in order to make further discoveries. They were very much addicted to abstractions and generalizations, as Tocqueville predicted they would be. They believed in scientific progress and appeared (there may have been an element of boasting and self-irony in this) to be convinced that they were on the verge of a historic breakthrough in the social sciences, equivalent to that scored in the sixteenth and seventeenth centuries in the natural sciences by Galileo, Kepler, Descartes and Newton, which would make earlier social science as irrelevant as was Ptolemy after Copernicus. These teachers were literally inebriated by the unconscious and values. And they were also sure that scientific progress would be related to social and political progress. All were either Marxists or New Deal liberals. The war against the Right had been won domestically at the polls, and in foreign affairs on the battlefield. The decisive question of principle had been resolved. Equality and the welfare state were now a part of the order of things, and what remained was to complete the democratic project. Psychotherapy would make individuals happy, as sociology would improve societies.

I do not believe any of these professors noticed the darker side of Freud and Weber, let alone the Nietzsche-Heidegger extremism lying somewhere beneath the surface. Or rather, if they did notice, they found it of autobiographical rather than scientific interest. It is amazing to me that the irrational source of all conscious life in Freud, and the relativity of all values in Weber, did not pose a problem for them and their optimism about science. Freud was very dubious about the future of civilization and the role of reason in the life of man. He certainly was not a convinced advocate of democracy or equality. And Weber, much more thoughtful than Freud about science, morals and politics, lived in an atmosphere of permanent tragedy. His science was formulated as a doubtful dare against the chaos of things, and values certainly lay beyond its limits. This is what the very precarious, not to say imaginary, distinction between facts and values meant. Reason in politics leads to the inhumanity of bureaucracy. Weber found it impossible to prefer rational politics to the politics of irrational commitment; he believed that reason and science themselves were value commitments like any other commitments, incapable of asserting their own goodness, thus having lost what had always been most distinctive in them. Politics required dangerous and uncontrollable semireligious value positing, and Weber was witnessing a struggle of the gods for possession of man and society, the results of which were unpredictable. Calculating reason would end up in dried-up, heartless and soulless administration of things without community-forming and sustaining values; feeling would lead to selfish indulgence in superficial pleasures; political commitment would likely foster fanaticism, and it was questionable whether there was enough value-positing energy left in man. Everything was up in the air, and there was no theodicy to sustain him in his travail. Weber, along with many others in Germany under Nietzsche's influence, saw that all that we care for was threatened by his insight and that we were without intellectual or moral resources to govern the outcome. We require values, which in turn require a peculiar human creativity that is drying up and in any event has no cosmic support. Scientific analysis itself concludes that reason is powerless, while dissolving the protective horizon within which men can value. None of this is peculiar to Weber or comes simply from his distressed personality, which he had at least partly because of the bleak perspective that lay before him. There is no doubt that value relativism, if it is true and it is believed in, takes one into very dark regions of the soul and very dangerous political experiments. But on enchanted American ground the tragic sense has little place, and the early proponents of the new social science gaily accepted the value insight, sure that their values were just fine, and went ahead with science. Compare the character and concerns of Talcott Parsons with those of Max Weber and you have the measure of the distance between the Continent and us. In Parsons you see the routinization of Weber. It was not until the sixties that the value insight began to have its true effects in the United States, as it had had in Germany thirty or forty years earlier. Suddenly a new generation that had not lived off inherited value fat, that had been educated in philosophic and scientific indifference to good and evil, came on the scene representing value commitment and taught their elders a most unpleasant lesson.

The image of this astonishing Americanization of the German pathos can be seen in the smiling face of Louis Armstrong as he belts out the words of his great hit "Mack the Knife." As most American intellectuals know, it is a translation of the song "Mackie Messer" from *The Threepenny Opera*, a monument of Weimar Republic popular culture, written by two heroes of the artistic Left, Bertolt Brecht and Kurt Weill. There is a strange nostalgia among many of the American intelligentsia for this moment just prior to Hitler's coming to power, and Lotte Lenya's rendition of this song has long stood with Marlene Dietrich's singing *"Ich bin von Kopf bis Fuss auf Liebe eingestellt"* in the *Blue Angel* as the symbol of a charming, neurotic, sexy, decadent longing for some hazy fulfillment not quite present to the consciousness. Less known to our intelligentsia is an aphorism in Nietzsche's *Thus Spake Zarathustra*, a book well known to Brecht, entitled "On the Pale Criminal," which tells the story of a neurotic murderer, eerily resembling Raskolnikov in *Crime and Punishment*, who does not know, cannot know, that he committed murder out of a motive as legitimate as any other and useful in many important situations, but delegitimized in our pacific times: he lusted after "the joy of the knife." This scenario for "Mack the Knife" is the beginning of the supra-moral attitude of expectancy, waiting to see what the volcano of the id will spew forth, which appealed to Weimar and its American admirers. Everything is all right as long as it is not fascism! With Armstrong taking Lenya's place, as Mai Britt took Dietrich's, it is all mass-marketed and the message becomes less dangerous, although no less corrupt. All awareness of foreignness disappears. It is thought to be folk culture, all-American, part of the American century, just as "stay loose" (as opposed to uptight) is supposed to have been an insight of rock music and not a translation of Heidegger's *Gelassenheit.* The historical sense and the distance on our times, the only advantages of Weimar nostalgia, are gone, and American self-satisfaction—the sense that the scene is ours, that we have nothing important to learn about life from the past—is served.

This image can be seen in our intellectual history, if only one substitutes Mary McCarthy for Louis Armstrong and Hannah Arendt for Lotte Lenya, or David Riesman for Armstrong and Erich Fromm for Lenya, and so on through the honor roll of American intellectuals. Our stars are singing a song they do not understand, translated from a German original and having a huge popular success with unknown but wide-ranging consequences, as something of the original message touches something in American souls. But behind it all, the master lyricists are Nietzsche and Heidegger.

In short, after the war, while America was sending out its blue jeans to unite the young of all nations, a concrete form of democratic universalism that has had liberalizing effects on many enslaved nations, it was importing a clothing of German fabrication for its souls, which clashed with all that and cast doubt on the Americanization of the world on which we had embarked, thinking it was good and in conformity with the rights of man. Our intellectual skyline has been altered by German thinkers even more radically than has our physical skyline by German architects.[3]

My insistence on the Germanness of all this is intended not as a know-nothing response to foreign influence, the search for a German intellectual under every bed, but to heighten awareness of where we must look if we are to understand what we are saying and thinking, for we are in danger of forgetting. The great influence of a nation with a powerful intellectual life over less well endowed nations, even if the armies of the latter are very powerful, is not rare in human experience. The most obvious cases are the influence of Greece on Rome and of France on Germany and Russia. But it is precisely the differences between these two cases and the example of Germany and the United States that makes the

---

[3]Mies van der Rohe too was a figure around Chicago before he really got his chance to build, and the Bauhaus was another product of Weimar, closely allied with the currents of thought I have been describing.

latter so problematic for us. Greek and French philosophy were universalistic in intention and fact. They appealed to the use of a faculty potentially possessed by all men everywhere and at all times. The proper noun in *Greek* philosophy is only an inessential tag, as it is in *French* Enlightenment. (The same is true of *Italian* Renaissance, a rebirth that is proof of the accidental character of nations and of the universality of Greek thinkers.) The good life and the just regime they taught knew no limits of race, nation, religion or climate. This relation to man as man was the very definition of philosophy. We are aware of this when we speak of science, and no one seriously talks of German, Italian or English physics. And when we Americans speak seriously about politics, we mean that our principles of freedom and equality and the rights based on them are rational and everywhere applicable. World War II was really an educational project undertaken to force those who did not accept these principles to do so.

But German philosophy after Hegel cast doubt on them, and there was some relationship between German politics and German thought. Historicism has taught that the mind is essentially related to history or culture. Germanness is, according to later German philosophers, an essential part of them. For Nietzsche and those influenced by him, values are the products of folk minds and have relevance only to those minds. The possibility of translation itself, as I have mentioned, is doubted by Heidegger. For him the Latin translations of the Greek philosophical terms are superficial and do not convey the essence of the translated text. German thought tended not toward liberation from one's own culture, as did earlier thought, but toward reconstituting the rootedness in one's own, which has been shattered by cosmopolitanism, philosophical and political. We are like the millionaire in *The Ghost (Geist) Goes West* who brings a castle from brooding Scotland to sunny Florida and adds canals and gondolas for "local color." We chose a system of thought that, like some wines, does not travel; we chose a way of looking at things that could never be ours and had as its starting point dislike of us and our goals. The United States was held to be a nonculture, a collection of castoffs from real cultures, seeking only comfortable self-preservation in a regime dedicated to superficial cosmopolitanism in thought and deed. Our desire for the German things was proof we could not understand them. The decisive character of peoples and their values that was decreed by historicism of all kinds, but particularly by Nietzsche's radical historicism, makes the

German case the opposite of the Greek one. The difference can be seen in the way Cicero treats Socrates as opposed to the way Nietzsche does. For Cicero, Socrates is a friend and contemporary; for Nietzsche he is an enemy and an ancient. Given our country's extreme Enlightenment universalism, nothing could be more unwelcome to Nietzsche and Heidegger than our embrace.

Whether this value relativism is harmonious with democracy is a question that is dealt with by never being raised. The social sciences have dealt with Nazism as a psychopathology, a result of authoritarian or other-directed personalities, a case for psychiatrists, as presented by Woody Allen. Social science denies that thought, especially serious thought, even the very thought at its own root, could have had anything to do with Hitler's success. But the Weimar Republic, so attractive in its left-wing version to Americans, also contained intelligent persons who were attracted, at least in the beginning, to fascism, for reasons very like those motivating the Left ideologues, reflections on autonomy and value creation. Once one plunges into the abyss, there is no assurance whatsoever that equality, democracy or socialism will be found on the other side. At very best, self-determination is indeterminate. But the conditions of value creation, particularly its authoritative and religious or charismatic character, would seem to militate against democratic rationalism. The sacred roots of community are contrary to the rights of individuals and liberal tolerance. The new religiosity connected with community and culture influenced people who look at things from the perspective of creativity to lean toward the Right. On the Left there was only an assertion that Marx would, after his revolution, produce exactly what Nietzsche promised, while on the Right there was meditation on what we know of the conditions of creativity. I shall not comment on the Nazi period of the now de-Nazified Heidegger, other than to remark that the ever more open recognition that he was the most interesting thinker of our century, formerly chastely displaced in admiration for his various proxies, gives evidence that we are playing with fire. His interest in new gods led him, as it did Nietzsche, in his teaching to honor immoderation over moderation and to ridicule morality. Both helped to constitute that ambiguous Weimar atmosphere in which liberals looked like simpletons and anything was possible for people who sang of the joy of the knife in cabarets. Decent people became used to hearing things about which they would have in the past been horrified to think, and which would not have been allowed public expression. An extreme outcome in the struggle between Right and Left in Weimar was inevitable.

The great mystery is the kinship of all this to American souls that were not prepared by education or historical experience for it. Pierre Hassner once asked whether the fantastic success of Freud in America was due simply to the fact that so many of his disciples took refuge from Hitler there and were very effective propagandists, or whether there was some special need for him in a country he did not much care for. As a Chicago boy, I was always particularly struck by the fact that Marshall Field III, the scion of the great merchandising family, the archetypical success story of what Weberians call the Protestant Ethic, was psychoanalyzed by Gregory Zilboorg, one of the earliest influential Freudians in the United States, and emerged as an ardent supporter of left-wing causes who lost fortunes on fellow-traveling newspapers. There was evidently much more going on in the store's basement than we had suspected. Was there something that the American self-understanding had not sufficiently recognized or satisfied?

Once Americans had become convinced that there is indeed a basement to which psychiatrists have the key, their orientation became that of the *self*, the mysterious, free, unlimited center of our being. All our beliefs issue from it and have no other validation. Although nihilism and its accompanying existential despair are hardly anything but a pose for Americans, as the language derived from nihilism has become a part of their educations and insinuated itself into their daily lives, they pursue happiness in ways determined by that language. There is a whole arsenal of terms for talking about nothing—caring, self-fulfillment, expanding consciousness, and so on, almost indefinitely. Nothing determinate, nothing that has a referent, as we saw in Allen and Riesman. There is a straining to say something, a search for an inwardness that one knows one has, but it is still a cause without an effect. The inner seems to have no relation to the outer. The outer is dissolved and becomes formless in the light of the inner, and the inner is a will-o'-the-wisp, or pure emptiness. No wonder the mere sound of the Existentialists' Nothing or the Hegelians' Negation has an appeal to contemporary ears. American nihilism is a mood, a mood of moodiness, a vague disquiet. It is nihilism without the abyss.

Nihilism as a state of soul is revealed not so much in the lack of firm beliefs but in a chaos of the instincts or passions. People no longer believe in a natural hierarchy of the soul's varied and conflicting inclinations, and the traditions that provided a substitute for nature have crumbled. The soul becomes a stage for a repertory company that changes plays regularly —sometimes a tragedy, sometimes a comedy; one day love, another day politics, and finally religion; now cosmopolitanism, and again rooted loyalty; the city or the country; individualism or community; sentimentality or brutality. And there is neither principle nor will to impose a rank order on all of these. All ages and places, all races and all cultures can play on this stage. Nietzsche believed that the wild costume ball of the passions was both the disadvantage and the advantage of late modernity. The evident disadvantage is the decomposition of unity or "personality," which in the long run will lead to psychic entropy. The advantage hoped for is that the richness and tension present in the modern soul might be the basis for comprehensive new worldviews that would take seriously what had previously been consigned to a spiritual ashcan. This richness, according to Nietzsche, consisted largely in thousands of years of inherited and now unsatisfied religious longing. But this possible advantage does not exist for young Americans, because their poor education has impoverished their longings, and they are hardly aware of the great pasts that Nietzsche was thinking of and had within himself. What they do have now is an unordered tangle of rather ordinary passions, running through their consciousnesses like a monochrome kaleidoscope. They are egotists, not in a vicious way, not in the way of those who know the good, just or noble, and selfishly reject them, but because the ego is all there is in present theory, in what they are taught.

We are a bit like savages who, having been discovered and evangelized by missionaries, have converted to Christianity without having experienced all that came before and after the revelation. The fact that most of us never would have heard of Oedipus if it were not for Freud should make us aware that we are almost utterly dependent on our German missionaries or intermediaries for our knowledge of Greece, Rome, Judaism and Christianity; that, however profound that knowledge may be, theirs is only one interpretation; and that we have only been told as much as they thought we needed to know. It is an urgent business for one who seeks self-awareness to think through the meaning of the intellectual dependency that has led us to such an impasse. The following explanatory dictionary of our current language is meant to be a small contribution to that undertaking.

TWO REVOLUTIONS AND TWO
STATES OF NATURE

The discovery of the soul's basement, exploration into it, and ʲ ʳaction to its dark contents have long been Continental specialties. Obscure longings and search for the elusive grounds of all things are pervasive themes of nineteenth- and twentieth-century French, German, and (prior to the revolution) Russian literature. Continental "depth" was thought by intellectuals to be opposed to American "superficiality." American souls were, so to speak, constructed without a basement, more reconciled to this world and not addicted to looking beyond it, not haunted by a sense of the groundlessness of their experience. Thus, when Americans became able to afford the luxury of indulging in Continental literature, as in Continental cuisine, we had to wonder whether their appetite was real and how they would digest the fare.

The issue between the Continent and us can be summed up by the word "bourgeois." The new man of the new democratic political regime has been labeled bourgeois by Continental philosophers and artists for more than two hundred years. This originally meant a diminished, egotistical, materialistic being without grandeur or beauty of soul, and it has maintained that negative sense—best known to Americans because of Marx—up to our day. Yet long after Nietzsche claimed the theme had already become boring, Continental thinkers have been obsessed with bourgeois man as representing the worst and most contemptible failure of modernity, which must at all costs be overcome. Nihilism in its most palpable sense means that the bourgeois has won, that the future, all foreseeable futures, belong to him, that all heights above him and all depths beneath him are illusory and that life is not worth living on these terms. It is the announcement that all the alternatives or correctives—for example, idealism, romanticism, historicism, and Marxism—have failed. Americans, on the other hand, have generally believed that the modern democratic project is being fulfilled in their country, can be fulfilled elsewhere, and that that project is good. They do not naturally apply the term "bourgeois" to themselves, or to anyone else for that matter. They do like to call themselves middle class, but that does not carry with it any determinate spiritual content. It is rather a good thing to be. If there is a failure here, it is that there are poor people. The term "middle class" does not have any of the many opposites that bourgeois has, such as aristocrat, saint, hero, or artist—all good—except perhaps for proletarian or socialist. The spirit is at home, if not entirely satisfied, in America.

Modernity is constituted by the political regimes founded on freedom and equality, hence on the consent of the governed, and made possible by a new science of nature that masters and conquers nature, providing prosperity and health. This was a self-conscious philosophical project, the greatest transformation of man's relations with his fellows and with nature ever effected. The American Revolution instituted this system of government for Americans, who in general were satisfied with the result and had a pretty clear view of what they had done. The questions of political principle and of right had been solved once and for all. No further revolution would be necessary, if revolution means changing of the fundamental principles of legitimacy, in accordance with reason and the natural order of things, and requiring armed combat against those who adhere to old orders and their unjust forms of rule. Revolution, a new word in the political vocabulary, which first referred to the Glorious Revolution of 1688 in England, made in the name of very much the same principles as ours, is akin to the movement of the sun from night to day.

The French Revolution, called a new dawn by Kant, was a much greater event than the American Revolution in the eyes of the world at that time because it concerned one of the two great powers in it, the veritable school of Europe, with one of the oldest and most civilized peoples. It was fought and won for freedom and equality, as were the English and American revolutions. It would seem to have completed the irresistible triumph of modern philosophy's project and to give a final proof of the theodicy of liberty and equality. But, unlike its predecessors, it gave birth to a dazzling array of interpretations and set off reactions in all directions that have not yet exhausted the impulse it lent to them. The Right—in its only serious meaning, the party opposed to equality (not economic equality but equality of rights)—at first wanted to undo the Revolution in the name of Throne and Altar, and this reaction probably breathed its last only with Francisco Franco in 1975. Another form of the Right, as it were a progressive Right, wanted to create and impose a new kind of inequality, a new European or German aristocracy, on the world, and it was blasted out of existence in Berlin in 1945. The Left, which intended to complete the Revolution by abolishing private property, is still quite alive but has never succeeded in doing so in those nations, particularly France, most influenced by the French Revolution. It was the Center, the bourgeois solution, which in the long run won out, but after so many regrets and so many disappointed aspirations, in France, Germany, Austria, Belgium, Italy, Spain and Portugal, as it had in England and the United States. The last really great bourgeois-haters died at about the same time: Sartre, De Gaulle, and Heidegger. (Americans are not sufficiently aware that hatred of the bourgeois is at least as much a thing of the Right as of the Left.) One can expect a certain literary afterglow, since bourgeois-baiting is almost a reflex among writers and is unlearned with great difficulty, as was proved when so many kept at it even though there were Nazis and Communists around who might have merited their attention. In order to keep that flame alive, many literary persons interpreted Hitler as a bourgeois phenomenon, an interpretation that they have made stick by force of repetition.

We may now have run out of the new revolutions, and the new metaphysics required to justify them, which were intended to rectify the French Revolution's *perceived* failures; but the reconciliation with reality is more fatigued than enthusiastic. I use the word "perceived" because, on the basis of the variety of readings of the French Revolution—by monarchists, Catholics, liberals, socialists, Robespierreans, Bonapartists—which were not idle academic exercises but life-forming and action-engendering, Nietzsche concluded that there was no text here but only interpretation. This observation is the foundation of the currently popular view that there is no *is* but only perspectives on *becoming,* that the perception is as much reality as there is, that things are what they are perceived to be. This view is, of course, allied with the notion that man is a value-creating, not a good-discovering, being. It is not surprising to find its source at least partially in the greatest events of modern politics.

The misunderstanding between America and the Continent is that where Americans saw a solution, Continentals saw a problem. The American Revolution produced a clear and unified historical reality; the French Revolution, a series of questions and problems. Americans have tended to look at the French Revolution with indulgence. It represented the good things, akin to ours, but did not succeed in providing a stable institutional framework for them. A large segment of intellectual opinion on the Continent, the most influential segment,[4] regarded the French Revolution as a failure not because it was not successful in establishing a liberal democracy but because it had been entirely too successful in producing the liberal democratic type of man—i.e., the bourgeois—and giving his class, the bourgeoisie, power in society. Even so pro-American and pro-liberal a writer as Tocqueville, who understood the French difficulty to be indeed its incapacity to adapt to liberal institutions, was melancholy about the prospects for a fully human life within them.

Americans found little to charm them in the *ancien régime* in France. Its throne and altar were the very reality of, respectively, the unjust inequality and the prejudice that the American regime was intended to replace in the world. America, they believed, would succeed in its project with relative ease because we began here with the equality of conditions. Americans did not have to kill a king, displace an aristocracy that would stay around and cause trouble, or disestablish a church and perhaps abolish it. But the need to do all this, plus the presence of the Parisian mob, which could not accept the rule of law, prevented the French from attaining the reasonable consensus required for orderly democratic government.

But another view of these events dominated public discussion on the Continent. To some Europeans, the Americans represented an intolerable narrowing of the human horizon, and the price paid for their decent order and prosperity was too high. The French aristocracy had a nobility, bril-

---

[4]Thinkers like Tocqueville who, in a qualified way, supported the American solution, are little read or cared for in France; and Montesquieu, that Frenchman who is closest to the English and American tradition of political philosophy and most influenced the American Founders, is the one of France's truly great writers who least affects French consciousness.

liance and taste that contrasted sharply with the pettiness and grayness of liberal society's commercial life and motives. The loss of what that aristocracy represented would impoverish the world. More important, the religion that was dismantled could be thought to express the depth and seriousness of life. If the noble and the sacred cannot find serious expression in democracy, its choiceworthiness becomes questionable. These are the arguments, the special pleading of the reactionaries, the disinherited of the *ancien régime*.

More serious for us are the arguments of the revolutionaries who accepted our principles of freedom and equality. Many believed that we had not thought through these cherished ideals. Can equality really only mean equal opportunity for unequal talents to acquire property? Should shrewdness at acquisition be better rewarded than moral goodness? Can private property and equality sit so easily together when even Plato required communism among equals? Communism or socialism never really made much headway against the respect for private property in the United States. Locke's definition of property suited, and still suits, our tempers perfectly, and Rousseau's critique of it made almost no impression here, although it was and remains very potent in Europe. And freedom for us meant merely acting as one pleases, restricted only by the minimum demands of social existence. We had not adequately understood what really setting laws for ourselves required, nor had we gone beyond the merely negative freedom of satisfying brutish impulsion. As for religion, the domesticated churches in America preserved the superstition of Christianity, overcoming of which was perhaps the key to liberating man. Should a good regime be atheistic, or should it have a civil religion? And, finally, what in the world can we do with the Napoleonic —heroic ambition and military glory—other than ignore or debunk it?

Such were the questions raised on the slaughter-bench of History by the French Revolution, questions that we were not eager to hear. They provided the material for a century of serious philosophy on the Continent, to which the spirit of philosophy had repaired from England. Even Mill, the heir of utilitarianism, which was a still narrower and more self-satisfied version of earlier liberal thought, had to turn to a German thinker, Humboldt, for the notion of spontaneity, to give an attractive modern account of the essence of liberty and protect it from the dangers of the tyranny of the majority. Philosophy begins, it seems, in the confrontation with the fundamental political alternatives. Of the truly great philosophers since the French Revolution, only Kant was a friend of liberal democracy. And he felt constrained to reinterpret it in ways that made it both unrecognizable and unattractive to us. He developed a new epistemology that makes freedom possible when the science of nature is deterministic, a new morality that makes the dignity of man possible when human nature is understood to be composed of selfish natural appetites, and a new esthetics that saves the beautiful and the sublime from mere subjectivity. None of this concerned the earlier egalitarian thought of the founders of liberalism.

What was acted out in the American and French Revolutions had been thought out beforehand in the writings of Locke and Rousseau, the scenarists for the drama of modern politics. These Columbuses of the mind—Thomas Hobbes led the way, but Locke and Rousseau followed and were considered more reliable reporters—explored the newly discovered territory called the state of nature, where our forefathers all once dwelled, and brought the important news that by nature all men are free and equal, and that they have rights to life, liberty and the pursuit of property. This is the kind of information that causes revolutions because it pulls the magic carpet out from under the feet of kings and nobles. Locke and Rousseau agreed on these basics, which became the firm foundation of modern politics. Where they disagreed, the major conflicts within modernity were to occur. Locke was the great practical success; the new English and American regimes founded themselves according to his instructions. Rousseau, probably the greatest literary success of all time, inspired all the later attempts in thought and deed, private and public, to alter, correct or escape from the fatality of Locke's complete victory.

It is now fashionable to deny that there ever was a state of nature. We are like aristocrats who do not care to know that our ancestors were once savages who, motivated only by fear of death and scarcity, killed one another in quarrels over acorns. But we continue to live off the capital passed on to us by these rejected predecessors. Everyone believes in freedom and equality and the rights consequent to them. These were, however, brought to civil society from the state of nature; in the absence of any other ground for them, they must be just as mythical as the tale of the state of nature told by the unreliable travelers. Instructed by the new natural science that provided their compass, they went to the origin and not to the end, as did the older political philosophers. Socrates *imagined* a shining city in speech; Hobbes discovered an isolated individual whose life was "mean, nasty, brutish and short." This opens up a very different perspective on what one wants and hopes for from politics. Prudence points not toward regimes dedicated to the cultivation of rare and difficult, if not impossible, virtues, but toward a good police force to protect men from one another and allow them to preserve themselves as well as possible. Hobbes, Locke and Rousseau all found that one way or another nature led men to war, and that civil society's purpose was not to cooperate with a natural tendency in man toward perfection but to make peace where nature's imperfection causes war.

The reports from the state of nature mixed bad news and good news. Perhaps the most important discovery was that there was no Garden of Eden; the Eldorado of the spirit turned out to be both desert and jungle. Man was not provided for at the beginning, and his current state is not a result of his sin, but of nature's miserliness. He is on his own. God neither looks after him nor punishes him. Nature's indifference to justice is a terrible bereavement for man. He must care for himself without the hope that good men have always had: that there is a price to be paid for crime, that the wicked will suffer. But it is also a great liberation—from God's tutelage, from the claims of kings, nobles and priests, and from guilt or bad conscience. The greatest hopes are dashed, but some of the worst terrors and inner enslavements are dispelled.

Unprotectedness, nakedness, unsuccored suffering and the awfulness of death are the prospects that man without illusions must face. But, looking at things from the point of view of already established society, man can be proud of himself. He has progressed, and by his own efforts. He can think well of himself. And now, possessing the truth, he can be even freer to be himself and improve his situation. He can freely make governments that, untrammeled by mythical duties and titles to rule, serve his interests. The explorations of Hobbes, Locke and Rousseau of the origins made possible a new beginning in theory, a project for the reconstruction of politics, just as the exploration and discovery of the New World promised a new beginning in practice. The two new beginnings coincided and produced, among other wonders, the United States.

From his reflection on the state of nature, Locke drew the formula of Enlightenment, with its particular combination of natural and political science. Its starting point is the untrammeled use of reason. In this he simply follows the oldest opinions of the philosophers. Freedom for man consists in ordering his life according to what he can see for himself through his most distinctive faculty, liberated from the force of tyrants and the authority of lies, i.e., myths. Through unaided reason, man as man, as opposed to the man of this place or time, nation or religion, can know the causes of things, can know nature for himself. Autonomy does not mean, as is now generally thought, the fateful, groundless decision in the void, but governing oneself according to the real. There must be an outside for the inside to have meaning.

So thought Locke and his philosophic predecessors and successors. What distinguished Enlightenment from earlier philosophy was its intention to extend to all men what had been the preserve of only a few: the life lived according to reason. It was not "idealism" or "optimism" that motivated these philosophers but a new science, a "method," and allied with them, a new political science. A clear and distinct mathematical science of the movement of bodies, discovered by the use of a simple method readily understood by ordinary men, could make the knowledge of nature accessible to them, if not provide them with the genius to discover that knowledge. The various mythic or poetic views of the whole that set the horizons for the nations of man, and within which the philosophers had always lived alone and misunderstood, would be dispensed with, and the fundamental difference in perspective between scientist and nonscientist overcome. Further, if man himself is taken out of the shadows of the kingdom of darkness and examined in the light of science, he sees that by nature he belongs to the realm of bodies in motion, and that he, like all other bodies, wishes to preserve his motion, that is, his life. Every man has a powerful fear of death, that corresponds to the way of nature. Critical, scientific, methodical examination of the other ends prescribed for man can show that they belong to the realm of the imagination, of false opinion, or derive from this primary end. Such critical examination, of which all men are capable if given guidance by philosophers, and which is supported by powerful inclinations in all men, results in a salutary unity of purpose and a useful simplification of the human problem: vulnerable man must seek the means to his preservation. Since this is what all men really want, whatever arrangements help them get food, clothing, shelter, health and, above all, protection from one another will, if they are properly educated, win their consent and their loyalty.

Once the world has been purged of ghosts or spirits, it reveals to us that the critical problem is scarcity. Nature is a stepmother who has left us unprovided for. But this means we need have no gratitude. When we revered nature, we were poor. Since there was not enough, we had to take from one another; and as a result of this competition, there was inevitably war, the greatest threat to life. But if, instead of fighting one another, we band together and make war on our stepmother, who keeps her riches from us, we can at the same time provide for ourselves and end our strife. The conquest of nature, which is made possible by the insight of science and by the power it produces, is the key to the political. The old commandment that we love our brothers made impossible demands on us, demands against nature, while doing nothing to provide for real needs. What is required is not brotherly love or faith, hope and charity, but self-interested rational labor. The man who contributes most to relieving human misery is the one who produces most, and the surest way of getting him to do so is not by exhorting him, but by rewarding him most handsomely to sacrifice present pleasure for the sake of future benefit, or to assure avoidance of pain through the power so gained. From the point of view of man's well-being and security, what is needed is not men who practice the Christian virtues or those of Aristotle, but rational (capable of calculating their interest) and industrious men. Their opposite numbers are not the vicious, wicked or sinful, but the quarrelsome and the idle. This may include priests and nobles as well as those who most obviously spring to mind.

This scheme provides the structure for the key term of liberal democracy, the most successful and useful political notion of our world: *rights*. Government exists to protect the product of men's labor, their property, and therewith life and liberty. The notion that man possesses inalienable natural rights, that they belong to him as an individual prior, both in time and in sanctity, to any civil society, and that civil societies exist for and acquire their legitimacy from ensuring those rights, is an invention of modern philosophy. Rights, like the other terms discussed in this chapter, are new in modernity, not a part of the common-sense language of politics or of classical political philosophy. Hobbes initiated the notion of rights, and it was given its greatest respectability by Locke. Unlike the other terms, however, we understand rights perfectly and have immediate access to the thought underlying them. The others are alien, problematic; and to understand them requires a great effort that, I am arguing, we do not make. But rights are ours. They constitute our being; we live them; they are our common sense. Right is not the opposite of wrong, but of duty. It is a part of, or the essence of, freedom. It begins from man's cherished passion to live, and to live as painlessly as possible. An analysis of universal needs and their relation to nature as a whole demonstrates that this passion is not merely an imagination. It can be called a right and converted into a term of political relevance when a man is fully conscious of what he needs most, recognizes that he is threatened by others and that they are threatened by him. The spring that makes the social machinery tick is this recognition, which generates the calculation that, if he agrees to respect the life, liberty and property of others (for which he has no natural respect), they can be induced to reciprocate. This is the foundation of rights, a new kind of morality solidly grounded in self-interest.

To say, "I've got my rights," is as instinctive with Americans as breathing, so clear and evident is this way of looking at things. It signifies the rules of the game, within which men play peacefully, the necessity of which they see and accept, and the infringement of which arouses moral indignation. It is our only principle of justice. From our knowledge of our rights flows our acceptance of the duties to the community that protects them. Righteousness means for us respect for equal rights equally guaranteed by the force of government. Everyone in the world today speaks of rights, even the communists, the heirs of Marx, who ridiculed "bourgeois rights" as a sham and in whose thought there is no place for rights. But almost every thoughtful observer knows that it is in the United States that the idea of rights has penetrated most deeply into the bloodstream of its citizens and accounts for their unusual lack of servility. Without it we would have nothing, only chaotic selfishness; and it is the interested source of a certain disinterestedness. We feel people's interests should be respected.

This scheme represented a radical break with the old ways of looking at the political problem. In the past it was thought that man is a dual being, one part of him concerned with the common good, the other with private interests. To make politics work, man, it was thought, has to overcome the selfish part of himself, to tyrannize over the merely private, to be virtuous. Locke and his immediate predecessors taught that no part of man is naturally directed to the common good and that the old way was both excessively harsh and ineffective, that it went against the grain. They experimented with using private interest for public interest, putting natural freedom ahead of austere virtue. Self-interest is hostile to the common good, but *enlightened* self-interest is not. And this is the best key to the meaning of enlightenment. Man's reason can be made to see his vulnerability and to anticipate future scarcity. This rational awareness of the future and its dangers is enough to set the passions in motion. In the past men were members of communities by divine commandment and by attachments akin to the blood ties that constitute the family. They were, to use Rousseau's phrase, "denatured." Their loyalties were fanatic and repressive of their natures. Clear reasoning wiped that slate clean in order to inscribe on it contracts calmly made with expectation of profit involving the kinds of relations found in business. Calculated work is the sum of the whole affair. Thomas Watson said it all with the motto he placed on the walls of his offices and factories: "Think"; for he was addressing himself to men who were already working.

Americans are Lockeans: recognizing that work is necessary (no longing for a nonexistent Eden), and will produce well-being; following their natural inclinations moderately, not because they possess the virtue of moderation but because their passions are balanced and they recognize the reasonableness of that; respecting the rights of others so that theirs will be respected; obeying the law because they made it in their own interest. From the point of view of God or heroes, all this is not very inspiring. But for the poor, the weak, the oppressed—the overwhelming majority of mankind—it is the promise of salvation. As Leo Strauss put it, the moderns "built on low but solid ground."

Rousseau believed that Hobbes and Locke did not go far enough, that they had not reached the Indies of the spirit, although they thought they had. They found exactly what they set out to look for: a natural man whose naturalness consisted in having just those qualities necessary to constitute society. It was too simple to be true.

> Natural man is entirely for himself. He is numerical unity, the absolute whole which is relative only to itself or its kind. Civil man is only a fractional

unity dependent on the denominator; his value is determined by his relation to the whole, which is the social body. . . .

He who in the civil order wants to preserve the primacy of the sentiments of nature does not know what he wants. Always in contradiction with himself, always floating between his inclinations and his duties, he will never be either man or citizen. He will be good neither for himself nor for others. He will be one of these men of our days: a Frenchman, an Englishman, a *bourgeois*. He will be nothing. *(Emile,* pp. 39–40, ed. Bloom, Basic Books, 1979)

It was Locke who wanted to preserve the primacy of the sentiments of nature in the civil order, and the result of his mistake is the bourgeois. Rousseau invented the term in its modern sense, and with it we find ourselves at the great source of modern intellectual life. The comprehensiveness and subtlety of his analysis of the phenomenon left nothing new to be said about it, and the Right and the Left forever after accepted his description of modern man as simply true, while the Center was impressed, intimidated, and put on the defensive by it. So persuasive was Rousseau that he destroyed the self-confidence of the Enlightenment at the moment of its triumph.

It must not be forgotten that Rousseau begins his critique from fundamental agreements with Locke, whom he greatly admired, about the animal man. Man is by nature a solitary being, concerned only with his preservation and his comfort. Rousseau, moreover, agrees that man makes civil society by contract, for the sake of his preservation. He disagrees with Locke that self-interest, however understood, is in any automatic harmony with what civil society needs and demands. If Rousseau is right, man's reason, calculating his best interest, will not lead him to wish to be a good citizen, a law-abiding citizen. He will either be himself, or he will be a citizen, or he will try to be both and be neither. In other words, enlightenment is not enough to establish society, and even tends to dissolve it.

The road from the state of nature was very long, and nature is distant from us now. A self-sufficient, solitary being must have undergone many changes to become a needy, social one. On the way, the goal of happiness was exchanged for the pursuit of safety and comfort, the means of achieving happiness. Civil society is surely superior to a condition of scarcity and universal war. All this artifice, however, preserves a being who no longer knows what he is, who is so absorbed with existing that he has forgotten his reason for existing, who in the event of actually attaining full security and perfect comfort has no notion of what to do. Progress culminates in the recognition that life is meaningless. Hobbes was surely right to look for the most powerful sentiments in man, those that exist independently of opinion and are always a part of man. But fear of death, however powerful it may be and however useful it may be as a motive for seeking peace and, hence, law with teeth in it, cannot be the fundamental experience. It presupposes an even more fundamental one: that life is good. The deepest experience is the *pleasant* sentiment of existence. The idle, savage man can enjoy that sentiment. The busy bourgeois cannot, with his hard work and his concern with dealing with others rather than being himself.

Nature still has something of the greatest importance to tell us. We may be laboring to master it, but the reason for mastering nature comes from nature. The fear of death on which Hobbes relied, and which is also decisive for Locke, insists on the negative experience of nature and obliterates the positive experience presupposed by it. This positive experience is somehow still active in us; we are full of vague dissatisfactions in our forgetfulness, but our minds must make an enormous effort to find the natural sweetness of life in its fullness. The way back is at least as long as the one that brought us here. For Hobbes and Locke nature is near and unattractive, and man's movement into society was easy and unambiguously good. For Rousseau nature is distant and attractive, and the movement was hard and divided man. Just when nature seemed to have been finally cast out or overcome in us, Rousseau gave birth to an overwhelming longing for it in us. Our lost wholeness is there. One is reminded of Plato's *Symposium*, but there the longing for wholeness was directed toward knowledge of the *ideas*, of the ends. In Rousseau longing is, in its initial expression, for the enjoyment of the primitive *feelings*, found at the origins in the state of nature. Plato would have united with Rousseau against the bourgeois in his insistence on the essential humanness of longing for the good, as opposed to careful avoidance of the bad. Neither longing nor enthusiasm belongs to the bourgeois. The story of philosophy and the arts under Rousseau's influence has been the search for, or fabrication of, plausible objects of longing to counter bourgeois well-being and self-satisfaction. Part of that story has been the bourgeois' effort to acquire the culture of longing as part of its self-satisfaction.

The opposition between nature and society is Rousseau's interpretation of the cause of the dividedness of man. He finds that the bourgeois experiences this dividedness in conflict between self-love and love of others, inclination and duty, sincerity and hypocrisy, being oneself and being alienated. This opposition between nature and society pervades all modern discussion of the human problem. Hobbes and Locke made the distinction in order to overcome all the tensions caused in man by the demands of virtue, and then to make wholeness easy for him. They thought that they had reduced the distance between inclination and duty by deriving all duty from inclination; Rousseau argued that, if anything, they had increased that distance. He thus restored the older, pre-modern sense of the dividedness of man and hence of the complexity of his attainment of happiness, the pursuit of which liberal society guarantees him while making its attainment impossible. But the restoration takes place on very different grounds, as can be seen in the fact that in the past men traced the tension to the irreconcilable demands of body and soul, not of nature and society. This too opens up a rich field for reflection on Rousseau's originality. The blame shifts, and the focus of the perennial quest for unity is altered. Man was born whole, and it is at least conceivable that he become whole once again. Hope and despair of a kind not permitted by the body-soul distinction arise. What one is to think of oneself and one's desires changes. The correctives range from revolution to therapy, but there is little place for the confessional or for mortification of the flesh. Rousseau's *Confessions* were, in opposition to those of Augustine, intended to show that he was born good, that the body's desires are good, that there is no original sin. Man's nature has been maimed by a long history; and now he must live in society, for which he is not suited and which makes impossible demands on him. There is either an uneasy acquiescence to the present or the attempt in one way or another to return to the past, or the search for a creative synthesis of the two poles, nature and society.

These are the essence of the social and political thought of the nineteenth and twentieth centuries that took off from Rousseau's critique of liberalism. The nature-society distinction is more than familiar to all of us. We know it best from Freud, in whose account of the unconscious is to be found lost nature, as well as the whole harsh history that took us out of nature; in whose account of the neuroses one sees the effects of civilization's demands on us; and in whose account of the reality principle one recognizes grim adjustment to bourgeois society. The easy solution to man's dividedness in early modern thought is rejected, but a solution is still expected. The search for solutions, easy or difficult, to problems is the stamp of modernity, while antiquity treated the fundamental tensions as permanent.

The first reaction to the self's maladaptation to society, its recalcitrance to the rationality of preservation and property, is the attempt to recover the self's pristine state, to live according to its first inclinations, to "get in touch with one's feelings," to live naturally, simply, without society's artificially generated desires, dependencies, hypocrisies. The side of Rousseau's thought that arouses nostalgia for nature came to the United States early on, in the life and writings of Thoreau. Recently, joined to many other movements, it came to full flower and found a wide public. Anarchism in one form or another is an expression of this longing, which arises as soon as politics and laws are understood to be repressions, perhaps necessary, but nonetheless repressions of our inclinations rather than perfections of them or modes of satisfying them. For the first time in the history of political philosophy, no natural impulse is thought to lead toward civil society, or to find its satisfaction within it. Yet those who first drew the distinction between nature and society (which obviously means society is completely of human making, not in any way natural), thought that the preference would be immediately and without hesitation for society. As a matter of fact, the distinction was made in order to emphasize how desirable civil society is, how fragile man's existence naturally is, and thus to extinguish those passions based on imagining that protection comes from nature or God, that rebel against civil society. Man, if he is sensible, separates himself from nature and becomes its master and conqueror. This was and still is the prevailing belief of liberal democracies, with their peace, gentleness, prosperity, productivity and applied science, particularly medical science.

All of this was held to be a great advance over the brutish natural condition. Locke said that "a day-laborer in England is better clothed, housed, and fed than a king in America," meaning an Indian chief. But Tocqueville notes that there is nevertheless something impressive about the American king. Perhaps the savage gains something in the comparison if pride, independence, contempt for death, freedom from anxiety about the future and other such qualities are taken into consideration. From the point of view of this savage, nature begins to look good rather than bad. Nature that excludes man and his corrupting hand becomes an object of respect. It gives guidance where previously there was only man's whim. The old view that cities are properly the peaks of nature is never considered and is barely comprehensible. The city is cut loose from nature and is a product only of man's art. Very different values can be attached to cities, but both sides begin from the same premise. Now there are two competing views about man's relation to nature, both founded on the modern distinction between nature and society. Nature is the raw material of man's freedom from harsh necessity, or else man is the polluter of nature. Nature in both cases means dead nature, or nature without man and untouched by man—mountains, forests, lakes and rivers.

Our nation, a great stage for the acting out of great thoughts, presents the classic confrontation between Locke's views of the state of nature and Rousseau's criticism of them. On the one hand you have the farmer who never looked at America's trees, fields and streams with a romantic eye. The trees are to be felled, to make clearings, build houses and heat them; the fields are to be tilled to produce more food, or mined for whatever is necessary to make machines run; the streams are there to be used as waterways for transporting food, or as sources of power. On the other hand there is the Sierra Club, which is dedicated to preventing such violations of nature from going any further, and certainly seems to regret what was already done. More interesting is the coexistence of these opposing sentiments in the most advanced minds of our day. Nature is raw material, worthless without the mixture of human labor; yet nature is also the highest and most sacred thing. The same people who struggle to save the snail-darter bless the pill, worry about hunting deer and defend abortion. Reverence for nature, mastery of nature—whichever is convenient. The principle of contradiction has been repealed.

This is the direct result of the two state-of-nature teachings. Locke's is responsible for our institutions, justifies our absorption with private property and the free market, and gives us our sense of right. Rousseau's lies behind the most prevalent views of what life is about and how to seek healing for our wounds. The former teaches that adjustment to civil society is almost automatic; the latter that such adjustment is very difficult indeed and requires all kinds of intermediaries between it and lost nature. The two outstanding intellectual types of our day represent these two teachings. The crisp, positive, efficient, no-nonsense economist is the Lockean; the deep, brooding, somber psychoanalyst is the Rousseauan. In principle their positions are incompatible, but easygoing America provides them with a *modus vivendi*. Economists tell us how to make money; psychiatrists give us a place to spend it.

THE SELF

The domain now supervised by psychiatrists, as well as other specialists in the deeper understanding of man, is the *self*. It is another one of the discoveries made in the state of nature, perhaps the most important because it reveals what we really are. We are selves, and everything we do is to satisfy or fulfill our selves. Locke was one of the early thinkers, if not the earliest, to use the word in its modern sense. From the very beginning it has been difficult to define; and as Woody Allen helped teach us, it has become ever more difficult to do so. We are suffering from a three-hundred-year-long identity crisis. We go back and back, ever farther, hunting the self as it retreats into the forest, just a step ahead of us. Although disquieting, this may, from the point of view of its latest interpretation, be the essence of the self: mysterious, ineffable, indefinable, unlimited, creative, known only by its deeds; in short, like God, of whom it is the impious mirror image. Above all, it is individual, unique; it is *me*, not some distant man in general or man-in-himself. As Ivan Ilyich in Tolstoy's story explains, the "All men are mortal" in the famous syllogism that guarantees Socrates' death cannot apply to this Ivan Ilyich who had a striped leather ball when he was a child. Everyone knows that the particular as particular escapes the grasp of reason, the form of which is the general or the universal. To sum up, the self is the modern substitute for the soul.

All of this goes back to that audacious innovator Machiavelli, who spoke admiringly of men who cared more for their fatherland than for the salvation of their souls. The higher demands made on men by the soul inevitably lead them to neglect this world in favor of the other world. Millennia of philosophizing about the soul had resulted in no certitude about it, while those who pretended to know it, the priests, held power or influenced it, and corrupted politics as a result. Princes were rendered ineffective by their own or their subjects' opinions about the salvation of their souls, while men slaughtered each other wholesale because of differences of such opinion. The care of the soul crippled men in the conduct of their lives.

Machiavelli dared men literally to forget about their souls and the possibility of eternal damnation, to do so in theory as well as in practice, as did those men whom he praised. Hobbes, among others, took him up on the dare with a very new interpretation of the old Delphic inscription "Know thyself!," which Socrates had interpreted as an exhortation to philosophize, and Freud was to interpret as an invitation to psychoanalysis. Freud was unknowingly following in the line of Hobbes, who said that each man should look to what *he feels*—*feels*, not thinks; *he,* not another. Self is more feeling than reason, and is in the first place defined as the contrary of other. "Be yourself." Astonishingly, Hobbes is the first propagandist for bohemia and preacher of sincerity or authenticity. No wanderings to the ends of the universe on the wings of imagination, no metaphysical foundations, no soul ordering things as well as men. Man is perhaps a stranger in nature. But he is something and can get his bearings by his most powerful passions. "Feel!," Hobbes said. In particular you should imagine how you feel when another man holds a gun to your temple and threatens to shoot you. That concentrates all of the self in a single point, tells us what counts. At that moment one is a real self, not a false consciousness, not alienated by opinions of the church, the state or the public. This experience helps much more to "set priorities" than does any knowledge of the soul or any of its alleged emanations such as conscience.

Throughout the whole tradition, religious and philosophic, man had two concerns, the care of his body and the care of his soul, expressed in the opposition between desire and virtue. In principle he was supposed to long to be all virtue, to break free from the chains of bodily desire. Wholeness would be happiness; but it is not possible, at least in this life. Machiavelli turned things upside down. Happiness is indeed wholeness, so let's try the wholeness available to us in this life. The tradition viewed man as the incomprehensible and self-contradictory union of two substances, body and soul. Man cannot be conceived as body only. But if the function of whatever is not body in him is to cooperate in the satisfaction of bodily desire, then man's dividedness is overcome. Simple virtue is not possible, and love of virtue is only an imagination, a kind of perversion of desire effected by society's (i.e., others') demands on us. But simple desire is possible.

This absoluteness of desire uninhibited by thoughts of virtue is what is found in the state of nature. It represents the turn in philosophy away from trying to tame or perfect desire by virtue, and toward finding out what one's desire is and living according to it. This is largely accomplished by criticizing virtue, which covers and corrupts desire. Our desire becomes a kind of oracle we consult; it is now the last word, while in the past it was the questionable and dangerous part of us. This unity of man in desire is fraught with theoretical difficulties, but it is, as we would say, existentially persuasive because, unlike the incomprehensible and self-contradictory union of body and soul, it is affirmed by powerful experiences, such as fear of violent death, that do not require abstract reasonings or exhortations.

Hobbes blazed the trail to the self, which has grown into the highway of a ubiquitous psychology without the psyche (soul). But he, like Locke, did not develop the psychology of the self in its fullness, just as neither went very deeply into the state of nature, because the solution seemed to be on the surface. Once the old virtues were refuted—the piety of the religious or the honor of the nobles—Hobbes and Locke assumed that most men would immediately agree that their self-preservative desires are real, that they come from within and take primacy over any other desire. The true self is not only good for individuals but provides a basis for consensus not provided by religions or philosophies. Locke's substitute for the virtuous man, the rational and industrious one, is the perfect expression of this solution. It is not an ethic or a morality of a Protestant or any other kind of believer, but a frank admission of enlightened selfishness (selfishness that has learned from modern philosophy which goals are real and which imaginary), or self-interest rightly understood. Locke develops the opposite, the idle and the quarrelsome man—who, we see, may be the priest or the noble (i.e., pretenders to a higher morality)—to debunk virtue in a less provocative way than Hobbes did. Locke's rational and industrious man partakes, as a prototype, of the charm of the sincere man who acts as he thinks and, without fraudulent pieties, seeks his own good. Beneath his selfishness, of course, lies an expectation that it conduces more to the good of others than does moralism. The taste of the sincere expresses itself more in blame of Tartufferie than in praise of virtue.

Terror in the face of death, an immediate and overwhelming subjective experience of the self and what counts most for it, and the imperative following from this experience that death must be avoided, were confirmed by the new natural philosophy which sees in nature only bodies in motion, bodies blindly conserving their motion by the necessity of inertia. All higher purposiveness in nature, which might have been consulted by men's reason and used to limit human passion, has disappeared. Nature tells us nothing about man specifically and provides no imperatives for his conduct. But man can be seen to behave as all other bodies behave, and the imaginary constraints on his following his powerful inclinations —constraints which would cause him to behave differently from natural bodies—vanish. Irrational passion and rational science cooperate in a new way to establish natural law: Pursue peace. Man's passionate subjectivity gives assent to the premises of natural philosophy—nay, takes them as its principles of action—and philosophy finds that that assent accords with nature. Man remains somehow a part of nature, but in a different and much more problematic way than in, say, Aristotle's philosophy, where soul is at the center and what is highest in man is akin to what is highest in nature, or where soul is nature. Man is really only a part and not the microcosm. Nature has no rank order or hierarchy of being, nor does the self.

Lockean natural man, who is really identical to his civil man, whose concern with comfortable self-preservation makes him law-abiding and productive, is not all that natural. Rousseau quickly pointed out that Locke, in his eagerness to find a simple or automatic solution to the political problem, made nature do much more than he had a right to expect a mechanical, nonteleological nature to do. Natural man would be brutish, hardly distinguishable from any of the other animals, unsociable and neither industrious nor rational, but, instead, idle and nonrational, motivated exclusively by feelings or sentiments. Having cut off the higher aspirations of man, those connected with the soul, Hobbes and Locke hoped to find a floor beneath him, which Rousseau removed. Man tumbled down into what I have called the basement, which now appears bottomless. And there, down below, Rousseau discovered all the complexity in man that, in the days before Machiavelli, was up on high. Locke had illegitimately selected those parts of man he needed for his social contract and suppressed all the rest, a theoretically unsatisfactory procedure and a practically costly one. The bourgeois is the measure of the price paid, he who most of all cannot afford to look to his real self, who denies the existence of the thinly boarded-over basement in him, who is most made over for the purposes of a society that does not even promise him perfection or salvation but merely buys him off. Rousseau explodes the simplistic harmoniousness between nature and society that seems to be the American premise.

Rousseau still hoped for a soft landing on nature's true grounds, but one not easily achieved, requiring both study and effort. The existence of such a natural ground has become doubtful, and it is here that the abyss opened up. But it was Rousseau who founded the modern psychology of the self in its fullness, with its unending search for what is really underneath the surface of rationality and civility, its new ways of reaching the unconscious, and its unending task of constituting some kind of healthy harmony between above and below.

Rousseau's intransigence set the stage for a separation of man from nature. He was perfectly willing to go along with the modern scientific understanding that a brutish being is true man. But nature cannot satisfactorily account for his difference from the other brutes, for his movement from nature to society, for his *history*. Descartes, playing his part in the dismantling of the soul, had reduced nature to extension, leaving out of it only the ego that observes extension. Man is, in everything but his consciousness, part of extension. Yet how he is a man, a unity, what came to be called a *self*, is utterly mysterious. This experienced whole, a combination of extension and ego, seems inexplicable or groundless. Body, or atoms in motion, passions, and reason are some kind of unity, but one that stands outside of the grasp of natural science. Locke appears to have invented the self to provide unity in continuity for the ceaseless temporal succession of sense impressions that would disappear into nothingness if there were no place to hold them. We can know everything in nature except that which knows nature. To the extent that man is a piece of nature, he disappears. The self gradually separates itself from nature, and its phenomena must be treated separately. Descartes' ego, in appearance invulnerable and godlike in its calm and isolation, turns out to be the tip of an iceberg floating in a fathomless and turbulent sea called the id, consciousness an epiphenomenon of the unconscious. Man is self, that now seems clear. But what is self?

Our gaily embraced psychology leaves us with this question. It is important for us to know the unbearably complicated story behind it if we are to abandon ourselves to it. One thing is certain: if this psychology is to be believed, it came to us belatedly, in order to treat the parts of man which had been so long neglected in our liberal society, and it opens up a Pandora's box, our*selves*. Like Iago it tells us, "I never found a man who knew how to love himself." Modern psychology has this in common with what was always a popular opinion, fathered by Machiavelli—that selfishness is somehow good. Man is self, and the self must be selfish. What is new is that we are told to look more deeply into the self, that we assumed too easily that we know it and have access to it.

The ambiguity of human life always requires that there be distinctions between good and bad, in one form or another. The great change is that a good man used to be the one who cares for others, as opposed to the man who cares exclusively for himself. Now the good man is the one who knows how to care for himself, as opposed to the man who does not. This is most obvious in the political realm. For Aristotle, good regimes have rulers dedicated to the common good, while bad ones have rulers who use their positions to further their private interest. For Locke and Montesquieu there is no such distinction. A good regime has the proper institutional structures for satisfying while containing the selfish men who make it up, while a bad one does not succeed in doing this. Selfishness is presupposed; men are not assumed to be as they ought to be, but as they are. Psychology has distinctions only between good and bad forms of selfishness, like Rousseau's deliciously candid distinction between *amour de soi* and *amour-propre*, untranslatable into English because we would have to use self-love for both terms.

For us the most revealing and delightful distinction—because it is so unconscious of its wickedness—is between inner-directed and other-directed, with the former taken to be unqualifiedly good. Of course, we are told, the healthy inner-directed person will *really* care for others. To which I can only respond: If you can believe that, you can believe anything. Rousseau knew much better.

The psychology of the self has succeeded so well that it is now the instinct of most of us to turn for a cure for our ills back within ourselves rather than to the nature of things. Socrates too thought that living according to the opinions of others was an illness. But he did not urge men to look for a source for producing their own unique opinions, or criticize them for being conformists. His measure of health was not sincerity, authenticity or any of the other necessarily vague criteria for distinguishing a healthy self. The truth is the one thing most needful; and conforming to nature is quite different from conforming to law, convention or opinion. Socrates spent his life discussing with other men and with himself opinions about what virtue is, what justice is, what piety is, rejecting those opinions that cannot be supported or are self-contradictory, investigating further those that seem stronger. Access to the nature of things is by way of thinking about what men say about them. Socrates was always among the Athenians but was not quite one of them, apparently never made uncomfortable by the fact that they did not trust him. He was neither solitary nor citizen. Rousseau, a figure of similar stature in the new tradition, was distressed by the hatred of mankind, and was both, at least in speech, the perfect citizen and the complete solitary. He was torn between the extremes, and there was no middle ground. Although a very great reasoner, his preferred means of learning about himself were the reverie, the dream, the old memory, a stream of associations unhampered by rational control. In order to know such an amorphous being as man, Rousseau himself and his particular history are, in his view, more important than is Socrates' quest for man in general or man in himself. The difference is made apparent by comparing the image of Socrates talking to two young men about the best regime, with the image of Rousseau, lying on his back on a raft floating on a gently undulating lake, sensing his existence.

CREATIVITY

The very expression *dignity of man*, even when Pico della Mirandola coined it in the fifteenth century, had a blasphemous ring to it. Man as man had not been understood to be particularly dignified. God had dignity, and whatever dignity man had was because he was made in God's image (as well as from dust) or because he was the rational animal whose reason could grasp the whole of nature and hence was akin to that whole. But now the dignity of man has neither of those supports; and the phrase means that man is the highest of the beings, an assertion emphatically denied by both Aristotle and the Bible. Man is elevated and alone. If this is to be plausible, man must be free—not in the sense of ancient philosophy, according to which a free man is one who participates in a regime where he rules as well as is ruled; nor in the sense of Hobbes and Locke, according to whom a free man is one who can follow his reason without having to obey God or man—but free in a much grander sense, that of legislating to himself and to nature, hence without guidance from nature.

The complement to and explanation of this view of freedom is *creativity*. We have become so accustomed to this word that it has no more effect on us than the most banal Fourth of July oratory. As a matter of fact, it has become our Fourth of July oratory. But when it was first used for man, it had the odor of blasphemy and paradox. God alone had been called a creator; and this was the miracle of miracles, beyond causality, a denial of the premise of all reason, *ex nihilo nihil fit*. What defines man is no longer his reason, which is but a tool for his preservation, but his art, for in art man can be said to be *creative*. There he brings order to chaos. The greatest men are not the knowers but the artists, the Homers, Dantes, Raphaels and Beethovens. Art is not imitation of nature but liberation from nature. A man who can generate visions of a cosmos and ideals by which to live is a *genius*, a mysterious, demonic being. Such a man's greatest work of art is himself. He who can take his person, a chaos of impressions and desires, a thing whose very unity is doubtful, and give it order and unity, is a *personality*. All of this results from the free activity of his spirit and his will. He contains in himself the elements of the legislator and the prophet, and has a deeper grasp of the true character of things than the contemplatives, philosophers, and scientists, who take the given order as permanent and fail to understand man. Such is the restoration of the ancient greatness of man against scientific egalitarianism, but how different he now looks! All this new language is a measure of the difference; and reflection on how the Greeks would translate and articulate the phenomena it describes is the task of a lifetime, which would pay rich rewards in self-understanding.

The vocabulary of self, culture, and creativity pretty much sums up the effects of what Rousseau began. It expresses the dissatisfactions with the scientific and political solutions of the Enlightenment. It turns around the understanding of what nature is. Somehow nature was always that by which men oriented themselves. However, no influential thinker has tried to return to the pre-Enlightenment understanding of nature, the so-called teleological view, in which nature is the fullness in its own kind that each of the beings strives to attain. The reaction to nature viewed as matter in motion, which can be conquered for the sake of man's needs, was twofold: a return to the notion that nature is good, but only the brute nature of the fields, forests, mountains and streams in which beasts live contentedly; or a transcendence of nature altogether in the direction of creativity. The latter solution conquered the Continent, and came from Germany to England by way of men like Coleridge and Carlyle. Very few thinkers were consistent or took seriously the full meaning of this revolution in thought. Hegel is the greatest exception. But everyone was affected by it, and its influence ran across the entire political spectrum, from Right to Left. Marxism as well as conservatism as we know them are unthinkable without what Rousseau did.

A small but illuminating example of the pervasiveness of anti-

Enlightenment thought today is how scientists themselves have taken to styling themselves as "creative." But nothing could be more contrary to the spirit of science than the opinion that the scientist fabricates rather than discovers his results. Scientists are to a man against creationism, recognizing rightly that, if there is anything to it, their science is wrong and useless. But they fail to see that creativity has exactly the same consequences. Either nature has a lawful order or it does not; either there can be miracles or there cannot. Scientists do not prove that there are no miracles, they assume it; without this assumption there is no science. It is easy today to deny God's creativity as a thing of the benighted past, overcome by science, but man's creativity, a thing much more improbable and nothing but an imitation of God's, exercises a strange attraction. In honoring it, the scientists' opinions are not the results of science or of any serious reflection on science. They are merely conforming to democratic public opinion, which has, unawares, been captured by Romantic notions adapted to flatter it (every man a creator). The artist, not the scientist, has become the admired human type; and science senses that it must assimilate itself to that type in order to retain its respectability intact. When every man was understood to be essentially a reasoner, the scientist could be understood to be a perfection of what all men wanted to be. That was Enlightenment's way of establishing the centrality of science and making it admired. This change in self-description shows how the *Zeitgeist* has altered and how science, instead of standing outside of it and liberating men from it, has been incorporated into it. The theoretical life has lost its status. Now the scientist scrambles to recover his position as the perfection of what all men want to be; but what all men want to be has changed, undermining the natural harmony between science and society.

Some may consider this labeling trivial, akin to C. P. Snow's calling science a "culture." Science may appear creative only because we forget what creativity really means and take it to be cleverness at proposing hypotheses, finding proofs or inventing experiments. From this perspective, science is unaffected, and we have just another example of the pollution of language. But this form of pollution, although less feared than the other kind, is really more deadly. It is the intellectual disorder of our age. The use of insignificant speech entails loss of clarity about what science and art are, weakening both in an impossible synthesis of opposites appealing to a society that wants to be told that it enjoys all good things.

There is here a sinister loss of confidence in the idea of science, if not its detailed practice, the idea which was at the foundation of democratic society and *the* absolute in a relativized world. These scientists know not what they do. Philosophy, despised and rejected by positive science, has its revenge when it is vulgarized into coarse public opinion and intimidates that science.

So the effects of Rousseau and his followers are everywhere around us, in the bloodstream of public opinion. Of course the use of words like "creativity" and "personality" does not mean that those who use them understand the thought that made their use necessary, let alone agree with it. The language has been trivialized. Words that were meant to describe and encourage Beethoven and Goethe are now applied to every school-child. It is in the nature of democracy to deny no one access to good things. If those things are really not accessible to all, then the tendency is to deny the fact—simply to proclaim, for example, that what is not art is art. There is in American society a mad rush to distinguish oneself, and, as soon as something has been accepted as distinguishing, to package it in such a way that everyone can feel included. Creativity and personality were intended to be terms of distinction. They were, as a matter of fact, intended to be the distinctions appropriate to egalitarian society, in which all distinction is threatened. The leveling of these distinctions through familiarity merely encourages self-satisfaction. Now that they belong to everyone, they can be said to mean nothing, both in common parlance and in the social science disciplines that use them as "concepts." They have no specific content, are a kind of opiate of the masses. They do, however, provide a focus for all the dissatisfactions that any life anywhere and at any time provides, particularly those fostered in a democratic society. Creativity and personality take the place of older words like virtue, industry, rationality and character, affect our judgments, provide us with educational goals. They are the bourgeois' way of not being bourgeois. Hence they are sources of snobbishness and pretentiousness alien to our real virtues. We have a lot of good engineers but very few good artists. All the honor, however, goes to the latter, or rather, one should say, those who stand in for the latter in the eyes of the many. The real artists don't need this kind of support and are instead weakened by it. The money-maker is not the most appetizing personality, but he is far preferable to the intellectual phony.

Thus what was intended as an elevation of taste and morality has merely become grist for our mill while sapping the mill's foundation. This was not the only result in Europe, where creativity had at times an inspiring effect and where the notion had more to feed off of. Even there, as we shall soon see, the balance sheet is arguably negative. But here I can see no benefits. And now the mother-word itself—culture—has also become part of empty talk, its original imprecision now carried to the point of pathology. Anthropologists can't define it although they are sure there is such a thing. Artists have no vision of the sublime, but they know culture (i.e., what they do) has a right to the honor and support of civil society. Sociologists and the disseminators of their views, the journalists of all descriptions, call everything a culture—the drug culture, the rock culture, the street-gang culture, and so on endlessly and without discrimination. Failure of culture is now culture. This is how the heroic response to the French Revolution fared when it immigrated to America. Our country is still a melting pot.

CULTURE

The interesting response to the nature-society tension, much more fertile than the return to, or nostalgia for, nature, can be summed up by the word "culture." It seems to mean something high, profound, respectable—a thing before which we bow. It joins nature as a standard for the judgment of men and their deeds but has even greater dignity. It is almost never used pejoratively, as are "society," "state," "nation" or even "civiliza-tion," terms for which culture is gradually substituted, or whose legitimacy is underwritten by culture. Culture is the unity of man's brutish nature and all the arts and sciences he acquired in his movement from the state of nature to civil society. Culture restores the lost wholeness of first man on a higher level, where his faculties can be fully developed without contradiction between the desires of nature and the moral imperatives of his social life.

"Culture" in the modern sense was first used by Immanuel Kant, who was thinking of Rousseau when he employed it, particularly about what Rousseau said of the bourgeois. The bourgeois is selfish, but without the purity and simplicity of natural selfishness. He makes contracts hoping to get the better of those with whom he contracts. His faithfulness to others and his obedience to law are founded on expectation of gain: "Honesty is the best policy." Thus he corrupts morality, the essence of which is to exist for its own sake. The bourgeois satisfies neither extreme, nature or morality. The moral demand is merely an abstract ideal if it asks for what nature cannot give. Brutish selfishness would be preferable to sham morality.

The progress of culture provides the link between inclination and duty. Kant uses the education of sexual desire as an example. Naturally man has the desire to have sexual intercourse and hence to procreate. But he has no desire to care for his children or educate them, even though the growth of their faculties requires prolonged maintenance and training. So the family is necessary. But natural desire does not point to the family. Desire is promiscuous and inclines man toward freedom. So desire is repressed. Man is commanded to abandon his desire. He is punished for it. Myths are created that haunt him, make him feel guilty and persuade him that he is sinful because of his natural desires. Marriage constrains both parties, and faithless deeds as well as desires habitually accompany it. In spite of all of society's machinery, untamed desire is always there. It is natural. It can be pushed down, but never completely, and it always has its revenge in one way or another.

A man in this condition can never be happy. But a man who is deeply in love with a woman both desires and, for the moment at least, really cares for another. If this latter condition can be made permanent, desire and morality practically coincide. The free choice of marriage and the capacity to stick to it, not merely outwardly but also inwardly, is a proof of culture, of desire informed by civility. It is also the proof of human freedom, of the overcoming of nature for the sake of morality, without making man unhappy. The exclusive preference for one person whose attraction is founded on ideas of beauty and virtue unknown to natural man makes sex sublime or sublimates it. This is love, and love seeks expression in poetry and music. Thus sublimated, sexual desire culminates in art. The children who are love's products make reflection about education necessary. And the family, its rights and its duties, its legal basis and its protection, finally connect what was once an isolated individual, concerned only with himself, to politics. Love, family and politics, which previously divided man and trapped him, can now be ordered in such a way as to fulfill and enhance natural desire and can therefore be unambiguously affirmed by the will. He is his own master again, but social or related to other men without being alienated by them. He is neither promiscuous nor repressed, because his sexual passion is fully expressed and satisfied. Both the world of nature and that of society are fulfilled. His intellectual acquisitions are not just extrinsic adornments but harmoniously serve and enrich his life. Such is the ideal of culture so far as sexual matters are concerned. Something of the kind must occur in all the aspects of man's life in order to produce a personality, the fully cultured human being.

This Rousseauan-Kantian vision is in essential agreement with the Enlightenment view of what is natural in man. But for the first time within philosophy, something other and higher than nature is found in man.

It should be noted that sex is a theme hardly mentioned in the thought underlying the American Founding. There it is all preservation, not procreation, because fear is more powerful than love, and men prefer their lives to their pleasures. This subordination or taming of the sexual and everything connected with it made it easier for society to satisfy nature's most powerful demands. The rehabilitation of sex made society's task more difficult and placed different demands on it. The primacy given to the sexual instinct in later modern thought as opposed to the preservative instinct among the early moderns accounts for much of the drama of our intellectual life, and for the varying expectations from social life. We are back to our economist and psychiatrist.

But what is the relation between Kant's use of the word culture and ours? It seems there are two different current uses that, while distinct, are linked. First, culture is almost identical to people or nation, as in French culture, German culture, Iranian culture, etc. Second, culture refers to art, music, literature, educational television, certain kinds of movies—in short, everything that is uplifting and edifying, as opposed to commerce. The link is that culture is what makes possible, on a high level, the rich social life that constitutes a people, their customs, styles, tastes, festivals, rituals, gods—all that binds individuals into a group with roots, a community in which they think and will generally, with the people a moral unity, and the individual united within himself. A culture is a work of art, of which the fine arts are the sublime expression. From this point of view, liberal democracies look like disorderly markets to which individuals bring their produce in the morning and from which they return in the evening to enjoy privately what they have purchased with the proceeds of their sales. In culture, on the other hand, the individuals are formed by the collectivity as are the members of the chorus of a Greek drama. A Charles de Gaulle or, for that matter, an Alexander Solzhenitsyn sees the United States as a mere aggregate of individuals, a dumping ground for the refuse from other places, devoted to consuming; in short, no culture.

Culture as art is the peak expression of man's creativity, his capacity to break out of nature's narrow bonds, and hence out of the degrading interpretation of man in modern natural and political science. Culture founds the dignity of man. Culture as a form of community is the fabric of relations in which the self finds its diverse and elaborate expression. It is the house of the self, but also its product. It is profounder than the modern *state*, which deals only with man's bodily needs and tends to degenerate into mere economy. Such a state is not a forum in which man can act without deforming himself. This is why in the better circles it always seems in poor taste to speak of love of country, while devotion to Western, or even American, culture is perfectly respectable. Culture restores "the unity in art and life" of the ancient polis.

The only element of the polis absent from culture is politics. For the ancients the soul of the city was the regime, the arrangements of and participation in offices, deliberation about the just and the common good, choices about war and peace, the making of laws. Rational choice on the part of citizens who were statesmen was understood to be the center of communal life and the cause of everything else. The polis was defined by its regime. Nothing of the kind is to be found in culture, and just what defines a culture is extremely difficult to discern. Today we are interested in Greek culture, not Athenian politics. Thucydides' version of Pericles' Funeral Oration is taken to be an archetypical expression of that culture, a splendid evocation—in the context of a religious ceremony—of Athenian love of beauty and wisdom. This interpretation makes some sense; but it is nonetheless a misreading; it is supposed to enrich us but it only confirms us in our prejudices, typical of our utter dependence on German interpretations of Greek things. Actually Pericles says nothing about the gods, or the poetry, history, sculpture or philosophy of which we think. He praises Athens' regime and finds beauty in its political achievement—its regime, and particularly its tyrannically held empire. The Athenians are the political heroes who surpass those in Homer, and the arts are implicitly understood to be imitations and adornments of that heroism. But we find what we look for, and do not see any of this. A Pericles thus interpreted would be too superficial for us.

The disappearance of politics is one of the most salient aspects of modern thought and has much to do with our political practice. Politics tends to disappear either into the subpolitical (economics) or what claims to be higher than politics (culture)—both of which escape the architectonic art, the statesman's prudence. Politics in the older sense encompassed and held together these two extremes. This opposition between economy and culture is but another formulation of the dualism in contemporary American intellectual life that keeps recurring in these pages and is their unifying theme.

The source can be found in one of the most remarkable passages in Rousseau's works, which marks the break with early modern statecraft and was decisive in the development of the idea of culture. It is his chapter on the Legislator in *The Social Contract* (II, 7). Rousseau directed men's attention back to the ancient polis as a corrective to the Enlightenment political teaching. Unlike many of those who came after him, he was hardheadedly political and saw statesmen's deeds as central to the life of a people. And it is precisely the very conditions for the existence of a people that Rousseau accuses his immediate predecessors of having misunderstood or ignored. Individual self-interest is not sufficient to establish a common good, he insists, but without it, political life is impossible, and men will be morally contemptible. The founder of a regime must first make a people to which the regime will belong. A people will not automatically result from individual men's enlightenment about their self-interest. A political deed is necessary. The legislator must

> so to speak change human nature, transform each individual, who by himself is a perfect and solitary whole, into a part of a greater whole from which that individual as it were gets his life and his being; weaken man's constitution to strengthen it; substitute a partial and moral existence for the physical and independent existence which we have all received from nature. He must, in a word, take man's own forces away from him in order to give him forces which are foreign to him and which he cannot use without the help of others. The more the natural forces are dead and annihilated, the greater and more lasting the acquired ones, thus the founding is solider and more perfect; such that if each citizen is nothing, can do nothing, except by all the others, and the force acquired by the whole is equal or superior to the sum of the natural forces of all the individuals, one can say that the legislation is at the highest point of perfection it can attain.

Rousseau with characteristic and refreshing frankness underlines the corporate character of the community and what is required to achieve it as over against the abstract individualism popularized by the Enlightenment. In elaborating the scheme Rousseau even puts in the popular festivals and all that. This complex nervous system constructed by the legislator is exactly what we call culture. Or rather, culture is the effect of the legislation without the legislator, without the political intention.

Rousseau's theoretical frankness, or harshness, about legislation put off succeeding generations of thinkers, who nonetheless wanted the results of that harshness, i.e., community. Or, more likely, Robespierre's practical harshness and the failure of his attempt at legislation scared off moderate observers. Changing human nature seems a brutal, nasty, tyrannical thing to do. So, instead, it began to be denied that there is such a thing as human nature. Rather, man grows and grows into culture; cultures are, as is obvious from the word, growths. Man is a culture being, not a natural being. What man has from nature is nothing compared to what he has acquired from culture. A culture, like the language that accompanies and expresses it, is a set of mere accidents that add up to a coherent meaning constitutive of man. Nature is gradually banished from the study of man; and the state of nature is understood to have been a myth, even though the notion of culture is inconceivable without the prior elaboration of the state of nature. The primacy of the acquired over the natural in man's humanity is the ground of the idea of culture; and that idea is bound up with the idea of history, understood not as the investigation into man's deeds but as a dimension of reality, of man's being. The very fact of movement from the state of nature to the civil state shows that there is history and that it is more important than nature. In Rousseau the tension between nature and the political order is maintained, and the legislator has to force the two into a kind of harmony. History is a union of the two in which each disappears.

Now, Rousseau, for all the adaptations made by the legislator, in order for his legislation to suit particular times and places, was still pursuing the same universal goal as were the thinkers of the Enlightenment: to secure the equal natural rights of all men within civil society. He simply argued that Hobbes and Locke did not succeed in doing so, that self-interest is not enough to found political morality on. The political solution was more complicated and demanding. Kant, who invented culture as part of a historical teaching, also had a similar universal goal. Although natural rights had become human rights in his teaching, those rights were the same ones, founded on a new basis; and the historical process he discerned in Rousseau's teaching moved toward the effective establishment of those rights in civil society. Universality and rationality were the hallmarks of all these teachings. But very quickly culture—which was for Kant and, speaking anachronistically, for Rousseau, singular—became *cultures*. That there were Englishmen, Frenchmen, Germans and Chinese was clear. That there is a cosmopolitan culture, either existing or coming into being, is unclear. The various unions of nature with the acquisitions of civilization are rare and difficult enough; that they should tend to the same end is improbable; we should cherish these creations and be happy that there is any culture at all. A charm was discovered in this diversity. Rousseau introduced rootedness as a condition of attaining the simple rational human goal. His historicist and romantic successors argued that such a goal undermined rootedness; rootedness became the goal.

Here again we live with two contradictory understandings of what counts for man. One tells us that what is important is what all men have in common; the other that what men have in common is low, while what they have from separate cultures gives them their depth and their interest. Both agree that life, liberty, and the pursuit of property, i.e., the interests of health and preservation, are what men share. The difference between them is the weight they give to being French or Chinese, Jewish or Catholic, or the rank order of these particular cultures in relation to the natural needs of the body. One is cosmopolitan, the other is particularistic. Human rights are connected with one school, respect for cultures with the other. Sometimes the United States is attacked for failing to promote human rights; sometimes for wanting to impose "the American way of life" on all people without respect for their cultures. To the extent that it does the latter, the United States does so in the name of self-evident truths that apply to the good of all men. But its critics argue that there are no such truths, that they are prejudices of American culture. On the other hand, the Ayatollah was initially supported by some here because he represented true Iranian culture. Now he is attacked for violating human rights. What he does is in the name of Islam. His critics insist that there are universal principles that limit the rights of Islam. When the critics of the U.S. in the name of culture, and of the Ayatollah in the name of human rights, are the same persons, which they often are, they are persons who want to eat their cake and have it, too.

Why, it might be asked, can't there be a respect for both human rights and culture? Simply because a culture itself generates its own way of life and principles, particularly its highest ones, with no authority above it. If there were such an authority, the unique way of life born of its principle would be undermined. The idea of culture was adopted precisely because it offered an alternative to what was understood to be the shallow and dehumanizing universality of rights based on our animal nature. The folk mind takes the place of reason. There is a continuing war between the universality of the Enlightenment and the particularity that resulted from the teachings of Enlightenment's critics. Their criticism appealed to all the old attachments to family, country and God that were uprooted by Enlightenment, and gave them a new interpretation and a new pathos. Such criticism provided a philosophic basis for resisting philosophy.

The question is whether reasonings really take the place of instincts, whether arguments about the value of tradition or roots can substitute for immediate passions, whether this whole interpretation is not just a reaction unequal to the task of stemming a tide of egalitarian, calculating individualism, which the critics themselves share, and the privileges of which they would be loath to renounce. When one hears newly divorced persons extolling the extended family, unaware of all the sacred bonds and ancestral tyranny that it required in order to exist, it is easy to see what they think is missing from their lives, but hard to believe they are aware of what they would have to sacrifice to achieve it. When one hears men and women proclaiming that they must preserve their *culture*, one cannot help wondering whether this artificial notion can really take the place of the God and country for which they once would have been willing to die.

The "new ethnicity" or "roots" is just another manifestation of the concern with particularity, evidence not only of the real problems of community in modern mass societies but also of the superficiality of the response to it, as well as the lack of awareness of the fundamental conflict between liberal society and culture. This attempt to preserve old cultures in the New World is superficial because it ignores the fact that real differences among men are based on real differences in fundamental beliefs about good and evil, about what is highest, about God. Differences of dress or food are either of no interest or are secondary expressions of deeper beliefs. The "ethnic" differences we see in the United States are but decaying reminiscences of old differences that caused our ancestors to kill one another. The animating principle, their soul, has disappeared from them. The ethnic festivals are just superficial displays of clothes, dances and foods from the old country. One has to be quite ignorant of the splendid "cultural" past in order to be impressed or charmed by these insipid folkloric manifestations (which, by the way, unite the meanings of culture—people and art). And the blessing given the whole notion of cultural diversity in the United States by the culture movement has contributed to the intensification and legitimization of group politics, along with a corresponding decay of belief that the individual rights enunciated in the Declaration of Independence are anything more than dated rhetoric.

The idea of culture was established in an attempt to find the dignity of man within the context of modern science. That science was materialistic, hence reductionist, and deterministic. Man can have no dignity if his status is not special, if he is not essentially different from the brutes. There must be something else in man to account for the fullness of his being and prevent political and economic arrangements that presuppose his brutishness from reducing him to it. Those who attempted to establish the dignity of man did not hope or try to transform the new natural science. It was a question of coexistence. They invented dualisms with which we still live—nature-freedom, nature-art, science-creativity, natural science-humanities—in which the latter term of the pair is supposed to be of higher dignity, but the groundedness of which has always turned out to be problematic. Freedom is a postulate, a possibility in Kant, not a demonstration; and that remains the difficulty. Culture, although it claims to be comprehensive, to include all of man's higher activities, does not really include natural science, which did not need the notion, which was doing just fine in the older democratic arrangement it had helped to found, and by which it was encouraged. Psychology today includes an important school for which man is nothing other than a brute, e.g., B. F. Skinner's behavioralism; another in which the fact that man is an animal practically disappears, e.g., Jacques Lacan's existential analysis; and various incoherent mixtures, e.g., Freud's psychoanalytic theory, which wants to found itself on biology and at the same time to account for spiritual phenomena, to the detriment of both. In general, everyone wants to be scientific and at the same time to respect the dignity of man.

VALUES

We have come back to the point where we began, where *values* take the place of good and evil. But now we have made at least a hasty tour of the intellectual experiences connected with modern politics that made such a response compelling. How it looked to thoughtful Germans is most revealingly expressed in a famous passage by Max Weber, about God, science and the irrational:

> Finally, although a naive optimism may have celebrated science—that is, the technique of the mastery of life founded on science—as the path which would lead to happiness, I believe I can leave this entire question aside in light of the annihilating critique which Nietzsche has made of "the last men" who "have discovered happiness." Who, then, still believes in this, with the exception of a few big babies in university chairs or in editorial offices? *(Science as a Vocation)*

So penetrating and well informed an observer as Weber could say in 1919 that the scientific spirit at the heart of Western democracy was dead for all serious men and that Nietzsche had killed it, or had at least given it the *coup de grâce*. The presentation of "the last man" in *Thus Spake Zarathustra* was so decisive that the old-style Enlightenment rationalism need not even be discussed anymore; and, Weber implies, all future discussion or study must proceed with the certainty that the perspective was a "naive" failure. Reason cannot establish values, and its belief that it can is the stupidest and most pernicious illusion.

194

This means, simply, that almost all Americans at that time, thinking Americans in particular, were "big babies" and remained so, long after the Continent had grown up. One need only think of John Dewey to recognize that he fits Weber's description to a T, and then remember what his influence here once was. And not only Dewey, but everyone from the beginning of our regime, especially those who said, "We hold these *truths* to be *self-evident,* " shared the rationalist dream. Weber's statement is so important because he as much as or more than anyone brought us into contact with the most advanced Continental criticisms of liberal democracy, and was the intermediary between Nietzsche and us Americans who were the most recalcitrant to his insight, perhaps because according to it we represent the worst or most hopeless and are therefore loath to see ourselves in that mirror. A very dark view of the future has been superimposed on our incorrigible optimism. We are children playing with adult toys. They have proved too much for us to handle. But, in our defense, we are probably not the only ones for whom they are too much.

Weber points us toward Nietzsche as the common source for serious thinkers of the twentieth century. He also tells us what the single fundamental issue is: the relation between reason, or science, and the human good. When he speaks of happiness and the last man, he does not mean that the last man is unhappy, but that his happiness is nauseating. An experience of profound contempt is necessary in order to grasp our situation, and our capacity for contempt is vanishing. Weber's science presupposes this experience, which we would call subjective. After having encountered it in Nietzsche, he spent the greater part of his scholarly life studying religion in order to understand the noncontemptible, those who esteem or revere and are therefore not self-satisfied, those who have values or, to say the same thing, have gods, in particular those who create gods or found religions. From Nietzsche he learned that religion, or the sacred, is the most important human phenomenon, and his further study of it was made from Nietzsche's unorthodox perspective.

"God is dead," Nietzsche proclaimed. But he did not say this on a note of triumph, in the style of earlier atheism—the tyrant has been overthrown and man is now free. Rather he said it in the anguished tones of the most powerful and delicate piety deprived of its proper object. Man, who loved and needed God, has lost his Father and Savior without possibility of resurrection. The joy of liberation one finds in Marx has turned into terror at man's unprotectedness. *Honesty* compels serious men, on examination of their consciences, to admit that the old faith is no longer compelling. It is the very peak of Christian virtue that demands the sacrifice of Christianity, the greatest sacrifice a Christian can make. Enlightenment killed God; but like Macbeth, the men of the Enlightenment did not know that the cosmos would rebel at the deed, and the world become "a tale told by an idiot, full of sound and fury, signifying nothing." Nietzsche replaces easygoing or self-satisfied atheism with agonized atheism, suffering its human consequences. Longing to believe, along with intransigent refusal to satisfy that longing, is, according to him, the profound response to our entire spiritual condition. Marx denied the existence of God but turned over all His functions to History, which is inevitably directed to a goal fulfilling of man and which takes the place of Providence. One might as well be a Christian if one is so naive. Prior to Nietzsche, all those who taught that man is a historical being presented his history as in one way or another progressive. After Nietzsche, a characteristic formula for describing our history is "the decline of the West."

Nietzsche surveyed and summed up the contradictory strands of modern thought and concluded that victorious rationalism is unable to rule in culture or soul, that it cannot defend itself theoretically and that its human consequences are intolerable. This constitutes a crisis of the West, for everywhere in the West, for the first time ever, all regimes are founded on reason. Human founders, looking only to universal principles of natural justice recognizable by all men through their unaided reason, established governments on the basis of the consent of the governed, without appeal to revelation or tradition. But reason has also discerned that all previous cultures were founded by and on gods or belief in gods. Only if the new regimes are enormous successes, able to rival the creative genius and splendor of other cultures, could reason's rational foundings be equal or superior to the kinds of foundings that reason knows were made elsewhere. But such equality or superiority is highly questionable; therefore reason recognizes its own inadequacy. There must be religion, and reason cannot found religions.

This was already implicit in the first wave of criticism of Enlightenment. Rousseau said a civil religion is necessary to society, and the legislator has to appear draped in the colors of religion. Tocqueville concentrated on the centrality of religion to America. With the failure of Robespierre's kind of civil religion, there was a continuing effort to promote a revised or liberal Christianity, inspired by Rousseau's *Profes-*

sion of Faith of the Savoyard Vicar. The very idea of culture was a way of preserving something like religion without talking about it. Culture is a synthesis of reason and religion, attempting to hide the sharp distinction between the two poles.

Nietzsche examines the patient, observes that the treatment was not successful, and pronounces God dead. Now there cannot be religion; but inasmuch as man needs culture, the religious impulse remains. No religion but religiosity. This suffuses Nietzsche's analysis of modernity, and, unnoticed, it underlies the contemporary categories of psychology and sociology. He brought the religious question back to the center of philosophy. The critical standpoint from which to view modern culture is its essential atheism; and that more repulsive successor of the bourgeois, the *last man*, is the product of egalitarian, rationalist, socialist atheism.

Thus the novel aspect of the crisis of the West is that it is identical with a crisis of philosophy. Reading Thucydides shows us that the decline of Greece was purely political, that what we call intellectual history is of little importance for understanding it. Old regimes had traditional roots; but philosophy and science took over as rulers in modernity, and purely theoretical problems have decisive political effects. One cannot imagine modern political history without a discussion of Locke, Rousseau and Marx. Theoretical implausibility and decrepitude are, as everyone knows, at the heart of the Soviet Union's malaise. And the Free World is not far behind. Nietzsche is the profoundest, clearest, most powerful diagnostician of the disease. He argues that there is an inner necessity for us to abandon reason on rational grounds—that therefore our regime is doomed.

The *disenchantment* of God and nature necessitated a new description of good and evil. To adapt a formula of Plato about the gods, we do not love a thing because it is good, it is good because we love it. It is our *decision* to esteem that makes something estimable. Man is the esteeming being, the one capable of reverence and self-contempt, "the beast with red cheeks." Nietzsche claimed to have seen that the objects of men's reverence in no sense compel that reverence; frequently the objects do not even exist. Their qualities are projections of what is most powerful in man and serve to satisfy his strongest needs or desires. Good and evil are what make it possible for men to live and act. The character of their judgments of good and evil shows what they are.

To put it simply, Nietzsche says that modern man is losing, or has lost, the capacity to value, and therewith his humanity. Self-satisfaction, the desire to be adjusted, the comfortable solution to his problems, the whole program of the welfare state, are the signs of the incapacity to look up toward the heaven of man's possible perfection or self-overcoming. But the surest sign is the way we use the word "value," and in this Nietzsche not only diagnosed the disease but exacerbated it. He intended to point out to men the danger they are in, the awesome task they face of protecting and enhancing their humanity. As he understood it, men in our current decrepitude could take it easy if they believed God, nature or history provides values. Such belief was salutary as long as the objectified creations of man were still noble and vital. But in the present exhaustion of the old values, men must be brought to the abyss, terrified by their danger and nauseated by what could become of them, in order to make them aware of their responsibility for their fate. They must turn within themselves and reconstitute the conditions of their creativity in order to generate values. The self must be a tense bow. It must struggle with opposites rather than harmonize them, rather than turn the tension over to the great instruments of last manhood—the skilled bow unbenders and Jesuits of our days, the psychiatrists, who, in the same spirit and as part of the same conspiracy of modernity as the peace virtuosos, reduce conflict. Chaos, the war of opposites, is, as we know from the Bible, the condition of creativity, which must be mastered by the creator. The self must also bring forth arrows out of its longing. Bow and arrow, both belonging to man, can shoot a star into the heavens to guide man. Stripping away the illusions about values was required, so Nietzsche thought, by our situation, to disenchant all misleading hopes of comfort or consolation, thereby to fill the few creators with awe and the awareness that everything depends on them. Nihilism is a dangerous but a necessary and a possibly salutary stage in human history. In it man faces his true situation. It can break him, reduce him to despair and spiritual or bodily suicide. But it can hearten him to a reconstruction of a world of meaning. Nietzsche's works are a glorious exhibition of the soul of a man who might, if anybody can, be called *creative*. They constitute the profoundest statement about creativity, by a man who had a burning need to understand it.

Nietzsche was ineluctably led to meditation on the coming to be of God—on God-creation—for God is the highest value, on which the others depend. God is not creative, for God *is not.* But God as made by man reflects what man is, unbeknownst to himself. God is said to have made the world of concern to us out of nothing; so man makes something, God, out of nothing. The faith in God and the belief in miracles are closer to the truth than any scientific explanation, which has to overlook or explain away the creative in man. Moses, overpowered by the obscure drives within him, went to the peak of Sinai and brought back tables of values; these values had a necessity, a substantiality more compelling than health or wealth. They were the core of life. There are other possible tables of values—one thousand and one, according to Zarathustra—but these were the ones that made this people what it was and gave it a life-style, a unity of inner experience and outer expression or form. There is no prescription for creating the myths that constitute a people, no standardized test that can predict the man who will create them or determine which myths will work or are appropriate. There is the matter and the maker, like stone and sculptor; but in this case the sculptor is not only the efficient cause but the formal and final cause as well. There is nothing that underlies the myth, no substance, no cause. No search for the cause of values, either in the rational quest for knowledge of good and evil or in, for example, their economic determinants, can result in an accurate account of them. Only an openness to the psychological phenomena of creativity can bring any clarity.

This psychology cannot be like Freud's, which, beginning from Nietzsche's understanding of the unconscious, finds causes of creativity that blur the difference between a Raphael and a finger painter. Everything is in that difference, which necessarily escapes our science. The unconscious is a great mystery; it is the truth of God, and it—the id— is as unfathomable as was God. Freud accepted the unconscious, and then tried to give it perfect clarity by means of science. But the id produces science. It can produce many sciences. Freud's procedure is like trying to determine God's essence or nature from what he created. God could have created an infinity of worlds. If he had been limited to this one, he would not have been creative or free.

Understanding all of this is necessary if one is to understand creativity. The id is the source; it is elusive and unfathomable and produces world interpretations. Yet natural scientists, among whom Freud wished to be counted, do not take any of this seriously. Biologists cannot even account for consciousness within their science, let alone the unconscious. So psychologists like Freud are in an impossible halfway house between science, which does not admit the existence of the phenomena he wishes to explain, and the unconscious, which is outside the jurisdiction of science. It is a choice, so Nietzsche compellingly insists, between science and psychology. Psychology is by that very fact the winner, since science is the product of the psyche. Scientists themselves are gradually being affected by this choice. Perhaps science is only a product of our culture, which we know is no better than any other. Is science true? One sees a bit of decay around the edges of its good conscience, formerly so robust. Books like Thomas Kuhn's *The Structure of Scientific Revolutions* are popular symptoms of this condition.

This is where what I called the bottomless or fathomless self, the last version of the *self,* makes its appearance. Id, Nietzsche named it. The id mocks the ego when a man says, "*It* occurred to me." The sovereign consciousness waits on something down below, which sends up its food for thought. The difference between this version and the others is that they began from a common experience, more or less immediately accessible, that all men share, which establishes, if only intersubjectively, a common humanity that can be called human nature. Fear of violent death and desire for comfortable self-preservation were the first stop on the way down. Everybody knows them, and we can recognize one another in them. The next stop was the sweet sentiment of existence, no longer immediately accessible to civilized man but recoverable by him. When under its spell, we can with certainty say to ourselves, "This is what I really am, what I live for," with the further conviction that the same must be so for all other men. This, allied with a vague, generalized compassion, makes us a species and can give us guidance. At the next stop there turns out to be no stop, and the descent is breathtaking. If one finds anything at all, it is strictly one's own, what Nietzsche calls one's *fatum,* a stubborn, strong ass that has nothing to say for itself other than that it is. One finds, at best, oneself; and it is incommunicable and isolates each from all others, rather than uniting them. Only the rarest individuals find their own stopping point from which they can move the world. They are, literally, profound.

Though the values, the horizons, the tables of good and evil that originate in the self cannot be said to be true or false, cannot be derived from the common feeling of mankind or justified by the universal standards of reason, they are not equal, contrary to what vulgar teachers of value theory believe. Nietzsche, and all those serious persons who in one way or another accepted his insight, held that inequality among men is proved by the fact that there is no common experience accessible in principle to all. Such distinctions as authentic-inauthentic, profound-superficial, creator-created replace true and false. The individual value of one man becomes the polestar for many others whose own experience provides them with no guidance. The rarest of men is the creator, and all other men need and follow him.

Authentic values are those by which a life can be lived, which can form a people that produces great deeds and thoughts. Moses, Jesus, Homer, Buddha: these are the creators, the men who formed horizons, the founders of Jewish, Christian, Greek, Chinese, and Japanese culture. It is not the truth of their thought that distinguished them, but its capacity to generate culture. A value is only a value if it is life-preserving and life-enhancing. The quasi-totality of men's values consists of more or less pale carbon copies of the originator's values. Egalitarianism means conformism, because it gives power to the sterile who can only make use of old values, other men's ready-made values, which are not alive and to which their promoters are not *committed*. Egalitarianism is founded on reason, which denies creativity. Everything in Nietzsche is an attack on rational egalitarianism, and shows what twaddle the habitual talk about values is these days—and how astonishing is Nietzsche's respectability on the Left.

Since values are not rational and not grounded in the natures of those subject to them, they must be imposed. They must defeat opposing values. Rational persuasion cannot make them believed, so struggle is necessary. Producing values and believing in them are acts of the will. Lack of will, not lack of understanding, becomes the crucial defect. *Commitment* is *the* moral virtue because it indicates the seriousness of the agent. Commitment is the equivalent of faith when the living God has been supplanted by self-provided values. It is Pascal's wager, no longer on God's existence but on one's capacity to believe in oneself and the goals one has set for oneself. Commitment values the values and makes them valuable. Not love of truth but *intellectual honesty* characterizes the proper state of mind. Since there is no truth in the values, and what truth there is about life is not lovable, the hallmark of the *authentic self* is consulting one's oracle while facing up to what one is and what one experiences. *Decisions*, not deliberations, are the movers of deeds. One cannot know or plan the future. One must will it. There is no program. The great revolutionary must destroy the past and open up the future for the free play of creativity. Politics are revolutionary; but unlike the Glorious Revolution, the American Revolution, the French Revolution or the Russian Revolution, the new revolutions should be unprogrammatic. They are to be made by intellectually honest, committed, strong-willed, creative men. Nietzsche was not a fascist; but this project inspired fascist rhetoric, which looked to the revitalization of old cultures or the foundation of new ones, as opposed to the rational, rootless cosmopolitanism of the revolutions of the Left.

Nietzsche was a cultural relativist, and he saw what that means—war, great cruelty rather than great compassion. War is the fundamental phenomenon on which peace can sometimes be forced, but always in the most precarious way. Liberal democracies do not fight wars with one another because they see the same human nature and the same rights applicable everywhere and to everyone. Cultures fight wars with one another. They must do so because values can only be asserted or posited by overcoming others, not by reasoning with them. Cultures have different *perceptions*, which determine what the world is. They cannot come to terms. There is no communication about the highest things. (Communication is the substitute for understanding when there is no common world men share, to which they can refer when they misunderstand one another. From the isolation of the closed systems of self and culture, there are attempts to "get in contact," and "failures of communication." How individuals and cultures can "relate" to one another is altogether a mysterious business.) Culture means a war against chaos *and* a war against other cultures. The very idea of culture carries with it a value: man needs culture and must do what is necessary to create and maintain cultures. There is no place for a theoretical man to stand. To live, to have any inner substance, a man must have values, must be committed, or *engagé*. Therefore a cultural relativist must care for culture more than truth, and fight for culture while knowing it is not true.

This is somehow impossible, and Nietzsche struggled with the problem throughout his career, perhaps without a satisfactory resolution. But he knew that the scientific view is deadly to culture, and that the political or moral cultural relativist of the ordinary sort is doomed to have no culture. Cultural relativism, as opposed to relativism simply, teaches the need to believe while undermining belief.

Nietzsche appears to have taken over the idea of culture from his philosophical predecessors without much hesitation. Culture is, from his point of view, the only framework within which to account for what is specifically human in man. Man is pure becoming, unlike any other being in nature; and it is in culture that he becomes something that transcends nature and has no other mode of existence and no other support than a particular culture. The actuality of plants and the other animals is contained in their potentialities; but this is not true of man, as is indicated by the many cultural flowers, essentially unlike, produced from the same seed, man. Nietzsche's contribution was to draw with perfect intransigence the consequences of that idea and try to live with them. If there are many cultures, unsolicited by one perfect or complete culture in which man is man, simply—without prefix such as Greek, Chinese, Christian, Buddhist (i.e., if Plato's *Republic*, outlining the one best regime, is simply a myth, a work of Plato's imagination), then the very word "man" is a paradox. There are as many kinds of man as there are cultures, without any perspective from which man can be spoken of in the singular. This is true not only of his habits, customs, rituals, fashions, but above all of his mind. There must be as many different kinds of mind as there are cultures. If the mind itself is not included among the things that are relative to cultures, the observations of cultural relativism are trivial and have always been accepted. Yet everyone likes cultural relativism but wants to exempt what concerns him. The physicist wants to save his atoms; the historian, his events; the moralist, his values. But they are all equally relative. If there is an escape for one truth from the flux, then there is in principle no reason why many truths are not beyond it; and then the flux, becoming, change, history or what have you is not what is fundamental, but rather, being, the immutable principle of science and philosophy.

It is Nietzsche's merit that he was aware that to philosophize is radically problematic in the cultural, historicist dispensation. He recognized the terrible intellectual and moral risks involved. At the center of his every thought was the question "How is it possible to do what I am doing?" He tried to apply to his own thought the teachings of cultural relativism. This practically nobody else does. For example, Freud says that men are motivated by desire for sex and power, but he did not apply those motives to explain his own science or his own scientific activity. But if he can be a true scientist, i.e., motivated by love of the truth, so can other men, and his description of their motives is thus mortally flawed. Or if he is motivated by sex or power, he is not a scientist, and his science is only one means among many possible to attain those ends. This contradiction runs throughout the natural and social sciences. They give an account of things that cannot possibly explain the conduct of their practitioners. The highly ethical economist who speaks only about gain, the public-spirited political scientist who sees only group interest, the physicist who signs petitions in favor of freedom while recognizing only unfreedom—mathematical law governing moved matter—in the universe are symptomatic of the difficulty of providing a self-explanation for science and a ground for the theoretical life, which has dogged the life of the mind since early modernity but has become particularly acute with cultural relativism. Nietzsche, in response to this difficulty, self-consciously made dangerous experiments with his own philosophy, treating its source as the will to power instead of the will to truth.

Nietzsche's new beginning in philosophy starts from the observation that a shared sense of the *sacred* is the surest way to recognize a culture, and the key to understanding it and all of its facets. Hegel made this clear in his philosophy of history, and he had found the same awareness in Herodotus' studies of various peoples, Greek and barbarian. What a people bows before tells us what it is. But Hegel made a mistake; he believed there could be a thoroughly rational God, one who conciliated the demands of culture and those of science. Yet somehow he also saw that this was not so when he said that the owl of Minerva flies at dusk, meaning that only when a culture is over can it be understood. Hegel's moment of understanding of the West coincided with its end. The West had been demythologized and had lost its power to inspire and its view of the future. Therefore, it is evident that its myths are what animates a culture, and the makers of myths are the makers of cultures and of man. They are superior to philosophers, who only study and analyze what the poets make. Hegel admits that poetry has lost its prophetic power but consoles himself with the belief that philosophy will suffice.

The artists whom Nietzsche saw around him, those whose gifts were the greatest, attested to this loss. They were what he called decadents, not because they lacked talent or their art was not impressive, but because their works were laments of artistic impotence, characterizations of an ugly world that the poets believe they cannot influence. Immediately after the French Revolution there had been a stupendous artistic effervescence, and poets thought they could again be the legislators of mankind. The vocation provided for the artists in the new philosophy of culture heartened them, and a new classic age was born. Idealism and romanticism appeared to have carved out a place for the sublime in the order of things. But within a generation or two the mood had noticeably soured, and artists began to represent the romantic visions as a groundless hoax. Men like Baudelaire and Flaubert turned away from the public and made the moralism and romantic enthusiasm of their immediate predecessors look foolish. Adulteries without love, sins without punishment or redemption became the more authentic themes of art. The world had been disenchanted. Baudelaire presented sinning man as in the Christian vision, but without hope of God's salvation, piercing pious fraudulence, *hypocrite lecteur*. And Flaubert drowned in a venomous hatred of the bourgeoisie, which had conquered. Culture was just fodder for its vanity. The great dualisms had collapsed; and art, creativity and freedom had been swallowed up by determinism and petty self-interest. In his greatest creation, M. Homais, the pharmacist, Flaubert encapsulated everything that modernity was and is to be. Homais represents the spirit of science, progress, liberalism, anticlericalism. He lives carefully with an eye to health. His education contains the best that has been thought and said. He knows everything that ever happened. He knows that Christianity helped to free the slaves, but that it has outlived its historical usefulness. History existed to produce him, the man without prejudices. He is at home with everything, and nothing is beyond his grasp. He is a journalist, disseminating knowledge for the enlightenment of the masses. Compassion is his moral theme. And all this is nothing but petty *amour-propre*. Society exists to give him honor and self-esteem. Culture is his. There are no proper heroes to depict nor audiences to inspire. They are all one way or another in business. Emma Bovary is Homais' foil. She can only dream of a world and men who do not and cannot exist. In this sober world she is nothing but a fool. She, like the modern artist, is pure longing with no possible goal. Her only triumph and her only free act is suicide.

Nietzsche finds these decadents, pessimists or protonihilists revelatory, as he does the fakers of great deeds and passions who are the reverse side of the coin, in particular Wagner. He has contempt for the former, not because they lack honesty or because their characterization of the world around them is inaccurate, but because they know that once there were gods and heroes and that they were the products of poetic imagination—which means that poetic imagination can make them again—yet do not have the courage or the resolve themselves to create. Therefore they are hopeless. They alone can still long; but they are secret believers in the Christian God or, at least, in the Christian *worldview* and cannot believe in the really new. They are afraid to set sail on stormy, uncharted seas. Only Dostoyevski has a vitality of soul, proof against decadence. His unconscious, filtered through a Christian conscience, expresses itself in forbidden desires, crimes, acts of self-abasement, sentimentality and brutality; but he is alive and struggling and proves the continuing health of the animal and all that is in ferment down under.

The artist is the most interesting of all phenomena, for he represents creativity, the definition of man. His unconscious is full of monsters and dreams. It provides the pictures to consciousness, which takes them as given and as "world," and *rationalizes* them. Rationality is only the activity of providing good reasons for what has no reason or is unreasonable. We do what we do out of a fate that is our individuality, but we have to explain and communicate. This latter is the function of consciousness; and when it has been provided with a rich store by the unconscious, its activity is fruitful, and the illusion of its sufficiency is even salutary. But when it has chopped up and chewed over its inheritance, as mathematical physics has now done, there are not enough nourishing plants left whole. Consciousness now requires replenishment.

Thus Nietzsche opened up the great terrain explored by modern artists, psychologists and anthropologists, searching for refreshment for our exhausted culture in the depths of the darkest unconscious or darkest Africa. Not all that Nietzsche asserted is plausible, but its charm is undeniable. He went to the end of the road with Rousseau, and beyond. The side of modernity that is less interesting to Americans, which seeks less for political solutions than for understanding and satisfaction of man in his fullness or completeness, finds its profoundest statement in Nietzsche, who represents the culmination of that second state of nature. Above all he was a friend of artists, who were the first to recognize him when he was disreputable among academics; and among them his influence was clearly most fertile. One need only think of Rilke, Yeats, Proust and Joyce. The greatest philosophic tribute to him is Heidegger's book *Nietzsche,* the most important part of which is entitled "The Will to Power as Art."

Nietzsche restored something like the soul to our understanding of man by providing a supplement to the flat, dry screen of consciousness, which with pure intellect looks at the rest of man as something alien, a bundle of affects of matter, like any other object of physics, chemistry and biology. The unconscious replaces all the irrational things—above all divine madness and eros—which were part of the old soul and had lost significance in modernity. It provides a link between consciousness and nature as a whole, restoring therewith the unity of man. Nietzsche made psychology, as the most important study, possible again; and everything of interest in psychology during the last century—not only psychoanalysis but also Gestalt, phenomenology, and existentialism—took place within the confines of the spiritual continent he discovered. But the difference between the self and the soul remains great because of the change in the status of reason. The reconstitution of man in Nietzsche required the sacrifice of reason, which Enlightenment, whatever its failings, kept at the center. For all the charms of Nietzsche and all that he says to hearten a lover of the soul, he is further away from Plato in this crucial respect than was Descartes or Locke.

Nietzsche's psychology concerns the impulse toward God, for in that impulse the self arrays and displays all its powers; and his influence brought a new burst of religious interest, if not religion, to the intellectual world. God is myth, Nietzsche taught. Myths are made by poets. This is just what Plato says in the *Republic,* and for him it is equivalent to a declaration of war between philosophy and poetry. The aim of philosophy is to substitute truth for myth (which by its very definition is falsehood, a fact too often forgotten in our post-Nietzschean fascination with myth). Since myths are there first and give men their first opinions, philosophy means a critical destruction of myth in favor of truth for the sake of freedom and living naturally. Socrates, as depicted in the Platonic dialogues, questioning and confuting the received opinions, is the model of the philosophic life; and his death at the hands of his countrymen for not believing in their myths epitomizes the risks of philosophy. Nietzsche drew precisely the opposite conclusion from the same facts about myth. There is no nature and no such freedom. The philosopher must do the contrary of what Socrates did. So Nietzsche is the first philosopher ever to have attacked Socrates, because Socrates' life is not the model life, but a corrupt and monstrous one lacking in all nobility. The tragic life, which Socrates defused and purged, is the serious life. The new philosopher is the ally of the poets and their savior, or philosophy is itself the highest kind of poetry. Philosophy in the old mode *demythologizes* and *demystifies*. It has no sense of the sacred; and by *disenchanting* the world and *uprooting* man, it leads into a void. The revelation that philosophy finds nothingness at the end of its quest informs the new philosopher that mythmaking must be his central concern in order to make a world.

The transfusion of this religious mythmaking or value-positing interpretation of social and political experience into the American bloodstream was in large measure effected by Max Weber's language. His success here is, I am tempted to say, miraculous. A good example is his invention, the Protestant Ethic. I read his book of that name in my first social-science course at the University of Chicago when I was being initiated into the modern mysteries. This course was a survey of social-science "classics," among which was also Marx—not only the *Communist Manifesto* but also goodly chunks of *Capital*. Of course, neither Locke nor Smith, the official spokesmen for "capitalism," who might very well even be considered its founders, was on the list, because we were dealing with thinkers whom a contemporary social scientist could take seriously. Marx explained the emergence of capitalism as a historical necessity, in no one's control, the result of class conflict over material property relations. For him Protestantism was just an ideology reflecting capitalist control of the means of production. I did not see, and I am not sure that my teachers saw, that, if Weber was right, Marx—his economics and his revolution, in short, Marxism and the kinds of moral sympathies it inevitably engenders—was finished. Weber purported to demonstrate that there was no such material necessity, that men's "worldviews" or "values" determine their history, spirit compelling matter rather than the other way around. This has the effect of restoring the older view that individual men count for something, that there is human freedom and the need for leadership. Weber said it was Calvin's *charisma* and the vision allied to it, routinized by his followers, that was decisive for the development of capitalism. But how different

Weber's charismatic leader is from the rational statesmen looked to by Locke, Montesquieu, Smith and the *Federalist*. They strive for ends grasped by reason and self-evidently grounded in nature. No values, no creative visions are required for them to see what all reasonable men should see—that hard work is required to have sober, secure and prosperous freedom. Marx is arguably closer to the core of their belief in that respect; although men, according to him, are in the grip of the historical process, that process itself is rational and has as its end the rational freedom of man. Man remains, somehow, the rational animal.

Weber, on the other hand, denies the rationality of the "values" posited by the Calvinists; they are "decisions," not "deliberations," imposed on a chaotic world by powerful personalities, "worldviews" or "world-interpretations" with no foundation other than the selves of the Protestants. Those "values" made the world what it was for the Protestants. They are acts that are primarily of the will, and constitute the self and the world at the same time. Such acts must be unreasonable; they are based on nothing. In a chaotic universe, reason is unreasonable because self-contradiction is inevitable. The prophet becomes the pure model of the statesman—with very radical consequences. This was something new in American social science and should have, but did not, make it clear that a new kind of causality—entirely different from that known to natural science—had entered the scene.

In spite of this, the Weberian language and the interpretation of the world it brings with it have caught on like wildfire. I have read about the Japanese Protestant ethic, the Jewish Protestant ethic. The manifest absurdity of such locutions appears to have struck some, so now "work ethic" is gradually replacing "Protestant ethic," but this is merely an adjustment and barely disguises the point of view that still remains underneath it. Those interested in the free market do not seem to recognize, when they use this language, that they are admitting that their "rational" system needs a moral supplement in order to work, and that this morality is not itself rational—or at least the choice of it is not rational, as they understand reason. Delay of gratification may make sense for the system as a whole, but is it unarguably good for the individual? Is increase of wealth self-evidently superior to poverty for a Christian? If the work ethic is just one choice among many equally valid choices, then the free-market system itself is also just one choice among many. So proponents of the free market should not be surprised when they see that what was once generally agreed upon no longer compels belief. One has to go back to Locke and Adam Smith in a serious way, not just for a set of quotes, to find *arguments* for the rational moral basis of liberal society. This they no longer do; and because they have lost the habit of reading serious philosophic books or of considering them really essential, they probably could not do so. When the liberal, or what came to be called the utilitarian, teaching became dominant, as is the case with most victorious causes, good arguments became less necessary; and the original good arguments, which were difficult, were replaced by plausible simplifications—or by nothing. The history of liberal thought since Locke and Smith has been one of almost unbroken decline in philosophic substance. When the liberal economic thought or way of life was manifestly threatened, its proponents, in order to defend it, took whatever came to hand. A religion must, it seems, be invented for the sole purpose of defending capitalism, whereas the earliest philosophers associated with it thought that religion must, at least, be weakened in order to establish it. And religion, contrary to containing capitalism's propensities, as Tocqueville thought it should do, is now intended to encourage them.

It goes without saying that Weber never for a moment considered whether Calvin might actually have had a revelation from God—which would certainly change the looks of things. Weber's atheism was dogmatic, but he was not interested in proving that Calvin was a charlatan or a madman. He rather preferred to believe in the authenticity of Calvin and other such founding figures as representing peak psychological types who can live and act in the world, who know how to take *responsibility*, who have an inner sureness or commitment. The religious experience is the thing, not God. The old quarrel between reason and revelation is a matter of indifference, because both sides were wrong, had faulty self-understandings. However, revelation teaches us what man is and needs. Men like Calvin are the value producers and hence the models for action in history. We cannot believe in the ground (God) of their experience, but that experience is critical. We are not interested in finding out how they understood themselves but rather in searching in the *self* for the mysterious substitute for their ground. We cannot have, and do not want to have, their peculiar illusions; but we do want values and commitments. The result of this atheistic religiosity is the mysterious musings and language of Weber and many others (think of Sartre) about belief and action, which culminate in something very different from what either religious leaders or rational statesmen ever said or did. It fuses the two kinds of men, but with greater weight given to the former, to the necessity of faith and all that goes with it. The intellectual apparatus accompanying this analysis tends to obscure the alternatives to it, particularly the rational alternatives.

As a result there is a continuous skewing of the historical perspective toward religious explanations. *Secularization* is the wonderful mechanism by which religion becomes nonreligion. Marxism is secularized Christianity; so is democracy; so is utopianism; so are human rights. Everything connected with valuing must come from religion. One need not investigate anything else, because Christianity is the necessary and sufficient condition of our history. This makes it impossible to take Hobbes or Locke seriously as causes of that history, because we know that superficial reason cannot found values and that these thinkers were unconsciously transmitting the values of the Protestant ethic. Reason transmits, routinizes, normalizes; it does not create. Therefore Weber gives short shrift to the rational side of our tradition. Philosophy's claims are ignored; religious claims are revered. Dogmatic atheism culminates in the paradoxical conclusion that religion is the only thing that counts.

Out of this "worldview" issues the gaudy religious word "charisma," which has had such fateful political consequences while becoming one of the most tiresome buzzwords in America. In Chicago there is a Charisma Cleaners, and every street gang leader is called "charismatic." In America charisma is not just a description but something good that has to do with leadership. It even seems to confer an extralegal title to leadership by virtue of "something special" inhering in the leader. Although Weber was thinking of Moses and Buddha, or of Napoleon, the gang leader formally suits his definition of charisma. Weber sought to make a place in politics for things that political legalism excludes and that claim to have a title to attention although they are not founded on reason or consent—the only titles to rule in liberal democracy. It is not to be wondered at, then, that all the demagogic appetites frustrated by our constitutional system should latch on to a word that appears to legitimize and to flatter them. Moreover, democratic individualism does not officially provide much of a place for leaders in a regime where everyone is supposed to be his own master. Charisma both justifies leaders and excuses followers. The very word gives a positive twist to rabble-rousing qualities and activities treated as negative in our constitutional tradition. And its vagueness makes it a tool for frauds and advertising men adept at manipulating images.

Charisma, as Weber knew perfectly well, is God-given grace, which confers leadership through God's sanction. In keeping with his analysis in the *Protestant Ethic,* he treats the self's value-positing as the human truth of God-given grace. His account of it appears to be merely descriptive, but it becomes prescriptive. In passages deeply influenced by Nietzsche, he analyzes the state as a relation of domination of man by man, founded on legitimate violence—that is, violence that is *considered* to be legitimate. Men inwardly accept being dominated if they have certain beliefs. There is no more foundation to legitimacy than the inner justification the dominated make to themselves in order to accept the violence of those who dominate them. These justifications are, according to Weber, of three kinds: traditional, rational, and charismatic. Some men submit because that is the way it has always been; others consent to obey competent civil servants who follow rationally established rules; and others are enchanted by the extraordinary grace of an individual. Of the three, charismatic legitimacy is the most important. No matter what conservatives may think, traditions had a beginning that was not traditional. They had a founder who was not a conservative or a traditionalist. The fundamental values informing that tradition were his creation. The tradition is the continuing half-life of the charmed moment when a happy few could live on the heights of inspiration with the creator. Tradition adjusts that inspiration to the ordinary, universal motives of man, such as greed and vanity; it routinizes the charisma. It is what it is because of that original impulse. So charisma is the condition of both the charismatic and the traditional legitimacies. It is also the splendid form of legitimacy. The rational is not informed by charisma, and the civil servants—bureaucrats —are therefore unable to make real decisions or take responsibility. They cannot, as we would say, determine the broad outlines of policy or, put more classically, establish ends. Mere competence can only serve already established goals and decide according to the established rules. It must be at least supplemented by charismatic leadership in order to be pointed in the right, or any, direction. So again charisma comes out on top. Value creation, the activity that writes the table of laws by which a people is constituted and lives, is, as Nietzsche tells, the nut in the shell of existence.

Whatever the merit of Weber's analysis and categories, they became holy writ for hosts of intellectuals. They were, as Weber recognized, not only an academic exercise. They expressed his vision of the crisis of the twentieth century. This is a case where the alleged facts also spoke the values. The tradition-based regimes had exhausted their impulse and were on their way to extinction. The ones based on rationality were simply becoming the administration for "the last man," the intolerable negative pole. Imperative, then, was a stab at some form of charismatic leadership in order to revitalize the politics of the West. The whole undertaking rested on the assurance that Nietzsche was right that the last man is also the worst possible man, or more generally that his critique of reason was correct.

The problem with charismatic politics is that it is almost impossible to define. There may be examples of it in the past, but they are inimitable. If politics is like art styles (a thought picked up in Weber's invention of the term "life-style"), nothing can be prescribed to it beforehand. There are no fixed principles and no program of action. All that one can say is "Be yourself!"; "Be original!"; "Let go!" or something of the kind. *Charisma* is a formula for extremism and immoderation. Moreover, the leader must have followers, so there is every temptation for him to act out his role as they define it. And, finally, genuine charisma is so difficult to judge. Persuasive tests for the genuineness of the charismatic leader, whose grace comes from God, were notoriously hard to come by. The leader whose grace emanates from the much more enigmatic self proves practically impossible to test. The modern situation as diagnosed by Weber requires radical remedies, and the charismatic leader is such a prescription.

Just over the horizon, when Weber wrote, lay Hitler. He was a leader, *Führer,* who was certainly neither traditional nor rational-bureaucratic. He was the mad, horrible parody of the charismatic leader—the demagogue—hoped for by Weber. Hitler proved to the satisfaction of most, if not all, that the last man is not the worst of all; and his example should have, although it has not, turned the political imagination away from experiments in that direction. Weber was a good man of decent political instincts who would never have had anything but disgust at and contempt for Hitler. What he wanted was a moderate corrective to the ills of German politics—about the same as De Gaulle brought to French politics. But when one ventures out into the vast spaces opened up by Nietzsche, it is hard to set limits. Measure and moderation are the real aliens there. Weber was just one of many serious persons who were affected by Nietzsche and popularized him without believing in the extremism that Nietzsche himself asserted is the result of positioning oneself beyond good and evil. The open-ended future contains many surprises, and all these followers of Nietzsche prepared the way by helping to jettison good and evil along with reason, without assurance of what the alternatives might be. Weber is of particular interest to us because he was the chosen apostle for the American promised land. It is not only the popularity of the heavily freighted language he bequeathed us that is surprising, but also the persistence among supposedly serious persons of his articulation of the political phenomena. Hitler did not cause a rethinking of politics here or in Europe. All to the contrary—it was while we were fighting him that the thought that had preceded him in Europe conquered here. That thought, which gave him at least some encouragement and did nothing to prepare us to understand him, remains dominant.

During the thirties some German Social Democrats became aware that Hitler, as well as Stalin, just would not fit Weber's terms of analysis, which they had previously used; and they began to employ "totalitarian" to describe them. Whether this is a sufficient corrective to Weber's narrowly conceived political science is questionable. But "charismatic" did indeed fit Hitler, unless charismatic necessarily means something good —a favorable value judgment. I suspect that those who abandoned Weber in this way did so because they could not face how wrong he had been, or the possibility that the thought they had embraced and propagated might have helped to support fascism. Hannah Arendt gave perhaps unconscious witness to my suggestion, in her book *Eichmann in Jerusalem*, where she used the now celebrated phrase "the banality of evil," to describe Eichmann. It is not difficult to discern the "routinization of charisma" under this thin disguise. Hitler, then, must have been charismatic. After Hitler, everybody scurried back under the protective cover of morality, but practically no one turned to serious thought about good and evil. Otherwise our President, or the pope, for that matter, would not be talking about values.

This entire language, as I have tried to show, implies that the religious is the source of everything political, social and personal; and it still conveys something like that. But it has done nothing to reestablish religion—which puts us in a pretty pickle. We reject by the fact of our categories the rationalism that is the basis of our way of life, without having anything to substitute for it. As the religious essence has gradually become a thin, putrid gas spread out through our whole atmosphere, it has gradually become respectable to speak of it under the marvelously portentous name *the sacred.* At the beginning of the German invasion of the United States, there was a kind of scientific contempt in universities for the uncleanness of religion. It might be studied in a scholarly way, as part of the past that we had succeeded in overcoming, but a believer was somehow benighted or ill. The new social science was supposed to take the place of morally and religiously polluted teachings just as Galileo, Copernicus, Newton, et al., had, according to the popular mythology, founded a natural science that crushed the superstitions of the Dark Ages. The Enlightenment, or Marxist, spirit still pervaded the land; and religion vs. science was equal to prejudice vs. truth. Social scientists simply did not see that their new tools were based on thought that did not accept the orthodox dichotomies, that not only were the European thinkers looking for something akin to religious actors on the political scene but that the new mind itself, or the self, had at least as much in common with Pascal's outlook as it did with that of Descartes or Locke. The sacred—as the central phenomenon of the self, unrecognizable to scientific consciousness and trampled underfoot by ignorant passers-by who had lost the religious instinct—was, from the outset of the value teaching, taken seriously by thinkers in Germany. That was because they understood what "value" really means. It has taken the softening of all convictions and the blurring of all distinctions for the sacred to be thought to be undangerous and to come into its own here.

Of course, as we use it, it has no more in common with God than does value with the Ten Commandments, commitment with faith, charisma with Moses, or life-style with Jerusalem or Athens. The sacred turns out to be a need, like food or sex; and in a well-ordered community, it must get its satisfactions like the other needs. In our earlier free-thinking enthusiasm, we tended to neglect it. A bit of ritual is a good thing; sacred space[5] along with some tradition must be provided for, as a generation

[5]Note how space—used to mean one's apartment, workshop, office or whatever—has become a trendy word.

ago culture was thought to be a useful supplement. The disproportion between what all these words really mean and what they mean to us is repulsive. We are made to believe that we have everything. Our old atheism had a better grasp of religion than does this new respect for the sacred. Atheists took religion seriously and recognized that it is a real force, costs something and requires difficult choices. These sociologists who talk so facilely about the sacred are like a man who keeps a toothless old circus lion around the house in order to experience the thrills of the jungle.

THE NIETZSCHEANIZATION OF
THE LEFT OR VICE VERSA

I have spoken little of Marx and referred to few of his terms so far, although the whole world is divided into two parts, one of which traces its intellectual lineage back to Locke and the other to Marx, and the latter is much readier to acknowledge its parent than is the former. But this relative neglect is inevitable when one begins with the souls of young Americans, for Marx does not speak to them, and the so-called Marxist teachers who attempt to influence them do not use Marxist language. To put it crudely, Marx has become boring—and not only to American youngsters. In some backwaters, grim autodidacts may still thrill to the rhetoric of "Workers of the world . . ." while Third World presidents of one-party states focus their resentments by invoking the authority of Marx. But in the centers where people keep up-to-date and ideologies are made, Marx has been dead for a long time. The *Manifesto* seems naive. *Capital* just does not persuade its readers that it is the truth about economics or about the inevitable future of man, and therefore worth the hard work it demands to be digested. A few brilliant essays still charm but are not enough on which to found a worldview. The intellectual death of their eponymous hero has not stopped much of the Left from continuing to call itself Marxist, for he represents the poor in their perennial struggle against the rich, and their demand for more equality than liberal societies provide. But beyond that, the Left's nourishment comes from elsewhere. Nothing in Marx resonates in souls furnished by Sartre, Camus, Kafka, Dostoyevski, Nietzsche and Heidegger. Rousseau can still overpower where Marx falls flat.

As an illustration of what has happened to Marx's influence, consider *ideology,* one of the few terms of his that has anything like the popular currency of Weber's terms. (I will discuss the American use of *dialectic* later.)

In Marx, ideology meant the false system of thought elaborated by the ruling class to justify its rule in the eyes of the ruled, while hiding its real selfish motives. Ideology was sharply distinguished in Marx from science, which is what Marx's system is—i.e., the truth based on disinterested awareness of historical necessity. In Communist society there will be no ideology. "The pure mind," to use Nietzsche's formulation, still exists in Marx's thought, as it had in all philosophy—the possibility of knowing the ways things are, an intellectual capacity irreducible to anything else. Ideology is a term of contempt; it must be seen through in order to be seen for what it is. Its meaning is not in itself but requires translation back into the underlying reality of which it is a misleading representation. The man without ideology, the one possessing science, can look to the economic infrastructure and see that Plato's political philosophy, which teaches that the wise should rule, is only a rationalization for the aristocrats' position in a slave economy; or that Hobbes's political philosophy, which teaches man's freedom in the state of nature and the resulting war of all against all, is only the cover for the political arrangements suitable for the rising bourgeoisie. This point of view provides the foundation for intellectual history, which tells the story behind the story. Instead of looking at Plato and Hobbes for information about what courage is—a subject important to us—we should see how their definitions of courage suited those who controlled the means of production.

But what applies to Plato and Hobbes cannot apply to Marx; otherwise the very assertion that these thinkers were economically determined would be itself a deception, simply the ideology for the new exploiters Marx happens to serve. The interpretation would self-destruct. He would not know what to look for in the thinkers who were inevitably and unconsciously in the grip of the historical process, for he would be in the same condition as they were. There are certainly historical preconditions of Marx's science; but they do not detract from the truth of his insight, which is therefore a kind of absolute moment in history that no further history can alter. This truth is the warrant for revolution, and the moral equivalent of the natural rights that warranted the American Revolution. Without it all the killing is unjust and frivolous.

However, by 1905, Lenin was speaking of Marxism as an ideology, which means that it too can make no claim to truth. In less than half a century Marx's absolute had been relativized. The implausibility—on which Nietzsche insisted in his radical historicism—of the absolute moment and of a standpoint outside history had become commonly acknowledged and made Marx a fossil. This was the beginning of the inner rot that has finally made Marxism unbelievable to anyone who thinks. Marxism itself became ideology. The historicization of Marx's thought, the turning of his method against him, now looked like the resolute taking of a stand within the universal flux, the sign of the creative man, a defiance of the meaninglessness of things—that is, it looked this way to those who had fallen under Nietzsche's spell. A parody of this new look is to be found in the person of Sartre, who had all those wonderful experiences of nothingness, the abyss, nausea, commitment without ground—the result of which was, almost without fail, support of the Party line.

Ideology today, in popular speech, is, in the first place, generally understood to be a good and necessary thing—unless it is bourgeois ideology. The evolution of the term was made possible by the abandonment, encouraged by Nietzsche, of the distinction between true and false in political and moral matters. Men and societies need myths, not science, by which to live. In short, ideology became identical to values, and that is why it belongs on the honor roll of terms by which we live. If we examine Weber's three forms of legitimacy—tradition, reason and charisma—which cause men to accept a domination by other men founded on violence, we see immediately that we would call them ideologies, as well as values. Weber, of course, meant that all societies or communities of human beings require such violent domination—as the only way order emerges from chaos in a world with no ordering force in it other than man's creative spirituality—while Marxists still vaguely hope for a world where there are values without domination. This is all that remains of their Marxism, and they can and do fellow-travel with the Nietzscheans a goodly *bout de chemin.* One sees their plight in the fact that ideology no longer has its old partner, science, in their thought, but stands in lonely grandeur.

Moreover, ideology is no longer very distinctly tied to economics, nor is it simply determined. It has been cut loose from necessity's apron strings in creativity's realm. Rational causality just does not, since Nietzsche, seem sufficient to explain the historically unique event or thought. Capitalist ideology is now instinctively taken to be something more like the Protestant ethic than what is described in *Capital*. When one talks to Marxists these days and asks them to explain philosophers or artists in terms of objective economic conditions, they smile contemptuously and respond, "That is vulgar Marxism," as if to ask, "Where have you been for the last seventy-five years?" No one likes to be considered vulgar, so people tend to fall back into embarrassed silence. Vulgar Marxism is, of course, Marxism. Nonvulgar Marxism is Nietzsche, Weber, Freud, Heidegger, as well as the host of later Leftists who drank at their trough—such as Lukacs, Kojève, Benjamin, Merleau-Ponty and Sartre—and hoped to enroll them in the class struggle. To do this, they had to jettison that embarrassing economic determinism. The game is surely up when Marxists start talking about "the sacred."

Very early in this century the effects of the encounter with Nietzsche began to be felt within Marxism. An example is the significance of revolution. Revolution and the violence that accompanies it are, as we have seen, justified in modern political philosophy and provide the most arresting spectacles of modern political history. Revolution took the place of rebellion, faction, or civil war, all of which are obviously bad things, while revolution is the best and greatest event—officially and in the popular imagination of Englishmen, Americans, Frenchmen and Russians. Germany was the only one of the great powers not to have had one, and Marxism was partly invented to provide a bigger and better revolution for Germany, the natural fulfillment of German philosophy, as French philosophy culminated in the French Revolution. Of course, the spilling of blood is involved in revolution, proof of men's preferring liberty to life. But great amounts of blood were not required, and the violence was not thought to be good in itself. The old regime was tottering and needed a push; behind it were the developed conditions for the new order, an order fully justified by nature, reason and history.

More recently, however, this has changed. The violence has a certain charm of its own, the joy of the knife. It proves decision or *commitment*. The new order is not waiting, but has to be imposed by the will of man; it is supported by nothing but the will. *Will* has become the key word, both Right and Left. In the past it was, to be sure, thought that will is necessary but secondary—that the cause came first. Nietzsche formulated the new way most provocatively when he said, "A good war makes sacred every cause." The causes have no status; they are values. It is the positing that is essential. The transformation of violence from a means to at least a kind of end helps to show the difference, and the link, between Marxism and Fascism. Georges Sorel, the author of *Reflections on Violence*, was a man of the Left who influenced Mussolini. The crucial thought goes back to Nietzsche by way of Bergson: If creativity presupposes chaos—hence strife and overcoming—and man is now creating an order of peace in which there is no strife, is successfully rationalizing the world, the conditions for creativity, i.e., humanity, will be destroyed. Therefore chaos must be willed, as against the peace and order of socialism. Marx himself recognized that man's historical greatness and progress came from contradictions he had to struggle to overcome. If, as Marx promises, there are to be no more contradictions after the revolution, will there be man? Older revolutionaries were willing peace, prosperity, harmony and reason, i.e., the last man. The newer breed wills chaos. Hardly anyone swallowed what Nietzsche prescribed whole, but the argument was infectious. It surely was impressive to Italian and German intellectuals in whose eyes the Fascist and Nazi "movements" found favor. *Self-assertion*, not justice or a clear view of the future, was the crucial element.

Thus determination, will, commitment, caring (here is where this now silly expression got its force), concern or what have you become the new virtues. The new revolutionary charm became evident in the U.S. in the sixties, much to the distaste of old Marxists. There is also something of this in the current sympathy for terrorists, because "they care." I have seen young people, and older people too, who are good democratic liberals, lovers of peace and gentleness, struck dumb with admiration for individuals threatening or using the most terrible violence for the slightest and tawdriest reasons. They have a sneaking suspicion that they are face to face with men of real commitment, which they themselves lack. And commitment, not truth, is believed to be what counts. Trotsky's and Mao's correction of Marx in calling for "permanent revolution" takes account of this thirst for the *act* of revolution, and its appeal lies therein. The radical students of the sixties called themselves "the movement," unaware that this was also the language used by young Nazis in the thirties and was the name of a Nazi journal, *Die Bewegung*. *Movement* takes the place of progress, which has a definite direction, a good direction, and is a force that controls men. Progress was what the old revolutions were evidence of. Movement has none of this naive, moralistic nonsense in it. Motion rather than fixity is our condition—but motion without any content or goal not imposed on it by man's will. Revolution in our times is a mixture of what it was earlier thought to be and what André Gide called a gratuitous act, represented in one of his novels by the unprovoked and unmotivated murder of a stranger on a train.

The continuing effort of the mutant breed of Marxists has been to derationalize Marx and turn Nietzsche into a leftist. Nietzsche's colossal political failure is attested to by the facts that the Right, which was his only hope that his teaching would have its proper effect, has utterly disappeared, and he himself was tainted in its ugly last gasp, while today virtually every Nietzschean, as well as Heideggerian, is a leftist. Georg Lukacs, the most prominent Marxist intellectual of this century, set the ball rolling. As a young man in Germany, he frequented the circle of Stefan George as well as that of Max Weber and was aware of the power of the things being discussed there about history and culture. This affected his later work and made him take a look back toward the much richer Hegel, who, for older Marxists, had been simply superseded by Marx.[6]

The mature Marx had almost nothing to say about art, music, literature or education, or about what the life of man would be when the yoke of oppression was lifted. His early "humanistic" writings were looked to by some for the inspiration lacking in the later ones, but they turned out to be thin and derivative stuff. Since the Nietzscheans spoke so marvelously well about all these things, why not just appropriate what they said? So they took over "the last man," whom they identified with Marx's bourgeois, and "the superman," whom they identified with the victorious proletarian after the revolution. The diminution of man and the impoverishment of his spiritual life as inimitably described by Nietzsche strengthened Marx's position, if one just believed that somehow or other

[6]Anyone wishing to see this now popular mixture of Marx with Hegel and Nietzsche-Heidegger in a philosophically serious expression must turn to the works of Alexandre Kojève, the most intelligent Marxist of the twentieth century. He was forced to treat Marx as a mere intellectual who disseminated with a few changes the thought of the real philosopher, Hegel. Moreover, Kojève faced "the last man" question squarely: Marxists, i.e., rationalists, must live with "the last man." He is the result of rational history, Kojève agrees with Nietzsche. Only mystifiers of one kind or another, promoting wild, irrational negativity, could, he thought, avoid this conclusion. Merleau-Ponty and Sartre were strongly influenced by him and took his hint.

capitalism was the cause of "the last man" and that, with capitalism removed, new energies would be released. Radical egalitarism is the cure for the evils of egalitarianism so marvelously portrayed by Nietzsche.

To take another example: Freud talked about interesting things not found anywhere in Marx. The whole psychology of the unconscious was completely alien to Marx, as was its inner motor, eros. None of this could be incorporated directly into Marx. But if Freud's interpretation of the cause of neuroses and his treatment of the maladjusted could itself be interpreted as bourgeois errors that serve enslavement to the capitalist control of the means of production, then Marx would move in on the Freudian scene. What Freud said were permanent contradictions between human nature and society could be set in motion dialectically, and in a socialist society there would be no need for the repression that causes neuroses. So Freud was neatly enrolled in the Marxist legions, adding to the charm of economics that of eros, and thereby providing a solution to the problem of what men are going to do after the revolution—a problem left unsolved by Marx. This is what we find in Marcuse and many others, who simply do not talk about the difficulty posed by the contradiction between Marx's fundamental principles and those of Freud. Two powerful systems are served up in a single package. Freud is the really meaty part of the concoction. Marx provides a generalized assurance that capitalism is indeed at fault and that the problems can be solved by more equality and more freedom, that the liberated people will possess all the virtues.

"The last man" interpretation of the bourgeois is reinforced by a certain ambiguity in the meaning of the word "bourgeois." Bourgeois is associated in the popular consciousness, especially in America, with Marx. But there is also the bourgeois as the enemy of the artists. The capitalist and the philistine bourgeois are supposed to be the same, but Marx presents only the economic side, assuming, without adequate warrant, that it can account for both the moral and esthetic deformities of the bourgeois described by the artists, and for the artists themselves. Doubt that this treatment of the bourgeois and the artist really works is one of the prime motives of those attracted to Nietzsche, whose central theme is the artist. As I have said many times and in many ways, most of the great European novelists and poets of the last two hundred years were men of the Right; and Nietzsche is in that respect merely their complement. For them the problem was in one way or another equality, which has no place for genius. Thus they are the exact opposite of Marx. But somehow he who says he hates the bourgeoisie can be seen to be a friend of the Left. Therefore when the Left got the idea of embracing Nietzsche, it got, along with him, all the authority of the nineteenth- and twentieth-century literary tradition. Goethe and Flaubert and Yeats hated the bourgeosie—so Marx was right: these writers simply had not recognized that the bourgeosie could be overcome by the proletariat. And Nietzsche, taken from the correct angle, can be said to be a proponent of the Revolution. When one reads the early *Partisan Review,* edited entirely by leftists, one sees its unlimited enthusiasm for Joyce and Proust, whom they were introducing to this country, apparently in the opinion that they represented the art of the socialist future, although these artists thought the future of art lay in the opposite direction.

The later Marxists in Germany were haunted by the idea of culture, repelled by the vulgarity of the bourgeoisie, and perhaps wondering whether they could still write out a blank check to culture in the socialist future. They wanted to preserve past greatness, of which they were much more conscious than their predecessors. Their Marxism had really shrunk back within the confines of the traditional hatred of the bourgeois, plus a vague hope that the proletariat would bring about cultural renewal or refreshment. One can easily see this in Adorno. But it is also easy to see that in Sartre and Merleau-Ponty, too, the bourgeois is the real concern. The working-class Marxists still thought about surplus value and other such authentic Marxist concerns. The intellectuals were obsessed by culture and, as Leszek Kolakowski has so aptly pointed out, found themselves without a proletariat. This is why the students of the sixties were so welcome to many of them. But so were they to Heidegger. They reminded him of something.

It is well to point out, in addition, that as prosperity increased, the poor began to become *embourgeoisé.* Instead of an increase in class consciousness and strife, there was a decrease. One could foresee a time, at least in the developed countries, when everybody would be a bourgeois. So another prop was knocked out from under Marxism. The issue is not really rich and poor but vulgarity. Marxists were coming perilously close to the notion that egalitarian man as such is bourgeois, and that they must join him or become culture snobs. Only an absolutely unsubstantiated dogma that the bourgeois worker is just an illness of our economic system and a product of *false consciousness* keeps them from saying, as did

Tocqueville, that this is the nature of democracy and that you must accept it or rebel against it. Any such rebellion would not be Marx's revolution. One might be tempted to assert that these advanced Marxists are just too cultured for egalitarian society. They only avoid that recognition by calling it bourgeois.

In general, sophisticated Marxism became cultural criticism of life in the Western democracies. For obvious reasons it generally stayed away from serious discussion of the Soviet Union. Some of that criticism was profound, some of it superficial and petulant. But none of it came from Marx or a Marxist perspective. It was, and is, Nietzschean, variations on our way of life as that of "the last man." If we look again at that psychology so influential in America of which I spoke in the beginning of this chapter, we are now in a position to see that tradition-directed, other-directed and inner-directed are just slight modifications of Weber's three kinds of legitimacy, with other-directed (read bourgeois) derived from economic or bureaucratic rationality guided by the demands of the market or public opinion, and inner-directed identical to charismatic, to the value-giving self. Weber's prophet is replaced by the socialist, egalitarian individual. There is not a single element of Marx in any of this, other than the absolutely unsubstantiated assertion that the socialist is the self-legislator. Discussion of the inner-directed man is empty. There are no examples that can be pointed to. Weber at least provided some examples, even though his definition may have been problematic. One wonders whether Weber's contention that the value giver is an aristocrat of the spirit is less plausible than that of those who say that just anyone is, if he has the right therapist, or if a socialist society is constructed for him. This egalitarian transformation of Weber permitted anyone who is not to the left to be diagnosed as mentally ill. Left critics of psychoanalysis called it a tool of bourgeois conformism; one wonders, however, whether the critics are not manipulators of psychological therapy in the service of Left conformism. Adorno's meretricious fabrication of the authoritarian and democratic personality types has exactly the same sources as the inner-directed–other-directed typology, and the same sinister implications.

So Nietzsche came to America. His conversion to the Left was easily accepted here as genuine, because Americans cannot believe that any really intelligent and good person does not at bottom share the Will Rogers *Weltanschauung*, "I never met a man I didn't like." Nietzsche's naturalization was accomplished in many waves: some of us went to

Europe to find him; he came with the emigrés; and most recently professors of comparative literature have gotten heavily into the import business, getting their goods from Paris, where deconstructing Nietzsche and Heidegger and reconstructing them on the Left has been the principal philosophical *métier* since the Liberation. From this last source Heidegger and Neitzsche now come under their own names, treading on the red carpet rolled out for them by their earlier envoys. Academic psychology, sociology, comparative literature and anthropology have been dominated by them for a long time. But their passage from the academy to the marketplace is the real story. A language developed to explain to knowers how bad we are has been adopted by us to declare to the world how interesting we are. Somehow the goods got damaged in transit. Marcuse began in Germany in the twenties by being something of a serious Hegel scholar. He ended up here writing trashy culture criticism with a heavy sex interest in *One Dimensional Man* and other well-known books. In the Soviet Union, instead of the philosopher-king they got the ideologist tyrant; in the United States the culture critic became the voice of Woodstock.

OUR IGNORANCE

In reflecting on the language about which I have just written, the thought behind it and the way it has been received in America, I am reminded of one of my teachers, who wrote a Ten Commandments for Americans that began, "I am the Lord thy God who brought thee out of the house of the European tyrants into my own land, America: Relax!" As we have seen, these words we have half digested are the distillations of great questions that must be faced if one is to live a serious life: reason-revelation, freedom-necessity, democracy-aristocracy, good-evil, body-soul, self-other, city-man, eternity-time, being-nothing. Our condition of doubt makes us aware of alternatives but has not until recently given us the means to resolve our doubt about the primacy of any of the alternatives. A serious life means being fully aware of the alternatives, thinking about them with all the intensity one brings to bear on life-and-death questions, in full recognition that every choice is a great risk with necessary consequences that are hard to bear. That is what tragic literature is about. It articulates all the noble things men want and perhaps need and shows how unbearable it is when it appears that they cannot coexist harmoniously. One need only remember what the choice between believing in God or rejecting Him used to entail for those who faced it. Or, to use a lesser but equally relevant example, think of Tocqueville, one of the rarest flowers of the old French aristocracy, choosing equality over the splendor of aristocracy because he believed it to be juster, even though it would never be salubrious for a Pascal, a man who consumed himself in the contemplation of God's existence, and even though the absence of such intransigent confrontation with the grounds of all things would impoverish the life of man and diminish his seriousness. These are real choices, possible only for one who faces real questions.

We, on the other hand, have taken these words, which point toward a rich lode of serious questions, and treated them as though they were answers, in order to avoid confronting them ourselves. They are not Sphinxlike riddles to which we must play the daring Oedipus, but facts behind which we need not go and which structure the world of concern to us. What has existentialism done to being-nothing for us? Or value to good-evil; history to eternity-time; creativity to freedom-necessity; the sacred to reason-revelation? The old tragic conflicts reappear newly labeled as assurances: "I'm OK, you're OK." *Choice* is all the rage these days, but it does not mean what it used to mean. In a free society where people are free—responsible—who can consistently not be "pro-choice"? However, when the word still had some shape and consistency, a difficult choice meant to accept difficult consequences in the form of suffering, disapproval of others, ostracism, punishment and guilt. Without this, choice was believed to have no significance. Accepting the consequences for affirming what really counts is what gives Antigone her nobility; unwillingness to do so is what makes her sister Ismene less admirable. Now, when we speak of the right to choice, we mean that there are no necessary consequences, that disapproval is only prejudice and guilt only a neurosis. Political activism and psychiatry can handle it. In this optic Hester Prynne and Anna Karenina are not ennobling exemplars of the intractability of human problems and the significance of choice, but victims whose sufferings are no longer necessary in our enlightened age of heightened consciousness. America has no-fault automobile accidents, no-fault divorces, and it is moving with the aid of modern philosophy toward no-fault choices.

Conflict is the evil we most want to avoid, among nations, among individuals and within ourselves. Nietzsche sought with his value philosophy to restore the harsh conflicts for which men were willing to die, to restore the tragic sense of life, at a moment when nature had been domesticated and men become tame. That value philosophy was used in America for exactly the opposite purpose—to promote conflict-resolution, bargaining, harmony. If it is only a difference of values, then conciliation is possible. We must respect values, but they must not get in the way of peace.[7] Thus Nietzsche contributed to what he was trying to cure. Conflict, the condition of creativity for Nietzsche, is for us a cry for therapy. I keep thinking of my Atlanta taxi driver and his Gestalt therapy. Kant argued that men are equal in dignity because of their capacity for moral choice. It is the business of society to provide the conditions for such choice and esteem for those who achieve it. With the intermediary of value relativism, we have been able to simplify the formula to: Men are equal in dignity. Our business is to distribute esteem equally. Rawls's *A Theory of Justice* is the instruction manual for such distribution. Kant's theory of justice makes it possible to understand *Anna Karenina* as a significant expression of our situation; Rawls's does the same for *Fear of Flying*.

Our desire for conflict reduction accounts for the great popularity of the word "dialectic"—in our sense, the Marxist sense—for, beginning in opposites it ends in synthesis, all charms and temptations united in harmony. In philosophy and morals the hardest and most essential rule is "You can't eat your cake and have it too," but dialectic overcomes this rule. Socratic dialectic takes place in speech and, although drawn forward by the search for synthesis, always culminates in doubt. Socrates' last word was that he knew that he knew nothing. Marx's dialectic takes place in deed and culminates in the classless society, which also puts an end to theoretical conflicts, now known as ideologies. Historical dialectic provides an absolute ground and happy resolution for our relative life-styles. Marx's formula that "Mankind never sets problems for itself which it cannot solve" suits one side of our national temper. Roosevelt said much the same thing when he announced, "We have nothing to fear but fear itself." This optimism is a national strength and is connected with our original project of mastering of nature. But that project itself is not unproblematic and makes sense only when kept within limits. One of these is the sanctity of human nature. It must not be mastered. Roosevelt's dictum is nonsense when blown up into cosmic proportions. Human nature must not be altered in order to have a problem-free world. Man is not just a problem-solving being, as behaviorists would wish us to believe, but a problem-recognizing and -accepting being.

Marx's appeal does, nonetheless, touch us close to home as the

[7]Nietzsche said that distrusting one's neighbor would be regarded as madness by last men, and they would go voluntarily to the madhouse if they suffered from it. Think of the use of the word "paranoid" today!

fulfillment of what we set out to do—solve problems that God and nature had previously seemed to make insoluble, and earlier men had made a virtue of living with. Man has always had to come to terms with God, love and death. They made it impossible to be perfectly at home on earth. But America is coming to terms with them in new ways. God was slowly executed here; it took two hundred years, but local theologians tell us He is now dead. His place has been taken by the sacred. Love was put to death by psychologists. Its place has been taken by sex and meaningful relationships. That has taken only about seventy-five years. It should not be surprising that a new science, thanatology, or death with dignity, is on the way to putting death to death. Coming to terms with the terror of death, Socrates' long and arduous education, learning how to die, will no longer be necessary. For death isn't what it used to be. What will take its place is not yet clear. Engels had a divination of what is needed when he said that the classless society would last, if not forever, a very long time. This reminds us of Dottore Dulcamare in *The Elixir of Love,* who says that he is known throughout the whole universe—and elsewhere. All one has to do is forget about eternity or blur the distinction between it and temporality; then the most intractable of man's problems will have been resolved. On Sunday mornings educated men used to be harangued about death and eternity, made to give them a bit of attention. This is not a danger to be run in doing battle with the Sunday *New York Times.* Forgetting, in a variety of subtle forms, is one of our primary modes of problem-solving. We are learning to "feel comfortable" with God, love and even death.

The way we digest the European things is well illustrated by the influence of Thomas Mann's *Death in Venice* on American consciousness. The story was enormously popular with generations of university students, for it seemed to express the mysteries and sufferings of sophisticated Europeans. It fit in with our preoccupation of Freud and with the artist; its homosexual theme attracted curiosity, and much more than curiosity in some, at a time when imagination had little to feed on so far as forbidden themes were concerned. It was a little like a compendium of the best that was being said around the turn of the century. In *Death in Venice,* with what I believe to be a rather heavy Freudian hand, Mann analyzes the favorite subject and hero of poets and novelists since the invention of culture—the artist, that is, himself. The setting and the action of the story suggest the decline of the West; and the decay and demise of its hero, Aschenbach, teach the failure of sublimation, the shakiness and hollowness of his cultural superstructure. Underlying it all are hidden drives, primal, untamed, which are the real motives of his higher endeavor. Awareness of this undermines his life work without providing any acceptable alternatives. Much of this is a gloss on Mann's famous statement in *Tonio Kröger* that "the artist is a bourgeois with a guilty conscience," which I take to mean that he was experiencing all the post-romantic doubts about the artist's ground or his access to the sublime, that he thought the reality is the bourgeois, but that the artist's troubled conscience leads him somewhere out above, from the point of view of morals, and somewhere down below, from the point of view of motives. Aschenbach is a writer, an heir to the German tradition, but clearly not the spiritual aristocrat Goethe was. His self-possession is based on lack of self-knowledge. In Venice he touches the roots, finds out what he really wants; but there is nothing noble or even tolerable he can do with his awareness. He withers away horribly, finally dying of the plague afflicting that beautiful but decadent city. The Freudian view of sublimation, as opposed to the Nietzschean, is that there is a fixed goal of sexuality, a natural reality toward which it is pointed. Accordingly, civilized behavior rests on that foundation, is a secondary satisfaction and, hence, really not choiceworthy if the primary satisfaction were available. Freud's account of sexuality cannot help making the careful observer regret civilization and long for direct sexual satisfaction. Nietzsche, on the other hand, thought that writing a poem could be as primary an erotic act as sexual intercourse. There is no fixed nature, just different levels of spirituality. From this point of view, Aschenbach represents both romanticism in its longing for lost nature and scientism in its bleak characterization of nature, with the addition of post-Nietzschean pathos. But *Death in Venice* does deal with the theme common to Freud and Nietzsche—the relation of sexual sublimation to culture. The coming to awareness of the infrastructure of culture is deadly to culture, and Mann is depicting the crisis of a civilization. Sublimation has lost its creative or molding power, and now there is desiccated culture and besmirched nature.

But I do not think this was how it was received by Americans. They were titillated and really took it as an early manifesto of the sexual-liberation movement. Even the most distinguished talents, or especially the most distinguished talents, suffer from these obscure longings repressed by society. There is nothing so bad about them; and people should not be intimidated by public opinion, should learn to accept themselves. They have nothing to fear but fear itself. In short, Aschenbach is a man aching to "come out of the closet." There may have been a bit of this in Mann, the need to be open about repressed desires, which, because of the climate of his time, had to come out in tragic garb, lacerating themselves, weeping and wailing. Surely Gide's Nietzscheanism was motivated largely by this. In order to be sexually liberated, so Gide seems to think, we must be supermen, beyond good and evil. He latches on to Nietzsche's immoralism for the sake of leveling bourgeois sexual morals, using a cannon to kill a gnat. Nietzsche would have had nothing but contempt for this. The man who said all greatness requires "semen in the blood" would not have sympathized with men obsessed by sexual repression, who could not make something sublime out of their eroticism, who longed for "natural" satisfaction and public approval to boot. To Nietzsche, Gide would have appeared to be a bourgeois in nihilistic drag. To the extent that such self-expression might have been Mann's intention, it would have been the sign of his own decadence, his creative impotence and desire to escape responsibility in aimless creature, as opposed to creator, pleasures.

The sexual interpretations of art and religion so powerfully made by Nietzsche, and less powerfully but more popularly made by Freud, had a corrupting effect on Americans. They noticed the sublime less than the sex in sexual sublimation. What in Nietzsche was intended to lead to the heights was used here to debunk the heights in favor of present desire. Any explanation of the higher in terms of the lower has that tendency, especially in a democracy, where there is envy of what makes special claims, and the good is supposed to be accessible to all. And this is one of the deep reasons why Freud found such an immediate audience in America. For all of the Continental *sturm und drang,* he believed in nature, and nature as Locke taught it, animal nature. He just added sex to work to compose his formula for healthy living—"love and work"—for he really could not explain love. This is what we were raised to believe. It accords with science rather than relying, as does Nietzsche, on poetic vapors. There is a solid ground, one that appeals to our native empiricism, in his interpretation of what eros really wants. Moreover, science rather than poetry is our preferred means of talking about the obscene. All this, plus the promise of some kind of satisfaction of our desires and relief from our miseries, made Freud a winner from the outset, the most accessible of all the great Continentals. He provided the license for the centrality of sex in public life, which is so characteristic of our day. He ultimately seemed too moralistic, not open enough. But all one had to do was imagine new social structures that demanded less repression for their functioning. This was where Marx was useful. Or one could simply forget about the problems concerning the relation between eros and culture, or else posit a natural harmony between the two. Freud, riding the crest of a wave of German philosophy, enabled Americans to think the satisfaction of their sexual desires was the most important element of happiness. He provided rationalization for instinct, although this was surely not his intention.

Sex immigrated to the United States with the special status given those who make scientific and literary contributions to our culture. But when it got here, it behaved just like everything else American. Gone was the plaintive tone, the poetry, the justification based on civilization's dependence on sublimation. Just as we had cut away the camouflage disguising economic needs—such as the Parthenon and Chartres—in order to concentrate efficiently on those needs themselves, so we demystified sexual desires, seeing them for what they really are, in order to satisfy them more efficiently. This brought into the Lockean world the second focus of human nature, the one concentrated on by Rousseau and those he influenced. The basic rights are "life, liberty, and the pursuit of property and sex." "Give us your poor, your sexually starved. . . ." Freud made it possible to consider sexual repression a medical complaint, and therefore endowed it with the prestige automatically enjoyed by anything having to do with health in a nation devoted to self-preservation. There is a tendency to neglect Rousseau's reminder that one does not die from not satisfying this hunger, and that even great seducers' lusts can be calmed by the certainty of the death penalty. Thus we demystify economy and sexuality, satisfying their primary demands, taking away what our philosophy tells us is their creative impulse, and then we complain we have no culture. We can always go to the opera between office and bed. In the Soviet Union they are dependent on operas from the bad old days, because tyranny prevents artistic expression; we are dependent on the same operas, because the thirsts that produced artistic need have been slaked. I cannot forget the Amherst freshman who asked in naive and good-natured bewilderment, "Should we go back to sublimation?" To the sugar-free diet substitute, as it were. This is what happened in America to the sublime, in all of the subtle meanings given to it from Rousseau and Kant to Nietzsche and Freud. I was charmed by the lad's candor but could not regard him as a serious candidate for culture. Because we have come to take the unnecessary to be necessary, we have lost all sense of necessity, either natural or cultural.

The crucial step was taken, however, when sex as life-style came on the scene. Up until then there was a certain rough-and-ready natural set of guidelines for sex. In the old America it was taken for granted that sex had a teleology—reproduction—and was treated as a means to this end. Everything not conducive to this is useless and even dangerous, to be forgotten or controlled by law, disapproval, conscience and, yes, reason. Freud had the effect of shaking sex loose from this definite connection. It is a force without an end, capable of serving many functions; and its wild, diffuse energies must be given some form if a person is to be happy. But Freud's real naturalism, underlying the explosive indeterminateness that he borrowed from Nietzsche, and the imperatives of health and the integrated personality provided limitations and a structure for legitimate sexual expression. There is no place in Freud for the satisfaction of the kinds of desire to which Mann gives voice in *Death in Venice*. They are explained and cured by Freud but not accepted on their own terms. In Mann they are somehow premonitory and like cries of the damned plunging into nothingness. Such desires search for significance—perhaps this is the case with everything erotic—but nothing in the world can give it to them. These desires are certainly not satisfied with the transfer of their cases from the tribunal of the judge and the priest to that of the doctor, or with being explained away. People can readily accept reductionism in everything except what most concerns them. Neither bourgeois society nor natural science has a place for the nonreproductive aspect of sex. With the slackening of bourgeois austerity and the concomitant emancipation of the harmless pleasures, a certain tolerance of harmless sex came into fashion. But this was not enough, because nobody really wants his dearest desires to be put in the same category as itching and scratching.

In America, especially, there is always a need for moral justification. Life-style—an expression that came out of the same school of thought as sublimation and was actually understood to be the product of sublimation, but had never been associated with it in America because of the division of labor that had Freud specializing in sublimation and Weber in life-style —turned out to be a godsend. "Life-style" justifies any way of life, as does "value" any opinion. It does away with the natural structure of the world, which is only raw material for the stylist's artistic hand. The very expression makes all moralisms and naturalisms stop short at the limit of the sacred ground, aware of their limits and respectful of creativity. Moreover, with our curious mixture of traditions, life-styles are accorded rights, so defense of them is a moral cause, justifying the sweet passions of indignation at the violators of human rights, against whom these tastes, before they became life-styles, were so politically and psychologically defenseless. Now they can call upon all the lovers of human rights throughout the world to join in their defense, for the threat to any group's rights is a threat to them all. Sadomasochists and Solidarity are bound together in the common cause of human rights, their fates depending on the success of the crusade in their favor. Sex is no longer an activity but a cause. In the past there was a respectable place for marginality, bohemia. But it had to justify its unorthodox practices by its intellectual and artistic achievement. Life-style is so much freer, easier, more authentic and democratic. No attention has to be paid to content.

Life-style was first popularized here to describe and make acceptable the lives of people who do attractive things that are frowned upon by society. It was identical to counterculture. Two great expressions in the American usage, draped in the authority lent by their philosophic genealogy, provided moral warrant for people to live exactly as they please. Counterculture, of course, enjoyed the dignity attaching to culture, and was intended as a reproach to the bourgeois excuse for a culture we see around us. What actually goes on in a counterculture or a life-style— whether it is ennobling or debasing—makes no difference. No one is forced to think through his practices. It is impossible to do so. Whatever you are, whoever you are, is the good. All this is testimony to the amazing power, about which Tocqueville speaks, of abstractions in a democratic society. The mere words change everything. It is also a commentary on our moralism. What begins in a search if not precisely for selfish pleasure —historians of the future will not look back on us as a race of hedonists who knew how to "enjoy," in spite of all of our talk about it—then at least for avoidance of and release from suffering or distress, transmogrified into a life-style and a *right*, becomes the ground of moral superiority. The comfortable, unconstrained life is morality.

One can see this in so many domains across the whole political spectrum. Self-serving is expressed as, and really believed to be, disinterested principle. When one looks at the earnest, middle-class proponents of birth control, abortion and easy divorce—with their social concern, their humorless self-confidence and masses of statistics—one cannot help thinking that all this serves them very well. This is not to deny the reality of the problems presented by too many children for the poor, the terrible consequences of rapes and battered wives. However, none of those problems really belongs to the middle classes, who are not reproducing themselves, are rarely raped or battered, but who are the best-rewarded beneficiaries of what they themselves propose. If one of their proposals entailed a sacrifice of freedom or pleasure for them or their class, they would be more morally plausible. As it is, all their proposals contribute to their own capacity to choose, in the contemporary sense of choice. Motives that could easily be so flawed should not be, but are, the basis for moral smugness. In this case, as in so many others, making sexual relations easy becomes identical to morality. I fear that the most self-righteous of Americans nowadays are precisely those who have most to gain from what they preach. This is made all the more distasteful when their weapons are constructed out of philosophic teachings the intentions of which are the opposite of theirs.

But what strikes me most about Mann's story, and makes me reflect on what has happened in America since such literature first attracted our attention, is his use of Plato. As Aschenbach becomes more and more obsessed by the boy on the beach, quotations from the *Phaedrus*, one of Plato's dialogues on love, keep coming into his head, expressing what he gradually and with horror recognizes is the character of his attraction. Plato had been incorporated into the German tradition, and the *Phaedrus* was probably one of the things Aschenbach was supposed to have read as a schoolboy while learning Greek. But its content, discourses on the love of a man for a boy, was not supposed to affect him. The dialogue, like so much that was in the German education, was another scrap of "culture," of historical information, which had not become a part of a vital, coherent whole. This is symptomatic of the deadness of Aschenbach's own cultural activity. Suddenly this scrap erupts into meaning, pointing the way down into the abyss of repressed desire. It is as a dream; and if you are a Freudian, you have keys for unlocking the meanings of dreams. Raw, physically unacceptable facts, inhabitants of the unconscious, express themselves in hidden ways, gaining covert satisfaction that way. They fasten themselves on consciously acceptable material, which then no longer really means what it seems to mean. It now does and does not express the true meaning. Plato's respectable dialogue is the intermediary between Aschenbach's good conscience and his carnality. Plato found a way of expressing and beautifying, of sublimating, perverse sexuality. So the story presents it. There is no indication that Mann thought one could learn much directly from Plato about eros. One could learn something by applying Freud's insights to Plato and seeing how desire finds rationalizations for itself. Plato was vile body for scientific dissection. Mann was too caught up by the novelty of the Freudian teaching to doubt whether sublimation can really account for the psychic phenomena it claims to explain. He was doctrinaire, or he was sure we know better than did older thinkers. They are mythologists.

Freud and Plato agree about the pervasiveness of eroticism in everything human. But there the similarity ends. Anyone who wished to lay aside his assurance about the superiority of modern psychology might find in Plato a richer explanation of the diversity of erotic expression, which so baffles us and has driven us to our present nonsense. He would see there a rewarding articulation of the possibilities and impossibilities of the fulfillment of erotic desires. Plato both enchants and disenchants eros, and we need both. At least in Mann the tradition in which we could refresh ourselves is present, if not exactly alive. With what he gives us we might embark on our own journey and find more interesting prey than is an Aschenbach. But in America that slender thread, which was already almost stretched to its limit in Mann, has broken. We have no more contact with the tradition. Eros is an obsession, but there is no thought about it, and no possibility of thought about it, because we now take what were only interpretations of our souls to be facts about them. Eros gradually becomes meaningless and low; and there is nothing good for man which is not informed by thought and affirmed by real choice, which means choice instructed by deliberation. Saul Bellow has described his own intention as "the rediscovery of the magic of the world under the debris of modern ideas." That gray net of abstraction, used to cover the world in order to simplify and explain it in a way that is pleasing to us, has become the world in our eyes. The only way to see the phenomena, rather than sterile distillations of them, to experience them in their ambiguity again, would be to have available alternate visions, a diversity of profound opinions. But our ideas have made it difficult to have such experiences in practice, and impossible in theory. How does a youngster who sees sublimation where Plato saw divination learn from Plato, let alone think Plato can speak to him? Souls artificially constituted by a new kind of education live in a world transformed by man's artifice and believe that all values are relative and determined by the private economic or sexual drives of those who hold them. How are they to recover the primary natural experience?

I suspect that if we were to make a law forbidding the use of any of the words on the imposing list in this section, a large part of the population would be silenced. Technical discourse would continue; but all that concerns right and wrong, happiness, the way we ought to live, would become quite difficult to express. These words are there where thoughts should be, and their disappearance would reveal the void. The exercise would be an excellent one, for it might start people thinking about what they really believe, about what lies behind the formulas. Would "living exactly as I please" be speakable as a substitute for "life-style"? Would "my opinion" do for "values"? "My prejudices" for my "ideology"? Could "rabble-rousing" or "simply divine" stand in for "charisma"? Each of the standard words seems substantial and respectable. They appear to justify one's tastes and deeds, and human beings need to have such justification, no matter what they may say. We have to have reasons for what we do. It is the sign of our humanity and our possibility of community. I have never met a person who says, "I believe what I believe; these are just my values." There are always arguments. Nazis had them; Communists have them. Thieves and pimps have them. There may be some people who don't feel they have to make a case for themselves, but they must be either tramps or philosophers.

However, these words are not reasons, nor were they intended to be reasons. All to the contrary, they were meant to show that our deep human need to know what we are doing and to be good cannot be satisfied. By some miracle these very terms became our justification:

nihilism as moralism. It is not the immorality of relativism that I find appalling. What is astounding and degrading is the dogmatism with which we accept such relativism, and our easygoing lack of concern about what that means for our lives. The one writer who does not appeal at all to Americans—who offers nothing for our Marxist, Freudian, feminist, deconstructionist, or structuralist critics to mangle, who provides no poses, sentimentalities or bromides that appeal to our young—is Louis-Ferdinand Céline, who best expresses how life looks to a man facing up to what we believe or don't believe. He is a far more talented artist and penetrating observer than the much more popular Mann or Camus. Robinson, the hero he admires in *Journey to the End of the Night,* is an utterly selfish liar, cheat, murderer for pay. Why does Ferdinand admire him? Partly for his honesty, but mostly because he allows himself to be shot and killed by his girlfriend rather than tell her he loves her. He believes in something, which Ferdinand is unable to do. American students are repelled, horrified by this novel, and turn away from it in disgust. If it could be force-fed to them, it might motivate them to reconsider, to regard it as urgent to think through their premises, to make their implicit nihilism explicit and examine it seriously. As an image of our current intellectual condition, I keep being reminded of the newsreel pictures of Frenchmen splashing happily in the water at the seashore, enjoying the paid annual vacations legislated by Léon Blum's Popular Front government. It was 1936, the same year Hitler was permitted to occupy the Rhineland. All our big causes amount to that kind of vacation.

What is so paradoxical is that our language is the product of the extraordinary thought and philosophical greatness at which this cursory and superficial survey has done nothing more than hint. There is a lifetime and more of study here, which would turn our impoverishing certitudes into humanizing doubts. To return to the reasons behind our language and weigh them against the reasons for other language would in itself liberate us. I have tried to provide the outline of an archeology of our souls as they are. We are like ignorant shepherds living on a site where great civilizations once flourished. The shepherds play with the fragments that pop up to the surface, having no notion of the beautiful structures of which they were once a part. All that is necessary is a careful excavation to provide them with life-enhancing models. We need history, not to tell us what happened, or to explain the past, but to make the past alive so that it can explain us and make a future possible. This is our educational crisis and opportunity. Western rationalism has culminated in a rejection of reason. Is this result necessary?

Many will say that my reports of the decisive influence of Continental, particularly German, philosophy on us are false or exaggerated and that, even if it were true that all this language comes from the source to which I attribute it, language does not have such effects. But the language is all around us. Its sources are also undeniable, as is the thought that produced the language. We know how the language was popularized. I need only think of my Amherst student or my Atlanta taxi driver to be persuaded that the categories of the mind determine the perceptions. If we can believe that Calvinist "worldviews" made capitalism, we can also credit the possibility that the overpowering visions of German philosophers are preparing the tyranny of the future.

I must reiterate that Rousseau, Kant, Hegel and Nietzsche are thinkers of the very highest order. This is, in fact, precisely my point. We must relearn what this means and also that there are others who belong in the same rank.

PART THREE

---◆---

THE UNIVERSITY

FROM SOCRATES' *APOLOGY* TO
HEIDEGGER'S *REKTORATSREDE*

When I was fifteen years old I saw the University of Chicago for the first time and somehow sensed that I had discovered my life. I had never before seen, or at least had not noticed, buildings that were evidently dedicated to a higher purpose, not to necessity or utility, not merely to shelter or manufacture or trade, but to something that might be an end in itself. The Middle West was not known for the splendor of its houses of worship or its monuments to political glory. There was little visible reminiscence of the spiritual heights with which to solicit the imagination or the admiration of young people. The longing for I knew not what suddenly found a response in the world outside.

It was, surely, the fake Gothic buildings. In the course of my education I have learned that they were fake, and that Gothic is not really my taste. But they pointed toward a road of learning that leads to the meeting place of the greats. There one finds examples of a sort not likely to be seen around one, without which one could neither recognize one's own capacities nor know how wonderful it is to belong to the species. This imitation of styles of faraway lands and ages showed an awareness of lack of, and a respect for, the substance expressed by those styles. These buildings were a bow to the contemplative life by a nation addicted more than any other to the active life. The pseudo-Gothic was much ridiculed, and nobody builds like that anymore. It is not authentic, not an expression of what we are, so it was said. To me it was and remains an expression of what we are. One wonders whether the culture critics had as good an instinct about our spiritual needs as the vulgar rich who paid for the buildings. This nation's impulse is toward the future, and tradition seems more of a shackle to it than an inspiration. Reminiscences and warnings from the past are our only monitor as we career along our path. Those despised millionaires who set up a university in the midst of a city that seems devoted only to the American goals paid tribute to what they had neglected, whether it was out of a sense of what they themselves had missed, or out of bad conscience about what their lives were exclusively devoted to, or to satisfy the vanity of having their names attached to the enterprise. (What feeds a man's vanity teaches as much about him as anything.) Education was an American thing, and not only technical education.

For me the promise of these buildings was fully kept. From the moment I became a student there, it seemed plausible to spend all my time thinking about what I am, a theme that was interesting to me but had never appeared a proper or possible subject of study. In high school I had seen many of the older boys and girls go off to the state university to become doctors, lawyers, social workers, teachers, the whole variety of professions respectable in the little world in which I lived. The university was part of growing up, but it was not looked forward to as a transforming experience—nor was it so in fact. No one believed that there were serious ends of which we had not heard, or that there was a way of studying our ends and determining their rank order. In short, philosophy was only a word, and literature a form of entertainment. Our high schools and the atmosphere around them put us in this frame of mind. But a great university presented another kind of atmosphere, announcing that there are questions that ought to be addressed by everyone but are not asked in ordinary life or expected to be answered there. It provided an atmosphere of free inquiry, and therefore excluded what is not conducive to or is inimical to such inquiry. It made a distinction between what is important and not important. It protected the tradition, not because tradition is tradition but because tradition provides models of discussion on a uniquely high level. It contained marvels and made possible friendships consisting in shared experiences of those marvels. Most of all there was the presence of some authentically great thinkers who gave living proof of the existence of the theoretical life and whose motives could not easily be reduced to any of the baser ones people delight in thinking universal. They had authority, not based on power, money or family, but on natural gifts that properly compel respect. The relations among them and between them and students were the revelation of a community in which there is a true common good. In a nation founded on reason, the university was the temple of the regime, dedicated to the purest use of reason and evoking the kind of reverence appropriate to an association of free and equal human beings.

The years have taught me that much of this existed only in my youthful and enthusiastic imagination, but not so much as one might suppose. The institutions were much more ambiguous than I could have suspected, and they have proved much frailer when caught in contrary winds than it seemed they would be. But I did see real thinkers who opened up new worlds for me. The substance of my being has been informed by the books I learned to care for. They accompany me every minute of every day of my life, making me see much more and be much more than I could have seen or been if fortune had not put me into a great university at one of its greatest moments. I have had teachers and students such as dreams are made on. And most of all I have friends with whom I can share thinking about what friendship is, with whom there is a touching of souls and in whom works that common good of which I have just spoken. All of this is, of course, mixed with the weaknesses and uglinesses that life necessarily contains. None of it cancels the low in man. But it informs even that low. None of my disappointments with the university—which is after all only a vehicle for contents in principle separable from it—has ever made me doubt that the life it gave me was anything other than the best one available to me. Never did I think that the university was properly ministerial to the society around it. Rather I thought and think that society is ministerial to the university, and I bless a society that tolerates and supports an eternal childhood for some, a childhood whose playfulness can in turn be a blessing to society. Falling in love with the idea of the university is not a folly, for only by means of it is one able to see what can be. Without it, all these wonderful results of the theoretical life collapse back into the primal slime from which they cannot re-emerge. The facile economic and psychological debunking of the theoretical life cannot do away with its irreducible beauties. But such debunking can obscure them, and has.

Tocqueville on Democratic Intellectual Life

Tocqueville taught me the importance of the university to democratic society. His noble book, *Democracy in America*, gave voice to my inchoate sentiments. His portrait of the "Intellectual Life of the Americans" is the mirror in which we can see ourselves. But, because the broader perspective he brings is alien, we do not immediately recognize ourselves. In my experience, students at first are bored by Tocqueville's account of the American mind, but, if they are really made to pay attention, they are finally riveted and alarmed by it. No one likes to believe that what he can see is limited by circumstances, no matter how easily he recognizes this fact in others. Tocqueville shows how a democratic regime causes a particular intellectual bent which, if not actively corrected, distorts the mind's vision.

The great democratic danger, according to Tocqueville, is enslavement to public opinion. The claim of democracy is that every man decides for himself. The use of one's natural faculties to determine for oneself what is true and false and good and bad is the American philosophic method. Democracy liberates from tradition, which in other kinds of regimes determines the judgment. Prejudices of religion, class and family are leveled, not only in principle but also in fact, because none of their representatives has an intellectual authority. Equal political right makes it impossible for church or aristocracy to establish the bastions from which they can affect men's opinions. Churchmen, for whom divine revelation is the standard, aristocrats in whom the reverences for antiquity are powerful, fathers who always tend to prefer the rights of the ancestral to those of reason, are all displaced in favor of the equal individual. Even if men seek authority, they cannot find it where they used to find it in other regimes. Thus the external impediments to the free exercise of reason have been removed in democracy. Men are actually on their own in comparison to what they were in other regimes and with respect to the usual sources of opinion. This promotes a measure of reason. However, since very few people school themselves in the use of reason beyond the calculation of self-interest encouraged by the regime, they need help on a vast number of issues—in fact, all issues, inasmuch as everything is opened up to fresh and independent judgment—for the consideration of which they have neither time nor capacity. Even the self-interest about which they calculate—the ends—may become doubtful. Some kind of authority is often necessary for most men and is necessary, at least sometimes, for all men. In the absence of anything else to which to turn, the common beliefs of most men are almost always what will determine judgment. This is just where tradition used to be most valuable. Without being seduced by its undemocratic and antirational mystique, tradition does provide a counterpoise to and a repair from the merely current, and contains the petrified remains of old wisdom (along with much that is not wisdom). The active presence of a tradition in a man's soul gives him a resource against the ephemeral, the kind of resource that only the wise can find simply within themselves. The paradoxical result of the liberation of reason is greater reliance on public opinion for guidance, a weakening of independence.

Altogether, reason is exposed at the center of the stage. Although every man in democracy thinks himself individually the equal of every other man, this makes it difficult to resist the collectivity of equal men. If all opinions are equal, then the majority of opinions, on the psychological analogy of politics, should hold sway. It is very well to say that each should follow his own opinion, but since consensus is required for social and political life, accommodation is necessary. So, unless there is some strong ground for opposition to majority opinion, it inevitably prevails. This is the really dangerous form of the tyranny of the majority, not the kind that actively persecutes minorities but the kind that breaks the inner will to resist because there is no qualified source of nonconforming principles and no sense of superior right. The majority is all there is. What the majority decides is the only tribunal. It is not so much its power that intimidates but its semblance of justice. Tocqueville found that Americans talked very much about individual right but that there was a real monotony of thought and that vigorous independence of mind was rare. Even those who appear to be free-thinkers really look to a constituency and expect one day to be part of a majority. They are creatures of public opinion as much as are conformists—actors of nonconformism in the theater of the conformists who admire and applaud nonconformity of certain kinds, the kinds that radicalize the already dominant opinions.

Reason's exposedness in the rational regime is exacerbated by the absence of class in the old sense, based on principles or convictions of right. There is a general agreement about the most fundamental political principles, and therefore doubts about them have no status. In aristocracies there was also the party of the people, but in democracy there is no aristocratic party. This means that there is no protection for the opponents of the governing principles as well as no respectability for them. There were in the past also parties representing ecclesiastical interests against those of monarchs or aristocrats. These too provided a place for dissenting opinions to flourish. In the heat of our political squabbles we tend to lose sight of the fact that our differences of principle are very small, compared to those over which men used to fight. The only quarrel in our history that really involved fundamental differences about fundamental principles was over slavery. But even the proponents of slavery hardly dared assert that some human beings are made by nature to serve other human beings, as did Aristotle; they had to deny the humanity of the blacks. Besides, that question was really already settled with the Declaration of Independence. Black slavery was an aberration that had to be extinguished, not a permanent feature of our national life. Not only slavery, but aristocracy, monarchy and theocracy were laid to rest by the Declaration and the Constitution. This was very good for our domestic tranquility, but not very encouraging for theoretical doubts about triumphant equality. Not only were the old questions of political theorizing held to have been definitively answered, but the resources that nourished diversity concerning them were removed. Democratic conscience and the simple need to survive combine to suppress doubt. The kinds of questions that Tocqueville put to America—the answers to which allowed him to affirm the justice of equality more reasonably and more positively than most of us can do—came out of an experience that we cannot have: his direct experience of an alternative regime and temper of soul—aristocracy. If we cannot in any way have access to something like that experience, our understanding of the range of human possibilities is impoverished, and our capacity to assess our strengths and weaknesses is diminished.

To make that range of possibilities accessible, to overcome the regime's tendency to discourage appreciation of important alternatives, the university must come to the aid of unprotected and timid reason. The university is the place where inquiry and philosophic openness come into their own. It is intended to encourage the noninstrumental use of reason for its own sake, to provide the atmosphere where the moral and physical superiority of the dominant will not intimidate philosophic doubt. And it preserves the treasury of great deeds, great men and great thoughts required to nourish that doubt.

Freedom of the mind requires not only, or not even especially, the absence of legal constraints but the presence of alternative thoughts. The most successful tyranny is not the one that uses force to assure uniformity but the one that removes the awareness of other possibilities, that makes it seem inconceivable that other ways are viable, that removes the sense that there is an outside. It is not feelings or commitments that will render a man free, but thoughts, reasoned thoughts. Feelings are largely formed and informed by convention. Real differences come from difference in thought and fundamental principle. Much in democracy conduces to the assault on awareness of difference.

In the first place, as with all regimes, there is what might be called an official interpretation of the past that makes it appear defective or just a step on the way to the present regime. An example of this is the interpretation of Rome and the Roman empire in Augustine's *City of God.* Rome is not forgotten, but it is remembered only through the lens of victorious Christianity and therefore poses no challenge to it.

Second, sycophancy toward those who hold power is a fact in every regime, and especially in a democracy, where, unlike tyranny, there is an accepted principle of legitimacy that breaks the inner will to resist, and where, as I have said, there is no legitimate power other than the people to which a man can turn. Repugnance at the power of the people, at the fact that the popular taste should rule in all arenas of life, is very rare in a modern democracy. One of the intellectual charms of Marxism is that it explains the injustice or philistinism of the people in such a way as to exculpate the people, who are said to be manipulated by corrupt elites. Thus a Marxist is able to criticize the present without isolating himself from present and future. Almost no one wants to face the possibility that "bourgeois vulgarity" might really be the nature of the people, always and everywhere. Flattery of the people and incapacity to resist public opinion are the democratic vices, particularly among writers, artists, journalists and anyone else who is dependent on an audience. Hostility and excessive contempt for the people is the vice of aristocracies, and is hardly our problem. Aristocracies hate and fear demagogues most of all, while democracies in their pure form hate and fear "elitists" most of all, because they are unjust, i.e., they do not accept the leading principle of justice in those regimes. Hence each regime discounts those who are most likely to recognize and compensate for its political and intellectual propensities, while it admires those who encourage them. But, to repeat, this tendency is more acute in democracy because of the absence of a nondemocratic class. In every regime there is a people; there is not necessarily any other class.

Third, the democratic concentration on the useful, on the solution of what are believed by the populace at large to be the most pressing problems, makes theoretical distance seem not only useless but immoral. When there is poverty, disease and war, who can claim the right to idle in Epicurean gardens, asking questions that have already been answered and keeping a distance where commitment is demanded? The for-its-own-sake is alien to the modern democratic spirit, particularly in matters intellectual. Whenever there is a crunch, democratic men devoted to thought have a crisis of conscience, have to find a way to interpret their endeavors by the standard of utility, or otherwise tend to abandon or deform them. This tendency is enhanced by the fact that in egalitarian society practically nobody has a really grand opinion of himself, or has been nurtured in a sense of special right and a proud contempt for the merely necessary. Aristotle's great-souled man, who loves beautiful and useless things, is not a democratic type. Such a man loves honor but despises it because he knows he deserves better, whereas democratic vanity defines itself by the honors it seeks and can get. The lover of beautiful and useless things is far from being a philosopher—at least as far as is the lover of the useful, who is likely to be more reasonable—but he has the advantage of despising many of the same things the philosopher does and is likely to admire the philosopher for his very uselessness, as an adornment. Great and unusual undertakings are more natural to him than to the lover of the useful, and he believes in and reveres motives that are denied existence by utilitarian psychology. He can take for granted the things that are the ends of most men's strivings—money and status. He is free, and must look for other fulfillments, unless he spends, as in the democratic view he should do, his life helping others to get what he already has. Knowing as fulfillment in itself rather than as task required for other fulfillments is immediately intelligible to him. Finality as opposed to instrumentality, and happiness as opposed to the pursuit of happiness, appeal to the aristocratic temperament. All of this is salutary for the intellectual life, and none of it is endemic to democracy.

Thus the mere announcement of the rule of reason does not create the conditions for the full exercise of rationality, and in removing the impediments to it some of its supports are also dismantled. Reason is only one part of the soul's economy and requires a balance of the other parts in order to function properly. The issue is whether the passions are its servitors, or whether it is the handmaiden of the passions. The latter interpretation, which is Hobbes's, plays an important role in the development of modern democracy and is a depreciation as well as an appreciation of reason. Older, more traditional orders that do not encourage the free play of reason contain elements reminiscent of the nobler, philosophic interpretation of reason and help to prevent its degradation. Those elements are connected with the piety that prevails in such orders. They convey a certain reverence for the higher, a respect for the contemplative life, understood as contemplation of God and the peak of devotion, and a cleaving to eternal beings that mitigates absorption in the merely pressing or current. These are images of philosophic magnificence—which, it must be stressed, are distortions of the original, and can be its bitterest enemies, but which preserve the order of the cosmos and of the soul from which philosophy begins. Tocqueville describes this marvelously well in his moving account of Pascal, whom he evidently regards as the most perfect of men. The possibility of such a human type, the theoretical type, is, according to Tocqueville, most threatened in democracy, and it must be vigorously defended if humanity is not to be grievously impoverished. Much of the theoretical reflection that flourishes in modern democracy could be interpreted as egalitarian resentment against the higher type represented by Pascal, denigrating it, deforming it and interpreting it out of existence. Marxism and Freudianism reduce his motives to those all men have. Historicism denies him access to eternity. Value theory makes his reasoning irrelevant. If he were to appear, our eyes would be blind to his superiority, and we would be spared the discomfort it would cause us.

It is to prevent or cure this peculiar democratic blindness that the university may be said to exist in a democracy, not for the sake of establishing an aristocracy but for the sake of democracy and for the sake of preserving the freedom of the mind—certainly one of the most important freedoms—for some individuals within it. The successful university is the proof that a society can be devoted to the well-being of all, without stunting human potential or imprisoning the mind to the goals of the regime. The deepest intellectual weakness of democracy is its lack of taste or gift for the theoretical life. All our Nobel prizes and the like do nothing to gainsay Tocqueville's appraisal in this regard. The issue is not whether we possess intelligence but whether we are adept at reflection of the broadest and deepest kind. We need constant reminders of our deficiency, now more than in the past. The great European universities used to act as our intellectual conscience, but with their decline, we are on our own. Nothing prevents us from thinking too well of ourselves. It is necessary that there be an unpopular institution in our midst that sets clarity above well-being or compassion, that resists our powerful urges and temptations, that is free of all snobbism but has standards. Those standards are in the first place accessible to us from the best of the past, although they must be such as to admit of the new, if it actually meets those standards. If nothing new does meet them, it is not a disaster. The ages of great spiritual fertility are rare and provide nourishment for other less fertile ones. What would be a disaster would be to lose the inspiration of those ages and have nothing to replace it with. This would make it even more unlikely that the rarest talents could find expression among us. The Bible and Homer exercised their influence for thousands of years, preserved in the mainstream or in backwaters, hardly ever being surpassed in power, without becoming irrelevant because they did not suit the temper of the times or the spirit of a regime. They provided the way out as well as the model for reform.

The university's task is thus well defined, if not easy to carry out or even keep in mind. It is, in the first place, always to maintain the permanent questions front and center. This it does primarily by preserving—by keeping alive—the works of those who best addressed these questions. In the Middle Ages, Aristotle was very much present in the minds of the leading elements of society. He was used as an authority almost on a level with the Church Fathers and was assimilated to them. This was, of course, an abuse of Aristotle, who thought that authority is the contrary of philosophy. His own teaching ought always to be approached with questions and doubts, not faith. The essence of philosophy is the abandonment of all authority in favor of individual human reason. Nevertheless, Aristotle was there, his moderate and sensible views had an effect on the world, and he could be a guide to those who came to have philosophic doubt. In our time, freedom from authority and the independence of reason are commonplaces. Aristotle, however, instead of being properly used—now that we have the proper disposition—has to all intents and purposes disappeared. We would hardly be able to use Aristotle, as did Hegel, to grasp the character of modernity. Instead we are more and more restricted to the narrow experience of the here and now, with a consequent loss of perspective. The disappearance of Aristotle has much less to do with his intrinsic qualities than with a political distaste for him, joined with the lack of intellectual discipline that results from a sense of self-sufficiency. Reason has become a prejudice for us. Rousseau noted that in his time many men were liberals who a century earlier would have been religious fanatics. He concluded that they were not really reasonable, but, rather, conformists. Reason transformed into prejudice is the worst form of prejudice, because reason is the only instrument for liberation from prejudice. The most important function of the university in an age of reason is to protect reason from itself, by being the model of true openness.

Hence, without having the answers, the university knows what openness is and knows the questions. It also knows the regime within which it lives, and the kinds of threats this regime poses to its activity. In a democracy it risks less by opposing the emergent, the changing and the ephemeral than by embracing them, because the society is already open to them, without monitoring what it accepts or sufficiently respecting the old. There the university risks less by having intransigently high standards than by trying to be too inclusive, because the society tends to blur standards in the name of equality. It also risks less by concentrating on the heroic than by looking to the commonplace, because the society levels. In an aristocracy the university would probably have to go in a direction opposite to the one taken in a democracy in order to liberate reason. But in an aristocracy the university is a less important institution than in a democratic society, because there are other centers for the life of the mind, whereas in a democracy there is practically no other center, practically no way of life, calling or profession, that requires or encourages or even permits cultivation. This is increasingly the case in the late twentieth century. The university as an institution must compensate for what individuals lack in a democracy and must encourage its members to participate in its spirit. As the repository of the regime's own highest faculty and principle, it must have a strong sense of its importance outside the system of equal individuality. It must be contemptuous of public opinion because it has within it the source of autonomy—the quest for and even discovery of the truth according to nature. It must concentrate on philosophy, theology, the literary classics, and on those scientists like Newton, Descartes, and Leibniz who have the most comprehensive scientific vision and a sense of the relation of what they do to the order of the whole of things. These must help preserve what is most likely to be neglected in a democracy. They are not dogmatisms but precisely the opposite: what is necessary to fight dogmatism. The university must resist the temptation to try to do everything for society. The university is only one interest among many and must always keep its eye on that interest for fear of compromising it in the desire to be more useful, more relevant, more popular.

The university's task is illustrated by two tendencies of the democratic mind to which Tocqueville points. One is abstractness. Because there is no tradition and men need guidance, general theories that are produced in a day and not properly grounded in experience, but seem to explain things and are useful crutches for finding one's way in a complicated world, have currency. Marxism, Freudianism, economism, behavioralism, etc., are examples of this tendency, and there are great rewards for those who purvey them. The very universality of democracy and the sameness of man presupposed by it encourage this tendency and make the mind's eye less sensitive to differences. All the terms discussed in Part Two are evidences of this abstractness, simulacra of thought and experience, hardly better than slogans, which take the place of reflection. In aristocracies men take the experiences of their nations as unique and superior and tend not to generalize, but rather to forget the natural community of men and the universality of thought. But they do really pay attention to their experiences, to the diversity of phenomena that is homogenized by abstract "mind-sets." This is another thing the democratic university must learn from aristocracies. Our temptation is to prefer the shiny new theory to the fully cognized experience. Even our famous empiricism is more of a theory than an openness to experience. Producing theories is not theorizing, or a sign of the theoretical life. Concreteness, not abstractness, is the hallmark of philosophy. All interesting generalization must proceed from the richest awareness of what is to be explained, but the tendency to abstractness leads to simplifying the phenomena in order more easily to deal with them.

If, for example, one sees only gain as a motive in men's actions, then it is easy to explain them. One simply abstracts from what is really there. After a while one notices nothing other than the postulated motives. To the extent that men begin to believe in the theory, they no longer believe that there are other motives in themselves. And when social policy is based on such a theory, finally one succeeds in producing men who fit the theory. When this is occurring or has occurred, what is most needed is the capacity to recover the original nature of man and his motives, to see what does not fit the theory. Hobbes's mercenary account of the virtues, which won out in psychology, needs to be contrasted with Aristotle's account, which preserves the independent nobility of the virtues. Hobbes was thinking of Aristotle, which we never do, when he developed his teaching. In order to restore what was really a debate, and thereby restore the phenomenon *man,* one must read Aristotle and Hobbes together and look at what each saw in man. Then one has the material on which to reflect. For modern men who live in a world transformed by abstractions and who have themselves been transformed by abstractions, the only way to experience man again is by thinking these abstractions through with the help of thinkers who did not share them and who can lead us to experiences that are difficult or impossible to have without their help.

A related problem is a tendency in the social sciences to prefer deterministic explanations of events to those that see them as results of human deliberation and choice. Tocqueville explains this tendency as a consequence of the impotence of the individual in egalitarian society. Curiously, in democracy, the freest of societies, men turn out to be more willing to accept doctrines that tell them that they are determined, that is, not free. No one by himself seems to be able, or have the right, to control events, which appear to be moved by impersonal forces. In aristocracies, on the other hand, individuals born to high position have too great a sense of their control over what they appear to command, are sure of their freedom and despise everything that might seem to determine them. Neither the aristocratic nor democratic sentiment about the causes of events is simply adequate. In a democracy where men already think they are weak, they are too open to theories that teach that they *are* weak, which, by making individuals think that controlling action is impossible, have the effect of weakening them further. The antidote is again the classic, the heroic—Homer, Plutarch. At the outset they appear hopelessly naive to us. But it is our sophisticated naiveté that makes us think that. Churchill was inspired by his ancestor Marlborough, and his confidence in his own action is inconceivable without the encouragement provided by that model. Marlborough said that Shakespeare was essential to his education. And Shakespeare learned a large part of what he knew about statesmanship from Plutarch. This is the intellectual genealogy of modern heroes. The democratic revolution of the mind extinguishes such old family lines and replaces them with decision-making theory, in which there is no category for statesmanship, let alone heroes.

To sum up, there is one simple rule for the university's activity: it need not concern itself with providing its students with experiences that are available in democratic society. They will have them in any event. It must provide them with experiences they cannot have there. Tocqueville did not believe that the old writers were perfect, but he believed that they could best make us aware of our imperfections, which is what counts for us.

The universities never performed this function very well. Now they have practically ceased trying.

The Relation Between Thought and Civil Society

Although universities go back very far, the university as we know it, in its content and its aim, is the product of the Enlightenment. To enlighten is to bring light where there had previously been darkness, to replace opinion, i.e., superstition, by scientific knowledge of nature, beginning from phenomena available to all men and ending in rational demonstration possible for all men. All things must be investigated and understood by reason, i.e., science or philosophy (the distinction between the two is of recent origin, coming to currency only in the nineteenth century). Knowledge of the nature of all things is Enlightenment's goal. The past was characterized not by ignorance but by false opinions. Men always had opinions about everything, but those opinions were without ground and indemonstrable. Yet they governed the nations of men and were authoritative. Thus the problem of Enlightenment is not merely discovery of the truth but the conflict between the truth and the beliefs of men, which are incorporated into the law. Enlightenment begins from the tension between what men are compelled to believe by city and religion, on the one hand, and the quest for scientific truth on the other. To think and speak doubts about, let alone to propose substitutes for, the fundamental opinions was forbidden by every regime previously known to man. Doing so was thought to be, and in fact was, disloyal and impious.

Of course, the men of the Enlightenment were not the first to recognize this tension. It had existed and been known to exist since science emerged in Greece sometime between the eighth and sixth centuries B.C. Enlightenment thinkers were aware that there had been surpassingly great philosophers, mathematicians, astronomers and political scientists from that time on, who had suffered persecutions and been compelled to live on the fringes of society. The innovation of the Enlightenment was the attempt to reduce that tension and to alter the philosopher's relation to civil society. The learned society and the university, the publicly respected and supported communities of scientists—setting their own rules, pursuing knowledge according to the inner dictates of science, as opposed to civil or ecclesiastical authority, communicating freely among themselves—are the visible signs of that innovation. The earlier thinkers accepted the tension and lived accordingly. Their knowledge was essentially for themselves, and they had a private life very different from their public life. They were themselves concerned with getting from the darkness to the light. Enlightenment was a daring attempt to shine that light on all men, partly for the sake of all men, partly for the sake of the progress of science. The success of this attempt depended on scientists' freedom to associate with and speak to one another. And freedom could be won only if the rulers believed that the scientists were not a threat to them. Enlightenment was not only, or perhaps not even primarily, a scientific project but a political one. It began from the premise that the rulers could be educated, a premise not held by the Enlightenment's ancient brethren.

This project was a conspiracy, as d'Alembert said in the Preliminary Discourse of *l'Encyclopédie,* the premier document of the Enlightenment. It had to be, for, in order to have rulers who are reasonable, many of the old rulers had to be replaced, in particular all those whose authority rested upon revelation. The priests were *the* enemies, for they rejected the claim of reason and based politics and morals on sacred text and ecclesiastical authorities. The philosophers appeared to deny the very existence of God, or at least of the Christian God. The old order was founded on Christianity, and free use of reason simply could not be permitted within it, since reason accepts no authority above itself and is necessarily subversive. There was a public struggle for the right to rule; for, in spite of the modest demeanor of the philosophers, they at the very least require rulers who are favorable to them, who have chosen reason. The right to freedom of thought is a political right, and for it to exist, there must be a political order that accepts that right.

In other words, an argument had to be made that the free pursuit of science is good for society, in order to persuade the most powerful element of society and thus guarantee the protection of that pursuit. In a simple formula, it had to be shown that the progress of knowledge was parallel to political progress. This is by no means a self-evident proposition, as anyone who has read Rousseau's *Discourse on the Arts and Sciences*, a powerful attack on it, knows. But it is the leading principle of Enlightenment and the ultimate ground of the prejudice that most people have in favor of freedom of thought and inquiry. I say prejudice because the reasons have almost been forgotten, and other kinds of thought hostile to freedom of thought are current. The old order offered roots and salvation, and the very latest thought is marked by nostalgia for that old order. The Enlightenment thinkers proposed a political science that could be used by founders, such as in America, in establishing principles and arrangements for a sounder and more efficient politics, and a natural science that could master nature in order to satisfy men's needs. These promises are what make reason not only acceptable within civil society but even central to it. A society based on reason needs those who reason best. The scientists were to be the most respected of men, taking the place of kings and prelates, because they are the evident sources of the good things for life, liberty and the pursuit of property. It was not precisely replacing one faith by another, because the new science, if it cannot be practiced by just anyone, can be understood by anyone, if he is trained in its method, and knowledge of the rights and duties of man requires the use of his reason.

The Enlightenment was a daring enterprise. Its goal was to reconstitute political and intellectual life totally under the supervision of philosophy and science. No conqueror, prophet or founder ever had a broader vision, and none had more stunning success. There is practically no contemporary regime that is not somehow a result of Enlightenment, and the best of the modern regimes—liberal democracy—is entirely its product. And throughout the world all men and all regimes are dependent on and recognize the science popularized by the Enlightenment. The Enlightenment inexorably defeated all opponents it targeted at the outset, particularly the priests and all that depends on them, by a long process of education that taught men, as Machiavelli put it, about "the things of this world." One need only read Adam Smith's *Wealth of Nations,* Book V, on education, to see how the reform of universities, particularly the overcoming of the theological influence, was essential to the emergence of modern political economy and the regime founded on it. Thus the academies and universities are the core of liberal democracy, its foundation, the repository of its animating principles and the continuing source of the knowledge and education keeping the machinery of the regime in motion.

The regime of equality and liberty, of the rights of man, is the regime of reason. The free university exists only in liberal democracy, and liberal democracies exist only where there are free universities. Marxists are right to say that the "bourgeois university" is essentially related to "bourgeois society," but not in the sense they intend. The university does not defend that society because the university merely reflects its interests, but because the balance of forces within this kind of society is such as most to need, respect and, hence, protect, freedom of thought. Earlier associations of thinkers were under theological-political supervision by unquestioned right. Fascism rejected reason and controlled the universities. When Hitler came to power, Karl Schmitt said, "Today Hegel died in Germany." Hegel was arguably the greatest university man there ever was. And communism asserts that the people, under the guise of the vanguard party, has become rational, so that the university no longer needs a special status—i.e., it can be controlled by the Party. Only in liberal democracy is the primacy of reason accepted, even though its citizenry is not understood to be simply and always reasonable. It assures a special status for the university, an exemption from the ordinary moral and political limitations on what can be thought and said in civil society. The university is not the beneficiary of the freedom of thought accorded to all the members of society. All to the contrary, in the original project of modern society, the general freedom of thought was believed to be desirable in order to support the kind of thought proper to philosophers and scientists, which alone strictly deserves the name of "thought." At the outset the primary freedom was freedom of thought, both because reason is the highest faculty and because it is most necessary to the good society. Hobbes, Descartes, Spinoza, Bacon, Locke and Newton had to be free to think and propagate what they learned if there was to be a new kind of society, a new dispensation for mankind.

The very special status of what came to be called academic freedom has gradually been eroded, and there hardly remains an awareness of what it means. There is barely a difference recognized in popular and even university consciousness between academic freedom and job security guaranteed by government, business or unions. It has become assimilated to the economic system and looks like self-interest of a kind that is sometimes approved of and sometimes disapproved of. The rights of science are now not distinguishable from the rights of thought in general, of any description whatsoever. Freedom of speech has given way to freedom of expression, in which the obscene gesture enjoys the same protected status as demonstrative discourse. It is all very wonderful; everything has become free, and no invidious distinctions need to be made. But it is too good to be true. All that has really happened is that reason has been knocked off its perch, is less influential and more vulnerable as it joins the crowd of less worthy claims to the attention and support of civil society. The semitheoretical attacks of Right and Left on the university and its knowledge, the increased demands made on it by society, the enormous expansion of higher education, have combined to obscure what is most important about the university.

The original intention of the reformed academies and universities was to provide a publicly respectable place—and a means of support—for theoretical men, of whom at best there are only a few in any nation, to meet, exchange their thoughts and train young persons in the ways of science. The academies and universities were to be engines in the progress of science. The right that reformers attempted to establish was for scientists to be unhindered in the use of their reason, in the areas in which they are competent, to solve the problems posed by nature. Reason and competence are to be underlined here. "Intellectual honesty," "commitment" and that kind of thing have nothing to do with the university, belong in the arenas of religious and political struggle, only get in the way of the university's activity, and open it to suspicion and criticism of which it has no need. Freedom of thought and freedom of speech were proposed in theory, and in the practice of serious political reformers, in order to encourage the still voice of reason in a world that had always been dominated by fanaticisms and interests. How freedom of thought and speech came to mean the special encouragement and protection of fanaticism and interests is another of those miracles connected with the decay of the ideal of the rational political order. The authors of *The Federalist* hoped their scheme of government would result in the preponderance of reason and rational men in the United States. They were not particularly concerned with protecting eccentric or mad opinions or life-styles. Such protection, which we now often regard as the Founders' central intention, is only an incidental result of the protection of reason, and it loses plausibility if reason is rejected. These authors did not respect the many religious sects or desire diversity for its own sake. The existence of many sects was permitted only to prevent the emergence of a single dominant one.

The moment of the Enlightenment's success seems also to have been the beginning of its decay. The obscuring of its intention as a result of its democratization is symptomatic of the inner difficulties of its project. That project entailed freedom for the rare theoretical men to engage in rational inquiry in the small number of disciplines that treat the first principles of all things. This requires an atmosphere where the voice of reason is not drowned by the loud voices of the various "commitments" prevailing in political life. Knowledge is the goal; competence and reason are required of those who pursue it. The disciplines are philosophy, mathematics, physics, chemistry, biology and the science of man, meaning a political science that discerns the nature of man and the ends of government. This is the academy. Dependent on it are a number of applied sciences—particularly engineering, medicine and law—that are lower in dignity and derivative in knowledge, but produce the fruits of science that benefit the unscientific and make them respectful of science. Thus the advantage of the knowers, who want to pursue knowledge, and that of those who do not know, those who want to pursue their well-being, are served simultaneously, establishing a harmony between them. And thus the age-old gulf separating the wise from those who hold power is bridged, and *the* problem of the wise in civil society is solved. The project was a unity reflecting the unity of the intelligible order of nature, its parts organized according to the order of the parts of the whole, joined together finally in a survey of the articulated whole made by the culminating science—philosophy.

This project has lost its unity and is in crisis. Reason is unable to establish its unity, to decide what should be in it, to divide up the intellectual labor. It floats without compass or rudder.

If the university is indeed the product of the Enlightenment and is its visible presence in modern democracy, and if Enlightenment was a political project that undertook to alter the age-old character of the relation between wisdom and power, knowledge and society, it might be suspected that the crisis of knowledge that has become politically useful —i.e., the crisis of the university—and the crisis of liberal democracy, the political order dependent on knowledge, have something to do with the new relationship between the two promoted by Enlightenment.

I have included among the Enlightenment philosophers men like Machiavelli, Bacon, Montaigne, Hobbes, Descartes, Spinoza and Locke, along with the eighteenth-century thinkers like Montesquieu, Diderot and Voltaire, whose teachings are usually held to constitute the Enlightenment, because these latter were quite explicit about their debt to the originators of what the Enlightenment was in large measure only popularizing. The men of the Enlightenment proper were the first whose teachings were addressed not only, or primarily, to other philosophers or potential philosophers of the same rank, and who were concerned not only with those who understand but also with changing the opinions of mankind at large. Enlightenment was the first philosophically inspired "movement," a theoretical school that is a political force at the same time. The very word Enlightenment conveys this mixture of elements, as does Marxism, whereas Platonism and Epicureanism refer strictly to theories—which may have had this or that effect but whose essence is only theoretical. Although Plato and Aristotle had political philosophies, there is no regime to which one can point as a Platonic or an Aristotelian regime, in the sense that either thinker had founded the movement or party that actually established the regime. But Enlightenment is certainly responsible for liberal democracy, as is Marxism for communism. Intellectual historians have frequently been too impressed by these recent events in philosophy and politics to recognize how recent they are, that they constitute a new phenomenon in both domains, and that what is most profound and interesting about Enlightenment is its radical and self-conscious break with the philosophical tradition in the mode and degree of its political activity.

The Enlightenment thinkers understood themselves to be making a most daring innovation: according to Machiavelli, modern philosophy was to be politically effective, while Plato and Aristotle, and all the ancients who followed them since Socrates founded political philosophy were politically ineffective. Machiavelli claimed that he taught the effective truth, and he and practically all those who followed him endeavored to be politically effective. Machiavelli follows Callicles in Plato's *Gorgias,* who ridicules Socrates for being unable to defend himself, to avert insults or slaps in the face. The vulnerability of the philosopher would seem to be the starting place for the new reflection and the renewal of philosophy. This may seem trivial to many today, but the entire philosophic tradition, ancient and modern, took the relation of mind to society as the most fruitful beginning point for understanding the human situation. Certainly the first philosophy of which we have a full account begins with the trial and execution of the philosopher. And Machiavelli, the inspirer of the great philosophical systems of modernity, starts from this vulnerability of reason within the political order and makes it his business to correct it.

Some might say it was not concern with the fate of philosophers but the wish, in Bacon's phrase, to ease man's estate that motivated the modern thinkers. This, however, comes down to the same thing—a criticism of the ancient philosophers for their impotence, and a reflection on the relation of knowledge to civil society. The ancients were always praising virtue, but men were not made more virtuous as a result. Everywhere there were rotten regimes, tyrants persecuting peoples, rich exploiting poor, nobles keeping down commoners, men insufficiently protected by laws or arms, etc. Wise men saw clearly what was wrong in all this, but their wisdom did not generate power to do anything about it. The new philosophy claimed to have discovered the means to reform society and to secure the theoretical life. If the two purposes were not identical, they were intended to be complementary.

It must be remembered that this was a dispute within philosophy and that there was an agreement among the parties to it about what philosophy is. The moderns looked to and disagreed with the Greek philosophers and their heirs, the Roman philosophers. But they shared the view that philosophy, and with it what we call science, came to be in Greece and had never, so far as is known, come to be elsewhere. Philosophy is the rational account of the whole, or of nature. Nature is a notion that itself is of Greek origin and requisite to science. The principle of contradiction guided the discourse of all, and the moderns presented reasoned arguments against those of their predecessors with whom they disagreed. The moderns simply took over a large part of ancient astronomy and mathematics. And they, above all, agreed that the philosophic life is the highest life. Their quarrel is not like the differences between Moses and Socrates, or Jesus and Lucretius, where there is no common universe of discourse, but more like the differences between Newton and Einstein. It is a struggle for the possession of rationalism by rationalists. This fact is lost sight of, partly because scholasticism, the use of Aristotle by the Roman Catholic Church, was the phantom of philosophy within the old order that was violently attacked by the modern philosophers, more out of antitheological ire than by dislike of ancient philosophy. Another reason why the essential agreement between ancients and moderns is no longer clear is the modern science of intellectual history, which tends to see all differences of opinion as differences of "worldview," which blurs the distinction between disagreements founded on reason and those founded on faith.

The very term Enlightenment is connected with Plato's most powerful image about the relation between thinker and society, the cave. In the *Republic*, Socrates presents men as prisoners in a dark cave, bound and forced to look at a wall against which are projected images that they take to be the beings and that are for them the only reality. Freedom for man means escaping the bonds, civil society's conventions, leaving the cave and going up to where the sun illuminates the beings and seeing them as they really are. Contemplating them is at once freedom, truth and the greatest pleasure. Socrates' presentation is meant to show that we begin from deceptions, or myths, but that it is possible to aspire to a nonconventional world, to nature, by the use of reason. The false opinions can be corrected, and their inner contradictions impel thoughtful men to seek the truth. Education is the movement from darkness to light. Reason projected on to the beings about which at first we only darkly opine produces enlightenment.

The moderns accepted that reason can comprehend the beings, that there is a light to which science aspires. The entire difference between ancients and moderns concerns the cave, or nonmetaphorically, the relation between knowledge and civil society. Socrates never suggests that, even in the unlikely event that philosophers should be kings and possess absolute wisdom, the nature of the cave could be altered or that a civil society, a people, a *dēmos,* could do without false opinions. The philosophers who returned to the cave would recognize that what others take to be reality is only image, but they could not make any but the happy few able to see the beings as they really are. They would guide the city reasonably, but in their absence the city would revert to unreason. Or to put it in another way, the unwise could not recognize the wise. Men like Bacon and Descartes, by contrast, thought that it was possible to make all men reasonable, to change what had always and everywhere been the case. Enlightenment meant to shine the light of being in the cave and forever to dim the images on the wall. Then there would be unity between the people and the philosopher. The whole issue turns on whether the cave is intractable, as Plato thought, or can be changed by a new kind of education, as the greatest philosophic figures of the seventeenth and eighteenth century taught.

As Plato tells us, Socrates was charged with impiety, of not holding the same gods the city held, and he was found guilty. Plato always presents Socrates as the archetypical philosopher. The events of Socrates' life, the problems he faced, represent what the philosopher as such must face. The *Apology* tells us that *the* political problem for the philosopher is the gods. It makes clear that the images on the wall of the cave about which men will not brook contradiction represent the gods. Socrates' reaction to the accusation is not to assert the right of academic freedom to pursue investigations into the things in the heavens and under the earth. He accepts the city's right to demand his belief. His defense, not very convincing, is that he is not a subversive. He asserts the great dignity of philosophy and tries as much as possible to reduce the gap between it and good citizenship. In other words, he temporizes or is insincere. His defense cannot be characterized as "intellectually honest" and is not quite to contemporary taste. He only wants to be left alone as much as possible, but is fully aware that a man who doubts what every good citizen is supposed to know and spends his life sitting around talking about virtue, rather than doing virtuous deeds, comes into conflict with the city. Characteristically, Socrates lives with the essential conflicts and illustrates them, rather than trying to abolish them. In the *Republic* he attempts to unite citizenship with philosophy. The only possible solution is for philosophers to rule, so there would be no opposition between the city's commands and what philosophy requires, or between power and wisdom. But this outline of a solution is ironic and impossible. It only serves to show what one must live with. The regime of philosopher-kings is usually ridiculed and regarded as totalitarian, but it contains much of what we really want. Practically everyone wants reason to rule, and no one thinks a man like Socrates should be ruled by inferiors or have to adjust what he thinks to them. What the *Republic* actually teaches is that none of this is possible and that our situation requires both much compromise and much intransigence, great risks and few hopes. The important thing is not speaking one's own mind, but finding a way to have one's own mind.

Contrary to common opinion, it is Enlightenment that was intent on philosophers' ruling, taking Socrates' ironies seriously. If they did not have the title of king, their political schemes were, all the same, designed to be put into practice. And they were put into practice, not by begging princes to listen to them but by philosophy's generating sufficient power to force princes to give way. The rule of philosophy is recognized in the insistence that regimes be constructed to protect the rights of man. The anger we experience on reading Socrates' censorship of the poets is unself-conscious, if we agree, as we willy-nilly do, that children must be taught the scientific method prior to any claims of the imagination on their belief or conduct. Enlightenment education really does what Socrates only tentatively proposes. Socrates, at least, tries to preserve poetry, whereas Enlightenment is almost indifferent to its fate. The fact that we think there should be poetry classes as well as education in reasoning helps us to miss the point: What happens to poetic imagination when the soul has been subjected to a rigorous discipline that resists poetry's greatest charms? The Enlightenment thinkers were very clear on this point. There is no discontinuity in the tradition about it. They were simply solving the problem to the advantage of reason, as Socrates wished it could be solved but thought it could not. Enlightenment is Socrates respected and free to study what he wants, and thereby it is civil society reconstituted. In the *Apology*, Socrates, who lives in thousandfold poverty because he neither works nor has inherited, proposes with ultimate insolence that he be fed at public expense at city hall. But what is the modern university, with its pay and tenure, other than a free lunch for philosophy and scientists?

Moreover, the Enlightenment's explicit effort to remove the religious passion from politics, resulting in distinctions like that between church and state, is motivated by the wish to prevent the highest principle in political life from being hostile to reason. This is the intention in the *Republic* of Socrates' reform of the stories about the gods told by the poets. Nothing that denies the principle of contradiction is allowed to be authoritative, for that is the reef against which Socrates foundered. But Socrates did not think that church and state could be separated. He would have treated both terms as artificial. The gods are believed to be the founders of every city and are its most important beings. He would not have dared to banish them in defense of himself.

The Enlightenment thinkers took on his case and carried on a war against the continuing threat to science posed by first causes that are irrational or beyond reason. The gradual but never perfect success of that war turns the desire to be reasonable into the right to be reasonable, into academic freedom. In the process, political life was rebuilt in ways that have proved intolerable to many statesmen and thinkers, and have gradually led to the reintroduction of religion and the irrational in new and often terrifying guises. This is what Socrates would have feared.

But here I am only indicating the unity of the tradition, that Enlightenment is an attempt to give political status to what Socrates represents. The academy and the university are the institutions that incorporate the Socratic spirit more or less well. Yet the existence of these institutions underlines at the same time how they differ from Socrates, who founded no institutions and had only friends. And the attacks on these institutions made first by Rousseau and then by Nietzsche are attacks on Socratic rationalism made in a Socratic spirit. The history of Western thought and learning can be encapsulated in the fate of Socrates, beginning with Plato defending him, passing through the Enlightenment institutionalizing him, and ending with Nietzsche accusing on him. The cherishing, for two and a half millennia, of the memory of this man, who was put to death by the city for philosophizing, ends with his spiritual execution in the name of culture at the hands of the latest of the great philosophers. Both city and culture are authorized by the sacred.

The meditation on Socrates is the inspiring theme of philosophy from Plato and Aristotle, through Farabi and Maimonides, Machiavelli, Bacon, Descartes, Spinoza, Locke, Rousseau and Hegel, to Nietzsche and Heidegger. Socrates is the complementary man whose enigmatic being leads to reflection on the nature of the knowers.

The Philosophic Experience

The character of the experience Socrates represents is important because it is the soul of the university. That experience and the relation to civil society of those who have it—which is the general formula for the problem of the university—is the continuous theme of Plato's and Xenophon's writings, which give us a flesh-and-blood Socrates, presenting the ambiguous material for judging him ourselves, showing us how such a man lives, the questions he raises, the different kinds of friends he has, his relations to the rulers, the laws and the gods, and the effects he has on the world around him. This forces us to ask, for example, what influence Socrates' humiliation of the political men had on the young Alcibiades, who was destined to become prominent among them. Socrates was not the first philosopher to have collided with the city, but he is the first to have benefited from a dramatic, poetic representation of his way of life, which placed him among the heroes and permitted, or rather necessitated, reflection not only about what he taught but also about the man himself and how he fitted into the city. This rich drama of the early philosopher who came to the attention of the city because he was a philosopher, presents all the questions of freedom of thought from all the angles, without any kind of doctrinairism, and hence provides us with a fresh view of the importance and also of the difficulties of such freedom. From the *Republic,* which really takes seriously only the demands of knowledge, to the *Laws,* which gives full attention to the competing demands of political life, Socrates as perfecter and as dissolver of the community reveals all the facets of his activity. The difficulty he and the other philosophers contend with from the law is not to be confounded with society's prejudice against outsiders, dissenters or nonconformists but is, at least apparently, a result of an essential opposition between the two highest claims on a man's loyalty—his community and his reason. That opposition can only be overcome if the state is rational, as in Hegel, or if reason is abandoned, as in Nietzsche. However that may be, we have a record, unparalleled in its detail and depth, of this first appearance of philosophy, and we can apprehend the natural, or at least primitive, responses to it, prior to philosophy's effect on the world. This provides a view of the beginning at a time when we may be witnessing the end, partly because we no longer know that beginning.

The poetry written about Socrates by Plato and Xenophon is already in the defensive mode, a rehabilitation of the condemned man. The first statement of the city's reaction to Socrates is made by Aristophanes. What luck Socrates had! Not only did he command the pens of Plato and Xenophon; he also was the central figure of the greatest work of the consummate genius of comedy. *The Clouds* often arouses indignation in those who care little for Socrates but think serious matters are not laughing matters. Socrates' fate and Aristophanes' possible contribution to it trouble them. But Socrates was probably not of their persuasion. He laughed and joked on the day of his death. He and Aristophanes share a certain levity. Aristophanes does present a ridiculous Socrates and takes the point of view of the vulgar, to whom Socrates does look ridiculous. But Aristophanes also ridicules the vulgar. Reading him we, indeed, laugh at the wise as do the ignorant, but we also laugh at the ignorant as do the wise. Above all we laugh at the anger of the ignorant against the wise.

The Socrates of *The Clouds* is a man who despises what other people care about and cares about what they despise. He spends his life investigating nature, worrying about gnats and stars, denying the existence of the gods because they are not to be found in nature. His maps have only a tiny dot where Athens looms large to its citizens. Law and convention *(nomos)* mean nothing to him, because they are not natural but manmade. His companions are pale-faced young men totally devoid of common sense. In this academy, which has established itself in the free atmosphere of Athens, these eccentrics carry on their activities without appearing to be other than harmless cranks. They are poor, without any fixed means of support. Socrates receives gifts and apparently countenances minor thefts, literally to keep body and soul together. There is no morality, but they are not vicious people, because their only concern is their studies. Socrates is utterly indifferent to honor or luxury.

Aristophanes recaptures for us the absurdity of a grown man who spends his time thinking about gnats' anuses. We have been too persuaded of the utility of science to perceive how far the scientist's perspective is from that of a gentleman, how shocking and petty the scientist's interests appear to a man who is concerned with war and peace, justice, freedom and glory. If science is just for curiosity's sake, which is what theoretical men believe, it is nonsense, and immoral nonsense, from the viewpoint of practical men. The world loses its proportions. Only Swift has rivalled Aristophanes in picturing the comedy of science. His description of a woman's breast seen through a microscope shows what science means, not in order to denigrate science but to make clear the harsh disproportion between the world most men cling to and the one inhabited by theoretical men.

What Aristophanes satirizes is the exterior of science, how the scientist appears to the nonscientist. He can only hint at the dignity of what the scientist does. His Socrates is not individualized; he is not *the* Socrates we know. He is a member of the species philosopher, student of nature, particularly of astronomy. The first known member of this species was Thales. He was the first man to have seen the cause of, and to predict, an eclipse of the sun. This means he figured out that the heavens move in regular ways that accord with mathematical reasoning. He was able to reason from visible effects to invisible causes and speculate about the intelligible order of nature as a whole. He at that moment became aware that his mind was in accord with the principles of nature, that he was the microcosm.

This moment contains many elements: satisfaction at having solved a problem; pleasure in using his faculties; fullness of pride, more complete than that of any conqueror, for he surveys and possesses all; certitude drawn from within himself, requiring no authorities; self-sufficiency, not depending, for the fulfillment of what is highest in himself, on other men or opinions or on accidents such as birth or election to power, on anything that can be taken from him; a happiness that has no admixture of illusion or hope but is full of actuality. But perhaps most important for Thales was seeing that the poetic or mythical accounts of eclipses are false. They are not, as men believed prior to the advent of science, a sign from the gods. Eclipses are beyond the power of the gods. They belong to nature. One need not fear the gods. The theoretical experience is one of liberation, not only negatively—freeing the thinker from fear of the gods—but also positively, simultaneously a discovery of the best way of life. Maimonides describes the experience of the philosophic use of reason as follows: "This then will be a key permitting one to enter places the gates to which were locked. And when these gates are opened and these places are entered into, the soul will find rest therein, the eyes will be delighted, and the bodies will be eased of their toil and of their labor." What had previously been checked in man's soul comes into full play. Freedom from the myths and their insistence that piety is best permits man to see that knowing is best, the end for which everything else is done, the only end that without self-contradiction can be said to be final. The important theoretical experience leads necessarily toward the first principles of all things and includes an awareness of the good. Man as man, regardless of nation, birth or wealth, is capable of this experience. And it is the only thing men surely have spiritually in common: the demonstrations of science come from within man, and they are the same for all men. When I think the Pythagorean theorem, I know that what is in me at that moment is precisely the same as what is within anyone else who is thinking that theorem. Every other supposedly common experience is at best ambiguous.

Some of this experience still remains within the contemporary natural sciences, and it has a fugitive existence within the humanities. The unity of it all is hardly anywhere to be found or appreciated because philosophy hardly exists today. But it was always understood by philosophers, because they share the experience and are able to recognize it in others. This sense of community is more important for them than any disagreements about the final things. Philosophy is not a doctrine but a way of life, so the philosophers, for all the differences in their teachings, have more in common with one another than with anyone else, even their own followers. Plato saw this in Parmenides, Aristotle in Plato, Bacon in Aristotle, Descartes in Bacon, Locke in Descartes and Newton, and so on.

The tiny band of men who participate fully in this way of life are the soul of the university. This is true in historical fact as well as in principle. Universities came to be where men were inspired by the philosophers' teachings and examples. Philosophy and its demonstration of the rational contemplative life, made possible and, more or less consciously, animated scholarship and the individual sciences. When those examples lost their vitality or were overwhelmed by men who had no experience of them, the universities decayed or were destroyed. This, strictly, is barbarism and darkness. I do not mean that philosophers were ordinarily present in universities any more than prophets or saints are ordinarily present in houses of worship. But because those houses of worship are dedicated to the spirit of the prophets and saints, they are different from other houses. They can undertake many functions not central to that spirit, but they remain what they are because of what they look up to, and everything they do is informed by that reverence. But if the faith disappears, if the experiences reported by the prophets and saints become unbelievable or matters of indifference, the temple is no longer a temple, no matter how much activity of various kinds goes on in it. It gradually withers and at best remains a monument, the inner life of which is alien to the tourists who pass idly through it. Although the comparison is not entirely appropriate, the university is also informed by the spirit, which very few men can fully share, of men who are absent, but it must preserve respect for them. It can admit almost anyone, but only if he or she looks up to and can have an inkling of the dignity of what is going on in it. It is itself always in danger of losing contact with its animating principle, of representing something it no longer possesses. Although it may seem wildly implausible that this group of rare individuals should be the center of what really counts for the university, this was recognized in the universities until only yesterday. It was, for example, well known in the nineteenth-century German university, which was the last great model for the American university. However bad universities may have been, however extraneous accretions may have weighed them down, there was always a divination that an Aristotle or a Newton was what they were all about.

The philosophic life is not the university. Until the nineteenth century most philosophers had nothing to do with universities, and perhaps the greatest abhorred them. One cannot imagine Socrates as a professor, for reasons that are worthy of our attention. But Socrates is of the essence of the university. It exists to preserve and further what he represents. In effect, it hardly does so anymore. But more important is the fact that as a result of Enlightenment, philosophers and philosophy came to inhabit the universities exclusively, abandoning their old habits and haunts. There they have become vulnerable in new ways and thus risk extinction. The classical philosophers would not, for very good reasons, have taken this risk. Understanding these reasons is invaluable for our peculiar predicament.

Although the philosophic experience is understood by the philosophers to be what is uniquely human, the very definition of man, the dignity and charm of philosophy have not always or generally been popularly recognized. This is not the case with the other claimants to the throne, the prophet or the saint, the hero or the statesman, the poet or the artist, whose claims, if not always accepted, are generally recognized to be serious. They were always present, apparently coeval with civil society, whereas philosophers appeared late on the scene and had to make their way. And this has something to do with the problem, but it may be symptom rather than cause. I doubt that the people have much greater access to the typical experiences of prophets, kings and poets than to those of the philosophers. Great imagination, inspiration, intrepidity in the pursuit of glory are further from the ordinary lives of ordinary men than is the experience of reasoning found in the practical arts in daily use, like farming, building, shoemaking, and which is despised by the higher men. Socrates always has to remind his aristocratic interlocutors of these crafts and uses them as models of the knowledge aristocrats lack. But this may indicate part of the difficulty: the people want something higher, something exalted, to admire. And certainly Socrates' person, at first sight anyway, does not provide such an object of admiration, as Aristophanes' comedy makes abundantly clear. Moreover, and more important, the prophets, kings and poets are clearly benefactors of mankind at large, providing men with salvation, protection, prosperity, myths and entertainment. They are the noble bulwarks of civil society, and men tend to regard as good what does good to them. Philosophy does no such good. All to the contrary, it is austere and somewhat sad because it takes away many of men's fondest hopes. It certainly does nothing to console men in their sorrows and their unending vulnerability. Instead it points to their unprotectedness and nature's indifference to their individual fates. Socrates is old, ugly, poor, of no family, without prestige or power in the city, and babbles about Ether's taking Zeus's place.

The kings praised by poetry and illustrated in sculpture are ambiguous. On the one hand they seem to exist for their own sake, beauty in which we do not participate and to which we look up. On the other hand, they are in our service—ruling us, curing us, perhaps punishing us, but for our sakes, teaching us, pleasing us. Achilles is perfection, what most men can only dream about being, and is therefore their superior and properly their master. But he is also their warrior protector, who in order to save Greece overcomes the fear of death that other men cannot overcome. All the heroes are in the business of taking care of and flattering men, the *dēmos*, receiving admiration and glory as their pay. In some sense they are fictions of civil society, whose ends they serve. Not that they do not do the deeds for which they are praised, but the goodness of those deeds is measured, alas, by utility, by the greatest good of the greatest number. The statesman possesses virtues that are supposed to be good in themselves; but he is measured by his success in preserving the people. Those virtues are means to the end of preservation, i.e., the good life is subordinate to and in the service of mere life. If the theoretical life is a good way of life, it cannot, at least in its most authentic expression, be, or seriously be understood to be, in the city's service. It therefore has an almost impossible public relations problem. Socrates hints at this in his *Apology* when, ridiculously—since he was never angry and since he distinguished himself as a soldier exclusively in retreats—he likens himself to Achilles.

The defenselessness of philosophy in the city is what Aristophanes points out and ridicules. He, the poet, has much sympathy with the philosopher's wisdom but prides himself on not being so foolish. He can take care of himself, win prizes from and be paid by the people. His stance is that of the wise guy in the face of the wise man; he is city smart. He warns the philosophers and proves prophetic in comically portraying the city's vengeance. The generation of great men who followed Socrates, including Plato, Xenophon and Isocrates, took the warning very much to heart. Philosophy, they recognized, is weak, precisely because it is new, not necessary, not a participant in the city's power. It is threatened and is a threat to all the beliefs that tie the city together and unite the other high types—priests, poets and statesmen—against philosophy. So Socrates' successors gathered all their strength and made a heroic effort to save and protect philosophy.

Socrates in Aristophanes' story minded his own business, was the subject of rumor and ridicule, until a father who was in debt because of his son's prodigality wanted to free himself of his obligations. Socrates' atheism was the right prescription for him, insofar as it meant that he need not fear Zeus's thunderbolt if he broke the law, if he perjured himself. The law is revealed to be merely manmade, and hence there is no witness to his misdeeds if he can escape the attention of other men. Philosophy liberates this foolish old man. His son, too, is liberated, but with the unexpected consequence that he loses reverence for his father and his mother, who are no longer under divine protection. This the father cannot stand and returns to his belief in the gods, who it turns out protect the family as well as the city. In a rage he burns down Socrates' school.

Aristophanes was prescient. The actual charges against Socrates were corrupting the youth and impiety, with the implication that the latter is the deepest cause of the former. And whatever scholars may say about the injustice of Aristophanes' or Athens' charges, the evidence supports those charges. In the *Republic,* for example, marriages are short-term affairs arranged only for reproduction, the family is dissolved, wise sons rule over and can discipline unwise fathers, and the prohibitions against incest are, to say the least, relaxed. The reverence for antiquity is replaced by reason, and the rule of fathers and the ancestral are disputed. This follows immediately from Socrates' procedures, and it entered into the bloodstream of the West, one of the innumerable effects of philosophy that, for better or worse, are to be found only there. Angry fathers are one of the constituencies mortally hostile to Socrates, who was not trying to achieve this result, or to reform the family. His example and the standards of judgment he invoked simply led to it.

Socrates collided not with culture, society or economy but with the law—which means with a political fact. The law is coercive. The human things impinge on the philosophers in the form of political demands. What philosophers need to survive is not anthropology, sociology or economics, but political science. Thus without any need for sophisticated reasons, political science was the first human science or science of human things that had to be founded, and remained the only one until sometime in the eighteenth century. The stark recognition that he depended on the city, that as he looked up to the heavens he lost his footing on the ground, compelled the philosopher to pay attention to politics, to develop a philosophic politics, a party, as it were, to go along with the other parties, democratic, oligarchic, aristocratic and monarchic, that are always present. He founded the truth party. Ancient political philosophy was almost entirely in the service of philosophy, of making the world safer for philosophy.

Moreover, the law against which Socrates collided was the one concerning the gods. In its most interesting expression the law is the divine law. The city is sacred, it is a theological-political entity. (This is, by the way, why the *Theological-Political Treatise* is for Spinoza *the* book about politics.) The problem for the philosophers is primarily religion. The philosophers must come to terms with its authoritative presence in the city. Socrates in the *Apology* makes some suggestions as to how the philosopher must behave. He must deny that he is an atheist, although he remains ambiguous as to the character of his belief. Any careful reading of the *Apology* makes clear that Socrates never says he believes in the gods of the city. But he does try to make himself appear to be a sign sent from the gods, commanded to do what he does by the Delphic god. Nonetheless he is condemned.

He states his problem succinctly in explaining his way of life to his jurors:

> If I tell you that I would be disobeying the god and on that account it is impossible for me to keep quiet, you won't be persuaded by me, taking it that I am ironizing. And if I tell you that it is the greatest good for a human being to have discussions everyday about virtue and the other things you hear me talking about, examining myself and others, and that the unexamined life is not livable for a human being, you will be even less persuaded.

The people recognize Socrates' irony, his talking down to them, and see how implausible his religious claims are. His irony appears as irony and is therefore not successful. But the truth, unadorned by the Delphic cover, is incomprehensible, corresponding to no experience his audience has. He would be closer to success in sticking to his first story. One can from this very description analyze the political situation. There are three groups of men: most do not understand him, are hostile to him, and vote for his condemnation; a smaller but not inconsiderable group also do not understand Socrates but glimpse something noble in him, are sympathetic to him and vote for his acquittal; finally, a very small group knows what he means when he says the greatest good for a human being is talking about —not practicing—virtue (unless talking about virtue is practicing it). The last group is politically inconsiderable. Therefore the whole hope for the political salvation of philosophy rests with the friendliness of the second group, good citizens and ordinarily pious, but somehow open.

And it was to such men, the gentlemen, that philosophy made its rhetorical appeal for almost two thousand years. When they ruled, the climate for philosophy was more or less salubrious. When the people, the *dēmos,* ruled, religious fanaticism or vulgar utility made things much less receptive to philosophy. Tyrants might be attracted to philosophers, either out of genuine curiosity or the desire to adorn themselves, but they are the most unreliable of allies. All of this rests on a psychological analysis that was forced on the philosophers, who had previously not paid much attention to men or their souls. They observed that the most powerful passion of most men is fear of death. Very few men are capable of coming to terms with their own extinction. It is not so much stupidity that closes men to philosophy but love of their own, particularly love of their own lives, but also love of their own children and their own cities. It is the hardest task of all to face the lack of cosmic support for what we care about. Socrates, therefore, defines the task of philosophy as "learning how to die." Various kinds of self-forgetting, usually accompanied by illusions and myths, make it possible to live without the intransigent facing of death—in the sense of always thinking about it and what it means for life and the things dear in life—which is characteristic of a serious life. Individuals demand significance for this individual life, which is so subject to accident. Most human beings and all cities require the unscientific mixture of general and particular, necessity and chance, nature and convention. It is just this mixture that the philosopher cannot accept and which he separates into its constituent parts. He applies what he sees in nature to his own life. "As are the generations of leaves, so are the generations of men,"—a somber lesson that is only compensated for by the intense pleasure accompanying insight. Without that pleasure, which so few have, it would be intolerable. The philosopher, to the extent that he really only enjoys thinking and loves the truth, cannot be disabused. He cherishes no illusion that can crumble. If he is comic, at least he is absolutely immune to tragedy. Nonphilosophic men love the truth only as long as it does not conflict with what they cherish—self, family, country, fame, love. When it does conflict, they hate the truth and regard as a monster the man who does not care for these noble things, who proves they are ephemeral and treats them as such. The gods are the guarantors of the unity of nature and convention dear to most men, which philosophy can only dissolve. The enmity between science and mankind at large is, therefore, not an accident.

This hostile relationship between the prevailing passions of the philosopher and those of the *dēmos* was taken by the philosophers to be permanent, for human nature is unchanging. As long as there are men, they will be motivated by fear of death. This passion is primarily what constitutes the cave, a horizon within which hope seems justified. Serving the community that lives in the cave, risking one's life for what preserves life, is honored. Vulgar morality is the code of this selfish collectivity, and whatever steps outside its circle is the object of moral indignation. And moral indignation, not ordinary selfishness or sensuality, is the greatest danger to the thinker. The fear that the gods who protect the city will be angered and withdraw their protection induces ecstasies of terror in men and makes them wildly vindictive against those who transgress the divine law. In the *Apology*, Socrates explains why he, such a good citizen, stayed out of Athens' political life. When he presided in the Council he refused to put to the vote—and was overridden—a motion to put to death the commanders of Athens' greatest naval victory because they had prudently refused to try to pick up the bodies of their dead from the water due to a storm that endangered the living. But divine law required the recovery of the bodies, and moral rage insisted on capital punishment for the commanders. Mere prudence cannot override the sacred. Socrates' philosophy has more in common with that prudence than it does with the popular moral fervor, which also caused his death, essentially for putting the prudent above the sacred. This fervor Socrates took to be the substrate of civil society, which would always in the end overpower and deform reason in civil society. Thus there are two possibilities: the philosopher must rule absolutely, or he, "like a man in a storm when dust and rain are blown about by the wind, stands aside under a little wall." There is no third way, or it belongs only to the intellectual, who attempts to influence and ends up in the power of the would-be influenced. He enhances their power and adapts his thought to their ends.

The philosopher wants to know things as they are. He loves the truth. That is an intellectual virtue. He does not love to tell the truth. That is a moral virtue. Presumably he would prefer not to practice deception; but if it is a condition of his survival, he has no objection to it. The hopes of changing mankind almost always end up in changing not mankind but one's thought. Reformers may often be intransigent or extreme in deed, but they are rarely intransigent in thought, for they have to be relevant. But the man who fits most easily into the conventions and is least constrained by struggle with them has more freedom for thought. The real radicalism of ancient thought is covered over by its moderation in political deed, and this misleads many modern scholars. The ancients had no tenure to protect them and wanted to avoid the prostitution to which those who have to live off their wits are prone. There is no moral order protecting philosophers or ensuring that truth will win out in the long, or the short, run.

So philosophers engaged in a gentle art of deception. There is no leaving civil society, no matter what Thoreau may have thought. But they cannot avoid being noticed. They are different. Therefore philosophers allied themselves with the gentlemen, making themselves useful to them, never quite revealing themselves to them, strengthening their gentleness and openness by reforming their education. Why are the gentlemen more open than the people? Because they have money and hence leisure and can appreciate the beautiful and useless. And because they despise necessity. Nietzsche said with some good reason that ancient gentlemen despised eating and sexual intercourse because these acts are forced on them by their animal nature, and they had the pride of the free. And although they tend to be reverent, they can be irreverent, and certainly are less prone to religious fanaticism than the many, because they are less in the grip of fear.

Aristotle in his *Ethics* shows how the philosopher appears as the ally of the gentlemen, speaking to them about the noble deeds that are their specialty (not his). All he apparently does is clarify for them what they already practice. But he makes slight changes that point toward philosophy. Piety is not even included in the list of the individual virtues. And shame, a quality of the noble and a great enemy of reason, is mentioned only in order to be banished from the canon. The virtuous man has nothing to be ashamed of, says Aristotle—an observation that fits Socrates' view of himself but is not typical of gentlemen. And gradually Aristotle turns his readers' attention to the theoretical life, not by seriously theorizing with them but by pointing to the direction in which it lies. He makes it godlike and the completion of their own incompleteness, which they used to achieve by admiring Achilles and revering the Olympian gods. Now they admire the theoretical men who contemplate a thinking god. It is an open question whether the gentleman grasped the essence of philosophy less accurately in this way than does the modern man who respects the scientist because he provides him with useful things.

Similarly in his *Poetics,* Aristotle explains to gentlemanly lovers of the theater what tragedy is and what they get from it. But here too he changes things a bit. The poet is not, as Homer presents himself, inspired by the Muses but is an imitator of nature, i.e., of the same thing the philosophers study, and hence does not depict a world alien to the one studied by philosophy, or one that results from causes in conflict with those admitted by science. Aristotle explicitly connects poetry with philosophy. And the end, the final cause, of tragedy is said to be the purgation of pity and fear, the two passions that combined lead to enthusiasm, religious possession or fanaticism. Socrates had attacked the poets for appealing to those passions that make men ecstatic from terror at what they can suffer and their unprotectedness in their suffering. It is just here, according to Socrates, that reason should be invoked, to face the necessary, to remind men of the order in things that exists in spite of the accidents that happen to them individually. Pity and fear cry out for satisfaction, for attention, for being taken seriously. Above all, the world men incline to see is full of benevolent and malevolent deities who take their cases seriously. Poetry to succeed must speak to these passions, which are more powerful than reason in almost all men. Because poetry needs an audience it is, in Socrates' view, too friendly to the enemies of reason. The philosopher has less need to enter into the wishes of the many or, as the wise of our time would put it, into the drama of history, or to be *engagé.* This is why Socrates heightens the enmity between philosophy and poetry.

Aristotle, actually following Socrates' lead, suggests that the poet can be the doctor of mortals who are so mad as to insist they should be immortal. The poet, not the philosopher, can treat the passions that are dangerous to philosophy, which Socrates had to his great cost ignored. He can arouse these passions in order to flush them out of the soul, leaving the patients more relaxed and calmer, more willing to listen to reason. Aristotle tells the poets they should present heroes who deserve their fates, whose sad ends are plausibly attributable to a flaw in their characters. Their suffering, while pitiable, is not promiscuous, a reproach to the moral order, or the lack of one, in the world. The effect of such drama would be to make men gentle and believers in the coherence of the world, in the rational relation of cause and effect. They are not made reasonable by this but are saved from hatred of reason and more disposed to accept it. Aristotle does not attempt to make scientists out of gentlemen, but he tempers their prevailing passions in such a way as to make them friends of philosophy. Socrates does much the same thing in the *Apology* when he addresses those who voted for his acquittal and tells them *myths* that tend to make death seem less terrible. The tales are not true, but they reinforce the gentleness that kept them from fearing and hence condemning Socrates. Socrates criticizes poetry in order to encourage it to be an ally of the philosophers instead of the priests.

Thus philosophy's response to the hostility of civil society is an educational endeavor, rather more poetic or rhetorical than philosophic, the purpose of which is to temper the passions of gentlemen's souls, softening the hard passions such as anger, and hardening the soft ones such as pity. The model for all such efforts is the dialogues of Plato, which together rival the *Iliad* and the *Odyssey,* or even the Gospels, introducing a new hero who excites admiration and imitation. To introduce a new hero, a new taste has to be established, and the taste for Socrates is unique, counter to all previous tastes. Plato turns the personage of *The Clouds* into one of those civilization-constituting figures like Moses, Jesus or Achilles, who have a greater reality in men's souls than do their own flesh-and-blood contemporaries. As Achilles is said to have formed Alexander the Great; Alexander, Caesar; and Caesar, Napoleon—reaching out to one another from the peaks across the valleys—so Socrates is the teacher of philosophers in an unbroken chain for two and a half millennia, extending from generation to generation through all the epochal changes. Plato insured this influence, not by reproducing Socrates' philosophy, in the manner of Aristotle or Kant, but by representing his action, more in the manner of Sophocles, Aristophanes, Dante and Shakespeare. Socrates is made to touch the prevailing passion of each of the different kinds of soul in such a way as appear to be divinatory of their longings and necessary to their self-understanding. There are dialogues that touch the pious; some move the ambitious and the idealistic; others excite the erotic and still others the warriors and the politicians; some speak to the poets, others to the mathematicians; lovers of money are no more forgotten than are lovers of honor. There is hardly anyone who is not made indignant by one aspect or another of Socrates' discourse, but there is also hardly anyone who is not moved and heartened by other aspects. Socrates stated the case for all human types better than they could have stated it for themselves. (He, of course, also stated the problem with each of those types and their aspirations.) Plato demonstrates the need for Socrates and in so doing makes the need felt in his readers. It is not only Alcibiades who felt incomplete without Socrates.

In almost no case was there a total conversion of a man. Certainly none is ever depicted in the dialogues. Plato himself, and a few others, were converted to philosophy, and their self-discovery was possible because Socrates was more or less tolerated in Athens. The toleration of philosophy requires its being thought to serve powerful elements in society without actually becoming their servant. The philosopher must come to terms with the deepest prejudices of men always, and of the men of his time. The one thing he cannot change and will not try to change is their fear of death and the whole superstructure of beliefs and institutions that make death bearable, ward it off or deny it. The essential difference between the philosopher and all other men is his facing of death or his relation to eternity. He obviously does not deny that many men die resolutely or calmly. It is relatively easy to die well. The question is how one lives, and only the philosopher does not need opinions that falsify the significance of things in order to endure them. He alone mixes the reality of death—its inevitability and our dependence on fortune for what little life we have—into every thought and deed and is thus able to live while honestly seeking perfect clarity. He is, therefore, necessarily in the most fundamental tension with everyone except his own kind. He relates to all the others ironically, i.e., with sympathy and a playful distance. Changing the character of his relationship to them is impossible because the disproportion between him and them is firmly rooted in nature. Thus, he has no expectation of essential progress. Toleration, not right, is the best he can hope for, and he is kept vigilant by the awareness of the basic fragility of his situation and that of philosophy.

Socrates allies himself with those who are powerful in the city and at the same time fascinated or charmed by him. But the charm only endures so long as he does not confront their most important concerns. Crito, the family man, thinks of Socrates as a good family man. Laches, the soldier, thinks of Socrates as a good soldier. Those who get angry at Socrates and accuse him always see something the more gently disposed miss. Thrasymachus sees that Socrates does not respect the city. He sees the truth about Socrates, but he cannot, at least in the beginning, appreciate him. The others appreciate him, but partly because they are blind to what is most important to him. This provides the model for the political tactics followed by the philosophers from Plato up to Machiavelli. None was primarily political, for there was a definite limit on what one could expect from politics, and it was essential not to make the pursuit of the truth dependent on what is politically relevant. Politics was a serious study to the extent that one learned about the soul from it. But the practical politics of all the philosophers, no matter how great their theoretical differences, were the same. They practiced an art of writing that appealed to the prevailing moral taste of the regime in which they found themselves, but which could lead some astute readers outside of it to the Elysian Fields where the philosophers meet to talk. They frequently became the interpreters of the traditions of their nations, subtly altering them to make them open to philosophy and philosophers. They were always suspect, but they also always had their well-placed friends.

For this reason the form and content of the writings of men like Plato, Cicero, Farabi and Maimonides appear very different, while their inner teachings may be to all intents and purposes the same. Each had a different beginning point, a different cave, from which he had to ascend to the light and to which he had to return. Thus they appeared to be "relevant" without forming their minds to the prejudices of the day. This protected them from the necessity or the temptation to conform to what is most powerful. Classical philosophy was amazingly robust and survived changes as great as are imaginable, such as that from paganism to the revealed Biblical religions. Marsilius of Padua was as Aristotelian as was Aristotle, proving that the problems are permanent but their expressions are changing. We moderns think that a comparatively minor change, like that wrought by the French Revolution, necessitates new thought. The ancients held that a man must never let himself be overcome by events unless those events taught something *essentially* new. They were more intent than were any men before or since on preserving the freedom of the mind. This was their legacy to the university. They, however, never let the principle become a dogma and never counted on its having any other ground than their wits. They were ever mindful of the responsibilities and the risks of their enterprise.

In sum, the ancient philosophers were to a man proponents of aristocratic politics, but not for the reasons intellectual historians are wont to ascribe to them. They were aristocratic in the higher sense of the word, because they thought reason should rule, and only philosophers are fully devoted to reason. But this is just a theoretical argument, since philosophers never really do rule. They were aristocratic in the vulgar sense, favoring the power of those possessing old wealth, because such men are more likely to grasp the nobility of philosophy as an end itself, if not to understand it. Most simply, they have the money for an education and time to take it seriously. Only technology, with its attendant problems, makes universal education possible, and therefore opens the prospect of a different kind of relationship of philosophy to politics.

The Enlightenment Transformation

The thinkers of the Enlightenment, as I have said, reproached all earlier philosophers for their powerlessness to help men and themselves. The *Republic*'s formula, that power and wisdom must *coincide* if evils are ever to cease in the cities, is the perfect expression of what the Enlighteners meant. The necessary unity of power and wisdom is only a coincidence for the ancients, i.e., dependent on chance completely out of the philosopher's control. Knowledge is not in itself power, and though it is not in itself vulnerable to power, those who seek it and possess it most certainly are. Therefore the great virtue for the philosophers in their political deeds was moderation. They were utterly dependent on the prejudices of the powerful and had to treat them most delicately. They subjected themselves to a fierce discipline of detachment from public opinion. Although they inevitably had to try to influence political life in their favor, they never seriously thought of themselves as founders or lawgivers. The mixture of unwise power and powerless wisdom, in the ancients' view, would always end up with power strengthened and wisdom compromised. He who flirts with power, Socrates said, will be compelled to lie with it.

The uncompromisable difference that separates the philosophers from all others concerns death and dying. No way of life other than the philosophic can digest the truth about death. Whatever the illusion that supports ways of life and regimes other than the philosophic one, the philosopher is its enemy. There can never be a meeting of minds on this question, as both ancients and moderns agreed. It seemed only natural to the ancients to find their allies among the vulgarly courageous, i.e., those willing to face death with endurance and even intrepidity, although they required unfounded beliefs about the noble, which made them forget about the good. They share the common ground with the philosophers on which something higher than *mere* life rests. But they have no good *reason* for their sacrifice. Achilles' laments and complaints about why he must die for the Greeks and for his friend are very different from Socrates' arguments and the reasoning that underlies them for accepting death—because he is old, because it is inevitable, and because it costs him almost nothing and *might* be useful to philosophy. Anger characterizes Achilles; calculation, Socrates. Whatever sympathy there might be between the two kinds of men is founded, to speak anachronistically, on Achilles' misunderstanding Socrates.

The extraordinary device contrived by the new philosophy that produces harmony between philosophy and politics was to exchange one misunderstanding for another. *All* men fear death and passionately wish to avoid it. Even the heroes who despised it do so against a background of fear, which is primary. Only religious fanatics who believe certainly in a better life after death march gaily to death. If, instead of depending on the rare natures who have a noble attitude toward death, which goes against nature's grain, philosophy could without destroying itself play the demagogue's role—i.e., appeal to the passion that all men have and that is most powerful—it could share in and make use of the power. Rather than fighting what appears to be human nature, by cooperating with it philosophy could control it. In short, if philosophy should be revealed to man not as his moral preceptor but as his collaborator in his fondest dreams, the philosopher could supplant priest, politician and poet in the affection of the multitude. This is what Machiavelli meant when he blamed the old writers for building imaginary principalities and republics that neglect how men actually live in favor of how they ought to live. He counsels writers to accommodate themselves to the dominant passions instead of exhorting men to practice virtues that they rarely perfect, whose goodness for the individuals who practice them is questionable, and the preachings of which are boring to everyone concerned. In a word, turn philosophy into a benefactor, and it will be thought to be good and will enjoy the power accruing to benefactors.

Philosophy can be used to conquer fortune, so Machiavelli announced. It was, of course, fortune—chance—that made it impossible for philosophers to rule, according to Plato. Fortune governs the relations between power and wisdom, which means that men cannot be counted on to consent to the rule of the wise, and the wise are not strong enough to force them to do so. The conquest of fortune meant for Machiavelli that thought and thinkers could compel and guarantee the consent of men. If this is possible, then the ancient philosophers' moderation looks like timidity. Daring in the political arena becomes the new disposition of the philosophers. Danton's *"de l'audace, encore de l'audace, toujours de l'audace,"* is but a pale, merely political, duplicate of Machiavelli's original call to battle. Bacon's assertion that the goal of science is to "ease man's estate," Descartes' assertion that science will make man "master and possessor of nature," and the commonplace that science is the conquest of nature are offsprings of Machiavelli's revolution and constitute the political face adopted by modern philosophy.

The strategy adopted for the assault on the old regime had two parts —one belonging to natural science and the other to political science. First, Descartes proposed that the humble doctor, one of Socrates' ordinary examples of a reasonable artisan, lacking in the political or religious splendor that brings men to the center of the human stage, could, if science were to increase his power to heal a thousandfold, promise enough —if not eternity, at least an ever-increasing longevity—to gain men's attachment and disenchant the priest. Then, Hobbes proposed that if another humble type, the policeman, who protects men against those who administer violent death, could be made effective in a new political order based on fear of violent death, founded by a new kind of political scientist who addresses the passions in a new way, he could ward off the real dangers for men who had been made to look those dangers in the face and thereby away from fear of invisible powers and their ministers. Doctor and policeman, enhanced by the application of science to their endeavors, were to be the foundations of a wholly new political undertaking. If the pursuit of health and safety were to absorb men and they were led to recognize the connection between their preservation and science, the harmony between theory and practice would be established. The actual rulers, after a couple of centuries of astute propaganda directing popular passions against throne and altar, would in the long run be constrained by their subjects and would have to enact the scientists' project. The scientists would, to use Harvey Mansfield's formula, be the hidden rulers. The ends pursued by politicians and the means they use would be determined by philosophers. Scientists would be free and get support, and scientific progress would be identical to political progress so conceived.

The scientists in this system belong to a world order of scientists, for national loyalties and customs are irrelevant to them as scientists. They are cosmopolitan. Gradually the political orders would have to be transformed, so that no particularity remains in the way of reason's operations or produces conflict between the scientist's loyalty to country and his loyalty to truth. There is only one science. It is the same everywhere and produces the same results everywhere. Similarly, there can, in principle, be only one legitimate political order, founded by, on, and for science. There may well remain individual nations with old but decaying traditions stemming from special experiences in the past, and attachment to them may tug at the scientists' cosmopolitanism. But the nations must all gradually become similar. They must respect the rights of man.

This doctrine of rights is the clear and certain rational teaching about justice that was intended to take the place of the ancient teachings, which were "like castles built on sand." In fact, rights are nothing other than the fundamental passions, experienced by all men, to which the new science appeals and which it emancipates from the constraints imposed on them by specious reasoning and fear of divine punishment. These passions are what science can serve. If these passions, given by nature, are what men have permission—a "right"—to seek satisfaction for, the partnership of science and society is formed. Civil society then sets as its sole goal that satisfaction—life, liberty and the pursuit of property—and men consent to obey the civil authority because it reflects their wants. Government becomes more solid and surer, now based on passions rather than virtues, rights rather than duties. These life-preserving passions act as the premises of moral and political reasoning, the form of which is as follows: "If I desire to preserve myself, then I must seek peace. If I seek peace, then . . . etc." On the basis of such evident and deeply felt premises, men's allegiance to government can be a matter of reason rather than passionate faith. Such imperatives are the very opposite extreme from those enunciated in the Ten Commandments, which provide no reasons for obeying their injunctions and do not affirm fundamental passions but inhibit them. Men now owe their clarity about their ends to reasoners. They obey on rational grounds the law that protects them. And they respect, and demand that the government respect, the scientists who most of all can, by the higher use of reason, understand and tame hostile nature, including human nature. Government becomes the intermediary between the scientists and the people.

The rights teachings established the framework and the atmosphere for the modern university. A regime founded on the inclinations of its members is one where freedom, rightly understood, is primary. And the right to know immediately follows from the right to pursue one's own preservation, and to be the judge of the means to that preservation. And the right to know, of those who desire to know and can know, has a special status. The universities flourished because they were perceived to serve society as it wants to be served, not as Socrates served it or Thales failed to serve it. Thus it is indeed true that there is a special kinship between the liberal university and liberal democracy, not because the professors are the running dogs of the "system," but because this is the only regime where the powerful are persuaded that letting the professors do what they want is good. Without this "liberal" framework, the rights that professors claim for themselves are meaningless. The very notion of rights was first enunciated by the founders of liberalism, and its only home is in liberal society, in both theory and practice.

All of this meant that the philosophers switched parties from the aristocratic to the democratic. The people, who were by definition uneducated and the seat of prejudice, could be educated, if the meaning of education were changed from experience of things beautiful to enlightened self-interest. The aristocrats, with their pride, their love of glory, their sense that they are born with the right to rule, now appear to be impediments to the rule of reason. The new philosophers dedicated themselves to reducing the aristocrats back into the commons, removing their psychological underpinnings and denigrating their tastes. This turn to the people can be understood as an appreciation of their decent desire for equality and willingness to contract not to do injustice in return for not suffering injustice, as opposed to the nobles' rejection of equality and willingness to risk suffering injustice in order to be first. Or it can be understood as a hardheaded strategy adopted in order to make use of the people's power. In this the modern philosophers imitated the ancient tyrants who found it easier to satisfy the people than the nobles who dared to rival them. No one has a naturally privileged position other than the knowers.

This turn should not be interpreted as a movement in philosophy from Right to Left. The emergence of a Right and a Left was a consequence of this turn to political activism, away from political accommodationism. The Left is the vehicle of modern philosophy and the Right is the opposition, largely religious, to it. Center is only the old liberalism, when a schism occurs in the philosophical party at the end of the eighteenth century, and a more radical egalitarianism threatens the project of science from within. Left means the transformation of society by Enlightenment, a possibility either not envisaged, or rejected, by all older thinkers. In modernity it is possible for there to be a right-wing philosopher, i.e., one who opposes the philosophic attempt to rationalize society; but in antiquity all philosophers had the same practical politics, inasmuch as none believed it feasible or salutary to change the relations between rich and poor in a fundamental or permanently progressive way. Democratic politics with a moral and intellectual foundation which commands the suffrage of the wise is strictly a modern invention, part and parcel of Enlightenment broadly conceived.

The philosophers, however, had no illusions about democracy. As I mentioned, they knew they were substituting one kind of misunderstanding for another. The gentleman thought that philosophic equanimity in the face of death comes from gentlemanly or heroic courage exercised for the sake of the noble. The man of the people, on the other hand, takes the philosopher's reasonableness about avoiding death to be a product of the passionate fear of death that motivates him. But the philosopher knows that the rational, calculating, economic man seeks immortality just as irrationally as, or even more so than, the man who hopes for eternal fame or for another life, of which the only sign or guarantee is lodged in his hopes but for which he organizes his life. The utilitarian behaves sensibly in all that is required for preservation but never takes account of the fact that he must die. He does everything reasonable to put off the day of his death—providing for defense, peace, order, health and wealth —but actively suppresses the fact that the day must come. His whole life is absorbed in avoiding death, which is inevitable, and therefore he might be thought to be the most irrational of men, if rationality has anything to do with understanding ends or comprehending the human situation as such. He gives way without reserve to his most powerful passion and the wishes it engenders. The hero and the pious man are at least taking account of eternity. Although their wishes may make them mythologize about it, the posture they assume is somehow more reasonable. The philosopher always thinks and acts as though he were immortal, while always being fully aware that he is mortal. He tries to stay alive as long as possible in order to philosophize, but will not change his way of life or his thought in order to do so. He is sensible in a way that heroes can never be; he looks at things under the guise of eternity, as the bourgeois can never do. Therefore he is at one with neither. Only the life devoted to knowing can unite these opposites. Socrates is the tragic hero whose mind is full of the things artisans think about.

The great modern philosophers were as much philosophers as were the ancients. They were perfectly conscious of what separates them from all other men, and they knew that the gulf is unbridgeable. They knew that their connection with other men would always be mediated by unreason. They took a dare on the peculiar form of reasoning that comes from the natural inclinations. They seem to have been confident that they could benefit from the rational aspect and keep the irrational one from overwhelming them. The theoretical life remained as distinct from the practical life in their view as in the ancient one—theory looking to the universal and unchangeable while understanding its relation to the partic-ular and changing; practice, totally absorbed by the latter, seeing the whole only in terms of it, as a theodicy or an anthropodicy, presented as God or History. Philosophy and philosophers always see through such hopes for individual salvation and are hence isolated. The modern philoso-phers knew that theory is pursued for its own sake but took an interest in promoting the opinion that, to paraphrase Clausewitz, theory is just practice pursued by other means.

The philosophers in their closets or their academies have entirely different ends than the rest of mankind. The vision of the harmony of theory and practice is only apparent. The moderns did not think, as did the ancients, that they would lose sight of the distinction between the two in identifying them. This is the most precise definition of their daring. What the ancients almost religiously kept apart, the moderns thought they could join without risk. The issue is: Does a society based on reason necessarily make unreasonable demands on reason, or does it approach more closely to reason and submit to the ministrations of the reasonable? The difficulty is illuminated by the popular contemporary misuse of a Greek word, *praxis*. It now means that there is no theory and no practice, that politics has been theoreticized and philosophy politicized. It expresses the overcoming of the distinction between the eternal and the temporal. This is surely a result of Enlightenment, although it goes counter to the intentions of the Enlighteners. The question is whether it is a necessary or only an accidental result.

It has long been fashionable in some quarters to treat the thinkers of the Enlightenment as optimistic and superficial. This was a view promoted in the wake of the French Revolution by reactionaries and romantics, the counter-coup of the religious and the poetic, which has had considerable and enduring success. The modern philosophers are alleged to have believed in a new dawn in which men would become reasonable and everything would be for the best. They did not, according to this popular view, understand the ineradicable character of evil, nor did they know, or at least take sufficient account of, the power of the irrational of which our later, profounder age is so fully aware. In these pages, I have tried to show that this is a skewed and self-serving interpretation. No one who looks carefully at the project these philosophers outlined can accuse them of being optimistic in the sense of expecting a simple triumph of reason or of underestimating the power of evil. It is not sufficiently taken into account how Machiavellian they were, in all senses of that word, and that they were actually Machiavelli's disciples. It was not by forgetting about the evil in man that they hoped to better his lot but by giving way to it rather than opposing it, by lowering standards. The very qualified rationality that they expected from most men was founded self-consciously on encouraging the greatest of all irrationalities. Selfishness was to be the means to the common good, and they never thought that the moral or artistic splendor of past nations was going to be reproduced in the world they were planning. The combination of hardness and playfulness found in their writings should dispel all suspicion of unfounded hopefulness. What they plotted was "realistic," if anything ever was.

And as to superficiality, everything turns on what the deepest human experience is. The philosophers, ancient and modern, agreed that the fulfillment of humanity is in the use of reason. Man is the particular being that can know the universal, the temporal being that is aware of eternity, the part that can survey the whole, the effect that seeks the cause. Whether it is wonder at the apprehension of being or just figuring things out, reason is the end for which the irrational things exist, and all that seems to be merely brutish in man is informed by his rational vocation —so thought the philosophers. Christopher Marlowe understood both philosophy and Machiavelli very well when he put in the latter's mouth the phrase, "I hold there is no sin but ignorance." There are other experiences, always the religious, and in modern times the poetic, which make competing claims. But it is not immediately evident that their claims are superior to those of philosophy. The issue comes back again to the relative dignity of reason vs. revelation. The fact that popularized rationalism is, indeed, superficial is no argument against the philosophers. They knew it would be that way. (And, even in this, the democratic citizen, knowing and exercising his rights, is not the most contemptible of beings.) They were trying to make the central human good central to society, and Enlightenment was and remains the only plausible scheme for doing so.

On the face of this, it seems absurd to me to say that Bacon, Descartes, Hobbes, Leibniz, Locke, Montesquieu and even Voltaire (who might be considered a mere popularizer of these others) were less deep than Jacques Maritain or T. S. Eliot—to mention two famous contemporaries from whose mouths I learned as a young man that the Enlightenment was shallow. Rousseau, who initiated the profound school of criticism of Enlightenment's effects, nevertheless says that Bacon, Descartes and Newton were very great men, and he speaks of the "wise Locke." He knew that these were his theoretical kin, although he disagreed with them in crucial respects. The vulgarity of modern society, the object of so many complaints by intellectuals, is something the philosophers were willing to live with. After all, as Socrates points out, all societies look pretty much the same from the heights, be they Periclean Athens or Des Moines, Iowa. A peaceful, wealthy society where the people look up to science and have enough money to support it is worth more than splendid imperia where there are slaves and no philosophy. Locke appears superficial because he was not a snob. There is no way he could make a parade of the magnificence of what he saw.

There is no doubt that these were serious men and that their contrivances have had a public effect unlike that of any philosophers or scientists before or since. The only comparable political events are the founding of what Machiavelli called new modes and orders by prophets—by Moses, Cyrus, Theseus, Romulus and (he implies) Jesus—which he called on the philosophers to imitate. Modernity is largely of these philosophers' making, and our self-awareness depends on understanding what they wanted to do and what they did do, grasping thus why our situation is different from all other situations. However contrary it may be to contemporary historical wisdom, the leading thread that runs through all the accidents of modern history is the philosophical doctrine of Enlightenment. Modern regimes were conceived by reason and depend on the reasonableness of their members. And those regimes required the reason of natural science in every aspect of their activity, and the requirements of scientific advance largely determine their policy. Whether it is called liberal democracy or bourgeois society, whether the regime of the rights of man or that of acquisitiveness, whether technology is used in a positive or a negative sense, everyone knows that these terms describe the central aspects of our world. They are demonstrably the results of the thought of a small group of men with deep insight into the nature of things, who collaborated in an enterprise the success of which is almost beyond belief. It penetrated and informed every detail of life. These are not men to be dismissed—but they can be questioned.

Swift's Doubts

One of the earliest questioners was Jonathan Swift, who saw what was intended and spoke up against it in the name of the ancients and of poetry. *Gulliver's Travels* is to early modern philosophy what Aristophanes' *The Clouds* was to early ancient philosophy. *Gulliver's Travels* is nothing but a comic statement of Swift's preference for antiquity, casting his ancients as giants and noble horses, his moderns as midgets and Yahoos. He addresses the aspect that most concerns us, the establishment of the academies and universities—the Republic of Letters, to use Pierre Bayle's expression—in the chapter entitled "A Voyage to Laputa." Gulliver, after observing modern politics in Lilliput, goes to Laputa to see modern science and its effects on life. Laputa is a flying island ruled by natural scientists. It is, of course, a parody of the British Royal Society, in Swift's time a relatively recent association of the philosophers and scientists who had been tempted more into public and public life by modern thought. In this strange new land Gulliver finds a theoretical preoccupation abstracted from primary human concerns, one whose beginning point was not the human dimension, but which ends up altering it. On the Flying Island the men have one eye turned inward, the other toward the zenith. They are perfect Cartesians—one egotistical eye contemplating the self, one cosmological eye surveying the most distant things. The intermediate range, which previously was the center of concentration and defined both the ego and the pattern for the study of the stars, is not within the Laputian purview. The only studies are astronomy and music, and the world is reduced to these two sciences. The men have no contact with ordinary sense experiences. This is what permits them to remain content with their science. Communication with others outside their circle is unnecessary. Rather than making their mathematics follow the natural shapes of things, they change things so as to fit their mathematics. Their food is cut into all sorts of geometrical figures. Their admiration for women, such as it is, is due to the resemblance of women's various parts to specific figures. Jealousy is unknown to them. Their wives can commit adultery before their eyes without its being noticed. This absence of eroticism is connected with an absence of poetic sensibility. These scientists cannot understand poetry, and hence, in Gulliver's view, their science cannot be a science of man.

Another peculiarity of these men is described by Gulliver as follows. "What I chiefly admired, and thought altogether unaccountable, was the strong disposition I observed in them towards news and politics, perpetually inquiring into public affairs, giving their judgments in matters of state and passionately disputing every inch of a party opinion. I have indeed observed the same disposition among most of the mathematicians I have known in Europe, although I could never discover the least analogy between the two sciences." Gulliver recognizes the political concern of theoretical science and doubts that it can comprehend the actual practice of politics. He also thinks the scientists have a sense of special right to manipulate politics. The Laputians' political power rests on the new science. The Flying Island is built on the principles of physics founded by Gilbert and Newton. Applied science can open new roads to political power. This island allows the king and the nobles to live free from conspiracies by the people—in fact, free from contact with them—while still making use of them and receiving the tribute that is necessary to the maintenance and leisure of the rulers. They can crush the terrestrial cities. Their power is almost unlimited and their responsibilities nil. Power is concentrated in the hands of the rulers; hence they are not forced even by fear to develop a truly political intelligence. They require no virtue. Everything runs itself, so there is no danger that their incompetence, indifference or vice will harm them. Their island allows their characteristic deformity to grow to the point of monstrosity. Science, in freeing men, destroys the natural conditions that make them human. Hence, for the first time in history, there is the possibility of tyranny grounded not on ignorance, but on science.

Swift objects to Enlightenment because it encourages a hypertrophic development of mathematics, physics and astronomy, thus returning to the pre-Socratic philosophy that Aristophanes had criticized for being unselfconscious or unable to understand man. Enlightenment rejected that moderate Socratic compromise between society and philosophy, poetry and science, which had governed intellectual life for so long and had made possible the foundation of political science. But, unlike pre-Socratic philosophy, which had no interest in politics at all, this science wished to rule and could rule. The new science had indeed generated sufficient power to rule, but in order to do so had had to lose the human perspective. In other words, Swift denied that modern science had actually established a human or political science. All to the contrary, it had destroyed it. Such a political science would, in the first place, have to understand man as man, and not as a geometric figure with flesh on it. In the second place, it would have to ensure the harmony between the good of science or scientists and that of a decent political community. On the Flying Island, neither condition is met. In particular, the scientists exploit the nonscientists so as to live their version of the contemplative life in safety and comfort.

More simply put, Swift says that the scientists in power and with power don't give a damn about mankind at large. The whole conspiracy is like any other. The potential tyrant speaks in the name of the common good but is seeking a private good. Bacon's House of Solomon in the *New Atlantis* is just propaganda for the Flying Island. The scientists want to live as they please—delighting in numbers, figures, and stars—and are no longer obliged to hide their desires. The people still have means of making themselves felt, but they are essentially enslaved to what scientists provide for them. The scientists can cut off the sun's light to the world below.

There were elements of uncanny prescience in Swift's misanthropic and cranky satire on science. Natural science very quickly withdrew from the Enlightenment project as a whole, leaving the human parts of it to fend for themselves. The laws of nature were scientific, but natural science no longer claimed to be able to legislate human laws, leaving political science out in the cold, without a rational or scientific basis. Instead of being real partners in the business of overthrowing the antiscientific regimes of the past, the scientists became fellow travelers. Once theological supervision was defeated and everyone accepted the need for scientists instead of priests, science was free and, in principle, indifferent to the political regimes that need and use them. Early Enlightenment thinkers appear to have believed that there was a perfect coincidence between rational consent of the governed and the freedom of science. But science could not rationalize all men, and turned out not to have to, inasmuch as it became able to force whatever rulers there are to support it and leave it alone. When there were still rulers who would in principle persecute a Galileo if they found out what he was up to—because his investigations undermined their legitimacy, founded on sacred texts—scientists were natural allies of all opponents of these rulers. The fascination of early modern thought with the ecclesiastical authority as the one great danger to freedom of thought caused the philosophers to believe that the alliance formed to overthrow it was permanent. In the event, it turned out that once there were secular rulers who had no absolute commitment to a nonrational or unscientific view of nature, the nonhuman part of the Enlightenment was immune. Self-interest, the great modern motivating principle, no longer dictated concern for the other thinkers, and science

or reason, which appeared now to belong utterly to the natural philosopher, no longer gave the political and moral thinkers any warrant. In short,
the common front presented by human and natural science in the name
of democracy became an ideology.

The condition of natural science in the Soviet Union is the dreadful
culmination of Swift's prediction. It is a tyranny founded on science. And
natural science, alone among the learned disciplines, and natural scientists, alone among human beings, have been able to force the tyrants to
leave them alone. A Soviet mathematician is as much a mathematician
as an American mathematician, whereas a historian or a political scientist
must be a sham, a party hack. Natural science can now flourish in the
Soviet Union, because the Soviet tyrants have finally recognized their
unconditional need of the scientists. They cannot endure the historians
or political scientists, and they do not have to. These latter are not of the
same species as the natural scientists, either in the eyes of the natural
scientists or those of the tyrants.

Most unpleasant of all is that this dreadful regime gets its power to
maintain its rule from the natural sciences. As sciences they are neutral,
except with respect to what concerns their interests, and cannot judge
Roosevelt to be superior to Stalin. This would have probably been true
of pre-Socratics too, but they did not generate political power. They were
indifferent to political regimes and provided aid and comfort to none. The
new scientists are the cause of all. The pre-Socratics lived in splendid
isolation as models of the theoretical life. Natural scientists now project
an ambiguous image. Although they may be truly theoretical, they do not
appear that way to untheoretical men. Their involvement in human
things gives them a public role as curers of diseases and inventors of
nuclear weapons, as bastions of democracy and bastions of totalitarianism.
Andrei Sakharov is humanly most impressive, but his stand for human
rights does not follow from his science and, to say the least, does not
guarantee him the fellowship of other Soviet scientists. The new dispensation has protected science; it has done nothing to give scientists control
over the uses of the results of science, or the wherewithal to know how
to use those results, if they were indeed able to gain control over them.
Natural science in the long run won out over the Party when its results
clashed with Marxist orthodoxy, but it could not control the Party's
political action. And no future tyrant is likely to imitate Hitler's mad

doctrinairism, which caused him to send Jewish scientists to his enemies to insure his defeat. Science in that sense moderates potential Hitlers—but only in that sense. In general it increases man's power without increasing his virtue, hence increasing his power to do both good and evil.

The total picture is one of great danger resulting from the political involvement of science. Some people assert that we have to reinvent politics in order to meet the danger. Swift tells us that politics was already reinvented by the founders of Enlightenment, and that is the problem. It turned out that natural science had nothing to say about human things, about the uses of science for life or about the scientist. When a poet writes about a poet, he does so as a poet. When a scientist talks about scientists, he does not do so as a scientist. If he does so, he uses none of the tools he uses in his scientific activity, and his conclusions have none of the demonstrative character he demands in his science. Science has broken off from the self-consciousness about science that was the core of ancient science. This loss of self-consciousness is somehow connected with the banishment of poetry.

Rousseau's Radicalization and the German University

Here Rousseau bursts on the scene, just at the moment of Enlightenment's victory and the establishment of the institutions of learning as the crown of society. An inverse Socrates, he reasserted the permanent tension between science and society, arguing that scientific progress corrupts morals and hence society, and he took the side of society. Virtue, "the science of simple souls," is what is most necessary, and science undermines virtue. It teaches a slack and selfish relation to other men and to civil society, it calls into question the principles of virtue, and it requires a luxurious and loose society in which to flourish.

The knowers who inhabit the academies lose sight of this, become easygoing and self-satisfied. The Ciceros and Bacons would not have been what they were if they had been professors. It was in living life as it really is, rather than in the artificially structured and protected universities, that they were able to grasp the human situation as a whole, recognize its inner tensions and take responsibility, without the protective cover of a faith in progress and without the vanity of society's ignorantly bestowed honors. Professors had made reason into a public prejudice and were now among the prejudiced. They represented an unsatisfactory halfway house between the two harsh disciplines that make a man serious—community and solitude.

Rousseau insisted on making explicit the ambiguity about the relative dignity of theory and practice implicit in Enlightenment. Enlightenment presented the thinker not as the best man but as the most useful one. Happiness is the most important thing; if thinking is not happiness, it must be judged by its relationship to happiness. It is, Rousseau argues, more than doubtful that science produces happiness. Moreover, although Hobbes and Locke teach that man is rational, his rationality is in the service of passions or sentiments, which are more fundamental than reason. Thinking through their position that man is naturally a solitary being results in the recognition that speech, the condition of reason, is not natural to man. Man's specific difference from the other animals cannot, therefore, be reason. Enlightenment misunderstands both reason and feeling.

Rousseau's reasoning and rhetoric were so potent that hardly anyone who thought, as well as many who did not, could avoid his influence. After him, community, virtue, compassion, feeling, enthusiasm, the beautiful and the sublime, and even imagination, the banished faculty, had their innings against modern philosophy and science. The fringe bohemian, the sentimentalist, the artist became at least as much the teacher and the model as the scientist. Inspired by Rousseau, Kant undertook a systematic overhauling of Enlightenment's project in such a way as to make coherent the relationship between theory and practice, reason and morality, science and poetry, all of which had been made so problematic by Rousseau. Kant's survey of the whole of knowledge can also be read as a project for the fruitful coexistence of the disciplines in the universities. Rousseau had pointed out that the ancient tension between the thinker and society, supposedly resolved by Enlightenment, had resurfaced in new and very dangerous ways. Kant tried again to resolve it.

He, too, agreed that natural science had read free, moral, artistic man out of nature. He did not try to reform natural science, to translate man back into nature after the fashion of the ancients. What he did was to demonstrate that nature, as understood by natural science, does not comprehend the whole of things. There are other realms, not grasped or graspable by natural science, which are real and leave a place for the reality of the experience of humanity. Reason does not have to be abandoned to defend humanity, for reason can demonstrate that science has limits that it did not know, and reason can demonstrate the possibility of a freedom illegitimately denied by natural science. *Possibility* and *ground* become the themes in Kant, for much that is human had begun to appear to be impossible and groundless.

Kant accepted Rousseau's reasoning that freedom must be what distinguishes man, that it is denied by the kind of causation accepted in natural science, and that therefore the practical life, the exercise of moral freedom, is higher than the theoretical life, the use of scientific reason. In one of the most arduous and powerful theoretical efforts undertaken by man, he tried to demonstrate that nature is not all, that reason and spontaneity are not contraries. All this is established by reason, not by passion against reason. That effort lives in the three Critiques, the last great statement of liberal Enlightenment, the other strand of rationalism that coexists in the universities with Baconian-Cartesian-Lockean rationalism. The primary effort is to set limits to pure reason, to say to "proud reason, 'this far and no further,' " in such a way that reason will submit rationally. Kant's critical philosophy does not dictate to science what it must discover; it establishes the limits within which pure reason operates. It does the same for practical reason, thus turning David Hume's distinction between the is and the ought from a humiliation for moral reasoning into the basis for its triumph and its dignity. It further establishes the faculty of judgment, which can again allow man to speak about ends and the beautiful.

In this system not only does natural science have a secure place in the order of the university, but so also do morals and esthetics. However, the unity of the university is now Kant. These three kinds of knowledge (the true, the good, the beautiful in new guises) are given their domains by the three Critiques, but are not unified by being knowledge of aspects of a single reality. Aristotle's human sciences are part of the science of nature, and his knowledge of man is connected to and in harmony with his knowledge of the stars, bodies in motion and animals other than man. This is not the case with the human sciences after Rousseau, which depend on the existence of a realm entirely different from nature. Their study is not part of the study of nature, and the two kinds of study have little to do with one another.

This new condition of the learned disciplines, which found its earliest expression in the German universities at the beginning of the nineteenth century and gradually spread throughout the Western universities, at first proved very fertile. The progress of the natural sciences, now unimpeded by theological or political supervision and emancipated from philosophy, continued and became even more rapid. And the human sciences, given a fresh vocation, came to a new flowering, especially in historical and philological studies. Man understood as a free, moral individual—as creative, as producer of cultures, as maker and product of history—provided a field for humane research taking man seriously as man, not reduced to the moved bodies that now constituted the realm of natural science. The serious goal that is necessary to make scholarship vital was provided by the sense that man could be understood by his historical origins; that moral and political standards could be derived from the historical traditions of the various nations, to replace the failed standards of natural right and law; that the study of high culture, particularly that of Greece, would provide the models for modern achievement; that a proper understanding of religion might provide a faith proof against critical reason. Scholars, for that moment, more than at any time since the Renaissance, seemed to be in the service of life, to be as useful as soldiers, doctors and workers. The great movements of careful historical research and textual criticism initiated in this heyday of the nineteenth century gave us nourishment which we have yet entirely to digest. The humanities took over the whole burden of instructing us about man, especially in morals and esthetics (the new science of the beautiful and the sublime).

However, the very condition of this exhilaration in the human sciences—the dualism nature-freedom—created problems from the outset and in the long run undermined the confidence of their practitioners or turned them back into mere erudites again. There was a haunting doubt as to the reality of the realm of freedom, which seemed to restore the richness of the phenomenon man. What are the relations between the two realms? At what point does the natural in man stop and the free begin? Is it really possible to limit the claims of natural science? Within Kant's system, if scientists can, as they claim, in the long run predict the behavior of all phenomena, can one plausibly postulate a noumenal freedom, the expressions of which are predictable in the phenomenal field? Does not natural science presuppose mechanical causation, determinism and the reduction of all higher phenomena to lower ones, the complex to the simple, and do not the successes of that science in astronomy, physics, chemistry and biology attest to the truth of its presuppositions? New discoveries or speculations such as evolution called into question the independent or nonderivative character of mind. The very faculty that made it possible to set the limits of science and reason in the *Critique of Pure Reason* proved to be just another accidental effect of evolving matter. The ground of morals and esthetics disappeared. Natural science continued to seem substantial, while romanticism and idealism inhabited imaginary cities, sublime hopes but little more. Pessimism as a philosophical school came onto the scene. Joined to the health and expansiveness of natural science was the recognition that humane learning had itself failed to generate moral and political standards. All the study of the facts of national history and the invention of "folk-minds" could not provide guidance for the future, or imperatives for conduct. The learning was impressive, but it looked more and more to be the product of idle curiosity rather than the quest for knowledge of what is most needful. Philosophy, no longer a part of, or required by, natural science, was nudged over toward the humanities and even became just another historical subject. Its claim to be the ruler in the university no longer earned respect. There was a condominium with no higher unity. The humane learning could argue for equal rights and was to some extent formally accorded them, but that began to be "academic" and have little to do with the way things looked in the real world. The natural scientist was both the image of the knower and the public benefactor; the humanist, a professor.

The problem of the knower in the perspective of the modern understanding was formulated over and over again from the beginning of the modern university dispensation by the man, not a member of the German university, who, along with Kant, most influenced it—Goethe. A classic summation of his views is to be found in *Faust,* the only modern book that can be said to have made a national heroic model to rival those of Homer, Virgil, Dante and Shakespeare. The scholar Faust, meditating in his cell, translates the first line of the Gospel According to John, "In the beginning was the word (logos)"; then, dissatisfied with the description he says "the feeling," which also does not quite do; finally and definitively he chooses to reinterpret it as "the deed." Action has primacy over contemplation, deed over speech. He who understands must imitate the beginnings. The act of the creator, not preceded and controlled by thought, is the first thing. The scholar with his reason misunderstands the origin because he lacks the vital force that lies behind the order of things. He trifles, piling up facts from which the informing principle has been extracted. Faust's relation to the perpetual studier Wagner, who says he already knows much but wants to know everything, is paradigmatic. Only knowledge that serves life is good, and life is in the first place constituted by dark action, by fatal impulse. Knowledge comes afterward and lightens the world made by the deed. As painted by Goethe, Wagner looks slight and feeble. His idle love of knowledge is superficial compared to Faust's inchoate impulses. Although the opposition between the *vita activa* and the *vita contemplativa* is as old as philosophy, if not older, Goethe's moment is the first where the side of action is taken by theory itself, thus announcing the end of the ancient opposition. The theoretical life is groundless because the first thing is not the intelligible order but the chaos open to creativity. There can be no contemplation where there is nothing to see. Goethe took full account of the modern situation of knower and poet and put a question mark after learning that is not subordinate to the ends of life enhancement. In antiquity there had also been mere scholars, studying Homer and Plato without knowing quite why, and without being interested in the questions the writers raised, fascinated by meters or the reliability of texts. But the objection to these scholars was that they lacked the urgent desire to know the most important things, whereas the modern objection to scholarship is that it lacks the urgency of commitment to action. Most simply, the historian—the very model of the modern scholar —chronicles deeds. But if deeds are the most important thing, then the scholar is by definition inferior to the doer. Moreover, such a reasoner is incapable of the leap into darkness that the deed demands. Finally, if the doer is not a thinker, then it is doubtful whether the thinker can understand the doer. Does one not have to be akin to Caesar to understand him? To say that one does not have to be Caesar to understand him is equivalent to saying that one does not have to be anything to understand everything. The hidden premise of the realm of freedom is that action has primacy over thought. As Goethe saw, the modern scholarly giant has feet of clay. It is also blind because it is lacking objects of cognition—as do all sciences—where there is only darkness.

The problem of scholarship is best illustrated in classical scholarship. The study of ancient Greece and Rome used to be the scholarly discipline par excellence, at times igniting brilliantly and illuminating the world, at others flickering and almost being extinguished. The study of the ancients has followed the ebb and flow of philosophic innovation in the West. Moments of great transformation have started with refreshment at the Greek source, its inspiration slaking a burning thirst. An overwhelming sense that something is missing is the serious motive for authentic, therefore careful and exhaustive, recovery of what has been lost. Greece provides the assurance that there was something better than what is. When the old treasures have been digested and the innovators are satisfied that they can walk on their own, the ancient seems less necessary and degenerates into habitual learning, a monument rather than a guiding light. The intoxicating atmosphere of the Renaissance, the rebirth of Greece, always possible because of its universality and the permanence of human nature, culminated in a specifically modern thought—beginning from Machiavelli's careful study and criticism of both Greeks and Romans—which could proudly assert its superiority to its ancient inspirers, winning the quarrel between the ancient and the modern.

Rousseau initiated a second Renaissance when he expressed his dissatisfaction with modernity, made possible by his knowledge of the Greek and Roman examples. "Ancient statesmen spoke endlessly of morals and virtue; ours speak only of commerce and money." Rousseau's use of his knowledge of antiquity—which was, although not scholarly, very profound—is a perfect model of the reason for having ancient thought available to those great individuals who, as Nietzsche put it, are untimely and need a vantage point from which to get their bearings and become the most timely of all. It is the old Greeks who make men both untimely and timely in crises. Nothing fancy, no infinite searching outside; the book in itself always intelligible, as long as human nature remains the same. This is the role played by the Greek authors throughout the wildly varying ages since they wrote, always Phoenix-like when they appear to have been consumed and are only ashes conserved by the scholars.

Rousseau's fervent appeal for modern man to look back to the ancient city, because it was whole and a true community, was the source of the romantic longing to breathe the fresh air of Greece again. Its moral and esthetic health was what Rousseau conveyed so convincingly. He gave the impulse to all kinds of attempts at new communitarian beginnings, from Robespierre to Owen to Tolstoy and the kibbutz, an impulse still alive in contemporary thought. But most of all, as I have discussed earlier, his observations on the tension between Enlightenment and decent politics gave birth to the idea of culture. It was to the study of Greece or Sparta or Athens as models of cultures that Rousseau's reflection led. The motive for this study—which flourished particularly in Germany, where Rousseau's influence was most strongly felt, precisely because of Kant's and Goethe's predominance there—was to understand culture, with a view to the founding of a German culture. It was primarily Greek and Roman poetry and secondarily history to which the German thinkers turned for inspiration, and the scholars followed. It was distinctly not Greek philosophy. This was evident in Rousseau himself. The philosophers whose theoretical reflection was necessary to him were Bacon, Descartes and Newton, not Plato and Aristotle. The latter two just did not know the truth about nature. Whatever interest later scholarship had in them was as parts of Greek culture, as typical expressions of it and less interesting than poets, who are culture founders. The Greek philosophers were not valid interlocutors. Rousseau admired Plato and thought he had deep insight into human things, but rather more as a poet than a philosopher or scientist. Plato was indeed the philosopher for lovers, but Rousseau, without consulting Plato, taught that eros is the child of sex and imagination. Its activity is poetry, the source of what Rousseau understood to be the life-creating and -enhancing illusions and thereby the source of the ultimate grounds of the folk-minds that make peoples possible. In Plato, eros led to philosophy, which in turn led to the rational quest for the best regime, the *one* good political order vs. the plurality of cultures. So the discovery of Greek "culture" was contrary to Greek philosophy. And this particular difference, concerning the best regime as opposed to culture, proved fatal to reason. We can recognize this in a preliminary way in Weber's assumption that it is values rather than reasons that found and sustain communities.

Thus from the outset of this second Renaissance, scholars treated Greek philosophers more as natural scientists treat atoms than as they treat other natural scientists. They were not invited to join the serious discussion of the scholars. All things Greek were subjected to our analysis based on the views of modern philosophy. This procedure alters radically what one expects to learn from them. Men of the Enlightenment looked down on Greek thinkers because they thought them wrong. Romantics respected them because their truth or falsity became a matter of indifference.

Schiller's distinction between naive and sentimental poetry is an example of the kind of categorization that became common. Homer's charm is a result of his not having seen what we see, his unawareness of the abyss. He still walked on enchanted ground, and his poetry lacked that reflectiveness imposed on us who know that the gods can depart. He was unaware of the death of gods and cultures as children are unaware of the death of men. He lived in the youth of the world. If we are to be whole and happy we must recover that direct relation to things men once had. But we must do it in the company of our awareness of the vulnerability of things. The artist has a greater responsibility than Homer knew because he does not merely imitate nature but creates it. A successful modern artist would be deeper, more fully self-conscious than was Homer.

The naive Homer belonged to a culture different from that of the sentimental Schiller, and has to be understood in his own cultural context. Naiveté consists in large measure in the lack of "historical consciousness," the belief that the greats are individuals to be understood individually and in the same way at all times. Plutarch believed he was showing forth images of greatness itself, while in fact his heroes are just Greeks and Romans, high expressions of their culture, from which they are inseparable. The awareness of this is the peculiarly modern superiority or insight.

Schiller was, of course, an unusually profound and sensitive reader. It is doubtful whether his reading of Homer teaches us very much about Homer, because it is too encumbered by what we now believe to be Romantic prejudices. But Homer, interpreted and misinterpreted by Schiller, contributed to his own artistic creation, which was founding a German literature and a German culture. It is an example of what some would call "creative misinterpretation." The faith in one's own vision, perhaps fed by the inspiration of others' visions, is what is important. An act uninformed by learning is the important thing. Implicit in what I am saying is that while Schiller's views are not true but are productive, there are true views, known presumably to scholars, which are not productive.

This is what Goethe implies. The scholar is an objective reasoner, the poet a subjective creator.

Here is where Nietzsche enters, arguing with unparalleled clarity and vigor that if we take "historical consciousness" seriously, there cannot be objectivity, that scholarship as we know it is simply a delusion, and a dangerous one, for objectivity undermines subjectivity. All of classical scholarship in Germany, with its exquisite sense of the historical determination of the mind, proceeded as though the mind of the German scholar were not so determined. The discovery of culture and the folk-mind means that there cannot be universal principles of understanding. Reason is a myth that makes mythmaking impossible to comprehend. Creativity and a science of human things cannot coexist, and since the science of human things admits that man is creative, the creative man wins the day. But scholars cannot behave creatively.

The discovery of culture as the element in which man becomes himself produces an imperative: Build and sustain culture. This the scholar cannot do. Culture is not only the condition of life, it is the condition of knowing. Without a German culture, the scholar in Germany cannot confront other cultures.

After the great moment in German thought—of Kant, Goethe, Schiller and Hegel, in which the rediscovery of Greece played so important a role—Greek scholarship retired to the universities, where it was again a dead piece of learning, unable itself to inspire or produce a compelling vision that could transform men. It became studied by bourgeois professors who educated bourgeois men for whom, as with Aschenbach, the Greeks were just "culture." The Greek splendor, which had formed such heroic figures just a half-century earlier, became a mystery. Nietzsche, acutely aware of this splendor and its disappearance from the scene, blamed the scholars, or rather blamed something that informed scholarship. A classical scholar who certainly would have been among the greatest who ever lived if he had not been called to philosophy, Nietzsche attempted the last great return to the Greeks. Like his German predecessors, he returned to Greek poetry in particular. But he coupled his taste for the tragedies with something very new—a radical attack on Socrates, the founder of the tradition of rationalism, which is the essence of the university. This is probably the first attack made by a philosopher on Socrates, and it is a violent one, continuing throughout Nietzsche's whole career. What is fascinating for us in this is that Nietzsche, and Heidegger following him, are the first modern thinkers since the days of Hobbes, Spinoza and Descartes to take Socrates—or any classical philosopher's teaching—really seriously as an opponent, as a living opponent[8] rather than as a cultural artifact. Socrates is alive and must be overcome. It is essential to recognize that this is *the* issue in Nietzsche. It is not a historical or cultural question. It is simply a classic philosophic disputation: Was Socrates right or wrong? Nietzsche's indictment of Socrates is that his rationalism, his utilitarianism, subverted and explained away that great stupidity which is noble instinct. He destroyed the tragic sense of life, which intuited man's true situation amidst things and allowed for creative forming of life against the terror of existence, unendowed with and unguided by any pre-existing forms or patterns. Instinct or fatality, prior to reason and vulnerable to reason, establishes the table of laws or valuations within which healthy reason works. A darkness on top of a void is the condition of life and creation, and it is dispelled in the light of rational analysis. The poet, in his act of creation, knows this. The scientist and the scholar never do. The act of creation is what forms cultures and folk-minds. There cannot be, as Socrates believed, the pure mind, which is trans-historical. This belief is the fundamental premise and error of science, an error that becomes manifestly fatal in dealing with human things. The method of the sciences is designed to see only what is everywhere and always, whereas what is particular and emergent is all that counts historically and culturally. Homer is not merely one example of an epic, or the Bible of a revealed text, but that is what science sees them as, and the only reason it is interested in them. The scholar turns away from them to comparative religion or comparative literature, i.e., either to indifference or to a flabby ecumenism compounded out of the lowest common denominator of a variety of old and incompatible creations. The scholar cannot understand the texts that he purports to interpret and explain. Schiller might be able to grasp the essence of the *Iliad* because as a creator he is akin to Homer. He could not understand Homer as Homer understood himself, because his mind was of a different historical epoch. But he could understand what it means to be a poet. A scholar can do neither. From the point of view of life, and from the point of view of

---

[8]Hegel, of course, studied ancient philosophy very well, but to incorporate it into modernity. It was not for him an enemy, and as a friend it was incomplete or imperfect.

truth, modern scholarship is a failure. Hegel ridicules the typical German gymnasium teacher who explains that Alexander the Great had a pathological love of power. The teacher proves the assertion by the fact that Alexander conquered the world. The teacher's freedom from this illness is attested to by the fact that he has not conquered the world. This story encapsulates Nietzsche's criticism of the German university and its classical scholarship. The scholar cannot understand the will to power, not a cause recognized by science, which made Alexander different from others, because the scholar neither has it nor does his method permit him to have it or see it. The scholar could never conquer the mind of man.

Nietzsche's return to the example of the ancients, and his rigorous drawing of the consequences of what German humane scholarship really believed, had a stunning effect on German university life and on the German respect for reason altogether. Artists received a new license, and even philosophy began to reinterpret itself as a form of art. The poets won the old war between philosophy and poetry, in which Socrates had been philosophy's champion. Nietzsche's war on the university led in two directions—either to an abandonment of the university by serious men, or to its reform to make it play a role in the creation of culture. The university ruled by Hegel, the modern Aristotle, had to be reconstituted, as the discredited medieval university had been made over by the now discredited Enlightenment university.

Nietzsche's effect was immediately felt by artists in all Western countries. He was the rage from 1890 on, and hardly any important painter, poet or novelist was immune to his charm. But his Hellenism had relatively little effect on that art. They took his characterization of modern culture and the conclusions of his arguments about the causes of its decadence and set about either popularizing them or attempting to found new cultures in various schools. They explored the freshly opened terrain of the id, seeking new forms. In the universities Nietzsche's first influences were to be found in relatively marginal or new disciplines like sociology or psychology, none of which was deeply influenced by Greek or Roman models. Within the study of classics a new generation of scholars turned more to the study of religion and poetry, concentrating on Greece prior to Socrates and on the irrational in its writers. In philosophy Nietzsche was the source of various schools of phenomenology and existentialism, and he finally became academically respectable.

But it was Heidegger, practically alone, for whom the study of Greek philosophy became truly central, a pressing concern for his meditation on being. Heidegger, following Nietzsche, had cast the most radical doubt on the whole enterprise of modern philosophy and science. A new beginning was imperative, and he turned with open mind to the ancients. But he did not focus on Plato or Aristotle—although he reflected on them and was a most ingenious interpreter of them—because Nietzsche had dealt with them by way of Socrates. Heidegger was drawn instead to the pre-Socratic philosophers, from whom he hoped to discover another understanding of being to help him replace the exhausted one inherited from Plato and Aristotle, which he and Nietzsche thought to be at the root of both Christianity and modern science.

Strangely, the Hellenism of Heidegger did not give a strong impulse to the study of Greek philosophy. This may have something to do with the effects of the war and Heidegger's disgrace. He, too, had to reenter respectability by literary backdoors and on the wings of the very respectable academic Left. Neither carrier was much interested in the profound reflection on the ancients, which gave him his perspective on the contemporary scene. This popularizing made hay out of his description of our situation. The intellectuals who admired Heidegger took for granted, as neither he nor Nietzsche did, that Plato and Aristotle are not worthy of our serious concern. But that is where the issue lies. Are Nietzsche and Heidegger right about Plato and Aristotle? They rightly saw that *the* question is here, and both returned obsessively to Socrates. Our rationalism is his rationalism. Perhaps they did not take seriously enough the changes wrought by the modern rationalists and hence the possibility that the Socratic way might have avoided the modern impasse. But certainly all the philosophers, the proponents of reason, have something in common, and more or less directly reach back to Aristotle, Socrates' spiritual grandchild. A serious argument about what is most profoundly modern leads inevitably to the conclusion that study of the problem of Socrates is the one thing most needful.[9] It was Socrates who made Nietzsche and Heidegger look to the pre-Socratics. For the first time in four hundred years, it seems possible and imperative to begin all over again, to try to figure out what Plato was talking about, because it might be the best thing available.

[9]Cf. Werner J. Dannhauser, *Nietzsche's View of Socrates,* Cornell, 1974.

The history of classics since the Renaissance has consisted in momentary glimpses of the importance of Greece for man as man, everywhere and always, followed by long periods of merely scholarly study without any sufficient reason for it, living off the gradually dying energy provided by the original philosophic dynamos. Up to Nietzsche, the neglect of and contempt for Plato and Aristotle was the result of a belief that what they tried to do could be done much better. That is why Socrates was always in good repute. He was the skeptical seeker after the way to knowledge by means of unaided reason. He was not tied to any solution or system and thus could be seen as the originator and the inspirer who did not constrain the freedom of posterity. The current contempt for Plato and Aristotle is of an entirely different kind, for it is allied to contempt for Socrates. He corrupted them; they did not pervert him. We did not progress from Socrates, but he marked the beginning of the decline. Reason itself is rejected by philosophy itself. Thus the common thread of the whole tradition has been broken, and with it the *raison d'être* of the university as we know it.

Thus it was no accident that Heidegger came forward just after Hitler's accession to power to address the university community in Freiburg as the new rector, and urged commitment to National Socialism. His argument was not without subtlety and its own special kind of irony, but in sum the *decision* to devote wholeheartedly the life of the mind to an emerging revelation of being, incarnated in a mass movement, was what Heidegger encouraged. That he did so was not a result of his political innocence but a corollary of his critique of rationalism. That is why I have entitled this section "From Socrates' *Apology* to Heidegger's *Rektoratsrede.*" The university began in spirit from Socrates' contemptuous and insolent distancing of himself from the Athenian people, his refusal to accept any command from them to cease asking, "What is justice? What is knowledge? What is a god?" and hence doubting the common opinions about such questions, and in his serious game (in the *Republic*) of trying to impose the rule of philosophers on an unwilling people without respect for their "culture." The university may have come near to its death when Heidegger joined the German people—especially the youngest part of that people, which he said had already made an irreversible commitment to the future—and put philosophy at the service of German culture. If I am right in believing that Heidegger's teachings are the most powerful intellectual force in our times, then the crisis of the German university, which everyone saw, is the crisis of the university everywhere.

It may be thought that I have devoted too much space to this idiosyncratic history of the university. But the university, of all institutions, is most dependent on the deepest beliefs of those who participate in its peculiar life. Our present educational problems cannot seriously be attributed to bad administrators, weakness of will, lack of discipline, lack of money, insufficient attention to the three R's, or any of the other common explanations that indicate things will be set aright if we professors would just pull up our socks. All these things are the result of a deeper lack of belief in the university's vocation. One cannot say that we must defend academic freedom when there are grave doubts about the principles underlying academic freedom. To march out to battle on behalf of the university may be noble, but it is only a patriotic gesture. Such gestures are necessary and useful for nations, but they do little for universities. Thought is all in all for universities. Today there is precious little thought about universities, and what there is does not unequivocally support the university's traditional role. In order to find out why we have fallen on such hard times, we must recognize that the foundations of the university have become extremely doubtful to the highest intelligences. Our petty tribulations have great causes. What happened to the universities in Germany in the thirties is what has happened and is happening everywhere. The essence of it all is not social, political, psychological or economic, but philosophic. And, for those who wish to see, contemplation of Socrates is our most urgent task. This is properly an academic task.

THE SIXTIES

"You don't have to intimidate us," said the famous professor of philosophy in April 1969, to ten thousand triumphant students supporting a group of black students who had just persuaded "us," the faculty of Cornell University, to do their will by threatening the use of firearms as well as threatening the lives of individual professors. A member of the ample press corps newly specialized in reporting the hottest item of the day, the university, muttered, "You said it, brother." The reporter had learned a proper contempt for the moral and intellectual qualities of professors. Servility, vanity and lack of conviction are not difficult to discern.

The professors, the repositories of our best traditions and highest intellectual aspirations, were fawning over what was nothing better than a rabble; publicly confessing their guilt and apologizing for not having understood the most important moral issues, the proper response to which they were learning from the mob; expressing their willingness to change the university's goals and the content of what they taught. As I surveyed this spectacle, Marx's overused dictum kept coming to my mind against my will: History always repeats itself, the first time as tragedy, the second as farce. The American university in the sixties was experiencing the same dismantling of the structure of rational inquiry as had the German university in the thirties. No longer believing in their higher vocation, both gave way to a highly ideologized student populace. And the content of the ideology was the same—value commitment. The university had abandoned all claim to study or inform about value—undermining the sense of the value of what it taught, while turning over the *decision* about values to the folk, the *Zeitgeist,* the relevant. Whether it be Nuremberg or Woodstock, the principle is the same. As Hegel was said to have died in Germany in 1933, Enlightenment in America came close to breathing its last during the sixties. The fact that the universities are no longer in convulsions does not mean that they have regained their health. As in Germany, the value crisis in philosophy made the university prey to whatever intense passion moved the masses. It went comfortably along until there was a popular fit of moralism, and then became aware that it had nothing to contribute and was persuaded by a guilty sense that its distance from the world made it immoral. Hardly any element in the university believed seriously that its distance was based on something true and necessary, the self-confident possession of the kinds of standpoint outside of public opinion that made it easy for Socrates to resist the pious fanaticism of the Athenian people who put their victorious generals to death after Arginusae, or to refuse to collaborate with the Athenian tyrants. Socrates thought it more important to discuss justice, to try to know what it is, than to engage himself in implementing whatever partial perspective on it happened to be exciting the passions of the day, causing the contemplative to be called unjust and impious.

Of course anyone who is a professional contemplative holding down a prestigious and well-paying job, and who also believes there is nothing to contemplate, finds himself in a difficult position with respect to himself and to the community. The imperative to promote equality, stamp out racism, sexism and elitism (the peculiar crimes of our democratic society), as well as war, is overriding for a man who can define no other interest worthy of defending. The fact that in Germany the politics were of the Right and in the United States of the Left should not mislead us. In both places the universities gave way under the pressure of mass movements, and did so in large measure because they thought those movements possessed a moral truth superior to any the university could provide. Commitment was understood to be profounder than science, passion than reason, history than nature, the young than the old. In fact, as I have argued, the thought was really the same. The New Left in America was a Nietzscheanized-Heideggerianized Left. The unthinking hatred of "bourgeois society" was exactly the same in both places. A distinguished professor of political science proved this when he read to his radical students some speeches about what was to be done. They were enthusiastic until he informed them that the speeches were by Mussolini. Heidegger himself, late in his life, made overtures to the New Left. The most sinister formula in his Rectoral Address of 1933 was, with only the slightest of alterations, the slogan of the American professors who collaborated with the student movements of the sixties: "The time for decision is past. The decision has already been made by the youngest part of the German nation."

At Cornell and elsewhere in the United States, it was farce because —whatever the long-range future of our polity—the mass of the country (there really was no mass but a citizenry) was at that moment unusually respectful of the universities, regarded them as resources for the improvement of Americans, and accepted the notion that scholarship should be left undisturbed and was likely to produce a great range of views that should be treated seriously and with tolerance. The nation was not ready for great changes and believed about universities the things professors professed to believe about them. A few students discovered that pompous teachers who catechized them about academic freedom could, with a little shove, be made into dancing bears. Children tend to be rather better observers of adults' characters than adults are of children's, because children are so dependent on adults that it is very much in their interest to discover the weaknesses of their elders. These students discerned that their teachers did not really believe that freedom of thought was necessarily a good and useful thing, that they suspected all this was ideology protecting the injustices of our "system," and that they could be pressured into benevolence toward violent attempts to change the ideology. Heidegger was fully aware that the theoretical foundations of academic freedom had been weakened and, as I have said, treated the mass movement he faced with a certain irony. The American professors were not aware of what they no longer believed, and they took ever so seriously the movements they were entangled with.

I became fully aware of this when I went to see Cornell's then provost (who later became president when the unfavorable national publicity continued and the usually passive trustees asked for the resignation of the incumbent because the national publicity about the guns appeared to be damaging the university's reputation), concerning a black student whose life had been threatened by a black faculty member when the student refused to participate in a demonstration. The provost was a former natural scientist, and he greeted me with a mournful countenance. He, of course, fully sympathized with the young man's plight. However, things were bad, and there was nothing he could do to stop such behavior in the black student association. He, personally, hoped there would soon be better communication with the radical black students (this was a few weeks before the guns emerged and permitted much clearer communication). But for the time being the administration had to wait to hear what the blacks wanted,[10] in the expectation that tensions could be reduced. He added that no university in the country could expel radical black students, or dismiss the faculty members who incited them, presumably because the students at large would not permit it.

I saw that this had been a useless undertaking on my part. The provost had a mixture of cowardice and moralism not uncommon at the time. He did not want trouble. His president had frequently cited Clark Kerr's dismissal at the University of California as the great danger. Kerr had not known how to conciliate the students. At the same time the provost thought he was engaged in a great moral work, righting the historic injustice done to blacks. He could justify to himself the humiliation he was undergoing as a necessary sacrifice. The case of this particular black student clearly bothered him.[11] But he was both more frightened of the violence-threatening extremists and also more admiring of them. Obvious questions were no longer obvious: Why could not a black student

[10]Up to that time there had only been hints of the following kind: the chairman of the Economics Department had been held hostage for several hours, along with his secretary, in further-ance of a demand that an assistant professor deemed racist be dismissed; the building housing a part of the Sociology Department had been forcibly seized, and its inhabitants as well as furnishings had been ejected; the president had been physically assaulted. In response to these communications, proofs of the bona fides of the following kind had been given to the students: the assistant professor disappeared from campus; and for good measure the black assistant dean, who had the misfortune of being an integrationist at a time when black power had come into vogue, was fired; the faculty of the College of Arts and Sciences received a memorandum from its dean informing the members that, although none were demonstrably overt racists, all were indeed institutional racists; classes for blacks only were established; the house that was being held by right of conquest was accorded to its new inhabitants by consent; a lavishly funded black studies center was established in the faculty appointments to which the black students were to have a voice. Such signs had not yet succeeded in establishing the kind of "dialogue" hoped for.

[11]The president himself appeared to be interested only in protecting himself and avoiding having to confront the black student association or any other radical group. He was of the moral stamp of those who were angry with Poland for resisting Hitler because this precipitated the war.

be expelled as a white student would be if he failed his courses or diso-
beyed the rules that make university community possible? Why could the
president not call the police if order was threatened? Any man of weight
would have fired the professor who threatened the life of the student. The
issue was not complicated. Only the casuistry of weakness and ideology
made it so. Ordinary decency dictated the proper response. No one who
knew or cared about what a university is would have acquiesced in this
travesty. It was no surprise that a few weeks later—immediately after the
faculty had voted overwhelmingly under the gun to capitulate to outrageous demands that it had a few days earlier rejected—the leading members of the administration and many well-known faculty members rushed
over to congratulate the gathered students and tried to win their approval.
I saw exposed before all the world what had long been known, and it was
at last possible without impropriety to tell these pseudo-universitarians
precisely what one thought of them.

It was also no surprise that many of those professors who had been
most eloquent in their sermons about the sanctity of the university, and
who had presented themselves as its consciences, were among those who
reacted, if not favorably, at least weakly to what was happening. They had
made careers out of saying how badly the German professors had reacted
to violations of academic freedom. This was all light talk and mock
heroics, because they had not measured the potential threats to the
university nor assessed the doubtful grounds of academic freedom. Above
all, they did not think that it could be assaulted from the Left or from
within the university, although serious examination of the events in Germany would have taught them that it was indeed the university youth, as
Heidegger pointed out, who had become disenchanted on theoretical
grounds with the old education, and that much of the same thing had
been going on here. The society at large had gradually been persuaded of
the justice of liberal notions of intellectual freedom just as the first waves
of doubt about them from Europe were smacking against our shores. A
conviction of the self-evidence of Enlightenment principles to all thinking
people, combined with simplistic economic and psychological explanations, permitted American professors to misinterpret the German experience and to avoid the fact that the theoretical critique of morality in all
its forms had been the precondition of the acceptability of certain kinds
of public speech in Germany during the twenties. These American profes-

sors were utterly disarmed, as were many German professors, when the constituency that they took for granted, of which they honestly believed they were independent, deserted or turned against them. Students and colleagues wanted to radicalize and politicize the university. To fulminate against Bible Belt preachers was one thing. In the world that counted for these professors, this could only bring approval. But to be isolated in the university, to be called foul names by their students or their colleagues, all for the sake of an abstract idea, was too much for them. They were not in general strong men, although their easy rhetoric had persuaded them that they were—that they alone manned the walls protecting civilization. Their collapse was merely pitiful, although their feeble attempts at self-justification frequently turned vicious. In Germany the professors who kept quiet had the very good excuse that they could not do otherwise. Speaking up would have meant imprisonment or death. The law not only did not protect them but was their deadly enemy. At Cornell there was no such danger. A couple of professors might have been hurt (inasmuch as those who had been dubbed racists,[12] a qualification equivalent to heretic in earlier times, were utterly abandoned by all but a few persons of decent instincts, and the president was in no way disposed to protect anyone other than himself), but one shot fired would have brought the civil authorities in. Those authorities were only restrained by respect for the special autonomous status of the university, which was being exploited to protect and encourage violators of academic freedom as well as of the law that governs ordinary mortals. There was essentially no risk in defending the integrity of the university, because the danger was entirely within it. All that was lacking was a professorial corps aware of the university's purpose, and dedicated to it. That is what made the surrender so contemptible. The official ideology became that there had been no danger to the threatened professors (thus no need for solidarity with them) and also that there was severe danger of violence and death (thus a need for capitulation).

One of the pious sermonizers who failed to speak out and who fancied himself a political philosopher wrote an article for *The New York Times Magazine* explaining to the world why capitulation had been

---

[12]Among those threatened over the university radio was the professor who had probably done more and risked more in the civil rights movement than anyone else at Cornell.

necessary at Cornell. The "social contract," he averred, was about to be broken, and we would have returned to "the state of nature," the war of all against all, the worst evil, so that anything to keep that from happening was justified. He proved therewith that he had never understood what he had been teaching, for the contract theorists (from whose teachings the American form of government was derived) all taught that the law must never be broken, that the strength of the law is the only thing that keeps us away from the state of nature, therefore that risks and dangers must be accepted for the sake of the law. Once the law is broken with impunity, each man regains the right to any means he deems proper or necessary in order to defend himself against the new tyrant, the one who can break the law. Such frivolous use, as was made by this professor, of the teachings that must be understood if there is to be a reasonable political order is emblematic of the real problem that lay behind all of this disruption of university life. Serious discussion of political problems and thought had almost been forgotten; and those to whom it was entrusted had no abiding concern for such discussion. The tradition was only a set of slogans or quotations from Bartlett's. Reflection about civil society and the university's role within it had withered away.

There were two results of the campus disruptions. The university was incorporated much more firmly into the system of democratic public opinion, and the condition of cavelike darkness amidst prosperity feared by Tocqueville was brought painfully near. When the dust settled it could be seen that the very distinction between educated and uneducated in America had been leveled, that even the pitiful remnant of it expressed in the opposition between highbrow and lowbrow had been annihilated. The real product was the homogenized persons described in Part One. The very ideas of truly different goals and motives of action that we can really take seriously, incarnated not only in systems of thought but in real and poetic models, began to disappear.

Freedom had been restricted in the most effective way—by the impoverishment of alternatives. Nothing that was not known to or experienced by those who constitute the enormous majority—which is ultimately the only authority in America—had any reality. Catering to democracy's most dangerous and vulgar temptations was the function of the famous "critical philosophy." Thus this fatal progress was accompanied by all the abstract substitutes for thought I discussed in Part Two.

They provided an artificial substitute for intellectual stimulation and confirmed that the way we are is the only way to be. They were just what the doctor ordered, as their enormous popularity suggests. All the radicalism of the sixties was intended to hasten our movement in the directions in which we were already going, and never really to question these directions. It was an exercise in egalitarian self-satisfaction that wiped out the elements of the university curriculum that did not flatter our peculiar passions or tastes of the moment. In short, the window to Europe, which was always the resource of free and oppressed spirits in America, was slammed shut, more definitively because Europeans were helping us do it while promising that they were opening it. What at the time appeared to be "elite" opinion current only among university intellectuals was in reality the next day's popular magazine feature. The longing for Europe has been all but extinguished in the young.

About the sixties it is now fashionable to say that although there were indeed excesses, many good things resulted. But, so far as universities are concerned, I know of nothing positive coming from that period; it was an unmitigated disaster for them. I hear that the good things were "greater openness," "less rigidity," "freedom from authority," etc.—but these have no content and express no view of what is wanted from a university education. During the sixties I sat on various committees at Cornell and continuously and futilely voted against dropping one requirement after the next. The old core curriculum—according to which every student in the college had to take a smattering of courses in the major divisions of knowledge—was abandoned. One professor of comparative literature—an assiduous importer of the latest Paris fashions—explained that these requirements taught little, really did not introduce students to the various disciplines, and bored them. I admitted this to be true. He then expressed surprise at my unwillingness to give them up. It was because they were, I said, a threadbare reminiscence of the unity of knowledge and provided an obstinate little hint that there are some things one must know about if one is to be educated. You don't replace something with nothing. Of course, that was exactly what the educational reform of the sixties was doing. The consequences are most visible now in the declining study of languages, but they are just as profound, or more so, in all of humane learning. The criticism of the old is of no value if there is no prospect of the new. It is a way of removing the impediments to vice presented by decaying virtue. In the sixties the professors were just hastening to fold up their tents so as to be off the grounds before the stampede trampled them. The openness was to "doing your own thing." It was, and I suppose still is, a sure sign of an authoritarian personality to believe that the university should try to have a vision of what an educated person is. "Growth" or "individual development" was all that was to be permitted, which in America meant only that the vulgarities present in society at large would overwhelm the delicate little plants kept in the university greenhouse for those who need other kinds of nourishment.

The reforms were without content, made for the "inner-directed" person. They were an acquiescence in a leveling off of the peaks, and were the source of the collapse of the entire American educational structure, recognized by all parties when they talk about the need to go "back to basics." This collapse is directly traceable to both the teachings and the deeds of the universities in the sixties. More important than the bad teachers and the self-indulgent doctrines was the disappearance of the reasons for and the models of—for example—"the king's English." The awareness of the highest is what points the lower upward. Now, it may be possible, with a lot of effort and political struggle, to return to earlier standards of accomplishment in the three R's, but it will not be so easy to recover the knowledge of philosophy, history and literature that was trashed. That was never a native plant. We were dependent on Europe for it. All of our peaks were derivative, with full self-awareness and without being ashamed of it. In the meantime, Europe itself, on which we could count if we faltered, has undergone an evolution similar to our own, and we cannot go there to train ourselves as once we could. Short of great new theoretical and artistic impulses rising up on their own here to replace the West's legacy to us, there is no way but tradition to have kept us in contact with such things. And one cannot jump on and off the tradition like a train. Once broken, our link with it is hard to renew. The instinctive awareness of meanings, as well as the stores of authentic learning in the heads of scholars, are lost. Neither aristocrats nor priests, the natural bearers of high intellectual tradition, exist in any meaningful sense in America. The greatest of thoughts were in our political principles but were never embodied, hence not living, in a class of men. Their home in America was the university, and the violation of that home was the crime of the sixties. Calming the universities down, stopping grade inflation, making students study, all of that may be salutary, but it does not go to the heart of the matter. There is much less in the university to study now.

Around the campus disruptions and the student movement there has grown up a mythology, an expression of the tastes of those for whom the atmosphere depicted in *Ten Days that Shook the World* is more stimulating than that in Hegel's Berlin lecture room would have been. One of the myths is that the fifties were a period of intellectual conformism and superficiality, whereas there was real excitement and questioning in the sixties. McCarthyism—invoked when Stalinism is mentioned in order to even the balance of injustice between the two superpowers—symbolizes those gray, grim years, while the blazing sixties were the days of "the movement" and, to hear its survivors tell it, their single-handed liberation of the blacks, the women and the South Vietnamese. Without entering into the strictly political issues, the intellectual picture projected is precisely the opposite of the truth. The sixties were the period of dogmatic answers and trivial tracts. Not a single book of lasting importance was produced in or around the movement. It was all Norman O. Brown and Charles Reich. This was when the real conformism hit the universities, when opinions about everything from God to the movies became absolutely predictable. The evidence brought from pop culture to bolster the case for the sixties—that in the fifties Lana Turner played torchy, insincere adulteresses while in the sixties we got Jane Fonda as an authentic whore; that before the sixties we had Paul Anka and after we had the Rolling Stones—is of no importance. Even if this characterization were true, it would only go to prove that there is no relation between popular culture and high culture, and that the former is all that is now influential on our scene.

The fact is that the fifties were one of the great periods of the American university, taking into account, of course, the eternal disproportion between the ideal and the real. Even the figures most seminal for "the movement," like Marcuse, Arendt and Mills, did what serious work they did prior to 1960. From 1933 on the American universities profited from the arrival of many of Europe's greatest scholars and scientists as well as a number of clever intellectuals of a sophistication beyond that known to their American counterparts. They were, for the most part, heirs of the German university tradition, which, as I have discussed, was the greatest expression of the publicly supported and approved version of the theoretical life. All were steeped in the general vision of humane education inspired by Kant and Goethe, whose thought and talents were of world historical significance and who intransigently and without compromise looked to the highest moral and artistic fulfillments within the new democratic order of things. They initiated us into a tradition that was living, and that penetrated the tastes and standards of society at large. Those who received this tradition had experience of the vast scholarship accumulated since its inception, as well as the advanced ideas that clustered around its inspiration. For better or worse, German ideas were where it was at—and where it still is—whether it be the ideas of Marx, Freud, Weber or Heidegger. In the chairs of philosophy in the German university there was an amazing correspondence between real talent and conventional respectability. Hegel, Husserl and Heidegger were the respected figures of their day, whose significance did not consist in their merely holding the chairs. An awareness of all this, and in many cases much more than an awareness, was brought by the refugees to the United States, which, speaking relatively, had been a backwater and a consumer. Much of what Americans previously had gone to seek elsewhere was now here. Although this was a mixed blessing in many respects, the fact that so many of the best physicists, mathematicians, historians, sociologists, classicists and teachers of philosophy were in the United States meant that we could learn here what one had to learn; or, rather, however defective what we had here, our quest for learning could no longer be better satisfied by the physical voyage to the Old World. In a word, before the dam burst, the American university had become largely independent of the contemporary European university. The refugees' students here were gradually taking the places of their teachers.

Of course, part of this independence was due to the decline of the Continental universities, especially the destruction of the German universities, the break in their intellectual tradition and the loss of inner confidence and the sense of high vocation they once possessed. But, no matter what the cause, in 1955 no universities were better than the best American universities in the things that have to do with a liberal education and arousing in students the awareness of their intellectual needs. And this was an extremely important fact for the civilization of the West. If in 1930 American universities had simply disappeared, the general store of learning of general significance would not have been seriously damaged, although it would surely not have been a good thing for us. But in 1960, inasmuch as most of intellectual life had long ago settled in universities and the American ones were the best, their decay or collapse was a catastrophe. Much of the great tradition was here, an alien and weak transplant, perched precariously in enclaves, vulnerable to native populism and vulgarity. In the mid-sixties the natives, in the guise of students, attacked.

Another aspect of the mythology is that McCarthyism had an extremely negative impact on the universities. Actually the McCarthy period was the last time the university had any sense of community, defined by a common enemy. McCarthy, those like him, and those who followed them, were clearly nonacademic and antiacademic, the barbarians at the gates. In major universities they had no effect whatsoever on curriculum or appointments. The range of thought and speech that took place within them was unaffected. Academic freedom had for that last moment more than an abstract meaning, a content with respect to research and publication about which there was general agreement. The rhetoric about the protection of unpopular ideas meant something, partly because the publicly unpopular ideas were not so unpopular in universities. Today there are many more things unthinkable and unspeakable in universities than there were then, and little disposition to protect those who have earned the ire of the radical movements. The old liberalism—belief in progress and the free market of ideas—had its last moment of vigor at that time. In the sixties, when things seemed to be going in the right direction, the old liberalism was understood more and more to be a part of bourgeois ideology, favoring and protecting the voices of reaction as opposed to those of progress. In the fifties the campuses were calm, most professors were against McCarthy (although, as one would expect in a democracy, some were for him; and, as one would also expect, human nature and professors being what they are, some who were against him were too timid to speak out). Professors were not fired, and they taught what they pleased in their classrooms. For that moment at least, there was a heightened awareness of the university's special status as a preserve against public opinion. That was a very healthy thing. In the sixties many professors, some of whom were notably silent during the McCarthy years, lost that awareness when the opinions they were attached to became more popular. The screen of academic freedom was no longer necessary now that the going was good. The American Association of University Professors' Cornell chapter applauded the black activists who infringed the rights of professors, and the national organization did nothing to protect academic freedom. Such groups abandoned merely formal freedom to support substantive causes. In short, in the fifties a goodly portion of the professors still held the views about freedom of thought put forward by Bacon, Milton, Locke and John Stuart Mill (this was just prior to the success in America of the Continental critique of these); another portion were of the Left, and they had a personal interest in the protection afforded them by those views. When the former lost their confidence, and the latter gained theirs, the strength of academic freedom declined drastically.

A final part of the mythology of the sixties is the alleged superior moral "concern" of the students. Morality became all the rage in the late sixties, succeeding the hard-nosed realism of the preceding years. But what was meant by morality has to be made clear. There is a perennial and unobtrusive view that morality consists in such things as telling the truth, paying one's debts, respecting one's parents and doing no voluntary harm to anyone. Those are all things easy to say and hard to do; they do not attract much attention, and win little honor in the world. The good will, as described by Kant, is a humble notion, accessible to every child, but its fulfillment is the activity of a lifetime of performing the simple duties prescribed by it. This morality always requires sacrifice. It sometimes entails danger and confrontation, but they are not of its essence and occur incidentally. Such morality, in order to be itself, must be for itself and not for some result beyond it. It requires resistance to the charms of feeling good about it and acclaim for it. This was not the morality that came into vogue in the sixties, which was an altogether more histrionic version of moral conduct, the kind that characterizes heroes in extreme situations. Thomas More's resistance to a tyrant's commands was the daily fare of students' imagination. Such challenges—which arise rarely, are always ambiguous in terms of both duty and motive, and require the subtlest reasoning as well as all the other virtues in the highest degree in order to be addressed justly—were the moral stuff on which these cubs teethed. It was not, of course, the complexity of such cases that was attractive but their brilliance, the noble pose. Somehow it was never the everyday business of obeying the law that was interesting; more so was breaking it in the name of the higher law. It was always Achilles and

Agamemnon. Conscience, a faculty thoroughly discredited in modern political and moral thought and particularly despised by Marx, made a great comeback, as the all-purpose ungrounded ground of moral determination, sufficient at its slightest rumbling to discredit all other obligations or loyalties. Hitler became the regulative principle of the conscience: "You wouldn't obey Hitler, would you?" So refined had the capacity for moral discrimination become, it followed that the elected American officials and the duly approved federal, state and local laws had no more authority than did Hitler. At Cornell, students were graced by the preachings of Father Daniel Berrigan, who explained that old ladies who work as secretaries for draft boards are the equivalent of the Beast of Belsen and deserve no more respectful treatment than she did. This was the temper of the moral revival. The models were a mixture of the makers of revolutions who hawk new moralities and liberate from prevailing constraint, and the heroes of popular existentialist literature whose morality consists in self-affirmation. One began to suspect that the new moralism was just a new dress for the antimorality of the preceding generation, which thought morality repression.

The content of this morality was derived simply from the leading notions of modern democratic thought, absolutized and radicalized. Equality, freedom, peace, cosmopolitanism were the goods, the only goods, without conflict among one another, available to us here and now. Not to be considered were natural differences in gifts or in habitual practice of the virtues, the restraints liberty must impose on itself, wars for the defense of democracy (other than wars of liberation). Devotion to family or country as a form of morality was the last refuge of reaction. There were two poles, supposed to be in perfect harmony, the self-development of the absolute individual and the brotherhood of all mankind. These goods or, rather, values, came on the winds. They were not the product of students' reasoning or study. They were inherent in our regime, they constituted its horizon. There was nothing new in it. The newness was in the thoughtlessness, the utter lack of need to argue or prove. Alternative views had no existence except as scarecrows.

This was an almost inevitable result of generations of teaching that the most instinctive of all questions—What is good?—has no place in the university, and that supersophisticated doctrines that dismiss and ridicule this question and the instinct animating it are the only things worthy of study. If the university's teachers cannot teach about the good, why should the students not teach it? The fact-value distinction admits that values are essential to life and shape the way facts are seen and used. Therefore values are primary. And if they do not come from reason, then they come from passionate commitment, the essence of morality. Of course, since commitment did not really produce values, the values adopted were the remnants of old reasoning, values with fallen arches, reaffirmed by claims of passionate commitment. The teachers were at first appalled by this return to old, bad ways of thought. But since they too were moral persons, and the values asserted were the ones they privately believed, finally they gave gay assent. David Easton's disgraceful presidential address to the American Political Science Association in 1966 said all this. Behavioralism (i.e., the social science founded on the fact-value distinction, devoted to the study of facts and contemptuous of philosophy) had not, he admitted, been sufficiently sensitive to moral issues. Now he promised a post-behavioralism in which the great achievements of social science would be put in the service of the right values. The piper would henceforward play the tune called by the students, and they were not even paying.

Indignation or rage was the vivid passion characterizing those in the grip of the new moral experience. Indignation may be a most noble passion and necessary for fighting wars and righting wrongs. But of all the experiences of the soul it is the most inimical to reason and hence to the university. Anger, to sustain itself, requires an unshakable conviction that one is right. Whether the student wrath against the professorial Agamemnons was authentically Achillean is open to question. But there is no doubt that it was the banner under which they fought, the proof of belonging.

Now, it has always been thought that moral conduct did not need precisely to be painful in order to be moral, but that it could not be itself if it were fun. However interpreted, it is connected with a self-overcoming that being wise or beautiful—or any other of the qualities for which human beings are thought to be enviable—do not require. That is why it commands special respect and also why there is so great a temptation to simulate it. The man who sacrifices his life for justice evidently has motives superior to those of most men, or a disinterestedness incomprehensible to them. They cannot help being impressed. In an admirable phrase Montesquieu encapsulated the moral taste that the student leaders

represented and on which they played: "Men, although they are individually rascals, are collectively a most decent lot: they love morality." This
is the formula for Tartuffe. The student moralism was a species of the
Tartuffe phenomenon, but a wholly new mutant of it. Unlike other
revolutionary movements, which tended to be austere and chaste—beginning with the first revolution, 1688, in England, which was really puritan
—this one was antipuritanical. The slogan was "Make love, not war."
Although the similarity of language was exploited, this is very different
from "Love thy neighbor," which is an injunction very difficult to fulfill.
"To make love" is a bodily act, very easy to perform and thought to be
pleasant. The word "obscene" was transferred out of sex into politics.
Somehow the students had touched on a whole set of desires previously
thought to be questionable, which had hardly dared to name themselves
but which were ripe for emancipation and legitimation. The ideology for
the revolution was already in place. Moderation of the infinite bodily
desires had become "repression" of nature, one of the forms of *domination,* the buzzword of the advanced thinkers and consciousness raisers.
All that was needed were the heroes willing to act out the fantasies the
public was now ready to accept as reality: the hero, as hedonist, who dares
to do in public what the public wants to see. It was *épater les bourgeois*
as a bourgeois calling. The practices of the late Roman empire were
promoted with the moral fervor of early Christianity and the political
idealism of Robespierre. Such a combination is, of course, impossible. It
is playacting, a role, and the students knew it. But that haunting sentiment was assuaged by the fact that this was the first revolution made for
TV. They were real because they could see themselves on television. All
the world had become a stage, and they were playing leads. The cure
proposed for the bourgeois disease really was its most advanced symptom.

A partial list of the sacrifices made by the students to their morality
will suffice to show its character: they were able to live as they pleased in
the university, as *in loco parentis* responsibilities were abandoned; drugs
became a regular part of life, with almost no interference from university
authorities, while the civil authority was kept at bay by the university's
alleged right to police its own precincts; all sexual restrictions imposed by
rule or disapproval were overturned; academic requirements were relaxed
in every imaginable way, and grade inflation made it difficult to flunk;
avoidance of military service was a way of life and a principle. All of these
privileges were disguised with edifying labels such as individual responsi-

bility, experience, growth, development, self-expression, liberation, concern. Never in history had there been such a marvelous correspondence between the good and the pleasant. Richard Nixon, with his unerring instinct for the high moral ground and the noble motive for consensus, assessed his student antagonists and ended the draft. Miraculously the student movement came to an end, although the war continued for almost three years thereafter.

A final note about an aspect of the students' motivation that has not received sufficient attention: In addition to the desire to live as they pleased, a covert elitism was at work among them. A permanent feature of democracy, always and everywhere, is a tendency to suppress the claims of any kind of superiority, conventional or natural, essentially by denying that there is superiority, particularly with respect to ruling. The Platonic dialogues are full of young men who passionately desire political glory and believe they have the talent to rule. Plato admits that he himself was once such a young man. And they lived in a city where their peculiar right to rule was denied them, where they would find it difficult to get ruling office, and where to do so they would have to make themselves into what the people wanted. They burned with that special indignation a man reserves for wrongs done to himself, and believed that their potential could not be fulfilled in democratic Athens. They constituted a subversive group in the city, unfriendly to the maintenance of its regime. Such were many of the companions of Socrates, and taming this instinct for rule was an essential part of the education he gave them. But he began by accepting, at least partially, the legitimacy of their longing and denying the unadulterated right of the many to rule over the few. He gave intellectual satisfaction to their complaint. And, more important, he took very seriously the element in their souls that made them ambitious. The aspiration to be number one and gain great fame is both natural in man and, properly trained, one of the soul's great strengths. Democracy in itself is hostile to such spiritedness and prevents its fulfillment. This was a problem for all ancient democracies. Coriolanus represents an extreme example of the man who refuses to ground his right to rule on any admixture of consent of the people, in this case a people ready to accept his right to rule. But he is not an entirely unadmirable man. The strength of his soul is a result of the part of it that makes him proud and ambitious, that seeks an autonomy not dependent on others' opinions or wills.

The problem of ambition in democracy is much aggravated by modern democracy. Ancient democracies were factually powerful, but they did not persuade the proud and the ambitious that the rule of the many is just. Inner confidence was not weakened by the sense that the master has right on his side, for there was neither a religion nor a philosophy of equality. The talented young could hope, and sometimes act, without guilt, to gain first place. This has been changed partially, but only partially, by Christianity. It asserted equality before God and condemned pride, but it left the inequalities of this world in place. More important was the work of modern philosophy, which established a rational teaching, making political equality the only just system of society. There is no intellectual ground remaining for any regime other than democracy. The soul cannot find encouragement for its longing anywhere. Moreover, the modern thinkers developed a scheme of things in which individual ambition would have little hope of success. The outline of this scheme is presented in Federalist X. The sheer size of this country, as well as its organization and its stability, has a disheartening effect on the potential ruler. Even more important have been the efforts of modern philosophers to root pride and great ambition out of the soul. At the outset, Hobbes's psychology treated what he called vainglory as a pathological condition based on ignorance of man's vulnerability, on unjustified confidence. This condition can, according to him, be cured by liberal doses of fear. One need only hear what is said today about competition among educators and in the press, and read Rousseau and Freud on related issues, to recognize how much of modernity is devoted to unmanning this disposition. Elitism is the catch-all epithet expressing our disapproval of the proud and the desire to be first.

But, unsupported and excoriated, this part of the soul lives on, dwelling underground, receiving no sublimating education. As with all repressed impulses, it has its daily effects on personality and also occasionally bursts forth in various disguises and monstrous shapes. Much of modern history can be explained by the search of what Plato called spiritedness for legitimate self-expression. Certainly compassion and the idea of the vanguard were essentially democratic covers for elitist self-assertion. Rousseau, who first made compassion the foundation of democratic sentiment, was fully aware that a sense of superiority to the sufferer is a component of the human experience of compassion. He actually was attempting to channel the inegalitarian impulse into egalitarian channels.

Similarly the avant-garde (usually used in relation to art) and the vanguard (usually used in relation to politics) are democratic modes of distinguishing oneself, of being ahead, of leading, without denying the democratic principle. The members of the vanguard have just a small evanescent advantage. They now know what everyone will soon know. This posture conciliates instinct with principle. And it was the one adopted by the students who feared assimilation to the democratic man. There they were in those few elite universities, which were being rapidly democratized. And their political futures were bleak, their educations not advantaging them for elective office, providing only the prospect of having to work their way up in the dreary fashion of such contemptible persons as Lyndon Johnson and Richard Nixon. But these universities were respected, looked to by the democratic press and were the alma maters of much of the powerful elite. These little places could easily be seized, just as a polis could have been seized. Using them as a stage, students instantly achieved notoriety. Young black students I knew at Cornell appeared on the covers of the national news magazines. How irresistible it all was, an elite short-cut to political influence. In the ordinary world, outside the universities, such youngsters would have had no way of gaining attention. They took as their models Mao, Castro and Che Guevara, promoters of equality, if you please, but surely not themselves equal to anyone. They themselves wanted to be the leaders of a revolution of compassion. The great objects of their contempt and fury were the members of the American middle class, professionals, workers, white collar and blue, farmers—all of those vulgarians who made up the American majority and who did not need or want either the compassion or the leadership of the students. They dared to think themselves equal to the students and to resist having their consciousness raised by them. It is very difficult to distinguish oneself in America, and in order to do so the students substituted conspicuous compassion for their parents' conspicuous consumption. They specialized in being the advocates of all those in America and the Third World who did not challenge their sense of superiority and who, they imagined, would accept their leadership. None of the exquisite thrills of egalitarian vanity were alien to them.

One could appreciate and even sympathize with the frustrated inclinations, the love of glory that could not be avowed, the quest for the recognition of excellence that were revealed in the sixties campus politics.

However, the hypocrisy of it all, and the ignorance of what a man has to know and to risk in order to be political, made the spectacle more repulsive than touching. Tyrannical impulses masqueraded as democratic compassion, and quest for distinction as love of equality. Self-knowledge was utterly lacking, and their conquest was so easy. The elite should really be elite, but these elitists were given the distinction they craved without having earned it. The university provided a kind of affirmative-action elitism. There had for a long time been a conspiracy in the universities to deny that there is a problem for the superior individual, particularly the one with the gift and the passion for ruling, in democratic society. Suddenly they found themselves confronted by potential rulers who accused them of complicity in the crime of ruling. It served them right.

It was with respect to precisely this problem that I had one of my greatest satisfactions as a teacher. The little Greek Civilization Program a group of professors set up against the currents had just gotten under way the year of the crisis. It consisted of about a dozen enthusiastic freshmen, and we had been reading Plato's *Republic* during the entire year. We had not finished it when the university became a chaos. Almost all classes ceased, as students and professors alike turned to the serious business of making the revolution, hanging about the campus and going from one crazy meeting to another. I had joined with a group of professors who announced they would not teach until the guns were off campus and some kind of legitimate order had been restored. But these students had become deeply involved with the story of the ambitious Glaucon, who was founding a city with the help of Socrates. So we continued to meet informally. They were really more interested in the book than the revolution, which in itself proved what kind of a counter-charm the university ought to provide to the siren calls of the contemporary scene. These students were rather contemptuous of what was going on, because it got in the way of what they thought it important to do. They wanted to find out what happened to Glaucon during his wonderful night with Socrates. They really *looked down* from the classroom on the frantic activity outside, thinking they were privileged, hardly a one tempted to join the crowd. I later found out that some of these students had indeed gone down from the library seminar room into the agora, where the action was. They had made copies of the following lines from the *Republic* and handed them out, competing with the hawkers of other kinds of tracts:

"Do you too believe, as do the many, that certain young men are corrupted by sophists, and that there are certain sophists who in a private capacity corrupt to an extent worth mentioning? Isn't it rather the very men who say this who are the biggest sophists, who educate most perfectly and who turn out young and old, men and women, just the way they want them to be?"

"But when do they do that?" he said.

"When," I said, "many gathered together sit down in assemblies, courts, theaters, army camps, or any other common meeting of a multitude, and, with a great deal of uproar, blame some of the things said or done, and praise others, both in excess, shouting and clapping; and, besides, the rocks and the very place surrounding them echo and redouble the uproar of blame and praise. Now in such circumstances, as the saying goes, what do you suppose is the state of the young man's heart? Or what kind of private education will hold out for him and not be swept away by such blame and praise and go, borne by the flood, wherever it tends so that he'll say the same things are noble and base as they do, practice what they practice, and be such as they are?" (*Republic* 491e–492b)

They had learned from this old book what was going on and had gained real distance on it, had had an experience of liberation. Socrates' magic still worked. He had diagnosed the complaint of the ambitious young and showed how to treat it.

The sixties have now faded from the current student imagination. What remains is a certain self-promotion by people who took part in it all, now in their forties, having come to terms with the "establishment" but dispersing a nostalgic essence in the media, where, of course, many of them are flourishing, admitting that it was unreal but asserting that it was the moment of significance. They stood for the good things. They seem to think they were responsible for great progress in relations between whites and blacks, that they played the key role in the civil rights movement. Without attempting to discuss what was decisive in the historic changes that took place in those relations in the years between 1950 and 1970—whether it was the doings of the courts, or of elected officials, or inspiration of the kind represented by Martin Luther King from within the black community that was most important—it is undeniable that the enthusiastic support of these changes by university students in the North played some role in creating the atmosphere that promoted the righting of old wrongs. But I believe the students' role was marginal and partook not a little of the histrionic morality of which I have been speaking. It consisted mostly in going off to marches and demonstrations that were vacationlike, usually during school term, with the confident expectation that they would not be penalized by their professors for missing assignments while they were off doing important deeds, in places where they had never been and to which they would never return, and where, therefore, they did not have to pay any price for their stand, as did those who had to stay and live there. Nor did they partake in the hard and low-profile labors of those who studied constitutional law and prepared legal briefs, those who spent lonely and frustrating years, whose lives were truly dedicated to a cause. I do not wish to denigrate the students' efforts, and people should not be blamed for inclinations that are truly good, although there should not be too much self-congratulation for what was easy and cost little. My point is, rather, that the student participation in the civil rights movement antedated the campus activism, and that the students' opinions were formed in the old, bad universities that they returned to destroy. The last significant student participation in the civil rights movement was in the march on Washington in 1964. After that, Black Power came to the fore, the system of segregation in the South was dismantled, and white students had nothing more to contribute other than to egg on Black Power excesses, the instigators of which did not want their help. The students were unaware that the teachings of equality, the promise of the Declaration of Independence, the study of the Constitution, the knowledge of our history and many more things were the painstakingly earned and stored-up capital that supported them. Racial justice is an imperative of our theory and historical practice, without which there would have been no problem and no solution. From what were claimed to be absolutely corrupt institutions serving "the system," students gained the awareness and learning that made their action possible and good. The most outrageous pretension of the students was that their commitments were their autonomous creations. Everything, but everything, was borrowed from the serious thought and beliefs about what America is and about good and bad in the university treasury. They could waste the capital because they did not know they were living off of it. They returned to the university, declared it bankrupt and thereby bankrupted it. They abandoned the grand American liberal traditions of learning. Under pressure from students the Founding was understood to be racist, and the very instrument that condemned slavery and racism was broken. The races in the Northern universities have grown more separate since the sixties. After the theory of the rights of man was no longer studied or really believed, its practice also suffered. The American university provided the intellectual inspiration for decent political deeds. It is very doubtful whether there is a teaching about justice within it now that could again generate anything like the movement toward racial equality. The very thing the sixties students prided themselves on was one of their premier victims.

THE STUDENT AND THE UNIVERSITY

Liberal Education

What image does a first-rank college or university present today to a teen-ager leaving home for the first time, off to the adventure of a liberal education? He has four years of freedom to discover himself—a space between the intellectual wasteland he has left behind and the inevitable dreary professional training that awaits him after the baccalaureate. In this short time he must learn that there is a great world beyond the little one he knows, experience the exhilaration of it and digest enough of it to sustain himself in the intellectual deserts he is destined to traverse. He must do this, that is, if he is to have any hope of a higher life. These are the charmed years when he can, if he so chooses, become anything he wishes and when he has the opportunity to survey his alternatives, not merely those current in his time or provided by careers, but those available to him as a human being. The importance of these years for an American cannot be overestimated. They are civilization's only chance to get to him.

In looking at him we are forced to reflect on what he should learn if he is to be called educated; we must speculate on what the human potential to be fulfilled is. In the specialties we can avoid such speculation, and the avoidance of them is one of specialization's charms. But here it is a simple duty. What are we to teach this person? The answer may not be evident, but to attempt to answer the question is already to philosophize and to begin to educate. Such a concern in itself poses the question of the unity of man and the unity of the sciences. It is childishness to say, as some do, that everyone must be allowed to develop freely, that it is authoritarian to impose a point of view on the student. In that case, why have a university? If the response is "to provide an atmosphere for learning," we come back to our original questions at the second remove. Which atmosphere? Choices and reflection on the reasons for those choices are unavoidable. The university has to stand for something. The practical effects of unwillingness to think positively about the contents of a liberal education are, on the one hand, to ensure that all the vulgarities of the world outside the university will flourish within it, and, on the other, to impose a much harsher and more illiberal necessity on the student—the one given by the imperial and imperious demands of the specialized disciplines unfiltered by unifying thought.

The university now offers no distinctive visage to the young person. He finds a democracy of the disciplines—which are there either because they are autochthonous or because they wandered in recently to perform some job that was demanded of the university. This democracy is really an anarchy, because there are no recognized rules for citizenship and no legitimate titles to rule. In short there is no vision, nor is there a set of competing visions, of what an educated human being is. The question has disappeared, for to pose it would be a threat to the peace. There is no organization of the sciences, no tree of knowledge. Out of chaos emerges dispiritedness, because it is impossible to make a reasonable choice. Better to give up on liberal education and get on with a specialty in which there is at least a prescribed curriculum and a prospective career. On the way the student can pick up in elective courses a little of whatever is thought to make one cultured. The student gets no intimation that great mysteries might be revealed to him, that new and higher motives of action might be discovered within him, that a different and more human way of life can be harmoniously constructed by what he is going to learn.

Simply, the university is not distinctive. Equality for us seems to culminate in the unwillingness and incapacity to make claims of superiority, particularly in the domains in which such claims have always been made—art, religion and philosophy. When Weber found that he could not choose between certain high opposites—reason vs. revelation, Buddha vs. Jesus—he did not conclude that all things are equally good, that the distinction between high and low disappears. As a matter of fact he intended to revitalize the consideration of these great alternatives in showing the gravity and danger involved in choosing among them; they were to be heightened in contrast to the trivial considerations of modern life that threatened to overgrow and render indistinguishable the profound problems the confrontation with which makes the bow of the soul taut. The serious intellectual life was for him the battleground of the great decisions, all of which are spiritual or "value" choices. One can no longer present this or that particular view of the educated or civilized man as authoritative; therefore one must say that education consists in knowing, really knowing, the small number of such views in their integrity. This distinction between profound and superficial—which takes the place of good and bad, true and false—provided a focus for serious study, but it hardly held out against the naturally relaxed democratic tendency to say, "Oh, what's the use?" The first university disruptions at Berkeley were explicitly directed against the multiversity smorgasbord and, I must confess, momentarily and partially engaged my sympathies. It may have even been the case that there was some small element of longing for an education in the motivation of those students. But nothing was done to guide or inform their energy, and the result was merely to add multilife-styles to multidisciplines, the diversity of perversity to the diversity of specialization. What we see so often happening in general happened here too; the insistent demand for greater community ended in greater isolation. Old agreements, old habits, old traditions were not so easily replaced.

Thus, when a student arrives at the university, he finds a bewildering variety of departments and a bewildering variety of courses. And there is no official guidance, no university-wide agreement, about what he *should* study. Nor does he usually find readily available examples, either among students or professors, of a unified use of the university's resources. It is easiest simply to make a career choice and go about getting prepared for that career. The programs designed for those having made such a choice render their students immune to charms that might lead them out of the conventionally respectable. The sirens sing *sotto voce* these days, and the young already have enough wax in their ears to pass them by without danger. These specialties can provide enough courses to take up most of their time for four years in preparation for the inevitable graduate study. With the few remaining courses they can do what they please, taking a bit of this and a bit of that. No public career these days—not doctor nor lawyer nor politician nor journalist nor businessman nor entertainer—has much to do with humane learning. An education, other than purely professional or technical, can even seem to be an impediment. That is why a countervailing atmosphere in the university would be necessary for the students to gain a taste for intellectual pleasures and learn that they are viable.

The real problem is those students who come hoping to find out what career they want to have, or are simply looking for an adventure with themselves. There are plenty of things for them to do—courses and disciplines enough to spend many a lifetime on. Each department or great division of the university makes a pitch for itself, and each offers a course of study that will make the student an initiate. But how to choose among them? How do they relate to one another? The fact is they do not address one another. They are competing and contradictory, without being aware of it. The problem of the whole is urgently indicated by the very existence of the specialties, but it is never systematically posed. The net effect of the student's encounter with the college catalogue is bewilderment and very often demoralization. It is just a matter of chance whether he finds one or two professors who can give him an insight into one of the great visions of education that have been the distinguishing part of every civilized nation. Most professors are specialists, concerned only with their own fields, interested in the advancement of those fields in their own terms, or in their own personal advancement in a world where all the rewards are on the side of professional distinction. They have been entirely emancipated from the old structure of the university, which at least helped to indicate that they are incomplete, only parts of an unexamined and undiscovered whole. So the student must navigate among a collection of carnival barkers, each trying to lure him into a particular sideshow. This undecided student is an embarrassment to most universities, because he seems to be saying, "I am a whole human being. Help me to form myself in my wholeness and let me develop my real potential," and he is the one to whom they have nothing to say.

Cornell was, as in so many other things, in advance of its time on this issue. The six-year Ph.D. program, richly supported by the Ford Foundation, was directed specifically to high school students who had already made "a firm career choice" and was intended to rush them through to the start of those careers. A sop was given to desolate humanists in the form of money to fund seminars that these young careerists could take on their way through the College of Arts and Sciences. For the rest, the educators could devote their energies to arranging and packaging the program without having to provide it with any substance. That kept them busy enough to avoid thinking about the nothingness of their endeavor. This has been the preferred mode of not looking the Beast in the Jungle in the face—structure, not content. The Cornell plan for dealing with the problem of liberal education was to suppress the students' longing for liberal education by encouraging their professionalism and their avarice, providing money and all the prestige the university had available to make careerism the centerpiece of the university.

The Cornell plan dared not state the radical truth, a well-kept secret: the colleges do not have enough to teach their students, not enough to justify keeping them four years, probably not even three years. If the focus is careers, there is hardly one specialty, outside the hardest of the hard natural sciences, which requires more than two years of preparatory training prior to graduate studies. The rest is just wasted time, or a period of ripening until the students are old enough for graduate studies. For many graduate careers, even less is really necessary. It is amazing how many undergraduates are poking around for courses to take, without any plan or question to ask, just filling up their college years. In fact, with rare exceptions, the courses are parts of specialties and not designed for general cultivation, or to investigate questions important for human beings as such. The so-called knowledge explosion and increasing specialization have not filled up the college years but emptied them. Those years are impediments; one wants to get beyond them. And in general the persons one finds in the professions need not have gone to college, if one is to judge by their tastes, their fund of learning or their interests. They might as well have spent their college years in the Peace Corps or the like. These great universities—which can split the atom, find cures for the most terrible diseases, conduct surveys of whole populations and produce massive dictionaries of lost languages—cannot generate a modest program of general education for undergraduate students. This is a parable for our times.

There are attempts to fill the vacuum painlessly with various kinds of fancy packaging of what is already there—study abroad options, individualized majors, etc. Then there are Black Studies and Women's or

Gender Studies, along with Learn Another Culture. Peace Studies are on their way to a similar prevalence. All this is designed to show that the university is with it and has something in addition to its traditional specialties. The latest item is computer literacy, the full cheapness of which is evident only to those who think a bit about what literacy might mean. It would make some sense to promote literacy literacy, inasmuch as most high school graduates nowadays have difficulty reading and writing. And some institutions are quietly undertaking this worthwhile task. But they do not trumpet the fact, because this is merely a high school function that our current sad state of educational affairs has thrust upon them, about which they are not inclined to boast.

Now that the distractions of the sixties are over, and undergraduate education has become more important again (because the graduate departments, aside from the professional schools, are in trouble due to the shortage of academic jobs), university officials have had somehow to deal with the undeniable fact that the students who enter are uncivilized, and that the universities have some responsibility for civilizing them. If one were to give a base interpretation of the schools' motives, one could allege that their concern stems from shame and self-interest. It is becoming all too evident that liberal education—which is what the small band of prestigious institutions are supposed to provide, in contrast to the big state schools, which are thought simply to prepare specialists to meet the practical demands of a complex society—has no content, that a certain kind of fraud is being perpetrated. For a time the great moral consciousness alleged to have been fostered in students by the great universities, especially their vocation as gladiators who fight war and racism, seemed to fulfill the demands of the collective university conscience. They were doing something other than offering preliminary training for doctors and lawyers. Concern and compassion were thought to be the indefinable X that pervaded all the parts of the Arts and Sciences campus. But when that evanescent mist dissipated during the seventies, and the faculties found themselves face to face with ill-educated young people with no intellectual tastes—unaware that there even are such things, obsessed with getting on with their careers before having looked at life—and the universities offered no counterpoise, no alternative goals, a reaction set in.

Liberal education—since it has for so long been ill-defined, has none of the crisp clarity or institutionalized prestige of the professions, but nevertheless perseveres and has money and respectability connected with it—has always been a battleground for those who are somewhat eccentric in relation to the specialties. It is in something like the condition of churches as opposed to, say, hospitals. Nobody is quite certain of what the religious institutions are supposed to do anymore, but they do have some kind of role either responding to a real human need or as the vestige of what was once a need, and they invite the exploitation of quacks, adventurers, cranks and fanatics. But they also solicit the warmest and most valiant efforts of persons of peculiar gravity and depth. In liberal education, too, the worst and the best fight it out, fakers vs. authentics, sophists vs. philosophers, for the favor of public opinion and for control over the study of man in our times. The most conspicuous participants in the struggle are administrators who are formally responsible for presenting some kind of public image of the education their colleges offer, persons with a political agenda or vulgarizers of what the specialties know, and real teachers of the humane disciplines who actually see their relation to the whole and urgently wish to preserve the awareness of it in their students' consciousness.

So, just as in the sixties universities were devoted to removing requirements, in the eighties they are busy with attempts to put them back in, a much more difficult task. The word of the day is "core." It is generally agreed that "we went a bit far in the sixties," and that a little fine-tuning has now become clearly necessary.

There are two typical responses to the problem. The easiest and most administratively satisfying solution is to make use of what is already there in the autonomous departments and simply force the students to cover the fields, i.e., take one or more courses in each of the general divisions of the university: natural science, social science and the humanities. The reigning ideology here is *breadth*, as was *openness* in the age of laxity. The courses are almost always the already existing introductory courses, which are of least interest to the major professors and merely assume the worth and reality of that which is to be studied. It is general education, in the sense in which a jack-of-all-trades is a generalist. He knows a bit of everything and is inferior to the specialist in each area. Students may wish to sample a variety of fields, and it may be good to encourage them to look around and see if there is something that attracts them in one of which they have no experience. But this is not a liberal education and does not satisfy any longing they have for one. It just teaches that there is no high-level generalism, and that what they are doing is preliminary to the real stuff and part of the childhood they are leaving behind. Thus they desire to get it over with and get on with what their professors do seriously. Without recognition of important questions of common concern, there cannot be serious liberal education, and attempts to establish it will be but failed gestures.

It is a more or less precise awareness of the inadequacy of this approach to core curricula that motivates the second approach, which consists of what one might call composite courses. These are constructions developed especially for general-education purposes and usually require collaboration of professors drawn from several departments. These courses have titles like "Man in Nature," "War and Moral Responsibility," "The Arts and Creativity," "Culture and the Individual." Everything, of course, depends upon who plans them and who teaches them. They have the clear advantage of requiring some reflection on the general needs of students and force specialized professors to broaden their perspectives, at least for a moment. The dangers are trendiness, mere popularization and lack of substantive rigor. In general, the natural scientists do not collaborate in such endeavors, and hence these courses tend to be unbalanced. In short, they do not point beyond themselves and do not provide the student with independent means to pursue permanent questions independently, as, for example, the study of Aristotle or Kant as wholes once did. They tend to be bits of this and that. Liberal education should give the student the sense that learning must and can be both synoptic and precise. For this, a very small, detailed problem can be the best way, if it is framed so as to open out on the whole. Unless the course has the specific intention to lead to the permanent questions, to make the student aware of them and give him some competence in the important works that treat of them, it tends to be a pleasant diversion and a dead end—because it has nothing to do with any program of further study he can imagine. If such programs engage the best energies of the best people in the university, they can be beneficial and provide some of the missing intellectual excitement for both professors and students. But they rarely do, and they are too cut off from the top, from what the various faculties see as their real business. Where the power is determines the life of the whole body. And the intellectual problems unresolved at the top cannot be resolved administratively below. The problem is the lack of any unity of the sciences and the loss of the will or the means even to discuss the issue. The illness above is the cause of the illness below, to which all the good-willed efforts of honest liberal educationists can at best be palliatives.

Of course, the only serious solution is the one that is almost universally rejected: the good old Great Books approach, in which a liberal education means reading certain generally recognized classic texts, just reading them, letting them dictate what the questions are and the method of approaching them—not forcing them into categories we make up, not treating them as historical products, but trying to read them as their authors wished them to be read. I am perfectly well aware of, and actually agree with, the objections to the Great Books cult. It is amateurish; it encourages an autodidact's self-assurance without competence; one cannot read all of the Great Books carefully; if one only reads Great Books, one can never know what a great, as opposed to an ordinary, book is; there is no way of determining who is to decide what a Great Book or what the canon is; books are made the ends and not the means; the whole movement has a certain coarse evangelistic tone that is the opposite of good taste; it engenders a spurious intimacy with greatness; and so forth. But one thing is certain: wherever the Great Books make up a central part of the curriculum, the students are excited and satisfied, feel they are doing something that is independent and fulfilling, getting something from the university they cannot get elsewhere. The very fact of this special experience, which leads nowhere beyond itself, provides them with a new alternative and a respect for study itself. The advantage they get is an awareness of the classic—particularly important for our innocents; an acquaintance with what big questions were when there were still big questions; models, at the very least, of how to go about answering them; and, perhaps most important of all, a fund of shared experiences and thoughts on which to ground their friendships with one another. Programs based upon judicious use of great texts provide the royal road to students' hearts. Their gratitude at learning of Achilles or the categorical imperative is boundless. Alexandre Koyré, the late historian of science, told me that his appreciation for America was great when—in the first course he taught at the University of Chicago, in 1940 at the beginning of his exile—a student spoke in his paper of Mr. Aristotle, unaware that he was not a contemporary. Koyré said that only an American could have the naive profundity to take Aristotle as living thought, unthinkable for most scholars. A good program of liberal education feeds the student's love of truth and passion to live a good life. It is the easiest thing in the world to devise courses of study, adapted to the particular conditions of each university, which thrill those who take them. The difficulty is in getting them accepted by the faculty.

None of the three great parts of the contemporary university is enthusiastic about the Great Books approach to education. The natural scientists are benevolent toward other fields and toward liberal education, if it does not steal away their students and does not take too much time from their preparatory studies. But they themselves are interested primarily in the solution of the questions now important in their disciplines and are not particularly concerned with discussions of their foundations, inasmuch as they are so evidently successful. They are indifferent to Newton's conception of time or his disputes with Leibniz about calculus; Aristotle's teleology is an absurdity beneath consideration. Scientific progress, they believe, no longer depends on the kind of comprehensive reflection given to the nature of science by men like Bacon, Descartes, Hume, Kant and Marx. This is merely historical study, and for a long time now, even the greatest scientists have given up thinking about Galileo and Newton. Progress is undoubted. The difficulties about the truth of science raised by positivism, and those about the goodness of science raised by Rousseau and Nietzsche, have not really penetrated to the center of scientific consciousness. Hence, no Great Books, but incremental progress, is the theme for them.

Social scientists are in general hostile, because the classic texts tend to deal with the human things the social sciences deal with, and they are very proud of having freed themselves from the shackles of such earlier thought to become truly scientific. And, unlike the natural scientists, they are insecure enough about their achievement to feel threatened by the works of earlier thinkers, perhaps a bit afraid that students will be seduced and fall back into the bad old ways. Moreover, with the possible exception of Weber and Freud, there are no social science books that can be said to be classic. This may be interpreted favorably to the social sciences by comparing them to the natural sciences, which can be said to be a living organism developing by the addition of little cells, a veritable body of knowledge proving itself to be such by the very fact of this almost unconscious growth, with thousands of parts oblivious to the whole, nevertheless contributing to it. This is in opposition to a work of imagination or of philosophy, where a single creator makes and surveys an artificial whole. But whether one interprets the absence of the classic in the social sciences in ways flattering or unflattering to them, the fact causes social scientists discomfort. I remember the professor who taught the introductory graduate courses in social science methodology, a famous historian, responding scornfully and angrily to a question I naively put to him about Thucydides with "Thucydides was a fool!"

More difficult to explain is the tepid reaction of humanists to Great Books education, inasmuch as these books now belong almost exclusively to what are called the humanities. One would think that high esteem for the classic would reinforce the spiritual power of the humanities, at a time when their temporal power is at its lowest. And it is true that the most active proponents of liberal education and the study of classic texts are indeed usually humanists. But there is division among them. Some humanities disciplines are just crusty specialties that, although they depend on the status of classic books for their existence, are not really interested in them in their natural state—much philology, for example, is concerned with the languages but not what is said in them—and will and can do nothing to support their own infrastructure. Some humanities disciplines are eager to join the real sciences and transcend their roots in the now overcome mythic past. Some humanists make the legitimate complaints about lack of competence in the teaching and learning of Great Books, although their criticism is frequently undermined by the fact that they are only defending recent scholarly interpretation of the classics rather than a vital, authentic understanding. In their reaction there is a strong element of specialist's jealousy and narrowness. Finally, a large part of the story is just the general debilitation of the humanities, which is both symptom and cause of our present condition.

To repeat, the crisis of liberal education is a reflection of a crisis at the peaks of learning, an incoherence and incompatibility among the first principles with which we interpret the world, an intellectual crisis of the greatest magnitude, which constitutes the crisis of our civilization. But perhaps it would be true to say that the crisis consists not so much in this incoherence but in our incapacity to discuss or even recognize it. Liberal education flourished when it prepared the way for the discussion of a unified view of nature and man's place in it, which the best minds debated on the highest level. It decayed when what lay beyond it were only specialties, the premises of which do not lead to any such vision. The highest is the partial intellect; there is no synopsis.

The Decomposition of the University

This became all too clear in the aftermath of the guns at Cornell, and I had a chance to learn something about the articulation of the university as it decomposed. In general, no discipline—only individuals—reacted very well to the assault on academic freedom and integrity. But various disciplines reacted in characteristic ways. The professional schools —engineering, home economics, industrial-labor relations and agriculture —simply went home and closed the shutters. (Some professors in the law school did indeed express indignation, and a group of them finally spoke out publicly for the dismissal of the president.) These faculties were supposed, in general, to be conservative, but they just did not want trouble and did not feel it was their fight. The complaints of the black students were not about them; and whatever changes in thought were to take place, they would be untouched. In spite of the common complaints about the great variety of disciplines unbalancing the university and causing it to lose its focus, everyone knows that the arts and sciences faculty is where the action is, that the other schools are ancillary to it, that it is the center of learning and prestige. This much of the old order has been preserved. The challenge at Cornell was issued to the College of Arts and Sciences, as was the case everywhere throughout the sixties. The problem thus had to be faced by the natural sciences, the social sciences and the humanities. They were asked to change their content and their standards, to eliminate elitism, racism and sexism as "perceived" by students. But the community of scholars proved to be no community. There was no solidarity in defense of the pursuit of truth.

The natural scientists were above the battle, an island unto themselves, and did not feel threatened. I believe that only one natural scientist at Cornell spoke out against the presence of guns or the bullying of professors. The university's most famous professor, a Nobel prizewinning physicist, became a leading spokesman in defense of the president without once consulting those professors whose lives had been threatened or posing the question of what was at stake. He deplored the violence but took no action or uttered any word indicating where a line should be drawn. As far as I know, none of the natural scientists was in cahoots with the thugs, as were some social scientists and humanists. It was the absolute independence of their work from the rest of the university's activity, and their trust that theirs is the important work, that made them indifferent. They did not share a common good with the rest of us. Walking to the meeting where the faculty capitulated to the students—a truly disgraceful event, a microcosm of cowardly acquiescence to the establishment of tyranny—in the company of a friend who had had to suffer the humiliation of leaving his home and hiding out with his family after receiving explicit threats, I heard a professor of biology loudly asking, perhaps for our benefit, "Do these social scientists really believe there is any danger?" My friend looked at me sadly and said, "With colleagues like that, you don't need enemies."

Because the student movements were so untheoretical, the natural sciences were not a target, as they had once been in high-grade fascism and communism. There were no Lenins thundering against positivism, relativity or genetics, no Goebbels alert to the falseness of Jewish science. There had been the beginnings of an offensive against the scientists' collaboration with the military-industrial complex, as well as their role in producing the technology that abets capitalism and pollutes the environment. But none of this went to the heart of the serious scientists' research. They were able to avoid the fury by distancing themselves from certain unpopular applications of their knowledge, by insulting the government which supported them, and by declaring themselves for peace and social justice. Here too the great Cornell physicist has, predictably, distinguished himself by making a habit of apologizing for physics' hand in producing thermonuclear weapons. But these scientists were not asked to change one thing in their studies, their classes or their laboratories. So they opted out.

This behavior was not merely selfishness and self-protectiveness, every man for himself, although there was a good deal of that, accompanied with the usual distasteful moralizing rhetoric. The atmosphere of crisis caused a not entirely conscious reassessment of natural science's relation to the university. Crises in the intellectual world as well as in the political one tend to bring to the surface tensions and changes in interest that it is easier not to face as long as things are calm. To break old alliances and form new ones is always a painful business, as, for example, when liberals broke with Stalinists at the beginning of the Cold War. The scientists found themselves confronted with the fact that they had no real connection with the rest of the university, and that to cast their lot with it was costly. One cannot imagine that biologists would have been so callous if chemistry had somehow become a target for cultural revolution, and young Red Guards monitored its teachings and terrorized its practitioners. Chemists are biologists' blood relations, and their knowledge is absolutely indispensable for the progress of biology. But it is not now conceivable that a physicist qua physicist could learn anything important, or anything at all, from a professor of comparative literature or of sociology. The natural scientist's connection with the rest of humane learning is not familial but abstract, a little like our connection with humanity as a whole. There may be a formulaic invocation of rights applicable to all, but nothing that moves with the burning immediacy of shared convictions and interests. "I can live without you" is the silent thought that steals into one's mind when such relations become painful.

The reality of separateness has existed since Kant, the last philosopher who was a significant natural scientist, and Goethe, the last great literary figure who could believe that his contributions to science might be greater than his contributions to literature. And, it should be remembered, it was not that they were philosopher and poet who happened to dabble in science, but that their writings were mirrors of nature and that their science was guided and informed by meditation on being, freedom and beauty. They represented the last gasp of the old unity of the questions before natural science became the Switzerland of learning, safely neutral to the battles taking place on the darkling plain. Henry Adams— whose life bridged the last epoch when gentlemen, such as Jefferson, thought science both attainable and useful for them, and the one where scientists speak an incomprehensible language that teaches nothing about life but is necessary to life as information—takes note of this change in his quirky way. When he was young he had studied natural science and had given it up; when as an old man he looked again in that direction, he found that he was in a new world. The old university traditions and ideals had concealed the fact that the ancient bonds had decayed and the marriage was washed up. The great scientists of the nineteenth century and twentieth century were in general cultivated men who had some experience of, and real admiration for, the other parts of learning. The increasing specialization of the natural sciences and the natural scientists gradually caused the protective fog to lift. Since the sixties the scientists have had less and less to say to, and to do with, their colleagues in the social sciences and humanities. The university has lost whatever polis-like character it had and has become like the ship on which the passengers are just accidental fellow travelers soon to disembark and go their separate ways. The relations between natural science, social science and humanities are purely administrative and have no substantial intellectual content. They only meet on the level of the first two years of undergraduate education, and there the natural scientists are largely concerned with protecting their interest in the young who will be coming their way.

A perfect illustration of this situation appeared a few years ago in a *New York Times* account of the visit of a professor of music to Rockefeller University. The life scientists working there brought bag lunches to the musicologist's lecture. The project was inspired by C. P. Snow's silly conceits about "the two cultures," the rift between which he proposed to heal by getting humanists to learn the second law of thermodynamics and physicists to read Shakespeare. This enterprise would, of course, be something other than an exercise in spiritual uplift only if the physicist learned something important for his physics from Shakespeare, and if the humanist similarly profited from the second law of thermodynamics. In fact, nothing of the sort ensues. For the scientist the humanities are recreation (often deeply respected by him, for he sees that more is needed than what he offers, but is puzzled about where to find it), and for the humanist the natural sciences are at best indifferent, at worst alien and hostile.

The *Times* quoted Joshua Lederberg, the president of Rockefeller University, from which philosophy had recently been banished, as saying after the lecture that C. P. Snow was on the right track but "counted wrong"—there are not two but many cultures, one example of which is that of the Beatles. This represents the ultimate trivialization of a trivial idea that was just a rest station on a downward slope. Lederberg saw in the humanities not the human knowledge that complements the study of nature but merely another expression of what was going on in the world. In the end, it is all more or less sophisticated show business. With a kind of wink at his audience Lederberg lets us know that in this sea of democratic relativism natural science stands out like Gibraltar. All the rest is a matter of taste.

This disposition affected the natural scientists' behavior at Cornell and everywhere else. In the attempt to use the admission of students and appointment of faculty as means for this or that social goal, which has lowered university standards and obscured the university's purpose, they cooperated with the new agenda, in their own way. They adopted the rhetoric of anti-elitism, antisexism and antiracism, and quietly resisted doing anything about the issues in their own domain. They passed the buck to the social scientists and the humanists, who proved more accommodating and could be more easily bullied. Natural scientists too are Americans, in general favorably disposed to the mood of the times. But they are also pretty sure of what they are doing. They cannot deceive themselves that they are teaching science when they are not. They have powerful operational measures of competence. And inwardly they believe, at least in my experience, that the only real knowledge is scientific knowledge. In the dilemma that faced them—mathematicians wanted, for example, to see more blacks and women hired but could not find nearly enough competent ones—they in effect said that the humanists and social scientists should hire them. Believing that there are no real standards outside of the natural sciences, they assumed that adjustments could easily be made. With the profoundest irresponsibility, scientists went along with various aspects of affirmative action, assuming, for example, that any minority students admitted without proper qualifications would be taken care of by other departments if they did not do well in science. The scientists did not anticipate large-scale failure of such students, with the really terrible consequences that would entail. They took it for granted that these students would succeed somewhere else in the university. And they were right. The humanities and social sciences were debauched and grade inflation took off, while the natural sciences remain largely the preserve of white males. Thus the true elitists of the university have been able to stay on the good side of the forces of history without having to suffer any of the consequences.

To find hysterical supporters of the revolution one had, not surprisingly, to go to the humanities. Passion and commitment, as opposed to coolness, reason and objectivity, found their home there. The drama included a proclamation from a group of humanities teachers threatening to take over a building if the university did not capitulate forthwith. A student told me that one of his humanities professors, himself a Jew, had said to him that Jews deserved to be put in concentration camps because of what they had done to blacks. Finally these men and women were in action instead of idling away their time in libraries and classrooms. But they worked to their own undoing, for it is the humanities that have suffered most as a result of the sixties. The lack of student interest, the near disappearance of language study, the vanishing of jobs for Ph.D.s, the lack of public sympathy, came from the overturning of the old order, where their place was assured. They have gotten what they deserved, but we have unfortunately all lost.

The reasons for this behavior on the part of many humanists are obvious and constitute the theme of this book. Cornell was in the forefront of certain trends in the humanities as well as in politics. It had for several years been a laundering operation for radical Left French ideas in comparative literature. From Sartre, through Goldmann, to Foucault and Derrida, each successive wave washed over the Cornell shores. These ideas were intended to give new life to old books. A technique of reading, a framework for interpretation—Marx, Freud, structuralism, and on and on —could incorporate these tired old books and make them a part of revolutionary consciousness. At last there was an active, progressive role for the humanists, who had been only antiquarians, eunuchs guarding a harem of aging and now unattractive courtesans. Moreover, the almost universal historicism prevailing in the humanities prepared the soul for devotion to the emergent. Added to this was the expectation that in such changes culture would take primacy over science. The intellectual anti-university ideology of which I have spoken found its expression in these conditions, as the university could be thought to be the stage of history. Lucien Goldmann told me a few months before his death that he was privileged to have lived to see his nine-year-old son throw a rock through a store window in the Paris of '68. His studies of Racine and Pascal culminated in this. *Humanitas redivivas!* Students took to the action but not to the books. They could work on the future without the assistance of the past or its teachers. The avant-garde's fond expectation that the revolution would introduce an age of creativity, that art rather than antiquarianism would flower, that imagination would finally have its innings against reason, did not find immediate fulfillment.

The professors of humanities are in an impossible situation and do not believe in themselves or what they do. Like it or not, they are essentially involved with interpreting and transmitting old books, preserving what we call tradition, in a democratic order where tradition is not privileged. They are partisans of the leisured and beautiful in a place where evident utility is the only passport. Their realm is the always and the contemplative, in a setting that demands only the here and now and the active. The justice in which they believe is egalitarian, and they are the agents of the rare, the refined and the superior. By definition they are out of it, and their democratic inclinations and guilt push them to be with it. After all, what do Shakespeare and Milton have to do with solving our problems? Particularly when one looks into them and finds that they are the repositories of the elitist, sexist, nationalist prejudice we are trying to overcome.

Not only did the thing in itself require a conviction and dedication not often really present in the professors, the clientele was disappearing. The students just were not persuaded that what was being offered them was important. The loneliness and sense of worthlessness were crushing, so these humanists jumped on the fastest, most streamlined express to the future. This meant, of course, that all the tendencies hostile to the humanities were radicalized, and the humanities, without reservations, were pitched off the train. Natural and social science found their seats by demonstrating a usefulness of one kind or another. This the humanities were unable to do.

The apolitical character of the humanities, the habitual deformation or suppression of the political content in the classic literature, which should be part of a political education, left a void in the soul that could be filled with any politics, particularly the most vulgar, extreme and current. The humanities, unlike the natural sciences, had nothing to lose, or so it was thought, and, unlike the social sciences, they had no knowledge of the intractableness of the political matter. Humanists ran like lemmings into the sea, thinking they would refresh and revitalize themselves in it. They drowned.

This left the social sciences as the battleground, both the point of attack and the only place where any kind of stand was made. They were the newest part of the university, the part that could least boast of great past achievement or contribution to the store of human wisdom, the part the very legitimacy of which was questionable and where genius had participated most modestly. But the social sciences were principally concerned with the human things, were supposed to be in possession of the facts about social life and had a certain scientific conscience and integrity about reporting them. The social sciences were of interest to everyone who had a program, who might care about prosperity, peace or war, equality, racial or sexual discrimination. This interest could be to get the facts—or to make the facts fit their agenda and influence the public.

The temptations to alter the facts in these disciplines are enormous. Reward, punishment, money, praise, blame, sense of guilt and desire to do good, all swirl around them, dizzying their practitioners. Everyone wants the story told by social science to fit their wishes and their needs. Hobbes said that if the fact that two and two makes four were to become a matter of political relevance, there would be a faction to deny it. Social science has had more than its share of ideologues and charlatans. But it has also produced scholars of great probity whose works have made it harder for dishonest policy to triumph.

Thus it was in social science that the radicals first struck. A group of black activists disrupted the class of an economics teacher, then proceeded to the chairman's office and held him and his secretary (who suffered from heart disease) hostage for thirteen hours. The charge, of course, was that the teacher was racist in using a Western standard for judgment of the efficiency of African economic performance. The students were praised for calling the problem to the attention of the authorities, the chairman refused to proffer charges against them, and the teacher disappeared miraculously from campus, never to be seen again.

This kind of problem-solving was typical, but some professors in the social sciences did not like it. Historians were being asked to rewrite the history of the world, and of the United States in particular, to show that nations were always conspiratorial systems of domination and exploitation. Psychologists were being pestered to prove the psychological damage done by inequality and the existence of nuclear weapons, and to show that American statesmen were paranoid about the Soviet Union. Political scientists were urged to interpret the North Vietnamese as nationalists and to remove the stigma of totalitarianism from the Soviet Union. Every conceivable radical view concerning domestic or foreign policy demanded support from the social sciences. In particular, the crimes of elitism, sexism and racism were to be exorcised from social science, which was to be used as a tool to fight them and a fourth cardinal sin, anticommunism. Nobody of course would dare to admit to any of these sins, and serious discussion of the underlying issue, equality itself, had long been banished from the scene. As in the Middle Ages, when everyone except for a few intrepid and foolish souls professed Christianity and the only discussion concerned what constituted orthodoxy, the major student activity in social science was to identify heretics. These were scholars who seriously studied sexual differentiation or who raised questions about the educational value of busing or who considered the possibility of limited nuclear war. It became almost impossible to question the radical orthodoxy without risking vilification, classroom disruption, loss of the confidence and respect necessary for teaching, and the hostility of colleagues. Racist and sexist were, and are, very ugly labels—the equivalents of atheist or communist in other days with other prevailing prejudices—which can be pinned on persons promiscuously and which, once attached, are almost impossible to cast off. Nothing could be said with impunity. Such an atmosphere made detached, dispassionate study impossible.

This suited many social scientists, but a new, tougher strain emerged out of the struggle. Some saw that their objectivity was threatened, and without respect and protection for scholarly inquiry any one of them might be put at risk. The pressure revived an old liberalism and awareness of the importance of academic freedom. Pride and self-respect, unwillingness to give way before menace and insult, asserted themselves. These social scientists knew that all parties in a democracy are jeopardized when passion can sweep the facts before it. Most of all, an instinctive disgust at loudspeakers blaring propaganda was roused in them. Such social scientists were not necessarily all of the same personal political persuasion. Their fellow feeling consisted in mutual respect for the motives of colleagues with whom they did not always agree but from whose disagreement they might profit, and in attachment to the institutions that protected their research. At Cornell one found social scientists of left, right and center—on the admittedly narrow spectrum that prevails in the American university—joining together to protest the outrage against academic freedom and against their colleagues that took place there and continues in more or less subtle forms everywhere. It is not an accident that the challenge to the university was mounted in its most political part, and that there it was best understood. The political perspective is the one in which the moral unity of learning naturally comes into focus and the goodness of science is tested.

I unfortunately cannot assert that this crisis has caused social science to broaden its concerns or has induced the other disciplines to reflect on their own situations. But it was inspiring to be momentarily with a band of scholars who were really willing to make a sacrifice for their love of truth and their studies, to discover that the pieties could be more than pieties, to sense community founded on conviction. The other disciplines have, in general, not put their professed attachment to free inquiry to the test. Their immunity is a large part of the story behind the fractured structure of our universities.

The Disciplines

How are they today, the big three that rule the academic roost and determine what is knowledge? Natural science is doing just fine. Living alone, but happily, running along like a well-wound clock, successful and useful as ever. There have been great things lately, physicists with their black holes and biologists with their genetic code. Its objects and methods are agreed upon. It offers exciting lives to persons of very high intelligence and provides immeasurable benefits to mankind at large. Our way of life is utterly dependent on the natural scientists, and they have more than fulfilled their every promise. Only at the margins are there questions that might threaten their theoretical equanimity—doubts about whether America produces synoptic scientific geniuses, doubts about the use of the results of science, such as nuclear weapons, doubts that lead to biology's need for "ethicists" in its experiments and its applications when, as scientists, they know that there are no such knowers as ethicists. In general, however, all is well.

But where natural science ends, trouble begins. It ends at man, the one being outside of its purview, or to be exact, it ends at that part or aspect of man that is not body, whatever that may be. Scientists as scientists can be grasped only under that aspect, as is the case with politicians, artists and prophets. All that is human, all that is of concern to us, lies outside of natural science. That should be a problem for natural science, but it is not. It is certainly a problem for us that we do not know what this thing is, that we cannot even agree on a name for this irreducible bit of man that is not body. Somehow this fugitive thing or aspect is the cause of science and society and culture and politics and economics and poetry and music. We know what these latter are. But can we really, if we do not know their cause, know what its status is, whether it even exists?

The difficulty is reflected in the fact that for the study of this one theme, man, or this *je ne sais quoi* pertaining to man, and his activities and products, there are two great divisions of the university—humanities and social science—while for bodies there is only natural science. This would all be very well if the division of labor were founded on an agreement about the subject matter and reflected a natural articulation within it, as do the divisions between physics, chemistry and biology, leading to mutual respect and cooperation. It could be believed and is sometimes actually said, mostly in commencement speeches, that social science treats man's social life, and humanities his creative life—the great works of art, etc. And, although there is something to this kind of distinction, it really will not do. This fact comes to light in a variety of ways. While both social science and humanities are more or less willingly awed by natural science, they have a mutual contempt for one another, the former looking down on the latter as unscientific, the latter regarding the former as philistine. They do not cooperate. And most important, they occupy much of the same ground. Many of the classic books now part of the humanities talk about the same things as do social scientists but use different methods and draw different conclusions; and each of the social sciences in one way or another attempts to explain the activities of the various kinds of artists in ways that are contrary to the way they are treated in the humanities. The difference comes down to the fact that social science really wants to be predictive, meaning that man is predictable, while the humanities say that he is not. The divisions between the two camps resemble truce lines rather than scientific distinctions. They disguise old and unresolved struggles about the being of man.

The social sciences and the humanities represent the two responses to the crisis caused by the definitive ejection of man—or of the residue of man extracted from, or superfluous to, body—from nature, and hence from the purview of natural science or natural philosophy, toward the end of the eighteenth century. One route led toward valiant efforts to assimilate man to the new natural sciences, to make the science of man the next rung in the ladder down from biology. The other took over the territory newly opened up by Kant, that of freedom as opposed to nature, separate but equal, not requiring the aping of the methods of natural science, taking spirituality at least as seriously as body. Neither challenged the champion, natural science, newly emancipated from philosophy: social science tried humbly to find a place at court, humanities proudly to set up shop next door. The result has been two continuous and ill-assorted strands of thought about man, one tending to treat him essentially as another of the brutes, without spirituality, soul, self, consciousness, or what have you; the other acting as though he is not an animal or does not have a body. There is no junction of these two roads. One must choose between them, and they end up in very different places, e.g., Walden II, known as Brave New World by the other side, and The Blessed Isles (a favorite retreat of Zarathustra), known as The Kingdom of Darkness by its opponents.

Neither of these solutions has fully succeeded. Social science receives no recognition from natural science.[13] It is an imitation, not a part. And the humanities shop has turned out to be selling diverse and ill-assorted antiques, decaying and ever dustier, while business gets worse and worse. Social science has proved more robust, more in harmony with the world dominated by natural science, and, while losing its inspiration and evangelical fervor, has proved useful to different aspects of modern life, as the mere mention of economics and psychology indicates. Humanities languish, but this proves only that they do not suit the modern world. It may very well be the indication of what is wrong with modernity. Moreover the language that in an unscholarly way influences life so powerfully today emerged from investigations undertaken in the realm of freedom. Social science comes more out of the school founded by Locke; humanities out

[13]Natural science simply does not care. There is no hostility (unless it is attacked) to anything that is going on elsewhere. It is really self-sufficient, or almost so. If some other discipline proved itself, satisfied natural science's standards of rigor and proof, it would be automatically admitted. Natural science does not boast, is not snobbish. It is genuine. As Swift pointed out, its only habitual and apparently necessary sortie from its own proper domain is into politics. This is where it itself, if only in confused fashion, recognizes that it is a part of a larger project, and that it is dependent on that project, which is not a product of its methods. Lowly, despised politics points toward the need for philosophy, as Socrates originally said, in such a way that even scientists have to admit it. Natural scientists have no respect for political science as a science, but they have a passionate concern for politics. This is a beginning point for rethinking everything. Is the danger of nuclear war or the imprisonment of Sakharov just an accident?

of that founded by Rousseau. But social science, while looking to natural science, has actually received a large part of its impulse in recent times from the nether world. One need only think of Weber, although Marx and Freud are similar cases. It cannot be avowed, but *man,* to be grasped, needs something the natural sciences cannot provide. Man is the problem, and we live with various stratagems for not facing it. The strange relations between the three divisions of knowledge in the present university tell us all about it.

To look at social science first, it might seem that it at least has a general outline of its field and a possible systematic ordering of its parts, proceeding from psychology to economics to sociology to political science. Unfortunately there is nothing to this appearance. In the first place, it leaves out anthropology, although I suppose that if I were desperate to make a case I could find a way of squeezing it in; and it also leaves out history, about which there is dispute as to whether it belongs to social science or humanities. More important, these various social sciences do not see themselves in any such order of interdependence. Largely they work independently, and if they, to use that hopeless expression, "interface" at all, they frequently turn out to be two-faced. Within most of the specialties, about half of the practitioners usually do not believe the other half even belong among them, and something of the same situation prevails throughout the discipline as a whole. Economics has its own simple built-in psychology, and that provided by the science of psychology is either really part of biology, which does not help much, or flatly contradicts the primacy of the motives alleged by economics. Similarly, economics tends to undermine the normal interpretation of political events that political science would make. It is possible to have an economics-guided or -controlled political science, but it is not necessary; and it is equally possible to have a psychology-guided political science, which would not be the same as the former. It is as though there were a dispute among the various natural sciences about which is primary. Actually each of the social sciences can, and does, make a claim to be the beginning point in relation to which the others can be understood—economics arguing for the economy or the market, psychology for the individual psyche, sociology for society, anthropology for culture, and political science for the political order (although this latter is the least assertive about its claim).

The issue is what is the social science atom, and each specialty can argue that the others are properly parts of the whole that it represents. Moreover each can accuse the other of representing an abstraction, or a construct, or a figment of the imagination. Is there ever a pure market, one not part of a society or a culture that forms it? What is a culture or society? Are they ever more than aspects of some kind of political order? Here political science is in the strongest position, because the reality of states or nations is undeniable, although they can in turn be considered superficial or compound phenomena. The social sciences actually represent a series of different perspectives on the human world we see around us, a series that is not harmonious, because there is not even agreement as to what belongs to that world, let alone as to what kinds of causes would account for its phenomena.

A further source of dispute within social science concerns what is meant by science. All agree that it must be reasonable, have some standards of verification and be based on systematic research. Moreover, there is a more or less explicit agreement that the kinds of causes admitted within natural science should somehow apply within social science. This means no teleology and no "spiritual" causes. Pursuit of salvation would, for example, need to be reduced to another kind of cause, like repressed sexuality, whereas pursuit of money would not. Search for material causes and reduction of higher or more complex phenomena to lower or simpler ones are generally accepted procedures. But to what extent the example of the most successful of the modern natural sciences, mathematical physics, can or should be followed within social science is a matter of endless discussion and quarreling. Prediction is the hallmark of modern natural science, and practically every social scientist would like to be able to make reliable predictions, although practically none have. Prediction appears to have been made possible in natural science by reducing phenomena in such a way as to be amenable to expression in mathematical formulas, and most social scientists want the same thing to happen in their discipline. The issue is whether various efforts in that direction cause distortion of the social phenomena, or lead to the neglect of some that are not easily mathematized and the preference for others that are; or whether they encourage the construction of mathematical models that are figments of the imagination and have nothing to do with the real world. A kind of continuous guerrilla war goes on between those who are primarily enthusiasts of science and those who are primarily attached to their particular subject matter.

Economics, held to be the most successful of the social sciences, is the most mathematized—both in the sense that its objects can be counted and that it can construct mathematical models for at least hypothetically predictive purposes. But some political scientists, for example, say that the Economic Man may be very nice for playing games with but that he is an abstraction who does not exist, while Hitler and Stalin are real and not to be played with. Economic analysis, they say, not only does not help us to understand such political actors but makes it more difficult to bring them within the purview of social science by systematically excluding or deforming their specific motives. Economists, seeking mathematical convenience, turn us away from the consideration of the most important social phenomena, assert the objectors (including the small, vociferous band of Marxist economists who are rigorously excluded from the core of the discipline, the only social science in which this has happened). So it goes between the various disciplines and within several of them where the adherents of the different approaches have no common universe of discourse.

Publicity aside, what students actually see today when they first encounter social science are two robust, self-sufficient, self-confident social sciences, economics and cultural anthropology, extremes forming the antipodes, having almost nothing to do with each other—while political science and sociology, quite heterogenous, not to say chaotic in their contents, are strung tensely between the two poles.[14] It should not be surprising that these two disciplines are more explicit than are the other social sciences about their founders: Locke and Adam Smith, on the one hand, and Rousseau on the other. For these sciences have as their clear presuppositions one or the other of the two states of nature. Locke argued

[14]Psychology is mysteriously disappearing from the social sciences. Its unheard-of success in the real world may have tempted it to give up the theoretical life. As the psychotherapist has taken his place alongside the family doctor, perhaps his education now belongs to something more akin to the medical school than to the sciences, and the research relevant for him is more directed to treatment of specific problems of patients than to the founding of a theory of the psyche. The Freudian theories have been incorporated into some aspects of sociology, political science and anthropology, and it appears that the self alone had nothing more to tell the social sciences. This leaves open the question of what the solid ground is on which therapy stands, and where its newer ideas come from. Serious academic psychology is left with the segment that has to all intents and purposes fused with physiology.

that man's conquest of nature by his work is the only rational response to his original situation. Locke emancipated greed and showed the illusory character of the countervailing motives. Life, liberty and the pursuit of property are the fundamental natural rights, and the social contract is made to protect these rights. These principles agreed upon, economics comes into being as *the* science of man's proper activity, and the free market as the natural and rational order (a natural order unlike other recognized natural orders in that it requires establishment by men, and they, as economists are constantly telling us, almost always get it wrong). Economists have in general stuck to this, are in general old liberals of one kind or another and supporters of liberal democracy, as the place where the market exists. Rousseau argued that nature is good and man far away from it. So the quest for those faraway origins becomes imperative, and anthropology is by that very fact founded. Lévi-Strauss is unambiguous about this. Civilization, practically identical to the free market and its results, threatens happiness and dissolves community. From this follows immediately admiration for tight old cultures that channel and sublimate the economic motive and do not permit the emergence of the free market. What economists believe to be things of the irrational past—known only as underdeveloped societies[15]—become the proper study of man, a diagnosis of our ills and a call to the future. Anthropologists have tended to be very open to many aspects of the Continental reflection, from culture on down, to which economists were completely closed (Nietzsche's influence was already evident more than fifty years ago in Ruth Benedict's distinction between Apollonian and Dionysian cultures); they have tended to the Left (because the extreme Right, equally viable in their system, had no roots here) and to be susceptible to infatuations with experiments tending to correct or replace liberal democracy. Economists teach that the market is the fundamental social phenomenon, and its culmination is money. Anthropologists teach that culture is the fundamental social phenomenon, and its culmination is the sacred.[16] Such is

[15]Undeveloped, bad; developing, better; developed, good—for man and for the science of economics.

[16]I am tempted to say that psychology teaches that sex is the primary phenomenon. It is closer to economics when understood as stimulus-response, closer to anthropology when understood as a hang-up. If one wants something more from psychology, one meets a road sign saying "To the Humanities."

the confrontation—man the producer of consumption goods vs. man the producer of culture, the maximizing animal vs. the reverent one—between old philosophic teachings present here but not addressed. The disciplines simply inhabit different worlds. They can be of marginal use to one another, but not in a spirit of community. There are few economists who also think of themselves as anthropologists, and vice versa, although there are, for example, many political scientists and sociologists who cross one another's borders, as well as those of economics and anthropology. The economists are the ones most ready to jump the social science ship and go it on their own, and think themselves closer than the others to having achieved a real science. They also have substantial influence on public policy. The anthropologists have no such influence beyond the academic world but have the charms of depth and comprehensiveness, as well as the possession of the latest ideas.

A few words about political science and its peculiarities might help to clarify the problems of social science as a whole. To begin with, it is, along with economics, the only purely academic discipline that, like medicine, engages a fundamental passion and the study of which could be understood as undertaken in order to ensure its satisfaction. Political science involves the love of justice, the love of glory and the love of ruling. But unlike medicine and economics, which are quite frank about their relations to health and wealth, and even trumpet them, political science turns modestly away from such avowals and would even like to break off these unseemly relations. This has something to do with the fact that she is a very old lady indeed, who would prefer not to show her age. Political science goes all the way back to Greek antiquity and has the dubious parentage of Socrates, Plato and Aristotle, all with bad reputations in the land of modern science. The other social sciences are of modern origin and part of the modern project, while political science persists, trying to modernize and get with it but unable entirely to control old instincts. Aristotle said that political science is the architectonic science, a ruling science, concerned with the comprehensive good or the best regime. But real science does not talk about good and bad, so that had to be abandoned. However, both medicine and economics really do talk about good and bad, so the abandonment of the old political goods had the effect only of leaving the moral field to health and wealth in the absence of the common good and justice. This accords with Locke's intention, which was not at all "value-free," but was to substitute lower but more solid, more easily attained goods for those that had been classically proposed. Political science's transformation into a modern social science did not further social science but did further the political intentions of modernity's founders. It has tried to reduce the specifically political motives into subpolitical ones, like those proposed in economics. Honor is not a real motive; gain is.

Of course Locke himself was still much more a political scientist than an economist, for the market (the peaceful competition for the acquisition of goods) requires the prior existence of the social contract (the agreement to abide by contracts and the establishment of a judge to arbitrate and enforce contracts) without which men are in a state of war. The market presupposes the existence of law and the absence of war. War was the condition of man prior to the existence of civil society, and the return to it is always possible. The force and fraud required to end war have nothing to do with the market and are illegitimate within it. The rational behavior of men at peace, in which economics specializes, is not the same as the rational behavior of men at war, as was so tellingly pointed out by Machiavelli. Political science is more comprehensive than economics because it studies both peace and war and their relations. The market cannot be the sole concern of the polity, for the market depends on the polity, and the establishment and preservation of the polity continuously requires reasonings and deeds which are "uneconomic" or "inefficient." Political action must have primacy over economic action, no matter what the effect on the market. This is why economists have had so little reliable to say about foreign policy, for nations are in the primitive state of war with each other that individuals were in prior to the social contract—that is, they have no commonly recognized judge to whom they can turn to settle their disputes. The policy advice of some economists during the Vietnam war attempted to set up a kind of market between the United States and North Vietnam, with the United States making the cost of South Vietnam prohibitive to North Vietnam; but the North Vietnamese refused to play. Political science, as opposed to economics, must always contemplate war with its altogether different risks, horrors, thrills, and gravity. Churchill formulated the difference between a political perspective and a market perspective in commenting on Coolidge's refusal to forgive the British war debts in the twenties. Coolidge said, "They hired the money, didn't they?" To which Churchill responded, "This is true, but not exhaustive." Political science must be exhaustive and this makes it a sticky subject for those who want to reform it so as to accord with the abstract projects of science. Consciously or unconsciously, economics deals only with the bourgeois, the man motivated by fear of violent death. The warlike man is not within its ken. Political science remains the only social science discipline which looks war in the face.

Political science has always been the least attractive and the least impressive of the social sciences, spanning as it does old and new views of man and the human sciences. It has a polyglot character. Part of it has joined joyfully in the effort to dismantle the political order seen as a comprehensive order and to understand it as a result of subpolitical causes. Economics, psychology and sociology as well as all kinds of methodological diagnosticians have been welcome guests. But there are irrepressible, putatively unscientific parts of political science. The practitioners of these parts of the discipline are unable to overcome their unexplained and unexplainable political instincts—their awareness that politics is the authoritative arena of effective good and evil. They therefore engage in policy studies whose end, whether it is stated or not, is action. Defense of freedom, avoidance of war, the furthering of equality—various aspects of justice in action—are hot subjects of study. The good regime has to be the theme of such political scientists, if only undercover, and they are informed by the question "What is to be done?" And, in a real peripety, it turns out that the area of political science where mathematics has had the greatest success is elections, the most exciting and decisive part of democratic life, where public opinion turns into government and policy. The most scientific element of political science is one that makes its practitioners friends and allies of real politicians, enlightening them and learning from them. Science here parallels the greatest political thrills and has no need of changing the perceived nature of its object to study it scientifically.

So political science resembles a rather haphazard bazaar with shops kept by a mixed population. This has something to do with its hybrid nature and its dual origins in antiquity and modernity. The reality with which it deals lends itself less to abstractions and makes more urgent demands than do any of the other social science disciplines, while the tension between objectivity and partisanship in it is much more extreme.

Everything in modern natural and social science militates against the assertion that politics is qualitatively different from other kinds of human association, but its practice repeatedly affirms the contrary. Its heterogeneity is perhaps debilitating, and one finds here choice theorists of the economic-models school, old-fashioned behavioralists, Marxists (who are never at home in economics), historians and policy researchers. Most unusual of all, political science is the only discipline in the university (with the possible exception of the philosophy department) that has a philosophic branch. This has long been an embarrassment to it, and political philosophy was scheduled for termination in the forties and fifties. "We want to be a real social science," cried the terminators with an exasperated stamp of the foot. But a combination of serious and fervent scholarship on the part of a few thinkers and the muscle of the rebellious students in the sixties gave political philosophy a reprieve that now looks permanent. It became, for the best and the worst of reasons, the bastion of the reaction against value-free social science and the new social science as a whole. It has, where its presence is at all serious, proved to be continuously the most attractive subject in the field for both graduate and undergraduate students. And as the new scientific persuasion has lost much of its élan and the field has fragmented in various directions dictated at least partly by fidelity to the political phenomena, many of those who were once fierce enemies of political philosophy have become its allies. Political philosophy is far from ruling, but it provides at least a reminiscence of those old questions about good and evil and the resources for examining the hidden presuppositions of modern political science and political life. Aristotle's *Politics* is still alive there, as well as Locke's *Treatise on Civil Government* and Rousseau's *Discourse on the Origins of Inequality*. Aristotle asserts that man is by nature a political animal, which means that he has an impulse toward civil society. Reading Aristotle helps to lay bare the hidden premise underlying modern social science, that man is by nature a solitary being, and could provide the basis for making a debate of it again.[17]

[17]History, sharing Greek origins with political science, also has elements of the ancients-moderns identity crisis, in addition to the other problems of the strictly modern social sciences. As already mentioned, both participants and observers are unsure whether it is a social science or one of the humanities. Its matter is resistant to the techniques of the behavioral sciences, since it is particular, and therefore not easily generalizable, deals with the past, and is therefore beyond

Obviously, then, the glory days of social science from the point of view of liberal education are over. Gone is the time when Marx, Freud and Weber, philosophers and interpreters of the world, were just precursors of what was to be America's intellectual coming of age, when youngsters could join the charms of science and self-knowledge, when there was the expectation of a universal theory of man that would unite the university and contribute to progress, harnessing Europe's intellectual depth and heritage with our vitality. Natural science was to culminate in human science; Darwin and Einstein would tell social science as much as they had told natural science. And modern literature—Dostoyevski, Joyce, Proust, Kafka—expressed our mood and provided the insights that social science would systematize and prove. Psychoanalysis provided the link between private experience and public intellectual endeavor. So unified was the experience that personal desire was intimately connected with intuition of the comprehensive order of things, a simulacrum of the old understanding of philosophy as a way of life. On a much less sophisticated level but expressing something of the same ethos, Margaret Mead had a new science that took one to exotic places, brought back new understandings of society and also proved the legitimacy of one's repressed sexual desires. To young people, the sociologists and psychologists who trod the university's grounds could look like heroes of the life of the mind. They were

---

controlled experiments; but it does not want to be merely literature. I believe that none of the other social sciences includes history as part of the social science schema, with the exception of that part of political science which is concerned with political practice as opposed to social science, e.g., some aspects of American politics and of international relations. History until the nineteenth century meant primarily political history; and it, unlike political science, was not refounded in early modernity. Its traditional role was enhanced during the new foundings because it told what happened, as opposed to old political science, which told what ought to have happened. Therefore history was understood to be closer to the truth of things. History had to wait until the nineteenth century for its modernization by historicism, which argued, as it were, that being, certainly man's being, is essentially historical. Historicism appears to have been a great boon for history, a radical step upward in status. But the appearance is somewhat deceptive. Historicism is a philosophical, not a historical, teaching, one not discovered by history. Rather than the prestige of philosophy adhering to history, the reverse occurred. All humanities disciplines are now historical—not philosophy, but history of philosophy, not art, but history of art, not science, but history of science, not literature, but history of literature. Thus history is all of these, but also none of them, because they are discrete disciplines in the humanities. History became the empty, universal category encompassing all the humanities, except insofar as it remained its modest, narrow political self. But because it does not have an anchor in political passion as does political science, it could float easily away from that dock under the influence of the prevailing winds, as politics was depreciated by so many other things, especially historicism. So, history, a wonderful, useful study, full of most learned individuals, is as a whole a medley of methods and goals, six disciplines in search of a self-definition.

initiated into the mysteries and might help us to become initiates too. Old-style philosophy had been overcome, but names like Hegel, Schopenhauer and Kierkegaard were thought to offer some of the experience required for our adventure.

Such an atmosphere as surrounded social science in the forties was obviously of ambiguous value for both students and professors. But something akin to it is necessary if American students are to be attracted to the idea of liberal education and the awareness that the university will cause them to discover new faculties in themselves and reveal another level of existence that had been hidden from them. American students, it must be remembered, if they have learned anything at all in high school, have learned natural science as a technique, not as a way of life or a means of discovering life. If anything other than routine specialized learning is to touch them, they must be given a shock treatment—even if it is only to make them think about their commitment to natural science and its meaning, inasmuch as their earlier training has been more of an indoctrination, more of a conformism, than the discovery of a vocation. The social science inebriation of the forties was not, I believe, the genuine article, but it reproduced something of the intellectual excitement surrounding theoretical new beginnings. It proved fertile for many students and scholars, generated its own ancillary bohemia and affected the substance of people's lives. It was not just a profession.

The hopes for a unity of social science have faded, and it cannot present a common front. It is a series of discrete disciplines and subdisciplines. Most are modest, and although there is a lot of nonsense, there are also a fair number of really useful parts practiced by highly competent specialists. The expectations are radically lowered. Economics is a specialty that has universal pretensions to explain and encompass everything, but they are not quite believed, and its popularity does not rest on them. Political science does not even try to make good its ancestral claim to comprehensiveness and only covertly and partially makes its special and rightful appeal to the political passion. Anthropology is the only social science discipline still exercising the charm of possible wholeness, with its idea of culture, which appears more really complete than does the economists' idea of the market. Both the superpolitical cultural part and the subpolitical economic part claim to be the whole, while neither sociology nor political science, apart from certain individuals, really seems to make any claims over the whole social science enterprise. There is no social science as an architectonic science. It is parts without a whole.

Similarly, with the possible exceptions of computer science as a model for man, and sociobiology, the expectation of substantive unity between natural science and social science has faded, leaving social science a consumer only of natural science method. Gone is the cosmic intention of placing man in the universe. In the direction of the humanities, it is again only anthropology that has maintained a certain opening, particularly to the merchandise being hawked in comparative literature, but also to serious studies, e.g., Greek religion. No other social scientists expect to get much from nineteenth- and twentieth-century art and literature, which fascinated many significant social scientists a generation ago, and there are fewer and fewer social scientists who have much familiarity with that sort of thing in a personal way. The social sciences have become an island in the university floating alongside the other two islands, full of significant information and hiding treasures of great questions that could be mined but are not. Notably, the social science intellectual in the German or French mold, looked upon as a kind of sage or wise man who could tell all about life, has all but disappeared.

The students are aware of this and do not turn to the social sciences in general for the experience of conversion. Particular things or particular professors may be of interest to them for one reason or another, but for any who might happen to be looking for the meaning of life, or who might be able to learn that that is what they should look for, social science is not now the place to go. Anthropology, to repeat myself, is something of an exception. The secret of social science's great early success with intelligent young Americans was that it was the only place in the university that seemed, however indirectly, to seek the answer to the Socratic question of how one should live. Even when it was most vigorously teaching that values cannot be the subject matter of knowledge, that very teaching taught about life, as shown by such once exciting contrivances as Weber's distinction between the ethics of intention and the ethics of responsibility. This was not textbook learning, but the real stuff of life. Nothing like this is to be found there today.

Moreover, a great disaster has occurred. It is the establishment during the last decade or so of the MBA as the moral equivalent of the MD or the law degree, meaning a way of insuring a lucrative living by the mere fact of a diploma that is not a mark of scholarly achievement. It is a general rule that the students who have any chance of getting a liberal education are those who do not have a fixed career goal, or at least those for whom the university is not merely a training ground for a profession. Those who do have such a goal go through the university with blinders on, studying what the chosen discipline imposes on them while occasionally diverting themselves with an elective course that attracts them. True liberal education requires that the student's whole life be radically changed by it, that what he learns may affect his action, his tastes, his choices, that no previous attachment be immune to examination and hence re-evaluation. Liberal education puts everything at risk and requires students who are able to risk everything.[18] Otherwise it can only touch what is uncommitted in the already essentially committed. The effect of the MBA is to corral a horde of students who want to get into business school and to put the blinders on them, to legislate an illiberal, officially approved undergraduate program for them at the outset, like premeds who usually disappear into their required courses and are never heard from again. Both the goal and the way of getting to it are fixed so that nothing can distract them. (Prelaw students are more visible in a variety of liberal courses because law schools are less fixed in their prerequisites; they are only seeking bright students.) Premed, prelaw and prebusiness students are distinctively tourists in the liberal arts. Getting into those elite professional schools is an obsessive concern that tethers their minds.

The specific effect of the MBA has been an explosion of enrollments in economics, the prebusiness major. In serious universities something like 20 percent of the undergraduates are now economics majors. Economics overwhelms the rest of the social sciences and skews the students' perception of them—their purpose and their relative weight with regard to the knowledge of human things. A premed who takes much biology does not, by contrast, lose sight of the status of physics, for the latter's influence on biology is clear, its position agreed upon, and it is respected by the biologists. None of this is so for the prebusiness economics major, who not only does not take an interest in sociology, anthropology or political

---

[18]It is to be noted that many students who come to the university intending to go into natural science change their intention while in college. It never, or almost never, happens that a student who was not interested in natural science before college discovers it there. This is an interesting reflection on the character of our high school education in general and science education in particular.

science but is also persuaded that what he is learning can handle all that belongs to those studies. Moreover, he is not motivated by love of the science of economics but by love of what it is concerned with—money. Economists' concern with wealth, an undeniably real and solid thing, gives them a certain impressive intellectual solidity not provided by, say, culture. One can be sure that they are not talking about nothing. But wealth, as opposed to the science of wealth, is not the noblest of motivations, and there is nothing else quite like this perfect coincidence between science and cupidity elsewhere in the university. The only parallel would be if there were a science of sexology, with earnest and truly scholarly professors, which would ensure its students lavish sexual satisfactions.

The third island of the university is the almost submerged old Atlantis, the humanities. In it there is no semblance of order, no serious account of what should and should not belong, or of what its disciplines are trying to accomplish or how. It is somehow the repair of man or of humanity, the place to go to find ourselves now that everyone else has given up. But where to look in this heap or jumble? It is difficult enough for those who already know what to look for to get any satisfaction here. For students it requires a powerful instinct and a lot of luck. The analogies tumble uncontrollably from my pen. The humanities are like the great old Paris Flea Market where, amidst masses of junk, people with a good eye found castaway treasures that made them rich. Or they are like a refugee camp where all the geniuses driven out of their jobs and countries by unfriendly regimes are idling, either unemployed or performing menial tasks. The other two divisions of the university have no use for the past, are forward-looking and not inclined toward ancestor worship.

The problem of the humanities, and therefore of the unity of knowledge, is perhaps best represented by the fact that if Galileo, Kepler and Newton exist anywhere in the university now it is in the humanities, as part of one kind of history or another—history of science, history of ideas, history of culture. In order to have a place, they have to be understood as something other than what they were—great contemplators of the whole of nature who understood themselves to be of interest only to the extent that they told the truth about it. If they were wrong or have been completely surpassed, then they themselves would say that they are of no interest. To put them in the humanities is the equivalent of naming a street after them or setting up a statue in a corner of a park. They are effectively dead. Plato, Bacon, Machiavelli and Montesquieu are in the same condition, except for that little enclave in political science. The humanities are the repository for *all* of the classics now—but much of the classic literature claimed to be about the order of the whole of nature and man's place in it, to legislate for that whole and to tell the truth about it. If such claims are denied, these writers and their books cannot be read seriously, and their neglect elsewhere is justified. They have been saved only on the condition of being mummified. The humanities' willingness to receive them has taken them off the backs of the natural and social sciences, where they constituted a challenge that no longer has to be met. On the portal of the humanities is written in many ways and many tongues, "There is no truth—at least here."

The humanities are the specialty that now exclusively possesses the books that are not specialized, that insist upon asking the questions about the whole that are excluded from the rest of the university, which is dominated by real specialties, as resistant to self-examination as they were in Socrates' day and now rid of the gadfly. The humanities have not had the vigor to fight it out with triumphant natural science, and want to act as though it were just a specialty. But, as I have said over and over again, however much the humane disciplines would like to forget about their essential conflict with natural science as now practiced and understood, they are gradually undermined by it. Whether it is old philosophic texts that raise now inadmissible questions, or old works of literature that presuppose the being of the noble and the beautiful, materialism, determinism, reductionism, homogenization—however one describes modern natural science—deny their importance and their very possibility. Natural science asserts that it is metaphysically neutral, and hence has no need for philosophy, and that imagination is not a faculty that in any way intuits the real—hence art has nothing to do with truth. The kinds of questions children ask: Is there a God? Is there freedom? Is there punishment for evil deeds? Is there certain knowledge? What is a good society? were once also the questions addressed by science and philosophy. But now the grownups are too busy at work, and the children are left in a day-care center called the humanities, in which the discussions have no echo in the adult world. Moreover, students whose nature draws them to such questions and to the books that appear to investigate them are very quickly rebuffed by the fact that their humanities teachers do not want or are unable to use the books to respond to their needs.

This problem of the old books is not new. In Swift's *Battle of the Books* one finds Bentley, the premier Greek scholar of the eighteenth century, on the side of the moderns. He accepted the superiority of modern thought to Greek thought. So why study Greek books? This question remains unanswered in classics departments. There are all sorts of dodges, ranging from pure philological analysis to using these books to show the relation between thought and economic conditions. But practically no one even tries to read them as they were once read—for the sake of finding out whether they are true. Aristotle's *Ethics* teaches us not what a good man is but what the Greeks thought about morality. But who really cares very much about that? Not any normal person who wants to lead a serious life.

All the things I have said about books in our time help to characterize the situation of the humanities, which are the really exposed part of the university. They have been buffeted more severely by historicism and relativism than the other parts. They suffer most from democratic society's lack of respect for tradition and its emphasis on utility. To the extent that the humanities are supposed to treat of creativity, professors' lack of creativity becomes a handicap. The humanities are embarrassed by the political content of many of the literary works belonging to them. They have had to alter their contents for the sake of openness to other cultures. And when the old university habits were changed, they found themselves least able to answer the question "Why?," least able to force students to meet standards, or to attract them with any clear account of what they would learn. One need only glance at the situation of the natural sciences in all these respects to see the gravity of the problem faced by the humanities. Natural science is sovereignly indifferent to the fact that there were and are other kinds of explanations of natural phenomena in other ages or cultures. The relation between Einstein and Buddha is purely for educational TV, in programs put together by humanists. Whatever its practitioners may say, they are sure its explanations are true, or truth. They do not have to give reasons "why," because the answer seems all too evident.

The natural sciences are able to assert that they are pursuing the important truth, and the humanities are not able to make any such assertion. That is always the critical point. Without this, no study can remain alive. Vague insistence that without the humanities we will no longer be civilized rings very hollow when no one can say what "civilized" means, when there are said to be many civilizations that are all equal. The claim of "the classic" loses all legitimacy when the classic cannot be believed to tell the truth. The truth question is most pressing and acutely embarrassing for those who deal with the philosophic texts, but also creates problems for those treating purely literary works. There is an enormous difference between saying, as teachers once did, "You must learn to see the world as Homer or Shakespeare did," and saying, as teachers now do, "Homer and Shakespeare had some of the same concerns you do and can enrich your vision of the world." In the former approach students are challenged to discover new experiences and reassess old; in the latter, they are free to use the books in any way they please.

I am distinguishing two related but different problems here. The contents of the classic books have become particularly difficult to defend in modern times, and the professors who now teach them do not care to defend them, are not interested in their truth. One can most clearly see the latter in the case of the Bible. To include it in the humanities is already a blasphemy, a denial of its own claims. There it is almost inevitably treated in one of two ways: It is subjected to modern "scientific" analysis, called the Higher Criticism, where it is dismantled, to show how "sacred" books are put together, and that they are not what they claim to be. It is useful as a mosaic in which one finds the footprints of many dead civilizations. Or else the Bible is used in courses in comparative religion as one expression of the need for the "sacred" and as a contribution to the very modern, very scientific study of the structure of "myths." (Here one can join up with the anthropologists and really be alive.) A teacher who treated the Bible naively, taking it at its word, or Word, would be accused of scientific incompetence and lack of sophistication. Moreover, he might rock the boat and start the religious wars all over again, as well as a quarrel within the university between reason and revelation, which would upset comfortable arrangements and wind up by being humiliating to the humanities. Here one sees the traces of the Enlightenment's political project, which wanted precisely to render the Bible, and other old books, undangerous. This project is one of the underlying causes of the impotence of the humanities. The best that can be done, it appears, is to teach "The Bible as Literature," as opposed to "as Revelation," which it claims to be. In this way it can be read somewhat independently of deforming scholarly apparatus, as we read, for example, *Pride and Prejudice.* Thus the few professors who feel that there is something wrong with the other approaches tend to their consciences.

Professors of the humanities have long been desperate to make their subjects accord with modernity instead of a challenge to it. One sees this in a puerile form in the footnotes to Paul Shorey's edition of Plato's *Republic,* on which I cut my teeth, where he is eager to show that Plato had already divined this or that discovery made by some American professor of psychology in 1911, while he remains studiously silent about Plato's embarrassing disagreements with current views. Much study in the humanities is just a more or less sophisticated version of the same thing. I do not deny that at least some professors love the works they study and teach. But there is a furious effort to make them up-to-date, largely by treating them as the matter formed by some contemporary theory—cultural, historical, economic or psychological. The effort to read books as their writers intended them to be read has been made into a crime, ever since "the intentional fallacy" was instituted. There are endless debates about methods—among Freudian criticism, Marxist criticism, New Criticism, Structuralism and Deconstructionism, and many others, all of which have in common the premise that what Plato or Dante had to say about reality is unimportant. These schools of criticism make the writers plants in a garden planned by a modern scholar, while their own garden-planning vocation is denied them. The writers ought to plant, or even bury, the scholar. Nietzsche said that after the ministrations of modern scholarship the *Symposium* is so far away that it can no longer seduce us; its immediate charm has utterly vanished. When it comes down to it, the humanities scholar is not motivated by inner necessity, by any urgency, certainly not one dictated by old books. The scholar who chooses to study Sophocles could just as well have chosen Euripides. And why a poet, and not a philosopher or a historian; or why, after all, a Greek, and not a Turk?

There are a few humanities departments in universities that have been able to escape respectably into the sciences, such as archeology and some aspects of the languages and linguistics. They have almost entirely broken off relations with the contents of books. Fine art and music are, of course, in large measure independent of the meanings of books, although the way of treating them does, at least to some extent, depend on the prevailing views about what art is and what is important in it. There is in humanities a great deal of purely scholarly work that is neutral, useful and intended to be used by those who have something to say, such as the making of dictionaries and the establishment of texts.

The list of departments is dominated by the long catalogue of the various departments of language and literature, usually one for each of the Western languages, and conglomerates for the others. Except for English, they all are responsible for teaching foreign languages. The teachers have had to learn a difficult language well and must teach it to a population of students who do not really want to learn languages very much. Now, in addition to the language, there are books written in that language, and the learning of the language entails reading those books. Hence, having learned the language in effect qualifies the teacher to teach the contents of the books, particularly since the books do not now belong anywhere else. However, the teachers' real knowledge of and affinity with those books is not ensured by their mastery of the language. The books are the important thing, but the language tail tends to wag the literature dog. These departments are the primary guardians of the classic literature and protect their dominion over their works ferociously. University convention submerges nature. It issues licenses, and hunting without one is forbidden. Moreover, because of these conventions the professors also listen to one another more attentively than to outsiders, and are listened to more attentively than others by outsiders, as doctors are more impressive to laymen in matters of health than are other laymen. A cozy self-satisfaction of specialists easily results (until there are rude jolts from the outside, such as occurred during the sixties). Professors of Greek forget or are unaware that Thomas Aquinas, who did not know Greek, was a better interpreter of Aristotle than any of them have proved to be, not only because he was smarter but because he took Aristotle more seriously.

This arrangement of the language and literature departments entails other structural difficulties. Do Greek poetry, history and philosophy belong together, or again, is not the secondary fact of the Greek language determining the articulation of the substance? And is it not possible that the proper connections go beyond Greece altogether, constituting such pairs as Plato and Farabi or Aristotle and Hobbes? Willy-nilly these departments are forced to adopt historical premises. Greek philosophers are of a piece and, more likely, the whole of Greek culture or civilization is a tightly woven tapestry of which the Greek scholar, not the philosopher or the poet, is the master. From the outset this arrangement answers the crucial questions about the relation between the mind and history before they are raised, and does so in a way contrary to the way Plato or Aristotle would answer them.

Most interesting of all, lost amidst this collection of disciplines, modestly sits philosophy. It has been dethroned by political and theoretical democracy, bereft of the passion or the capacity to rule. Its story defines in itself our whole problem. Philosophy once proudly proclaimed that it was the best way of life, and it dared to survey the whole, to seek the first causes of all things, and not only dictated its rules to the special sciences but constituted and ordered them. The classic philosophic books are philosophy in action, doing precisely these things. But this was all impossible, *hybris,* say their impoverished heirs. Real science did not need them, and the rest is ideology or myth. Now they are just books on a shelf. Democracy took away philosophy's privileges, and philosophy could not decide whether to fade away or to take a job. Philosophy was architectonic, had the plans for the whole building, and the carpenters, masons and plumbers were its subordinates and had no meaning without its plan. Philosophy founded the university, but it could no longer do so. We live off its legacy. When people speak vaguely about generalists vs. specialists, they must mean by the generalist the philosopher, for he is the only kind of knower who embraces, or once embraced, all the specialties, possessing a subject matter, necessary to the specialties, which was real—being or the good—and not just a collection of the matters of the specialties. Philosophy is no longer a way of life, and it is no longer a sovereign science. Its situation in our universities has something to do with the desperate condition of philosophy in the world today, and something to do with its peculiar history as a discipline in America. With respect to the former, although reason is gravely threatened, Nietzsche and Heidegger were genuine philosophers and able to face up to and face down both natural science and historicism, the two great contemporary opponents of philosophy. Philosophy is still possible. And on the Continent even now, schoolchildren are taught philosophy, and it seems to be something real. An American high school student knows only the word "philosophy," and it does not appear to be any more serious a life choice than yoga. In America, anyhow, everybody has a philosophy. Philosophy was not ever a very powerful presence in universities, although there were important exceptions. We began with a public philosophy that sufficed for us, and we thought that it was common sense. In America, Tocqueville said, everyone is a Cartesian although no one has read Descartes. We were almost entirely importers of philosophy, with the exception of Pragmatism. One need not have read a line of philosophy to be considered educated in this country. It is easily equated with hot air, much more so than any of the other humane disciplines. So it always had an uphill fight. Students who did seek it could, however, find some refreshment at its source.

But it has succumbed and probably could disappear without being much noticed. It has a scientific component, logic, which is attached to the sciences and could easily be detached from philosophy. This is serious, practiced by competent specialists, and responds to none of the permanent philosophic questions. History of philosophy, the compendium of dead philosophies that was always most lively for the students, has been neglected, and students find it better treated in a variety of other disciplines. Positivism and ordinary language analysis have long dominated, although they are on the decline and evidently being replaced by nothing. These are simply methods of a sort, and they repel students who come with the humanizing questions. Professors of these schools simply would not and could not talk about anything important, and they themselves do not represent a philosophic life for the students. In some places existentialism and phenomenology have gained a foothold, and they are much more attractive to students than positivism or ordinary language analysis. Catholic universities have always kept some contact with medieval philosophy, and hence, Aristotle. But, in sum, the philosophy landscape is largely bleak. That is why so much of the philosophic instinct in America used to lead toward the new social sciences and is now veering off toward certain branches of literature and literary criticism. As it stands, philosophy is just another humanities subject, rather contentless, without a thought of trying to take command in the crisis of the university. Actually it contains less of the exhilarating presence of the tradition in philosophy than do the other humanities disciplines, and one finds its professors least active of the humanists in attempts to revitalize liberal education. Although there was a certain modesty about ordinary language analysis—"We just help to give you clarity about what you are already doing"—

there was also smugness: "We know what was wrong with the whole tradition, and we don't need it anymore." Therefore the tradition disappeared from philosophy's confines.

All the language catalogued in Part Two was produced by philosophy and was in Europe known to have been produced by philosophy, so that it paved a road to philosophy. In America its antecedents remain unknown. We took over the results without having had any of the intellectual experiences leading to them. But the ignorance of the origins and the fact that American philosophy departments do not lay claim to them—are in fact just as ignorant of them as is the general public—means that the philosophic content of our language and lives does not direct us to philosophy. This is a real difference between the Continent and us. Here the philosophic language is nothing but jargon.

The evident weakness of the division of literature on the basis of the language in which it was written led, a half-century ago, to the sensible project of trying to reunite it. Thus comparative literature was founded. But as is the case with all such undertakings in our times, there was considerable perplexity about what the new discipline was trying to do, and it tended to generate systems of comparison that dominated the literary works, tributes to the ingenuity of their founders rather than openings through which the works could reveal themselves freed from arbitrary constraints. Comparative literature has now fallen largely into the hands of a group of professors who are influenced by the post-Sartrean generation of Parisian Heideggerians, in particular Derrida, Foucault and Barthes. The school is called Deconstructionism, and it is the last, predictable, stage in the suppression of reason and the denial of the possibility of truth in the name of philosophy. The interpreter's creative activity is more important than the text; there is no text, only interpretation. Thus the one thing most necessary for us, the knowledge of what these texts have to tell us, is turned over to the subjective, creative selves of these interpreters, who say that there is both no text and no reality to which the texts refer. A cheapened interpretation of Nietzsche liberates us from the objective imperatives of the texts that might have liberated us from our increasingly low and narrow horizon. Everything has tended to soften the demands made on us by the tradition; this simply dissolves it.

This fad will pass, as it has already in Paris. But it appeals to our worst instincts and shows where our temptations lie. It is the literary complement to the "life-styles" science I discussed in Part Two. Fancy German philosophic talk fascinates us and takes the place of the really serious things. This will not be the last attempt of its kind coming from the dispossessed humanities in their search for an imaginary empire, one that flatters popular democratic tastes.

Conclusion

These are the shadows cast by the peaks of the university over the entering undergraduate. Together they represent what the university has to say about man and his education, and they do not project a coherent image. The differences and the indifferences are too great. It is difficult to imagine that there is either the wherewithal or the energy within the university to constitute or reconstitute the idea of an educated human being and establish a liberal education again.

However, the contemplation of this scene is in itself a proper philosophic activity. The university's evident lack of wholeness in an enterprise that clearly demands it cannot help troubling some of its members. The questions are all there. They only need to be addressed continuously and seriously for liberal learning to exist; for it does not consist so much in answers as in the permanent dialogue. It is in such perplexed professors that at least the idea might persevere and help to guide some of the needy young persons at our doorstep. The matter is still present in the university; it is the form that has vanished. One cannot and should not hope for a general reform. The hope is that the embers do not die out.

Men may live more truly and fully in reading Plato and Shakespeare than at any other time, because then they are participating in essential being and are forgetting their accidental lives. The fact that this kind of humanity exists or existed, and that we can somehow still touch it with the tips of our outstretched fingers, makes our imperfect humanity, which we can no longer bear, tolerable. The books in their objective beauty are still there, and we must help protect and cultivate the delicate tendrils reaching out toward them through the unfriendly soil of students' souls. Human nature, it seems, remains the same in our very altered circumstances because we still face the same problems, if in different guises, and have the distinctively human need to solve them, even though our awareness and forces have become enfeebled.

After a reading of the *Symposium* a serious student came with deep melancholy and said it was impossible to imagine that magic Athenian atmosphere reproduced, in which friendly men, educated, lively, on a footing of equality, civilized but natural, came together and told wonderful stories about the meaning of their longing. But such experiences are always accessible. Actually, this playful discussion took place in the midst of a terrible war that Athens was destined to lose, and Aristophanes and Socrates at least could foresee that this meant the decline of Greek civilization. But they were not given to culture despair, and in these terrible political circumstances, their abandon to the joy of nature proved the viability of what is best in man, independent of accidents, of circumstance. We feel ourselves too dependent on history and culture. This student did not have Socrates, but he had Plato's book about him, which might even be better; he had brains, friends and a country happily free enough to let them gather and speak as they will. What is essential about that dialogue, or any of the Platonic dialogues, is reproducible in almost all times and places. He and his friends can think together. It requires much thought to learn that this thinking might be what it is all for. That's where we are beginning to fail. But it is right under our noses, improbable but always present.

Throughout this book I have referred to Plato's *Republic*, which is for me *the* book on education, because it really explains to me what I experience as a man and a teacher, and I have almost always used it to point out what we should not hope for, as a teaching of moderation and resignation. But all its impossibilities act as a filter to leave the residue of the highest and non-illusory possibility. The real community of man, in the midst of all the self-contradictory simulacra of community, is the community of those who seek the truth, of the potential knowers, that is, in principle, of all men to the extent they desire to know. But in fact this includes only a few, the true friends, as Plato was to Aristotle at the very moment they were disagreeing about the nature of the good. Their common concern for the good linked them; their disagreement about it proved they needed one another to understand it. They were absolutely one soul as they looked at the problem. This, according to Plato, is the only real friendship, the only real common good. It is here that the contact people so desperately seek is to be found. The other kinds of relatedness are only imperfect reflections of this one trying to be self-subsisting, gaining their only justification from their ultimate relation to this one.

This is the meaning of the riddle of the improbable philosopher-kings. They have a true community that is exemplary for all other communities.

This is a radical teaching but perhaps one appropriate to our own radical time, in which proximate attachments have become so questionable and we know of no others. This age is not utterly insalubrious for philosophy. Our problems are so great and their sources so deep that to understand them we need philosophy more than ever, if we do not despair of it, and it faces the challenges on which it flourishes. I still believe that universities, rightly understood, are where community and friendship can exist in our times. Our thought and our politics have become inextricably bound up with the universities, and they have served us well, human things being what they are. But for all that, and even though they deserve our strenuous efforts, one should never forget that Socrates was not a professor, that he was put to death, and that the love of wisdom survived, partly because of his *individual* example. This is what really counts, and we must remember it in order to know how to defend the university.

This is the American moment in world history, the one for which we shall forever be judged. Just as in politics the responsibility for the fate of freedom in the world has devolved upon our regime, so the fate of philosophy in the world has devolved upon our universities, and the two are related as they have never been before. The gravity of our given task is great, and it is very much in doubt how the future will judge our stewardship.

Afterword

Andrew Ferguson

He had gone public with his ideas. He had written a book—difficult but popular—a spirited, intelligent, warlike book, and it had sold and was still selling in both hemispheres and on both sides of the equator. The thing had been done quickly but in real earnest: no cheap concessions, no popularizing, no mental monkey business, no apologetics, no patrician airs. . . . His intellect had made a millionaire of him. It's no small matter to become rich and famous by saying exactly what you think—to say it in your own words, without compromise.

—*Ravelstein*, by Saul Bellow, 1996

Bellow's Ravelstein is a thinly fictionalized Allan Bloom, caught at the peak of life and rendered, so I'm told by Bloom's friends and students, with uncanny precision and ingenuity. We first see him dressed in a blue-and-white kimono, sashaying around the penthouse he's rented at the Hotel Crillon in the heart of Paris. His lover, a young man from Singapore named Nikki, lies asleep in bed. Bellow wants to impress upon the reader his subject's physicality. Abe Ravelstein's frame is long and angled and ungainly, but it's usually adorned in $5,000 suits. When he eats, you sense the pleasure with which he undertakes the task: "he was stoking his system," Bellow says, "and nourishing his ideas"; at dinner parties, hostesses are advised to place newspapers under his chair to gather the debris from his enthusiastic feeding. His baldness is "geological." He smokes constantly, twin spouts of tobacco smoke flowing dragonlike from his nostrils. Bellow stresses the physicality at the beginning of the novel because it lends poignancy to the wasting at the end, when Ravelstein endures a tortured death from AIDS, as did Bloom. He was carried off in 1992, only four years before Bellow immortalized him as Ravelstein and five after he published the book you hold in your hands.

Among much else, Bellow dramatizes the suddenness and unexpectedness of the wealth and fame that rained down on Bloom in the late 1980s. The course that Bloom's classic took on its way to boffo box office is singular even among the endless eruptions and craterings of the American book business. The proposal for the book was bought by one editor and midwived into print by another, with no more than modest expectations. The original title, *Souls Without Longing,* was lovely but uncommercial, so it was changed. The first print run, in February of 1987, was ten thousand copies. By spring it was selling twenty-five thousand copies a week. It hit the bestseller list in April, reached number one by summertime, and stayed there for two and a half months. It became beach reading! From the top of the list it beat back waves of challengers, including multiple celebrity memoirs, self-help books, and a particularly gloomy book-length warning about the "coming depression of the nineties." In March of the following year, *The Closing of the American Mind* was still a bestseller. By then nearly a million copies had been sold in the United States. Foreign sales were just as prodigious. The best minds in American publishing were boggled. Never in their experience had a book about Jean-Jacques Rousseau, Friedrich Nietzsche, and Martin Heidegger outsold books by Patty Duke, Shirley MacLaine, and Sam Donaldson.

Various attempts were made at the time to account for the runaway success. The nearest cause was a handful of spectacular early reviews. The book "hits with the approximate force and effect of what electric-shock therapy must be like," wrote the daily reviewer in the *New York Times,* rather awkwardly. "It commands one's attention and concentrates one's mind more effectively than any other book I can think of in the past five years." (Cut, print, and blurb.) The *Times's* Sunday reviewer, a college president, was similarly overwhelmed, calling the book "rich and absorbing." Ditto the *Washington Post's* reviewer, likewise from the *Chronicle of Higher Education,* and still more from *Time* and *Newsweek.*

But good reviews, even ecstatic reviews, aren't sufficient to sell a book, as any number of highly praised authors you've never heard of would be happy to tell you. Something else was happening here, but we didn't know what it was. James Atlas, in the *New York Times Magazine*, conjectured that the book acted as a kind of adult continuing education class: "It appeals to the student in us all." Bloom's editor at Simon & Schuster said the book tapped a large reservoir of underserved book buyers eager for intelligent discussion of profound issues. Louis Menand, a literature professor at Princeton and CUNY, was rather more sardonic in the *New Republic*: "It gratifies our wish to think ill of our culture (a wish that is a permanent feature of modernity) without thinking ill of ourselves."

Menand's review was part of a second surge of notices, far more critical than the first. It was the Revenge of the Eggheads, and when at last it came you couldn't help but wonder what took them so long. The *Wall Street Journal's* rapturous review arrived late enough to note how odd the early praise had been, sociologically and politically, coming as it did from the "cultural establishment" that had been squarely in Bloom's crosshairs: "Many of the reviewers who have praised Mr. Bloom's book have not faced up to the consequences of Mr. Bloom's ideas." The college president in the Sunday *Times* was singled out as an especially unlikely booster. His rave review for the book "shows no indication that the institution over which he presides stands fundamentally indicted by it." And not only this or that institution: Bloom was accusing an entire generation of humanities professors of academic dereliction.

They took the book as a personal affront and reacted accordingly. "Bad reviews are one thing," James Atlas wrote. "The responses to Bloom's book have been charged with a hostility that transcends the usual mean-spiritedness of reviewers." Tactics differed. There were attacks on Bloom's scholarship, his philosophical skill, and the empirical support for his broader claims. There were also sarcasm, invective, caricature, shaming, and, inevitably then as now, accusations of elitism, racism, sexism, and homophobia. Perhaps the most celebrated rebuttal to *Closing*, considered by many of Bloom's critics to be definitive, was one of the calmest and most measured. Written by the Harvard classicist Martha Nussbaum, it was a lengthy piece even by the standards of the magazine in which it appeared, the *New York Review of Books*. Her disputes with Bloom over the the ancient texts were too obscure for a layman to adjudicate, but to my mind her characterization of his general argument wasn't quite accurate and in places discredited itself. She tells us, for example, that in *Closing* "Bloom presents himself to us as a profoundly religious man." You could have fooled me. His pre-eminent teacher, the philosopher Leo Strauss, liked to make the distinction between Athens and Jerusalem—a life of philosophy versus a life of faith. After a few approving nods toward the Bible, *The Closing of the American Mind* shows Bloom to have been an Athens man all the way (not to mention a Jew, a homosexual, and a Hoosier. Truly, they broke the mold . . .).

The most subtle of Nussbaum's arguments poked at a contradiction lying half-buried in the book. Bloom opens with a patriotic celebration of America's foundation in natural rights, the guarantee of equality; by the end of the book he seems to argue that the only way to save America from its present course is for universities to recommit to promoting the philosophical life, a life accessible, he frankly acknowledges, only to a chosen few. The contradiction, if that's what it is, doesn't cripple his other arguments, but Nussbaum and the other second-wave academics thought it exposed an elitist, antidemocratic agenda that could easily darken into something much spookier—autocracy or worse, a new (or very old) kind of authoritarian rule.

One observer estimated that more than two hundred reviews of *Closing* were eventually published, and scores of these, in obscure quarterlies and highbrow opinion magazines alike, elaborated the theme of Bloom as authoritarian menace. In *Harpers*, the political scientist Benjamin Barber called the book "a most enticing, a most subtle, a most learned, a most dangerous tract." Americans were too susceptible to a "Philosopher Despot" like Bloom, Barber wrote. "Anxious about the loss of fixed points, wishing for simpler, more orderly times," they found in his work "a new Book of Truth for an era after God." This was a common assertion but a weak one, even on its own terms. In accusing Bloom of authoritarian tendencies, Barber and the others exposed their own horror at the common folk and made you wonder about their own faith in democracy. Who knew Americans were so easily duped? Toss them a few quotes from Herodotus and bitch about their college kids and they'll think you've given them the Book of Truth. Even Franco had to work harder than that! Maybe this whole idea of "government by the people" needs to be rethought . . .

In time the academic establishment's horror of Bloom grew too vast for mere paper and ink to contain. Conferences were held to declare him anathema. At one of these, in Manhattan, the associate headmaster of the

Dalton School called the book "Hitleresque." Richard Bernstein, then a reporter for the *Times*, chronicled a gathering sponsored by Duke and the University of North Carolina, where Bloom, though not in attendance, was "derided, scorned and laughed at" by a large group of humanities professors. "In some respects," Bernstein wrote, "the scene in North Carolina last weekend recalled the daily 'minute of hatred' in George Orwell's 1984, when citizens are required to rise and hurl invective at pictures of a man known only as Goldstein, the Great Enemy of the state."

It's worth noting that Duke's conference was held nearly *a year and a half* after Bloom's book was published. Some hatreds need more than a minute to burn themselves out. And among the establishment—deans and department chairs, the grim-faced apparatchiks at the American Council on Education and the American Association of University Professors—Bloom remained a pariah for the rest of what was left of his life. But he was a jaunty and cheerful pariah, as Bellow shows, for there were compensations: appearing endlessly on TV, accepting invitations to Chequers from Mrs. Thatcher and to the White House from President Reagan, and laughing in his kimono all the way to *la banque*.

I wonder whether all this fuss will seem bizarre to new and younger readers of *The Closing of the American Mind*. It's useful to recall the world Bloom and his book broke into and riled so. In material ways, the United States of America of 1987 seems as remote as Republican Rome. Our national wealth has more than tripled in the last twenty-five years. The digital revolution, with its upending of the habits and patterns of everyday life, was just getting underway. Music lovers delighted in the portability and convenience of their brick-sized Walkmans, never imagining the tiny wonders they would be slipping into their shirtpockets a decade hence. Cars, on the other hand, seem to have been roughly half their present size. You couldn't carry around a telephone unless you yanked it off the wall. Nintendo was as sophisticated as gaming systems came. And nobody used the word "gaming system."

Culturally, the country fretted. Culturally, of course, all countries, or some segments of them, are always fretting, and have been doing so since Cicero grieved over *O tempora, O mores*, up to and beyond Yeats's insistence that the center cannot hold. But by the end of the 1980s in the United States, there were numbers to underscore the worry.

In the previous thirty years, violent crime had increased 500 percent, the divorce rate had doubled, the teen suicide rate had tripled, and the number of "illegitimate births" (this was the last era when you could use the term) had increased 400 percent.

Beyond the numbers, the worriers readily found signs of the culture's degradation, if not its imminent collapse. On TV, Geraldo Rivera, Jerry Springer, and Sally Jesse Raphael had introduced a new kind of freak show that proved enormously popular, banishing modesty and discretion and making exhibitionism a virtue, qualifying adulterers and wifebeaters and cross dressers to strut their hour upon the stage set. (Eerie fact: exactly nine months after *Closing*'s publication date, Snooki Polizzi was born.) Popular fiction chronicled a generation of pampered youth lost to anomie and cocaine. As the Iran-Contra scandal shook the executive branch, pundits discovered among the people a loss of faith in their institutions. A devastating crash on Wall Street was credited to greed unchecked by law or moral obligation.

And as if all that weren't sufficient cause for alarm, one final word: Madonna.

The skittish American public in 1987 was well-prepped soil for a message like Bloom's. It helped that his subject, colleges and universities, shared in the general unease and were in fact one cause of it. Test scores at all levels of schooling, but particularly college entrance exams, had been falling since the late 1960s. Two generations earlier the GI Bill had begun to democratize higher education by making it available to cohorts that in earlier times would have never thought it necessary for a fulfilling life. To accommodate the swells of new students, and to absorb the subsidies that followed them, schools vastly expanded their housing stock, increased the number of classrooms, and, crucially, widened the range of their fields of study.

The purpose of a four-year liberal arts program—defended by Bloom as an exploration of the big questions that life presents to the fully conscious human being—became confused. What was the point of a bachelor of arts degree? Was it to plumb the depths and origins of Western civilization, which had after all invented the university, and to develop the student spiritually and morally? Or was the point to set the kid up to get a cushy job? Humanists in our universities lost confidence in the traditional answer. And their departments, the seat of liberal arts, suffered in the confusion, losing students to the social sciences and programs devoted to professional training, such as pre-law or business. The humanities responded by either aping the professional curriculum or shrinking still further into the theory and abstraction that Bloom devastatingly describes. Core courses were dropped. Teachers of literature or philosophy had difficulty describing what they did for a living, or why.

By the time Bloom's book was released the crisis in the humanities was acknowledged by everyone except the people who worked in the humanities. Parents in particular began to wonder why their college-age children were taking classes called "Hip-Hop Eshu: Queen Bitch 101" (at Syracuse University) or coming home after four years with degrees in "Peace Studies" that cost $100,000. Phrases that were used without irony by many profs in the humanities — "politically correct" (good) and "Dead White Males" (bad) — were captured by their critics and turned into short-hand for the leftwing orthodoxy that filled the vacuum in the liberal arts.

The crisis was made political fodder. The Reagan administration took a special interest and an especially acerbic tone. Lynne Cheney, chairman of the National Endowment for the Humanities, and the Secretary of Education, William Bennett, led the dyspeptic chorus. Both held doctorates in the humanities, which enhanced their influence with the higher-ed establishment not at all. When Cheney echoed Bloom in a widely publicized report — criticizing efforts by humanities departments to make themselves "relevant" by treating "great books as little more than the political rationalizations of dominant groups" — she earned many multiple minutes of hate all on her own.

With the publication of *Closing*, Bloom was placed alongside Bellow, Bennett, and later the jurist and Jeremiah, Robert Bork, in a convenient journalistic category: the Doom and Gloomers, or the Killer B's, or the Grumpy Old Men. (Cheney, alphabetically disqualified to serve with the Killer B's, was nevertheless an honorary Grump.) But this grouping wasn't fair to Bloom, not entirely — and it wasn't fair to the arguments developed in the book, which had a subtlety and depth that journalism and partisan politics can seldom capture.

Bloom was never a movement conservative. In electoral politics he was a moderately liberal Democrat, and more liberal still in personal and social matters. Unlike Bennett or Cheney, who considered themselves champions of ordinary American bourgeois life, Bloom viewed it with a disdain that runs just below the book's surface. He was no fan of the free market or the ceaseless getting and striving that it encourages. He worried that the life that awaited students after college would be just as enervating as their dismal and purposeless education. And he wasn't above invoking a brand-name cliché to drive the point home. In their "Brooks Brothers suits," he writes, "they will want to get ahead and live comfortably. But this life is as empty and false as the one they left behind." Elsewhere he speaks of the "intellectual deserts" of middle-class living and "the dreary professional training that awaits [liberal arts students] after the baccalaureate."

There is no element of moral uplift in his brief against modern life. Discussing the collapse of the traditional family, which has only accelerated since his time, he writes: "I am not arguing here that the old family arrangements were good or that we should or could go back to them." Bloom's discussion of rock music (see pages 68–81 if you've forgotten, though how could you?) was always adduced as Exhibit A in the charge of fuddy-duddyism—to most people under the age of thirty-five, his complaints sounded no more informed or intelligent than the bellowing of the old crank next door: "Turn it down!" But his case against rock was entirely his own; he worried that it deadened the passion required for real education. "My concern here," he wrote, "is not the moral effects of this music—whether it leads to sex, violence, or drugs." This placed Allan Bloom to the left of Tipper Gore, at the time an energetic crusader against the depredations of Mötley Crüe and Def Leppard.

In the last quarter-century, the reader will notice, Bloom's book has grown a few whiskers. Anachronisms are unavoidable. He wrote before the population of modernity's Holy Trinity—Marx, Freud, and Darwin—reduced by two-thirds. Marx lost his allure, at least nominally, after the collapse of the murderous regimes that claimed to have been built from his ideas. Freud was demoted from scientist to cultural observer, and an unreliable one besides. Some of Bloom's language is outdated: no professor today could use the word "Oriental" for "Asian" and long survive. He objects to squishy nonce words, but the examples he uses—"commitment," "values," "life-style"—are now so deeply embedded in everyday speech that no amount of ridicule will dislodge them. He's lucky he didn't live to see the infinitely elastic use of the now-meaningless word "issues." I was touched by his quaint mention of "Mack the Knife" as an example of American life's homogenizing effects: mass marketed by Louis Armstrong (I assume he couldn't bring himself to mention Bobby Darin), Brecht's leftist agitprop "becomes less dangerous, though no less corrupt." What would Bloom have made of the taming of the Village People's "YMCA"—a tribute to the joys of shower-room sodomy transformed into a surefire crowd-pleaser at middle-school pep rallies? The controversy over "affirmative action," which he treats at length, was settled by the subtler logic of "diversity." And the book gives little notice to the arrival on campus of gay rights, easily the most consequential social movement of the last three decades.

But I'm surprised by how few the anachronisms are. Most of Bloom's criticisms still apply. I can think of lots of reasons why *The Closing of the American Mind* deserves as many readers as it earned in the eighties—Bloom's sly wit and the torrential energy of his prose are worth the price of admission, in my opinion—but one carries a special urgency. The trends he tagged in higher education in 1987 have only intensified: toward weaker academic requirements for students, greater specialization in the departments, a rigid orthodoxy in the university's politics and cultural life. The university we face today is still the one he described, only more so.

At a minimum, what Bloom demands of us in response is aware-ness—thoughtfulness. He hated unthinking conformity above all. The contemporary university appalled him because it had conformed to the frivolous culture that surrounds it and from which it was meant to stand apart. The cheap relativism it absorbed led inevitably to the undoing of the liberal arts. The humanities retreated from the tradi-tional ways of teaching and learning when humanists stopped believ-ing the effort could reveal any truths about the perplexities of life. In liberal education, relativism is a universal corrosive.[1] No discipline can survive it. If there's no truth, finally, why study the work of dead people who were deluded enough to think there was? And without the pur-

---

1 I'm aware that defenders of relativism defend it by denying it exists: no one, they say, truly believes that one idea is ultimately as good as any other. And of course they're right that none of us act in our own lives as though we believed this. But most of us pro-fess it nonetheless. In a genial but harrowing review of *Closing*, a teacher named Michael Zuckert told how he canvassed the students in his American Political Thought class at Carleton College. He asked whether they agreed that the truths in the first lines of the Declaration of Independence were indeed "self-evident." Seven percent voted "yes." On further conversation, he wrote, it turned out "that they were convinced there is no such thing as 'truth,' self-evident or otherwise, in the sphere of claims of the sort raised in the Declaration." He would have gotten much the same response in a classroom today.

suit of what's finally true, higher education becomes post-secondary professional training—that's if we're lucky; a four-year booze cruise if we're not.

If I had reread *The Closing of the American Mind* ten years ago, when my own children were themselves under ten, I confess I would have thought Bloom's portrait of educational decline was overwrought. But then they grew up and went off to school.

Recall the passage on page 337. A freshman arrives on campus. "He finds a democracy of disciplines," Bloom wrote. "This democracy is really an anarchy because there are no recognized rules and no legitimate titles to rule. In short, there is no vision, nor is there a set of competing visions, of what an educated human being is." In the end the freshman will likely give up on a liberal education, opting for a major that will get him hired when he graduates and "picking up in elective courses a little of whatever is thought to make one cultured."

This observation from twenty-five years ago describes what a freshman encounters at a moderately selective university today, and with modest adjustments, even at smaller colleges that say they specialize in the liberal arts. It is what my own family found. Poring over the catalog of courses in the weeks before my son enrolled at our big state university (which I have come to think of, for reasons soon to become clear, as BSU), we discovered that no survey classes were available to him in American history, English literature, the history of science, ancient or modern philosophy. His "general education" requirements could be satisfied by a scattering of electives, none related to any other. He was required to enroll in a writing class, which was good. The writing classes offered were "*Mad Men* and American Society," "A History of the Sixties," and "Intro to Queer Theory." Which was not.

Last year, the Association of College Trustees and Alumni surveyed the catalogs of more than one thousand colleges and universities. Fewer than 20 percent of the schools required courses in American government, only a third required a literature survey class, and 15 percent required anything more than a beginner's level class in a foreign language. The "core curriculum," as at BSU, is largely a sham: a math class may be offered, a science class may be offered, but seldom are both required, and often the content of each has only a glancing relation to the study of math or science. The results have been predictable. The authors of *Academically Adrift*—the most devastating book about higher education since *Closing*—found that nearly half of undergraduates show no measurable improvement in learning or "critical thinking" after two years of college.

Perhaps the most famous image in *Closing*—certainly the least appetizing—is a cartoonish word picture of an MTV-watching, Walkman-wearing thirteen-year-old boy, the flower of American civilization, the human culmination of centuries of learning and sacrifice, nonetheless brought low by a degraded popular culture: "a pubescent child whose body throbs with orgasmic rhythms; whose feelings are made articulate in hymns to the joys of onanism or the killing of parents," and so on and so on, whose "life is made into a nonstop, commercially prepackaged masturbation fantasy."

I thought of that boy of thirteen when I finished rereading *The Closing of the American Mind* not long ago. He is now thirty-eight. His parents, I hope, survived his childhood unscathed; I won't speculate about the onanism. He likely has children of his own by now. And I hope by the time his own daughter is ready for college, he and all the youngsters he was meant to symbolize will have forgiven the author of this scandalous but all too realistic caricature. And when he disgorges tens of thousands of dollars to send his daughter to a school that has itself become a caricature of higher education, I am consoled to think that he will be able to consult Allan Bloom as to how such a thing could come to pass, thanks to a new edition of his maddening, haunting, towering book.

Index of
Proper Names

ABOUT THE AUTHOR

Allan Bloom was Professor in the Committee on Social Thought and the College and co-director of the John M. Olin Center for Inquiry into the Theory and Practice of Democracy at the University of Chicago. He taught at Yale, University of Paris, University of Toronto, Tel Aviv University, and Cornell, where he was the recipient of the Clark Teaching Award in 1967. His other books are Plato's *Republic* (translator and editor), *Politics and the Arts: Letter to M. d'Alembert on the Theatre* (translator and editor), Rousseau's *Emile* (translator and editor), and *Shakespeare's Politics* (with Harry V. Jaffa). He died in 1992.

CPSIA information can be obtained
at www.ICGtesting.com
Printed in the USA
LVHW041622190622
721443LV00003B/3